Work and Pay in Twentieth-Century Britain

Work and Pay in Twentieth-Century Britain

Edited by
Nicholas Crafts,
Ian Gazeley
and
Andrew Newell

OXFORD
UNIVERSITY PRESS

OXFORD

UNIVERSITY PRESS

Great Clarendon Street, Oxford OX2 6DP

Oxford University Press is a department of the University of Oxford.
It furthers the University's objective of excellence in research, scholarship,
and education by publishing worldwide in

Oxford New York

Auckland Cape Town Dar es Salaam Hong Kong Karachi
Kuala Lumpur Madrid Melbourne Mexico City Nairobi
New Delhi Shanghai Taipei Toronto

With offices in

Argentina Austria Brazil Chile Czech Republic France Greece
Guatemala Hungary Italy Japan Poland Portugal Singapore
South Korea Switzerland Thailand Turkey Ukraine Vietnam

Oxford is a registered trade mark of Oxford University Press
in the UK and in certain other countries

Published in the United States
by Oxford University Press Inc., New York

British Library Cataloguing in Publication Data

Data available

Library of Congress Cataloging in Publication Data

Data available

Typeset by Newgen Imaging Systems (P) Ltd., Chennai, India
Printed in Great Britain
on acid-free paper by
Biddles Ltd., King's Lynn, Norfolk

ISBN 978–0–19–928058–2
ISBN 978–0–19–921266–8 (Pbk.)

10 9 8 7 6 5 4 3 2 1

Contents

Contents

Introduction

Ian Gazeley and Andrew Newell

0.1 The big picture

This volume is about the evolution of pay and employment in Britain through the twentieth century. It is a collection of essays that establish what happened and why it happened. Most are concerned with change rather than continuity, which, given the relatively short temporal focus of the book, may at first seem surprising. In fact, very few of the individual essays highlight continuities of experience across the century. This is for three main reasons. First, the twentieth century—especially the first half—was fractured by world war and world slumps, which inevitably had profound consequences, but also tend to dwarf the events around them so that years before and after seem from different eras.

Secondly, and most enduringly, the twentieth century was a period of unrivalled technological progress that raised the productivity of an hour of labour by, roughly, a factor of four. This process forced massive increases in the standard of living, but it also wrought great transformations in what workers do and how they do it, and it resulted in large numbers of them being educated to levels attained by only a tiny elite in 1900. There is much about this process that is not fully understood. There does not yet exist a fully analytical historical account of twentieth-century technological change, and its relationship to the world economy on the one hand and to systematic scientific research on the other hand. Some elements of that history are known, however. The centre of technological innovation was the United States where the commercial pursuit of profitable innovation fused links between industries and universities to create and direct powerful research communities. From the perspective of the British labour market, by the 1920s there was a clearly established trend away from employment in the great industries of the industrial revolution towards employment in the manufacture of consumer goods using mass production techniques. This structural change slowed in the late 1930s as rearmament revived demand for the output of some of the older industries. The needs of war created a renaissance of demand for the products of nineteenth-century staple industries, which lasted into the early 1950s.

The pace of industrial change in employment was also slow in the two decades after 1945. These decades are sometimes referred to as the 'golden age'; a period of higher productivity growth, low unemployment, and a great extension of well-being as state education, social security system, and the National Health Service delivered fitter, stronger, and more highly skilled workers into the labour market. After 1965, and especially after 1980, structural change accelerated again. The market for manual work collapsed. Between 1965 and the end of the century the share of manual workers fell from 51 per cent to 31 per cent of employment, and the share of agriculture, mining, manufacturing, and construction fell from 50 to 22 per cent of employment. Over the same period, productivity growth initially slowed, but sped up again after the slump of the early 1980s.

Thirdly, the twentieth century is a period in which the pervasive intellectual framework oscillated. In terms of the political economy, this was from liberal laissez-faire at the beginning of the century, in which the role of the state was minimal, to active state intervention at mid-century, in which the state assumed responsibility for almost every aspect of the labour market. In 1900 a safety net was provided by the Poor Law and the state regulated working conditions with various Factories and Workshop Acts. By 1950 the situation had changed dramatically: the state ran agencies to enable individuals to find work; took responsibility for vocational training; provided welfare payments and minimum wage regulatory mechanisms; had established a corporatist framework for wage bargaining; managed employment in a large swath of British industry that was in direct government control; and had adopted a Keynesian macroeconomic commitment to maintaining high employment. At the end of the century, additionally, the state had legislated to outlaw wage discrimination by gender and race, but some, if by no means all, of the interventions of mid-century had been reversed. By the year 2000, the corporatist framework of government had been abandoned, state-owned industries had been largely privatized, and the macroeconomic commitment to low unemployment had been replaced by a low inflation target.

Why did these political changes occur? Some elements of the story are uncontroversial. Nineteenth-century social observers had highlighted the terrible conditions of the urban working classes during the later phases of industrialization. The perception of disadvantage steadily grew among the working class and found expression in campaigns for electoral reform, improved working conditions, and pay. In Britain, these movements found political expression in the Liberal Party and particularly, from 1906 onwards, the Labour Party. The First World War transformed the relationship between workers, employers, and the state. It was no longer the case that wars could be won with the endowment of men, armaments, and munitions available at the outset. By 1916, the war had become one of attrition in which the victor would be the power that was most able to harness the productive potential of economy to the objective of victory.

This necessity massively improved the bargaining position of labour and helped transform its political representation into a party in government by 1924.

The immediate post-war slump, followed by the high unemployment of the 1920s, particularly marked in areas dependent on the old staple industries, imparted a negative blow to the power of the trade unions. Unemployment, seen as a major social scourge, was the focus of much social research. Keynes wrote the General Theory (1936) partly as the intellectual foundation of the policy measures he advocated to relieve the problem. Keynes's work, and Beveridge's similarly motivated work (1942, 1944) on social security, were both crucial to the social and economic reforms of the late 1940s. The consequences of total war on economic organization during the Second World War were even more pronounced than they had been during the earlier conflict. From May 1940, the Churchill coalition brought leading Labour Party members and the leader of Britain's largest trade union into government. The Ministry of Labour directed labour to an unprecedented extent and at the same time workplace organization and union representation was greatly extended. During the war there was a change in the climate of the British political economy that resulted in a post-war settlement based upon a coporatist system of government. The fundamentals of this social contract between the state, organized labour, and employers were to last a generation or more.

The long boom of the golden age, partly caused by external forces, probably maintained the post-war settlement longer than it would otherwise have lasted. Nationalization, designed to allow for long-term economic stability, locked the British economy into an increasingly outdated industrial structure. Also, by offering greater job security, reinforced by employment protection legislation, nationalization shifted the balance of power in the workplace further towards employees and unions. Workplace unrest became an increasing feature of the British industrial landscape in the 1950s and 1960s.

These economic problems, of outdated nationalized industries and militant workforces, came to a head in the 1970s when days lost to industrial disputes were running at over 11 million per year. Much has been written about the degree to which Thatcher's governments of the 1980s set out to make all the reforms they eventually undertook. There was a series of reforms to trade unions, commencing with the Industrial Relations Act of 1981, which severely constrained union power. These changes were fiercely opposed by a trade union movement accustomed to being treated by government as a partner in decision making. The other big reform was privatization. Between 1983 and 1993 more than a million jobs were transferred from the public sector to the private sector. Prior to sale, employment was heavily reduced, again in the face of bitter union opposition, in several large public sector industries, most notably coal and steel. At the end of the century, the Labour government began a programme of increasing public sector employment again, but only within the state health and education systems. These policy-induced changes coincided with the last period of twentieth-century structural change. Technological advances, perhaps especially in information technology, created new opportunities in the internationalization of production that led to increasing British specialization in non-manual work and a further decline in traditional British manufacturing employment.

How did this history impact upon households? The most obvious change is in the proportion of women in the workforce. In 1901 we calculate that women accounted for about 29 per cent of the workforce,[1] whereas a century later the Labour Force Survey estimates this share at roughly 46 per cent. Another change, particularly affecting the last quarter of the twentieth century, is the demise of the breadwinner household. Define the breadwinner household as one where some adults work, but some do not. In 1975, General Household Survey data show that these were 36.8 per cent of all households, with 6.5 per cent workless households and 56.7 per cent of household where all adults were engaged in paid work. By 2001, the share of breadwinner households had more than halved, to 17.6 per cent, while workless household had grown to 16.6 per cent and all-worker households had grown to 65.8 per cent. The rise of the all-worker household is very likely to be caused by the same factors as the rise in women's participation. The rise in zero-earner households is likely to be related to longer retirement amongst other factors.

0.2 The book

Much of the literature that deals with the labour market in Britain is confined to the analysis of sub-periods of the twentieth century. This book provides a new, century-long perspective. We have noted that the increase in living standards in the twentieth century outstripped that of any other period in history. In Chapter 1, Nicholas Crafts unpacks the methodology for comparisons of living standards. He demonstrates how the standard method, of deflating household income by a consumer price index, is based on a narrow definition of living standards, and shows how a broader definition that takes into account changes in the quality of life undoubtedly raises these estimates. The rise in living standards did not occur smoothly through the century. The rate of growth after the Second World War was roughly twice the rate of the first part of the century. This is widely explained by the coincidence of a large number of technological innovations that interacted to cause rapid productivity growth, especially in the 1950s, 1960s, and 1990s. These innovations caused a shift in labour demand to non-manual work within industries and a shift in employment from the production industries to services. As mentioned above, the shift

---

[1] Underlying data taken from Feinstein (1972) and Table 3.1.

away from manufacturing to service employment happened mainly after 1965. In Chapter 2, Andrew Newell establishes these changes and then discusses their possible causes.

In Chapter 3, Ian Gazeley studies the progress of manual wages 1900–70. There were modest gains in real earnings in the first half of the century. Within manual work what stands out is the levelling of pay between the unskilled and skilled and to a lesser extent between men and women. Most of this levelling occurs during the two world wars. As discussed above, it seems that total war required the full mobilization of labour and the harnessing of the interests of organized labour to the war effort. This greatly strengthened the position of trade unions and a social contract emerged that favoured the unskilled and women workers, based on simple ideas of fair shares for all. The wars took mostly young men into the forces and consequently there was an expansion of participation, in particular of women's employment, and also a breaking down of formerly skilled tasks into sequences of semi-skilled and unskilled operations. In terms of the overall structure of employment, men's work continued to be concentrated in blue-collar employment. A notable feature of women's work in the first half of the century is the concentration in relatively few sectors, notwithstanding the temporary impact of both world wars.

The wartime narrowing of wage differentials was maintained if not reinforced during the two decades after the Second World War and especially in the 1970s with statutory flat rate incomes policies in force. Florence Kondylis and Jonathan Wadsworth, who employ data from the New Earnings Surveys, take up the story of wages after 1970 in Chapter 4. The trend of narrowing wage differentials by skill was sharply reversed after 1979. Although wages continued to grow from most workers, there was an unprecedented widening of pay differentials from 1980 to the mid-1990s. Two main causes for this have been identified: first, the global shift of labour demand away from less-skilled workers in advanced countries, and second, the institutional changes, particularly away from trade unionism, of the 1980s.

Part of the response of labour suppliers to the rise in real wages over the century has been a reduction in years of life in work for men and an increase for women. In Chapter 5, Paul Johnson and Asghar Zaidi describe and analyse the twentieth-century history of lifetime participation in work. Over the century annual hours fell for all workers. Why did women's participation increase over this period of unrivalled prosperity growth, particularly after the 1960s? As Chapter 5's Figure 5.2 shows, fewer women took shorter periods away from paid work to care for young children, as family size was reduced. Sara Horrell in Chapter 6 analyses the interaction between the household and the labour market. The reduction in family size is partly a response to falling infant mortality and also a response to the need to educate children longer, which delays the age at which they begin to earn. A big part of the story of increased participation must also be the extra freedom and control allowed by oral contraception, but perhaps also by the increased flexibility in household work allowed by new household technology. Additionally, on the demand side, the shift in employment to services, many of which were dominated by female employment, opened new opportunities. Of course these changes required parallel changes in social attitudes. These gathered pace from the 1960s onwards. Chapter 7, by Sara Connolly and Mary Gregory, charts the rise of working women since 1970 and discusses the roles of gender discrimination and the twin burdens of domestic and labour market responsibilities in accounting for women's patterns of work and pay.

Another possible contributory factor in the evolution of women's working lives is the development of the welfare state. As Pat Thane shows in Chapter 8, through the twentieth century the British state took over some of the welfare and support roles previously carried out by female members of the extended family. Welfare states developed in all the economically advanced countries during the twentieth century. Expansion was particularly marked after 1980. In Britain, the welfare state was based on a social insurance system that coexisted with basic minimum needs provision, the ancestry of which can be traced back to the Elizabethan Poor Law. From a labour market perspective, the provision of a provides a floor below which wages cannot fall, just like a statutory minimum wage. Minimum wages were also introduced for many trades early in the century. Unemployment insurance provides an additional wage floor, and has the effect of changing financial incentives to job search.

The other great twentieth-century labour market institution was the trade union movement. In Chapter 9, Chris Wrigley explains how the unionization of the workforce grew rapidly during the century. In 1913, just under a quarter of the workforce was unionized. This figure had nearly doubled by 1920, before falling back sharply during the inter-war period. Fresh impetus was given to union membership during the Second World War and the long post-war boom. Union density reached a peak in 1979 at just over 53 per cent of the workforce. The periods of war stand out as being important in both the development and expansion of trade unionism, but also for the way in which the state became embroiled in the system of industrial relations. During the wars a substantial proportion of the male labour force was withdrawn from civilian employment as the armed forces expanded rapidly. At its peak, the size of the armed forces represented about 25 per cent of the pre-war labour force during the First World War and about 20 per cent during the second conflict. This strengthened considerably the bargaining position of workers in civilian employment and during both wars there was a growth in collective bargaining and the widespread adoption of national agreements.

During the Second World War, Labour leaders planned for a corporatist post-war economy. This plan was loosely based on the government's pledge to maintain a high and stable level of employment after the war in the 1944 White Paper on Employment, and the 1942 Beveridge Report which aimed to provide every citizen with a basic level of minimum needs from 'the cradle to the grave'. In addition, a system of industrial relations was formalized between organized labour, employers' federations, and the state, most particularly through the National Economic Development Council, where trade union leaders delivered 'responsible' wage bargaining in return for the government's commitment to full employment and the provision of universal social security benefits.

Towards the end of the long post-war boom, this corporatist system came under increasing strain as trade union leaders were experiencing difficulties delivering 'responsible' wage bargaining by their membership. From the late 1950s, so-called 'wildcat' or unofficial strikes in support of wage claims characterized some sections of British manufacturing industry. From the employers' perspective, there was a desire to move away from implementing national wage agreements across all grades of worker and a modest growth in the incidence of plant-level bargaining, especially for skilled workers. After 1979, trade union density and collective bargaining declined in the more competitive labour market conditions of the 1980s and the pervasive background of an anti-trade union political climate. During the 1990s the trend away from collective bargaining at a national level continued, as many firms implemented plant-level agreements. By 1996, overall collective bargaining covered little more than a third of the workforce and the legal position of trade unions had been transformed by a series of legislative measures aimed at curbing trade union power.

Chapter 10, by Ian Gazeley and Andrew Newell, deals with unemployment. The course of British unemployment over the century was partially driven by world economic events. The long decline of the staple industries caused by a diminution of their nineteenth century competitive advantage, which was clear as early as 1920, set the regional pattern for British unemployment until 1990. The Great Depression of 1930/31, the small depression of 1958, the rise in unemployment in the mid-1970s, the 1980/81 depression, and the 1990/91 depression all had important external causes, even if they were not the whole story.

The second driver of British unemployment was British government policy. The most important policy element was probably monetary policy making. The 1920/21 depression and its long aftermath were partly due to the decision to return to the gold standard in 1918. Also, the British experience of the Great Depression was milder because of the abandonment of the gold standard in 1931. There is also wide agreement that monetary policy played a major role in the 1980/81 depression, the fall in unemployment in the late 1980s, and the 1990/91 depression. At various points in the century it has been suggested that labour market institutions have been crucial in determining British unemployment. For example, different authors and different times have ascribed movements of unemployment to: the extension of unemployment insurance during the inter-war period; the rise of national bargaining during the First World War; the rise of union power in the 1960s and 1970s, and its subsequent demise.

In Chapter 11, Michael Sanderson analyses the matching of education to the needs of the labour market. During the twentieth century the education system and labour force structure were reasonably well matched at various points. Immediately prior to the First World War, roughly 80 per cent of the labour force were manual workers and the education system was able to meet these needs. Compulsory elementary education had provided for near universal literacy rates among children and technical education was much improved compared with the position in the last quarter of the nineteenth century. Middle-class education was provided through fee-paying grammar schools, which were well able to meet the labour force needs for higher skills. Universities made a relatively limited contribution in keeping with the small size of professional and managerial occupations within the pre-First World War labour force.

Indeed, until about 1950, it appears that the education system and occupation structure were roughly in line, despite concerns about the provision of technical education during the inter-war period. It is likely, however, that the education system did not provide for significant occupational mobility. The 1918 Fisher Education Act raised the school leaving age to 14, thus ensuring a basic education for all children. The real crunch comes after the Second World War, when occupation structure and education seem increasingly out of line. In particular there was a decline in the provision of technical education. In 1951, 72 per cent of workers were manual workers and foremen, nearly 11 per cent were employers and managers, and just under 7 per cent professional workers. In 1950, 68 per cent of children received education at a secondary modern school, 28 per cent at grammar school, and only 4 per cent at secondary technical schools. By 1985 only 0.06 per cent of children were at technical schools, as a result of a sustained swing away from science and technology during the 1960s. After 1950, many writers point to a shortfall in vocational skills, industrial training, and apprenticeship. Yet this period was also when the economy was growing strongly.

In Chapter 12, Stephen Broadberry and Mary O'Mahony study Britain's productivity growth in international perspective. For many years Britain's relative economic decline over the century from 1870 dominated accounts of national progress. With hindsight, it seems rather curious to be focusing on Britain's relative position during a period of unprecedented growth of prosperity. Part of the story of relative decline for Britain in the twentieth century must be due to the process of other parts of the world catching up via capital accumulation, the spread of technology, and higher levels of education. Another part of the world picture was the extraordinary leap forward of the US economy which left the rest of the world way behind for a period in the middle of the twentieth century. This huge increase in US living standards was driven by the application of mass production techniques to an increasing proportion of economic activities as well as to the great explosion of technological advances centred in the USA.

These events set the context for the progress of well-being in Britain, but are far from the whole picture. Britain's relative manufacturing productivity level is steady, compared to other advanced countries over the century. This means that the decline in relative national productivity must be due to productivity trends in agriculture and services. In these latter sectors, the main story seems to be as outlined above, that is, of the rest of the world catching up on the one hand and on the other hand of the great innovations in agricultural technology having their earliest effects in the United States.

In manufacturing and industry in general, though, British relative productivity appears to be at its lowest in the two decades after the Second World War. It is tempting to line this observation up beside the fact that Britain's economic structural change, away from production and towards services, was arrested over the same period. There are two possible explanations from these events. First, it may be that post-Second World War reconstruction put demands on British industry that meant a greater focus on meeting demand than on raising efficiency. Secondly, it may be that the nationalization of large sections of British industry removed the commercial pressure to innovate and raise efficiency. Whatever the relative empirical weight of these two theories, both impediments to productivity growth had been removed by the middle 1980s, in time for the revival of productivity growth that took place from then on.

In Chapter 13, Dudley Baines analyses the relationship between the labour market and immigration policy. The relationship between immigration, emigration, and the labour market has varied during the course of the twentieth century and has been interwoven with political considerations, in terms of both Britain's relations with countries, or groups of countries like the Commonwealth, and domestic political reaction (in relation to perceived increases in immigration). Taking the twentieth century as a whole Britain, like much of Western Europe, experiences net emigration. After the Second World War when immigration gathered pace, net immigration was negative until the last twenty years of the century. Only 30 per cent of post-Second World War immigration was non-white. Attempts to control immigration in this period were ostensibly related to the needs of the labour market. For example the 1962 Commonwealth Immigrants Act controlled immigration using a voucher system that was related to the needs of the British economy. Not surprisingly, few vouchers were given to unskilled workers.

The extent to which migration affected the skill mix of the workforce remains unknown for most of the twentieth century as only from 1992 were Labour Force Survey data available. These data provide information on the qualifications and earnings of immigrants. Even at the end of the twentieth century when net immigration was positive, Baines maintains that the effects on the labour market are likely to have been qualitative rather than quantitative and most studies conclude that the average effect on skill mix was neutral.

0.3 Acknowledgements

Many thanks to Anita Ponari for editorial assistance and to Jennifer Wilkinson and the rest of the OUP team for their patience and helpfulness.

References

Beveridge, W. (1942). *Report on Committee on Social Insurance and Allied Services*. Cmd. 6404. London: HMSO.

—— (1944). *Full Employment in a Free Society*. London: Allen and Unwin.

Feinstein, C. H. (1972). *National Income, Expenditure and Output in the UK, 1855–1965*. Cambridge: Cambridge University Press.

Keynes, J. M. (1936). *The General Theory of Employment, Interest and Money*. London: Macmillan.

1

Living standards

Nicholas Crafts

1.1 Introduction

The central objective of this chapter is to answer the question 'how much did average British living standards increase during the twentieth century?' The aim is not to explain the observed trends but to explore the difficulties of measurement inherent in this question. Some attention will also be given to dispersion around the average.

The traditional approach of economic historians to measuring living standards has been through real wages. Here the most difficult issues concern the measurement of changes in the cost of living over the long run in the context of changes in the quality and range of goods and services available to consumers. In the last thirty years or so, many have found this approach inadequate and broader concepts of living standards have been proposed. For example, Floud and Harris (1997) adopted the Human Development Index (HDI), which takes account of income, life expectancy, and schooling and has been widely used in development economics. The rationale for this measure is not simply that education and longevity matter to people but also that their provision is typically financed by the state and does not depend on personal income.

If a broad concept of living standards embracing several aspects is adopted, the resulting measure will be in the form of an index of economic welfare. In order to construct such an index the question of how to value the various components has to be confronted. This issue of weighting, the 'index number problem', is the key to most arguments about changes in living standards. Since there may be no consensus over the weights to choose, it is important to review trends in each of the components individually as well as the overall index.

These methodological issues are reviewed in detail in the next section before the later sections of the chapter present the evidence on real wages and broader measures of living standards. The discussion points to a conclusion which may seem surprising to some, namely, that during the twentieth century living standards grew a good deal more rapidly than the traditional measures of real wages or real GDP per person suggest. If this is correct, it implies a strong contrast with the classic debate on the standard of living during the industrial revolution when living standards improved less quickly than national income.

1.2 Measurement issues

Before reviewing the evidence on various measures of living standards, it is important to be aware of several important issues that arise. Although this may seem rather technical or even boring, it is an essential preliminary for anyone wishing to evaluate the arguments set out in later sections.

1.2.1 *Real wages*

The traditional measure of living standards has been an index of real wages. This entails collecting evidence on money wages and then adjusting them for changes in purchasing power resulting from inflation. Thus real wages in period 1 relative to period 0 can be expressed as $RW_1/RW_0 = (MW_1/P_1)/(MW_0/P_0)$ or, equivalently, $(MW_1/MW_0)/(P_1/P_0)$. Conventionally, the indices of money wages, prices, and real wages are normalized to equal 100 in the base year.

The main issues here concern the price index numbers used to deflate the money wage series. All price index numbers have to confront questions of weighting. The weights assigned to the prices of different items typically reflect quantities purchased for a base period. For example, the price index number used to deflate a person's money wages compared with last year may use quantities from last year or this year (or even an average of the two). The former, a Laspeyres index number, is written as $P_L = \Sigma p_1 q_0 / \Sigma p_0 q_0$ and the latter, a Paasche index number, as $P_p = \Sigma p_1 q_1 / p_0 q_1$. Generally speaking, the rate of inflation depends on the weights used and these two indices will not be exactly the same.

A price index with fixed quantity weights is a COGI (cost of goods index), strictly speaking, rather than a COLI (true cost of living index). A COGI prices a fixed basket of goods and services and will generally overstate the amount of money required to maintain a given standard of living since when relative prices change it is usually possible to substitute now relatively cheaper for more expensive items. If the percentage increase in money wages is greater than that of the Laspeyres price index, the consumer is definitely better off and generally by more than this calculation of real wages will show. A similar point is illustrated in Figure 1.1.

In Figure 1.1 point *A* can be purchased for the same outlay both at original prices (budget line 1) and at new prices (budget line 2). At point *A* the

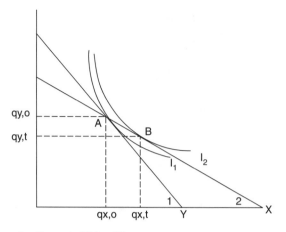

Figure 1.1 Measuring the cost of living (1)

consumer is on indifference curve I_1, which traces out combinations of goods X and Y which provide equal satisfaction to the consumer. After the change in prices with the same money income, although the consumer can still purchase the basket of point A, a higher level of satisfaction can now be attained by moving to point B on indifference curve I_2, which entails consuming more of the now cheaper good, X. So the cost of living has fallen in the sense that with the same cash outlay the consumer reaches a higher indifference curve. A true cost of living index (COLI) measures the expenditure required in order to maintain a given standard of living as prices change.

The difference between a COGI and a COLI is of fundamental importance when seeking to measure long-run changes in living standards since the difference between the two will be amplified by the introduction of new goods and services and by changes in quality that result from technological progress. When a new good becomes available it is necessary to re-compute the expenditure needed to maintain the reference standard of living if it embodies new features that consumers value. For example, in the nineteenth century railways offered faster travel and third-class passengers paid to ride on the train instead of walking. They were significantly better off because of the time that they saved and the invention of railways had decreased their true cost of living despite an increased price of transport (Leunig 2006).

In the recent past, it seems likely that there has been failure adequately to take account of the value of new goods and of quality improvements to consumers. The Boskin Commission in the United States concluded that this might well have led to an overstatement of increases in the cost of living of around 0.5 per cent per year between the 1970s and the 1990s and it seems likely that a similar bias would apply for the United Kingdom. A simple

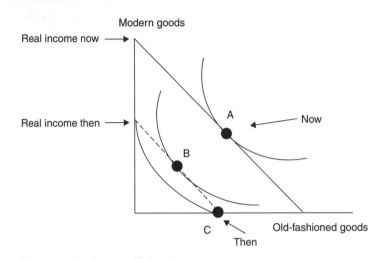

Figure 1.2 Measuring the cost of living (2)

thought experiment suggests that the consumer benefits of the vast increase in the range of goods and services over the long run are not adequately reflected in measures of real income. Real GDP per person at the prices of 1995 was £1,948 in 1870 compared with £12,525 in 2001. But modern goods were unavailable in that earlier period. So the material standard of living in 1870 was what could be obtained in 1995 with £1,948 spent entirely on goods and services already available in 1870. Cars, electric light, hip replacements, DVDs, antibiotics, etc. would not be on the menu.

As Figure 1.2 shows, that would be a much lower standard of living, constrained to be at point *C* rather than point *B*, which the deflation of money income by a 1995-based price index would seem to imply. It follows that the true cost of living has increased by less and living standards have risen by more than conventional methods of measuring inflation indicate.

1.2.2 *Leisure and life expectancy*

The idea that real income should be measured in utility terms, i.e. with reference to the true cost of living, as above, can be extended to consider aspects of life other than material consumption that people care about. Among the most obvious of these are leisure and life expectancy. The basic idea is that, if you earn the same income as another person but work fewer hours, or, if you earn the same income but have a lower risk of dying, you are better off.

Figure 1.3 illustrates how greater longevity could be incorporated into measures of living standards. The person whose preferences are represented in

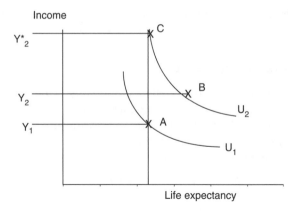

Figure 1.3 Life expectancy and the cost of living

Figure 1.3 regards both longer life and greater income as good things. In period 1 she is at point A and in period 2 at B. Income as conventionally measured has risen from Y_1 to Y_2. If, however, the improved life expectancy were taken away, she would need to be at point C to keep the standard of living represented by U_2; this would require an income of Y^*_2. Thus, the gain from lower risks of mortality is worth $(Y^*_2 - Y_2)$ and the total improvement in welfare is equivalent to $(Y^*_2 - Y_1)$ rather than $(Y_2 - Y_1)$.

This expresses the value of longer expected life in monetary terms. In effect, an increase in life expectancy is taken to be an exogenous change in the consumer's environment which cannot be bought but for which a price would willingly be paid (Usher 1980). This is not an unreasonable view of developments in the twentieth century where longer life became possible mainly as a result of improvements in medical science and public health measures. To make this approach operational requires estimates of how much people value reductions in mortality risks. Inferences can be made from studies of market behaviour in circumstances that involve safety considerations. For example, danger money is paid to steeplejacks.

To take account of reductions in work hours in a similar way, the simplest procedure is to value changes in hours worked at the wage rate that could have been earned (Beckerman 1980). These hours are now used for leisure or non-market work which is presumably worth at least as much as the wages forgone. It should be noted that this is probably a rather conservative approach in the sense that it makes no allowance for any improvement in capacity to enjoy leisure or to perform non-market work more effectively.

More generally, these examples could be extended, in principle, to cover other aspects of environmental conditions that matter, for example, risks of being a victim of violent crime. The key data requirements are to be able to measure the risk and willingness to pay to reduce the risk by a given amount.

1.2.3 *Human Development Index*

The Human Development Index (HDI) has become a popular measure of change in economic well-being. It is a broader measure of socio-economic welfare than either real GDP per person or real wages and also takes into account life expectancy and education. The formula for HDI has varied somewhat over time but the current version is as follows:

$$HDI = (E + I + L)$$

where

$E = 0.67LIT + 0.33ENROL$
$I = (\log y - \log 100)/(\log 40{,}000 - \log 100)$
$L = (e_0 - 25)/(85 - 25)$

where LIT is the adult literacy rate, ENROL is the percentage of the relevant age group enrolled in primary, secondary, and tertiary education, y is real GDP per person measured in 1999 purchasing-power-parity-adjusted dollars, and e_0 is years of life expectancy at birth. Each of E, I, and L has a value between 0 and 1, as does HDI. Values of HDI below 0.5 (above 0.8) are described as 'low (high) development'.

HDI measures development in terms of the fraction of the distance travelled between an assumed minimum and maximum value of the variable concerned. Income is included but is not the only thing that matters. Its origins are in an approach pioneered by Sen (1987) which sees underdevelopment as the lack of certain basic capabilities rather than the lack of income per se. The focus of HDI is on the escape from poverty and in this it is the lives that people lead that are taken to be of intrinsic importance. These outcomes depend substantially on the provision of public services as well as the level of private incomes which may therefore not be a good guide to economic welfare.

HDI is, of course, an index number and, as such, is not immune from 'the index number problem'. In fact, HDI embodies an implicit weighting scheme—or trade-off between its components which is nowhere justified and may not be acceptable to everyone. A one-unit increase in HDI results from an increase in literacy of 0.45 percentage points or of enrolment by 0.90 percentage points or of life expectancy by 0.18 years. The required gain in income depends on the level: at $1,000 it is about $18; at $5,000 about $90; at $10,000 about $180; and so on. This implies a high but not necessarily unreasonable valuation for gains in life expectancy (Crafts 2002*a*). Clearly, anything that is omitted has, in effect, a weighting of zero and there may be a number of excluded aspects of the socio-economic environment whose inclusion could be advocated on grounds similar to those on which education or life expectancy are rationalized, for example, the rights that a person has.

1.2.4 *Diagnostic indicators*

There also exist indicators which reflect well-being and perhaps capture aspects which conventional measures do not but which cannot be regarded as indices of living standards. These indicators, which can be thought of as useful diagnostics, include anthropometric and happiness measures.

Real wages do not take account of work effort or the health environment to which workers are exposed but heights, which are strongly influenced by net nutritional status, will be sensitive to these influences on well-being. In the context of British industrialization in the first half of the nineteenth century declining heights, especially of the urban population, are an important signal that rising real wages do not tell the whole story (Floud 1998).

It is clear that height is not of itself an acceptable direct index of the standard of living. Indeed, it is possible that in some circumstances height and economic well-being could move in opposite directions, for example, if the price of textiles falls and workers switch consumption away from nutrition towards clothing (Komlos 1989). While data on stature could in principle be used to adjust standard national accounts or real wages measures of economic welfare, in practice, the information requirements are severe and out of reach in two fundamental respects. First, a way would have to be found to avoid double counting of the impact on height of increased purchasing power and, second, the welfare implications of the remaining changes in height would have to be quantified. More precisely, estimates of willingness to pay for these extraneous influences on height are required, since height per se is not an aspect of the standard of living (Steckel 1995). This implies that height is a useful diagnostic but no more. Similar remarks apply to Body Mass Index (BMI) which is an indicator of an inappropriate diet in the sense that extreme values reflect poor health.

Over long periods of time, self-assessment of levels of happiness in responses to opinion polls have shown no tendency to improve even though real incomes as conventionally measured have risen substantially and at any point in time individuals with higher incomes do say that they are happier (Blanchflower and Oswald 2004). The solution to this paradox is probably that suggested by Easterlin (2001), namely, that as incomes increase over time the impact on happiness is offset by an increase in material aspirations. This argument is illustrated in Figure 1.4 where at the original level of aspirations (A_1) an increase in income from y_m to y_2 would raise well-being from U_m to U_2. If aspirations then rise to A_2, however, well-being remains at U_m.

That said, a further look at Figure 1.4 reveals that, if income now returned to its original level (y_m), utility would no longer be at U_m but would have fallen to

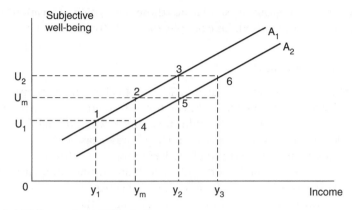

Figure 1.4 Welfare and material aspirations

U_1. So giving up increases in material consumption is not recommended. This is a 'hedonic treadmill'. Nevertheless, the key point is that the failure of happiness to go up does not mean that people would be indifferent to a return to old levels of consumption. On the contrary, being reduced to the real wages of our grandparents would be felt as a major reduction in living standards.

Research into the correlates of self-reported happiness is, however, very helpful in identifying what people regard as important components of their well-being. By comparing the impact of income on reported happiness with that of poor health or unemployment, it is possible to obtain a monetary valuation of these events. In principle, this might be extremely useful in constructing a broad index of economic welfare. In this context, a key finding of the happiness literature is the massive adverse impact of unemployment which is much greater than simply the loss of wage income (Blanchflower and Oswald 2004).

1.2.5 Poverty

It is, of course, possible that living standards have increased over time for the vast majority of the population but that a minority have been excluded and live in 'poverty'. Taking account of the distribution of the benefits of economic growth is clearly an important aspect of describing changes in economic well-being. In that context, it is striking that, throughout the twentieth century, budget studies always found a significant fraction of households below the poverty line.

Measuring poverty is, however, not entirely straightforward. The simplest approach, using an absolute income concept, would be to estimate the budget for each type of household that covers bare subsistence needs in terms of food, shelter, and clothing. If poverty were measured in this way, even at the start of the twentieth century few would have been below the poverty line, the number would have declined steadily over time, and in recent decades would have been approximately zero.

An alternative approach uses a relative income concept of poverty. Poverty might then be defined in terms of falling below a given proportion of median income, again normalizing for household composition. Such a criterion is essentially arbitrary and is perhaps best thought of as a value judgement about the acceptability of various degrees of income inequality. On a definition of this kind poverty is always present, however rapidly absolute living standards have increased. There may well be periods when the numbers in poverty rise, for example, if wage differentials increase or welfare benefits do not keep up with wages such that incomes are less equally distributed.

A more sophisticated concept of poverty is that a person is poor if they cannot participate fully in society (Sen 1979). This requires various consumption standards to be met, but these will change substantially over time as social conventions evolve and as technological progress makes new goods and services available. For example, not having a television was not to be excluded from anything in 1930 but fifty years later was a serious deprivation; social expectations and methods of communication had changed. Using this approach, the basket of goods and services that is required so as not to be poor changes over time and, in practice, requires a larger real outlay.

Early poverty investigators like Rowntree (1901, 1941) adopted so-called 'minimum needs' criteria. Right from the outset, these included expenditures that were occasioned in order to be 'respectable' and, not surprisingly, the consumption baskets proposed by researchers in this tradition evolve and the expenditures required rise over time. In effect, these writers were already adopting a Sen-like criterion. It may well be that the real income required to stay out of poverty from this perspective grows at a similar rate to median income. If so, the operative measure of the poverty line would look like a relative income measure but the underlying philosophy would be quite different.

For much of the post-war period, many investigators looked at poverty in terms of the government's own implicit criterion and estimated the number below 'national assistance' or 'supplementary benefit' levels of income or some ratio of this level such as 110 per cent (Piachaud 1988). From the late 1940s to the early 1980s this amounted, in effect, to a relative income measure as benefits rose in parallel with average earnings. Since then, however, benefits have been indexed to prices and have fallen sharply relative to wages so this approach has fallen out of favour. Most recent analyses have been based on relativist criteria such as percentage below half of mean income.

Finally, it should be noted that, although poverty was traditionally measured in terms of a headcount, it is also relevant to consider the poverty gap in the sense of asking how much more income in total would require to be transferred to eliminate poverty on the chosen criterion. This approach takes into account the severity of the problem of exclusion and is useful for the evaluation of welfare policies.

1.3 Real earnings

The twentieth century was an era of unprecedented economic growth. Although the UK experienced a relative economic decline in that income levels failed to keep pace with those in other OECD economies, nevertheless income levels rose substantially in absolute terms, as Table 1.1 reports. These tendencies were particularly noticeable during the so-called golden age of European economic growth (1950–73).

Over the long run the growth in average real wages tended to exceed that in real GDP per person. According to Table 1.1, the exception to this was in the quarter-century after the golden age, but this may be a bit deceptive since this is the period in which the Boskin Commission issues relating to the accuracy of

Table 1.1. Growth of real GDP per person and real wages

(*a*) Real GDP per person

	Level (1913 = 100)	% Western Europe		Growth rate (% per year)
1870	65	162.8		
1913	100	142.3	1870–1913	1.01
1950	141	151.5	1913–50	0.93
1973	244	105.3	1950–73	2.42
2001	409	104.5	1973–2001	1.86

Source: Maddison (2003).

(*b*) Real wages

	Level (1913 = 100)		Growth rate (% per year)
1873	67		
1901	96		
1913	100	1873–1913	1.01
1938	135		
1951	173	1913–51	1.46
1960	221		
1973	343	1951–73	3.16
1990	406		
2001	483	1973–2001	1.23

Source: Feinstein (1995) updated using *Economic Trends*.

price indices are most acute. Even so, real wage growth in all periods of the twentieth century, including the troubled inter-war period, was significant and, by the standards of earlier centuries, remarkable.

Clark (2005) has recently completed a comprehensive reappraisal of the growth of real wages over the very long run. He found that real wages of an unskilled worker in the 1860s were only about 20 per cent higher than 400 years earlier while in the following 100 years they increased by 250 per cent. Only in the era of modern economic growth since the industrial revolution have real wages grown at a rapid rate.

Real earnings depend not only on real wage rates but also on employment. Over the century as a whole employment grew a little bit faster than population and rose from 18.2 million in 1901 to 22.0 million in 1950 and 27.6 million in 2001. Equally, there is no long-run upward trend in the unemployment rate which, on a consistent basis, was 5.7 per cent in 1901 and 5.2 per cent in 2001 (Boyer and Hatton 2002). There is no reason to believe that globalization or technological progress have reduced employment opportunities in the aggregate, although, clearly, some jobs have disappeared.

Nevertheless, unemployment was very high in some periods of the twentieth century, as Table 1.2 reports. In both the 1930s and 1980s the economy experienced severe shocks which took many years to overcome given the nature of labour market institutions. By contrast, the golden age stands out as a halcyon era when not only was real wage growth at its all-time high but unemployment was remarkably low. Given that welfare losses from unemployment are very big (Blanchflower and Oswald 2004), the high rates of job loss and prevalence of long-term joblessness in these difficult decades are a major qualification to an optimistic interpretation of trends in real wages.

Table 1.1 displayed real wages for the average of all workers but it is also important to consider wage differentials, which have changed considerably over time, as Table 1.3 reports. Much attention has been given recently to the rapid increase in the dispersion between the top and bottom of the wage distribution as reflected in the ratio of the 90th decile over the 10th decile. For male

Table 1.2. Unemployment rate (%)

	Mean	Standard deviation
1871–91	5.5	1.83
1891–1913	6.2	1.31
1921–38	10.9	3.00
1947–73	2.1	0.69
1974–99	10.1	3.88

Note: Unemployment rates adjusted to historically consistent definition throughout.
Source: Boyer and Hatton (2002).

Table 1.3. Wage dispersion: ratio of 90th/10th decile

(a) All men

	Class 1A/Class 7	90th/10th
1913/14	5.21	
1935/36	4.91	
1955/56	3.54	
1970	2.54	2.46
1978	2.44	2.36
1993		3.25
2001		3.48

Sources: Routh (1980) and *New Earnings Survey.*

(b) Male manual workers

	90th/10th
1886	2.09
1906	2.36
1938	2.07
1960	2.06
1973	2.16
1993	2.55
2001	2.56

Source: Thatcher (1976) updated using *New Earnings Survey.*

Table 1.4. Annual hours worked

1870	2755
1913	2656
1950	2112
1973	1919
2001	1655

Sources: Huberman (2004); GGDC (2005).

workers this rose from 2.36 in 1978 to 3.48 in 2001. Real wages for the 10th decile male worker increased only very slowly in the last quarter of the century—by about 12 per cent between 1975 and 2000 (Machin 2003: 195). For female workers, these trends are similar but less marked with the 90/10 ratio rising from 2.94 to 3.79 over the same period with real wages at the 10th decile up by 48 per cent.

The increasing wage dispersion reflects trends in technological change and to a lesser extent competition from low-wage Asian workers which have undermined the demand for unskilled workers. These developments are quite recent and the relativity between top earners and the low skilled behaved very differently in the first three-quarters of the century. As an approximation to the 90/10 ratio for this period Table 1.3 uses the pay ratio between higher professionals (class 1A) and unskilled workers (class 7). This declined steadily from 5.21 in 1913/14 to 2.44 in 1978. Thus, over the twentieth century as a whole the ratio of wages between the top and bottom of the distribution described a U-shape which reached a low point in the mid-1970s. The ratio in 2001 was similar to that in the mid-1950s but well below that of Edwardian Britain.

Finally, it is worth noting trends in hours worked, which are reported in Table 1.4. During the twentieth century the work year fell by about 40 per cent. Over time people worked fewer hours per week—the 54-hour week became the 37-hour week—and took more holidays, with five weeks being quite normal at the end of the century compared with only two weeks forty years earlier. This reflects an income-elastic demand for leisure and is a reflection of technological change in the sense that the purchasing power of an hour of work has risen substantially.

1.4 Health

In moving beyond real wages to a broader concept of the standard of living the most obvious and important extension is to take account of measures of health. These may be seen as diagnostics or as potential components of a more comprehensive index of well-being.

1.4.1 *Height and body mass index*

The best available long-run estimates of these diagnostic indicators are reported in Table 1.5. They show that during the twentieth century both average height and then, a generation or so later, average weight increased. In the

Table 1.5. Mean height, weight, and body mass index of males, aged 19–25

Birth cohort	Height (metres)	Weight (kilograms)	BMI
1840–59	1.71	66.37	21.31
1860–79	1.71	65.07	21.03
1880–99	1.73	66.00	22.03
1900–19	1.73	63.45	21.07
1920–39	1.75	66.08	21.54
1940–59	1.76	71.40	23.00
1960–79	1.76	71.40	23.04

Note: BMI = weight/height^2.
Source: Floud (1998).

later decades average BMI also rose appreciably. As Floud (1998) pointed out, in the context of anthropometric history the fact that the average male was 3 per cent shorter and 10 per cent lighter a hundred years ago is a large difference. Unlike the early industrialization phase, the anthropometric data do not conflict with the positive picture of trends in living standards seen in the real wage series.

Seen in a longer-term perspective, the twentieth century finally saw heights return to and then exceed levels last seen in the early middle ages when northern European males averaged 1.73 metres. Over the millennium, European heights seem to have traced out a U-shape with the low point at about 1.66 metres in the late seventeenth/early eighteenth century (Steckel 2001). By the second half of the twentieth century the balance between nutrition and the disease environment had changed decisively as both aspects improved markedly.

1.4.2 Life expectancy

By 2001 life expectancy at birth was nearly double the level of 1870, as Table 1.6 reports. The huge reduction in mortality risks during the twentieth century is primarily the result of improvements in medical interventions and public health measures. A key breakthrough was the triumph of the germ theory of disease after 1865, and much-improved sanitation followed from public health measures initiated in the 1870s. In the twentieth century antibiotics and new vaccines became available and infectious disease ceased to be a major killer, while in recent times smoking has declined sharply (Cutler and Miller 2005).

Underlying all these improvements have been continuing and very substantial additions to the stock of scientific knowledge. In 1870, British mortality was adversely affected by an exceptionally high degree of urbanization but nowhere in the world was life expectancy at birth as high as 50 years (Crafts 1997). From the mid-sixteenth to the mid-nineteenth centuries any

Table 1.6 Life expectancy at birth and infant mortality

	Life expectancy at birth (years)	Infant mortality (per 1,000 live births)
1870	41.3	144.9
1913	53.4	108.2
1950	69.2	29.8
1973	72.0	16.8
2001	78.1	5.4

Source: Government Actuary's Department.

improvements in life expectancy were quite tenuous and e_0 fluctuated between a little over 30 and a little over 40 years (Wrigley et al. 1997). Until modern science came along high mortality was an inescapable fact of life. By the late twentieth century, across the world life expectancy at any income level was about twenty years more than in 1870 (Kenny 2005).

Life expectancy differs by social class, as it has throughout the period since 1870. Table 1.7 reports the Standardized Mortality Ratio (SMR) for a standard five class breakdown where I comprises professionals and V is unskilled. SMRs compare actual deaths in each group with the number to be expected on the basis of the age-specific mortality rates for the population as a whole. The most notable feature of Table 1.7 is the narrowing of health inequalities in the first half of the twentieth century followed by a sharp reversal of this trend in the second half. Presumably, the widening gap between class I and class V in recent decades derives from some combination of social deprivation, lifestyle choices, and differential ability to access medical treatment.

Understandably, many writers have seen these trends in SMRs as disturbing, especially since the rise in health inequalities has occurred in the era of the National Health Service. It also combines with the changes in wage differentials to underline that manual workers did relatively badly in the latter part of the twentieth century. However, this is not to say that life expectancy was declining absolutely; on the contrary between 1972/76 and 1997/2001 e_0 for social class V rose from 66.4 to 71.0 years, well above the average of all classes in 1950.

1.4.3 Retirement

The expected length of retirement depends both on life expectancy on and on decisions on when to cease work, themselves influenced by collective bargaining, labour market regulation, and pension arrangements. Table 1.8 reports

Table 1.7 Standardized mortality ratios by social class, males 15/20–64

	I	II	III	III	IV	V	Ratio: V/I
1871	81	119	96		111	137	1.69
1901	75	95	97		117	132	1.76
1921	82	94	95		101	125	1.52
1931	90	94	97		102	111	1.23
1951	86	92	101		104	118	1.37
1971	77	81	IIIN: 99	IIIM: 106	114	137	1.78
1991	66	72	IIIN: 100	IIIM: 117	116	189	2.86

Note: Data are for ages 15–64 except for 1991 which are for ages 20–64.
Sources: Woods and Williams (1995); Shaw et al. (1999).

Table 1.8 Expected years of retirement
for males at age 20

1881	1.76
1891	2.44
1901	2.84
1911	3.17
1921	3.96
1931	4.66
1941	5.72
1951	6.44
1961	6.83
1971	8.29
1981	10.29
1991	13.64
2001	15.62

Source: Crafts (2005).

that expected years of retirement for a 20-year-old male were about thirteen more in 2001 than in 1881, having risen from 1.76 to 15.62 years in that time.

This represents a significant improvement in living standards not only because of greater length but also better quality of the retirement period. In recent decades, retirement has come to be viewed much more positively as a time for enjoyment and creative experience (Costa 1998). Longer retirement has resulted mainly from longer life rather than earlier retirement. If mortality were still at the 1881 level, the expected retirement period for a 20-year-old male in 2001 would have been only 6.5 years; in other words, about two-thirds of the increase in the retirement period can be attributed to longer life expectancy (Crafts 2005).

The combination of longer retirement and shorter work years (as reported in Table 1.4) implies that today's 20-year-old can look forward to a work–life balance that seems much more attractive than the prospect that would have faced his great-great-great-grandfather in 1881. Then the expectation was that 46 per cent of waking hours would be spent at work, now only about 20 per cent. Put another way, expected hours of leisure time over the life cycle have approximately doubled in that time (Crafts 2005).

1.5 Broad measures of living standards

In this section the objective is to aggregate over various components of living standards to form an index of changes in economic welfare. This requires a set of weights or a method to value items other than income in income equivalents. There is no consensus on how best to proceed so what follows is illustrative rather than definitive.

1.5.1 *Human Development Index (HDI)*

To obtain HDI scores requires information on income, life expectancy, and education. The improvement over time in the first two has already been described. Table 1.9 reports estimates of educational standards which are required for the computation of HDI. Here too there is a substantial improvement over time, especially in terms of enrolment. In the early twentieth century few people went into secondary education—about 5 per cent of the age group were enrolled in 1913 and only 10 per cent in 1938—but by the end of the century about 70 per cent of 15- to 19-year-olds were in full-time education. Years of schooling of the labour force rose from 6.0 years in 1901 to 9.2 in 1951 and 12.7 in 2001 (Matthews et al. 1982; OECD 2004). It should be noted, however, that this measures quantity not quality of education, which has left much to be desired for less fortunate members of British society. In the mid-1990s about 23 per cent of the British labour force were found to be too badly educated to participate in a knowledge-based economy compared with 7 per cent in Sweden (OECD 2000).

Table 1.10 reports estimates of HDI. These show the UK just escaping from 'low' human development by 1870 and reaching 'high' human development during the golden age. Its score at the end of the twentieth century is fairly typical for an OECD country. The HDI index suggests steady progress away from low levels of development between 1870 and 1950 despite the turmoil of two world wars and the inter-war depression. Once a high level of development has been reached this is no longer a very useful indicator.

It should be remembered that, although HDI has been widely used, it is an index number and, as such, embodies a set of weights that do not necessarily command universal approval. In particular, HDI places a lot of emphasis on changes in life expectancy. Since this improved markedly from the late nineteenth century onwards, it is not surprising that HDI also did so. HDI is a

Table 1.9 Educational aspects of Human Development Index

	LIT	ENROL
1871	76	35.4
1913	96	43.1
1950	99	51.0
1973	99	66.7
2001	99	112.0

Note: ENROL is the proportion of the relevant age group enrolled in primary, secondary, and tertiary education.

Sources: Crafts (1997); UNDP (2003).

Table 1.10 Human Development Index

1870	0.500
1913	0.644
1950	0.766
1973	0.839
2001	0.930

Note: HDI $= (E + I + L)/3$
where $E = 0.67LIT + 0.33ENROL$
$I = (\log y - 100)/(\log 40{,}000 - \log 100)$
$L = (e_0 - 25)/(85 - 25)$
where e_0 is years of life expectancy at birth, y is
GDP per person in 1999 purchasing-power-
parity-adjusted dollars, LIT is the adult literacy
rate, ENROL is the proportion of the relevant
age group enrolled in primary, secondary, and
tertiary education.
Sources: Crafts (2002a); UNDP (2003).

distance measure so it does not permit a comparison of the growth rate of a broader measure of living standards with that of real wages or real GDP per person.

1.5.2 Augmented GDP

The basic ideas that are put into practice here were set out in principle in section 1.2.2. Changes in hours worked and mortality risks are given a monetary valuation and added to the change in GDP per person to calculate a growth rate for augmented GDP per person. The leisure calculation is based on the methodology of Beckerman (1980), as described earlier. The longevity calculation uses a technique suggested by Nordhaus (2002).

This method values improvements in life expectancy by taking the change in the population-weighted average of age-specific mortality rates multiplied by the estimated value of a death averted. This last is based, as has become normal in studies of this kind, on the value of a statistical life (VSL), a measure of willingness to pay for reductions in mortality risks.[1] A recent survey of the international evidence concluded that a good rule of thumb is that VSL is around 120 times GDP per person and grows at the same rate as real GDP per person; for the UK the best estimate is a multiple of 132 times per capita GDP with a range of 101 to 154 (Miller 2000). This would mean that VSL in 2001 was £1.92 million.

An extension to the Nordhaus methodology is to allow for age differences in the value of reductions in mortality risks. Generally, this would imply an

---

[1] VSL is the total price that the population is willing to pay to reduce its expected death toll by one. Thus, if 60 million people are each willing to pay 1.667 pence for a public health improvement that saves one life, VSL is £1 million.

Table 1.11 Illustrative imputations for improved life expectancy and leisure (% per year)

	Mortality unweighted	Mortality age weighted	Leisure
1870–1913	2.1	1.8	0.0
1913–50	2.4	1.7	0.3
1950–73	2.5	0.9	0.3
1973–2001	2.2	1.4	0.2

Sources: See text.

inverted U-shape over the life cycle in willingness to pay with a peak around age 30 and falling quite steeply in old age, based on the fact that earning power rises initially then falls while quality of life typically declines in the later years of life (Murphy and Topel 2005).

Table 1.11 reports estimates of the contribution to growth made by reduced mortality risks using the Nordhaus methodology in column (1) and adjusting for age weighting according to the schedule in Murray (1996) in column (2).[2] Lower and upper bounds on the estimates of column (1) based on letting VSL range between 101 and 154 times GDP per person would give a margin of about +/− 0.5 percentage points per year around the central estimate. The age-weighted estimates in column (2) give lower contributions to growth because mortality reductions have been skewed to the early and late years of life.

The clear message of Table 1.11 is that taking into account the welfare gains of longer life expectancy potentially makes a big difference to estimated growth in living standards. This conclusion is in line with that of Nordhaus (2002) for the United States and, although the exact numbers would change, quite robust to changes in the detail of the assumptions.

The imputation for leisure in Table 1.11 is relatively small. Nevertheless, if the contributions of both greater longevity and shorter work hours captured by columns (2) and (3) of Table 1.11 are added to the conventional growth rate of real GDP per person reported in Table 1.1, the augmented growth rate goes up from 1.0 to 2.8 per cent per year in 1870 to 1913, from 0.9 to 2.9 per cent from 1913 to 1950, from 2.4 to 3.6 per cent in 1950 to 1973 and from 1.9 to 3.5 per cent in 1973 to 2001.

1.6 Poverty

The extent of poverty depends on the concept adopted, as was discussed in section 2.5. The estimates in Table 1.12 are based on measures commonly used at

---

[2] Full details of the methodology are reported in Crafts (2005).

Nicholas Crafts

Table 1.12 Poverty lines and percentage in poverty

	Poverty line (£)	Poverty line (% average disposable income)	In poverty (%)
1899: Rowntree	53.10	115	10
1936: Rowntree Class A	56.45	91	8
1953: Benefits	69.40	109	5
1979: Benefits	121.60	111	6
1979: < 0.5 mean income	155.09	134	8
2000: < 0.5 mean income	243.21	124	21

Note: Poverty line is for man, woman, and three children in 2000 prices; percentage in poverty refers to persons.

Sources: Poverty line from Piachaud and Webb (2004) except 1936 from Piachaud (1988); percentage in poverty from Hills (2004a) except 1953 from Fiegehen et al. (1977).

the time. The selection can be thought of as broadly consistent with a social participation standard which converts to a fairly constant proportion of average disposable income, as proposed by Piachaud (1988).[3] The absolute income level at the poverty line rises by nearly five times over the twentieth century. Rowntree's work, which is based on surveys of York, has been revised by recent research. Gazeley (2003) suggests that a more accurate estimate for the percentage in poverty in 1899 is 6 per cent. Rowntree's third survey, of York in 1950, is known to be seriously flawed and its claims that poverty has fallen to below 2 per cent of the population are not credible (Hatton and Bailey 2000).

On this basis, it appears that the proportion in poverty did not change greatly during the first four-fifths of the twentieth century, varying between 5 and 8 per cent of the population, if York is representative of the UK which is probably an acceptable assumption. In the last two decades, however, there was a surge up to about 1 in 5 persons by the end of the century.

If the poverty line were kept at a constant absolute level, obviously, the picture would look very different. For example, on the 1899 standard poverty in 1936 was 4 per cent, and poverty in 1971 was 0.5 per cent on the 1953 standard. If a criterion of below 60 per cent of 1996/97 median income is adopted, then 18 per cent were in poverty in that year compared with 30 per cent in 1979 and only 10 per cent in 2002/03 (Hills 2004b). The recent surge in poverty would disappear if the poverty line were frozen at the 1979 level. The estimates reported in Table 1.12 do, however, represent the mainstream view.

What accounted for the late-century rise in poverty? In part, the answer comes from trends in the labour market discussed in section 1.3. These included rising unemployment and economic inactivity and the declining

[3] The 1936 figure for categories other than man, woman, and three children do support this remark.

relative wages of unskilled workers. Both these trends were seriously exacerbated by the poor quality of education of the socially disadvantaged. Demographic changes played a major role as well: in particular, lone parent families became much more common and there were more elderly people. Government policy also mattered since benefits were indexed to prices rather than wages.

The rise in poverty in the late twentieth century is an important qualification to an optimistic account of trends in living standards. It should not be seen as reflecting declines in absolute levels of income or health but it does represent a major break from what had hitherto been a more inclusive type of economic growth.

1.7 Conclusions

The basic conclusion of this chapter is that average living standards rose substantially during the twentieth century. The rate of advance far outstripped any previous period. Real wages grew at over 1 per cent per year during the first half of the century despite the turmoil of the depression and two world wars and at about 2 per cent per year in the second half. If it were possible to take full account of the value to consumers of improvements in the quality and range of goods and services over time, these estimates would surely be increased appreciably.

Other changes contributed to increased well-being. Since 1870 annual hours worked have nearly halved while life expectancy has nearly doubled. The latter is particularly important because people place a high value on reduction in mortality risks. If these changes are valued in terms of an equivalent increase in GDP, this would add considerably to growth. A measure of real GDP per person augmented to take account of these factors grew at about 3 per cent per year in the first half of the twentieth century and at about 3.5 per cent per year in the second half.

There are, however, some important qualifications to this optimistic picture. First, it should be noted that while growth in living standards might be described as 'inclusive' through the first three-quarters of the century this is a less apt description of the final quarter, which was marked by a big increase in the proportion living on less than half of average income from 8 to 21 per cent of the population. Secondly, some periods, notably the 1930s and 1980s, were seriously blighted by unemployment. Here too a significant minority of the population were excluded from the benefits of economic growth. The evidence suggests that welfare losses from involuntary unemployment are very large.

Also, there are inevitably technical limitations to this discussion. First, the issue of the future sustainability of the growth of living standards has not been addressed. Secondly, it has not been possible to adjust the national income accounts for all their limitations. That said, were this feasible, it is quite unlikely that the finding that average living standards rose appreciably throughout the century would be undermined (Crafts 2002b). Finally, there are, of course, serious index number problems in seeking to measure the growth of living standards, and the estimates discussed in this chapter might be challenged by an investigator taking a different stance on these issues.

References

Beckerman, W. (1980). 'Comparative Growth Rates of "Measurable Economic Welfare": Some Experimental Calculations', in R. C. O. Matthews (ed.), *Economic Growth and Resources*, vol. ii. London: Macmillan, 36–59.

Blanchflower, D. G., and Oswald, A. J. (2004). 'Well-Being over Time in Britain and the USA', *Journal of Public Economics*, 88: 1359–86.

Boyer, G. R., and Hatton, T. J. (2002). 'New Estimates of British Unemployment, 1870–1913'. *Journal of Economic History*, 62: 643–75.

Clark, G. (2005). 'The Condition of the Working Class in England, 1209–2004'. *Journal of Political Economy*, 113: 1307–40.

Costa, D. L. (1998). *The Evolution of Retirement*. Chicago: Chicago University Press.

Crafts, N. (1997). 'The Human Development Index and Changes in Standards of Living: Some Historical Comparisons'. *European Review of Economic History*, 1: 299–322.

—— (2002a). 'The Human Development Index, 1870–1999: Some Revised Estimates'. *European Review of Economic History*, 6: 395–405.

—— (2002b). 'UK Real National Income, 1950–1998: Some Grounds for Optimism'. *National Institute Economic Review*, 181: 87–95.

—— (2005). 'The Contribution of Increased Life Expectancy to the Growth of Living Standards in the UK, 1870–2001'. Mimeo, London School of Economics.

Cutler, D. M., and Miller, G. (2005). 'The Role of Public Health Improvements in Health Advances'. *Demography*, 42: 1–22.

Easterlin, R. A. (2001). 'Income and Happiness: Towards a Unified Theory'. *Economic Journal*, 111: 465–84.

Feinstein, C. H. (1995). 'Changes in Nominal Wages, the Cost of Living and Real Wages in the United Kingdom over Two Centuries, 1780–1990', in P. Scholliers and V. Zamagni (eds.), *Labour's Reward*. Aldershot: Edward Elgar, 3–36.

Fiegehen, G. C., Lansley, P. S., and Smith, A. D. (1977). *Poverty and Progress in Britain, 1953–1973*. Cambridge: Cambridge University Press.

Floud, R. (1998). 'Height, Weight and Body Mass of the British Population since 1820'. NBER Historical Paper 108.

—— and Harris, B. (1997). 'Health, Height, and Welfare: Britain, 1700–1980', in R. H. Steckel and R. Floud (eds.), *Health and Welfare during Industrialization*. Chicago: University of Chicago Press, 91–126.

Gazeley, I. S. (2003). *Poverty in Britain, 1900–1965*. Basingstoke: Palgrave Macmillan.

Groningen Growth and Development Centre (2005). *Total Economy Database*.

Hatton, T. J., and Bailey, R. E. (2000). 'Seebohm Rowntree and the Postwar Poverty Puzzle'. *Economic History Review*, 53: 517–43.

Hills, J. (2004a). *Inequality and the State*. Oxford: Oxford University Press.

Hills, J. (2004b). 'The Last Quarter Century: From New Right to New Labour', in H. Glennerster, J. Hills, D. Piachaud, and J. Webb (eds.), *One Hundred Years of Poverty and Policy*. York: Joseph Rowntree Foundation, 92–131.

Huberman, M. (2004). 'Working Hours of the World Unite? New International Evidence of Worktime, 1870–1913'. *Journal of Economic History*, 64: 964–1001.

Kenny, C. (2005). 'Why are we Worried about Income? Nearly Everything Else that Matters is Converging'. *World Development*, 33: 1–19.

Komlos, J. (1989). *Nutrition and Economic Development in the Eighteenth Century Habsburg Monarchy*. Princeton: Princeton University Press.

Leunig, T. (2006). 'Time is Money: A Reassessment of the Social Savings from Victorion British Railways'. *Journal of Economic History*, 66: 635–73.

Machin, S. (2003). 'Wage Inequality since 1975', in R. Dickens, P. Gregg, and J. Wadsworth (eds.), *The Labour Market under New Labour*. Bašingstoke: Palgrave Macmillan, 191–200.

Maddison, A. (2003). *The World Economy: Historical Statistics*. Paris: OECD.

Matthews, R. C. O., Feinstein, C. H., and Odling Smee, J. C. (1982). *British Economic Growth, 1856–1973*. Stanford, Calif.: Stanford University Press.

Miller, T. (2000). 'Variations between Countries in Values of Statistical Life'. *Journal of Transport Economics and Policy*, 34: 169–88.

Murphy, K. M., and Topel, R. H. (2005). 'The Value of Health and Longevity'. NBER Working Paper 11405.

Murray, C. (1996). 'Rethinking DALYs', in C. Murray and A. Lopez (eds.), *The Global Burden of Disease*. Cambridge, Mass.: Harvard University Press, 1–98.

Nordhaus, W. D. (2002). 'The Health of Nations: The Contribution of Improved Health to Living Standards'. NBER (National Bureau of Economic Research) Working Paper 8818.

OECD (Organization for Economic Cooperation and Development) (2000). *Literacy in the Information Age*. Paris: OECD.

—— (2004). *Education at a Glance*. Paris: OECD.

Piachaud, D. (1988). 'Poverty in Britain 1899 to 1983'. *Journal of Social Policy*, 17: 335–49.

—— and Webb, J. (2004). 'Changes in Poverty', in H. Glennerster, J. Hills, D. Piachaud, and J. Webb (eds.), *One Hundred Years of Poverty and Policy*. York: Joseph Rowntree Foundation, 29–47.

Routh, G. (1980). *Occupation and Pay in Great Britain, 1906–1979*. London: Macmillan.

Rowntree, B. S. (1901). *Poverty: A Study of Town Life*. London: Macmillan.

—— (1941). *Poverty and Progress*. London: Longmans, Green.

Sen, A. K. (1979). 'Issues in the Measurement of Poverty'. *Scandinavian Journal of Economics*, 81: 285–307.

—— (1987). *The Standard of Living*. Cambridge: Cambridge University Press.

Shaw, M., Dorling, D., Gordon, D., and Smith, G. D. (1999). *The Widening Gap: Health Inequalities and Policy in Britain*. Bristol: The Policy Press.

Steckel, R. H. (1995). 'Stature and the Standard of Living'. *Journal of Economic Literature*, 33: 1903–40.

—— (2001). 'Health and Nutrition in the Pre-Industrial Era: Insights from a Millennium of Average Heights in Northern Europe'. NBER (National Bureau of Economic Research) Working Paper 8542.

Thatcher, A. R. (1976). 'The New Earnings Survey and the Distribution of Earnings', in A. B. Atkinson (ed.), *The Personal Distribution of Income*. London: Allen and Unwin, 227–59.

UNDP (2003). *Human Development Report*. New York: United Nations.

Usher, D. (1980). *The Measurement of Economic Growth*. Oxford: Blackwell.

Woods, R., and Williams, N. (1995). 'Must the Gap Widen Before it Can be Narrowed? Long Term Trends in Social Class Mortality Differentials'. *Continuity and Change*, 10: 105–37.

Wrigley, E. A., Davies, R. S., Oeppen, J. E., and Schofield, R. S. (1997). *English Population History from Family Reconstitution, 1580–1837*. Cambridge: Cambridge University Press.

2

Structural Change

Andrew Newell

2.1 Introduction

This chapter presents and analyses the major structural changes, in terms of industry and occupation, that took place in the British labour market over the twentieth century. The engine driving these changes was technological progress, which completely transformed the occupations, industries, hours of work, and, most of all, the standard of living of British workers. These statements may seem to leave too little room for a long list of other influences such as the growth of education, industrial, economic, or social policy, or the campaigns of trade unions and other social activists concerned with working conditions. All these influences matter, of course, but, as we will see, the massive scale of the changes rules out any other influence as truly fundamental.

The case for viewing technological change as the primary cause of change is enhanced by taking an international perspective. The path of the British economy in the twentieth century is very similar to the paths taken by most of the advanced Western countries. Any theory of the direction of change must apply throughout the region, suitably modified for local conditions. Technological change meets this requirement.

The most obvious change is in the living standards available to workers. This is the topic of Chapter 1, but to emphasize the role of technology, it is worth noting that the best available estimates are of fourfold (400 per cent) increases in the standard of living and the level of productivity of the average British worker through the twentieth century. Exact comparisons of living standards over long periods are fraught with difficulties of interpretation, mostly related to the technological change that causes them. For instance, one hundred years ago many contemporary goods were not yet invented. Nevertheless, there is no doubt the twentieth century delivered massive increases in living standards in Britain (and the rest of the world) and these were far greater improvements than in any known previous century, see, again, Chapter 1 and also, *inter alia*, Lucas (2000).

Figure 2.1 Real wages and productivity, UK 1900–2003

Notes: Output per worker is GDP at constant prices divided by total employment. The real wage is an index of average weekly earnings divided by an index of retail prices.

Sources: Feinstein (1972); **www.statistics.gov.uk/STATBASE/**.

Figure 2.1 shows the bulk of this improvement came in the second half of the century. Wars and the macroeconomic disasters of the 1920s and 1930s slowed economic growth 1900–50. After 1950 a massive volume of technological change took place. What were these technological changes? Mowery and Rosenberg (1998) argue there were four main areas of innovation driving the direction of change in the advanced economies. These were: innovations related to the internal combustion engine, generating great reductions in transport costs; innovations in chemicals, especially related to agriculture, but also pharmaceuticals and plastics; innovations related to new uses of electrical power; and finally the electronics, information technology, and communications revolutions.

Most of these innovations changed the processes of making things, so that goods became cheaper, more reliable, or more desirable in other ways. Other innovations took the form of new products. Of course, these two forms of innovation interacted with one another. Mowery and Rosenberg (1998) also emphasize that innovation itself became an identifiable industry in the twentieth century, as commercial companies found it profitable to build research and development capacity and the university system expanded.

The biggest structural change in British employment has been the rise of non-manual work. This topic occupies the bulk of the chapter. Section 2.2 is a discussion of the relevant data. Section 2.3 is an analysis of the rise in non-manual employment *within* industries. Three causes are examined. First is a discussion of the extent to which the direction of technological change was biased against manual workers. This is followed by a discussion of the impact of increased competition in international trade on the occupational mix of

British employment. Finally there is a discussion of the rise of *outsourcing*, that is, multinational production within companies.

Section 2.4 investigates the great industrial shift of UK employment to services. The demand for services, and service workers, remained buoyant even though technical progress has ensured that many goods have become very cheap relative to the services for which they might be substitutes. The reason for this buoyancy must be that demand for services rises very strongly with income. This income elasticity may be partly due to the time-saving nature of some services. As real wages increase, the opportunity cost of domestic work rises, in turn raising the demand for time-saving services. This happens despite great technological progress in home production, via new domestic appliances and innovations in food preparation.

The remaining sections examine other aspects of industrial change. Section 2.5 discusses industrial change in employment in the inter-war years and the decline of the staple industries. Section 2.6 discusses the timing of industrial change, and concludes.

One industrial change not mentioned elsewhere in the chapter is the decline of agriculture. Throughout the century, agricultural employment has been shrinking (see Table 2.1). The kinds of arguments already outlined seem likely to apply to the case of agriculture. First, technological change, in the form of mechanization, new seed varieties, fertilizer, and pesticide technologies as well as more intensive animal husbandry, have raised labour productivity in the sector. Secondly, there is Engel's law. This states that food, the main output of the agricultural sector, declines as a share of consumer spending as incomes rise. These two arguments make a powerful combination of forces driving agricultural employment downward. Thirdly, the use of synthetic fabrics has reduced demand for wool. A final force driving workers out of agriculture might have been falling relative transport costs that, if allowed, increase the penetration into the UK market of agricultural products from lower-cost, less-developed countries.

2.2 Long-run trends in British employment

2.2.1 *Occupation*

Over the century the most dramatic change in the nature of the jobs performed by British workers has been the shift away from manual work (see Table 2.2). In 1921 around 61 per cent of workers performed manual work. By 2003 manual workers were only 31 per cent of the employed. Of course, this shift was not unique to Britain. A similar change is visible in other industrialized economies; see, for instance, the data for the United States in Table 2.3. Secondly, the change has been very pronounced in Britain. By the end of the century, there were fewer manual workers in Britain than in other major

Table 2.1. Employment by industry, UK 1901–2001

	Total	Agriculture, forestry, and fishing	Energy	Manufacturing	Construction	Distributive trades[a]	Transport	Public admin., education, and health	Financial and other services[a]
000s									
1901	18,680	2,420	1,120	5,990	1,090	1,990	1,450	1,600	3,020
1911	20,390	2,400	1,410	6,550	1,030	2,460	1,580	1,670	3,290
1920	20,297	1,741	1,510	7,208	927	2,352	1,641	2,242	2,676
1935	19,685	1,394	1,133	6,387	1,141	2,965	1,579	2,094	3,368
1950	23,303	1,186	1,221	8,133	1,476	2,841	1,840	3,759	2,847
1965	25,764	853	1,049	9,141	1,909	3,508	1,702	4,393	3,209
1980	27,067	634	683	6,797	1,927	5,602	1,732	5,598	4,095
1995	27,653	562	238	4,407	1,813	6,358	1,583	6,504	6,186
2001	29,728	469	219	4,075	1,902	6,836	1,832	6,886	7,509
%									
1901	100	13.0	6.0	32.1	5.8	10.7	7.8	8.6	16.2
1911	100	11.8	6.9	32.1	5.1	12.1	7.7	8.2	16.1
1920	100	8.6	7.4	35.5	4.6	11.6	8.1	11.0	13.2
1935	100	7.1	5.8	32.4	5.8	15.1	8.0	10.6	17.1
1950	100	5.1	5.2	34.9	6.3	12.2	7.9	16.1	12.2
1965	100	3.3	4.1	35.5	7.4	13.6	6.6	17.1	12.5
1980	100	2.3	2.5	25.1	7.1	20.7	6.4	20.7	15.1
1995	100	2.0	0.9	15.9	6.6	23.0	5.7	23.5	22.4
2001	100	1.6	0.7	13.7	6.4	23.0	6.2	23.2	25.2

[a] For 1901–65 hotels and restaurants are included with financial and other services. For 1980–2001 hotels and restaurants are included with distributive trades.

Sources: 1901 and 1911: Feinstein (1972: table 60); 1920–65: Feinstein (1972: table 59); 1980–2001: **www.statistics.gov.uk/STATBASE/**.

Table 2.2. Employment by occupational groups percentage shares: 1921–2003

	1921	1931	1951	1966	1977	2003[a]
Managerial, professional and technical	6.2	6.6	8.2	12.9	26.7	40.1
Personal services	11.4	12.1	9.4	12.1	11.0	7.6
Sales	9.1	13.7	9.8	9.7	6.3	7.9
Clerical	7.3	7.2	11.4	14.0	16.1	13.0
Skilled, semi-skilled, and unskilled manual	46.4	43.1	43.0	47.4	36.8	31.4
Agricultural	7.7	6.4	5.5	3.5	1.7	—
Other	11.8	10.8	12.7[b]	0.3	1.4	—
Total (000s)	19,371	21,773	22,595	23,916	23,756	28,206

Note: Early data from *British Labour Statistics: Historical Abstract*, table 102, show that the share of employment in non-manual intensive sectors rose from 24% in 1901 to 26% in 1921.

[a] Data refer to Great Britain, except for 2003, which refers to the United Kingdom. Agricultural workers were not separately identified in 2003.
[b] Includes armed forces.
Sources: 1921–51: Mitchell and Deane (1962); 1977, 2003: Labour Force Survey.

Table 2.3. The occupational distribution of the workforce in the USA, 1900–2002 (%)

	1900	1910	1920	1930	1940	1950	1960	1970	1983	2002
Prof. + tech.	4.3	4.7	5.4	6.8	7.5	8.6	10.8	14.3	15.7	19.4
Managerial	5.8	6.6	6.6	7.4	7.3	8.7	8.1	8.0	10.7	15.1
Clerical	3.0	5.3	8.0	8.9	9.6	12.3	14.1	17.6	16.3	13.3
Sales	4.5	4.7	4.9	6.3	6.7	7.0	7.1	7.0	11.7	11.9
Craft	10.5	11.6	13.0	12.8	12.0	14.2	13.6	13.7	12.2	10.7
Operatives	12.8	14.6	15.6	15.8	18.4	20.4	18.9	17.8	16.0[a]	13.0[a]
Labourers	12.5	12.0	11.6	11.0	9.4	6.6	5.2	4.7	—	—
Servants	5.4	5.0	3.3	4.1	4.7	2.6	2.7	1.5	1.0	0.6
Other services	3.6	4.6	4.5	5.7	7.1	7.9	8.5	11.2	12.8	13.5
Farmers	19.9	16.5	15.3	12.4	10.4	7.4	3.7	1.8	3.7[b]	2.5[b]
Farm labourers	17.7	14.4	11.7	8.8	7.0	4.4	2.3	1.3	—	—
All (000s)	29,030	37,291	42,206	48,686	51,742	58,999	67,990	80,603	100,834	136,485

[a] For 1983 and 2002 operatives and labourers are combined.
[b] For 1983 and 2002 farmers and farm labourers are combined.
Sources: 1900–70: Historical Statistics of the United States from Colonial Times to 1970, series D 183–232; 1983 and 2002: Statistical Abstract of the United States: 2003, table 615.

European economies (see Table 2.4). The share of manual and agricultural occupations among employees in 1998 was under 30 per cent in Britain and the USA, but substantially higher in Western European countries: 36 per cent in Germany, 39 per cent in France, and 40 per cent in Italy. Thirdly, looking back to Table 2.2 it is notable that whereas the decline in agricultural employment took place throughout the century, the decline in non-agricultural manual work only started in Britain after the mid-1960s.

Table 2.4. The occupational distribution of employees in four European countries, 1998

	Germany	France	Italy	UK
Managerial	3.3	4.6	1.9	14.2
Professional	12.0	10.1	10.5	15.1
Technical	20.5	18.7	14.3	8.2
Clerical	13.9	16.1	17.5	18.0
Service and sales	11.9	13.3	10.8	16.3
Agriculture	1.2	1.6	0.9	0.5
Craft	18.7	16.7	18.0	10.3
Operators	8.2	12.1	10.9	8.5
Elementary	7.9	8.9	10.2	8.4
Armed forces	0.7	1.6	1.3	0.5
No response	1.6	0.2	3.8	0.0
All	100.0	100.0	100.0	100.0

Source: Eurostat Labour Force Survey, Main Results 1998.

2.2.2 Industry

The industrial structure of employment has also undergone a great transition. Data on employment by industry (see Table 2.1) show a very large shift away from employment in the *production* industries (agriculture, mining, manufacturing, and construction) towards service employment. These four broad industry categories have always had much higher proportions of manual workers than the rest of the economy. In British Labour Force Survey data for 2003, for instance, the share of manual workers in total employment stood at 77.1, 71.3, 53.2, and 53.5 per cent in agriculture, construction, manufacturing, and transport respectively. By contrast, none of the major service sectors had more than 25 per cent manual employment. In parallel to the occupational changes and aside from the long-run agricultural trend, the main shift away from employment in production seems to take place after the mid-1960s.

However, there were contrasting trends within the production sector. Many older industries, i.e. agriculture, coal, iron and steel, mechanical engineering, especially shipbuilding and textiles, were in decline for much of the century. Other manufacturing industries, vehicles, electrical and electronic goods, for instance, all grew in importance in the early part of the century before declining in the final thirty years.

These shifts away from employment in production industries also took place in Europe (see Table 2.5) and in the USA (see Figure 2.2). Figure 2.2 also shows that the shift away from production industries seems to take place earlier in the USA, perhaps starting in the 1950s, whereas in the UK, as mentioned before, the share of production industries in employment fell fastest in the 1970s and 1980s.

Table 2.5. Percentage shares of employees by industry, selected European countries, 1960–98

	Germany			France			Italy			UK		
	Agric.	Industry	Service	Agric.	Industry	Service	Agric.	Industry	Service	Agric.	Industry	Service
1960	2.9	59.7	37.4	7.2	50.1	42.7	14.8	51.8	33.4	4.2	46.8	49.0
1973	1.1	52.4	46.5	2.4	44.7	52.9	7.0	52.8	40.2	1.6	45.2	53.2
1998	1.6	36.0	62.3	4.4	26.4	69.2	3.1	35.9	61.0	0.9	26.5	72.5

Source: Eurostat: Labour Force Survey Results, various issues.

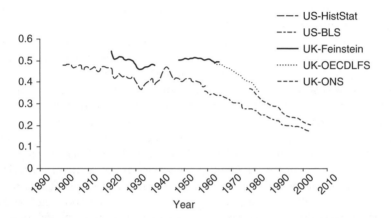

Figure 2.2 Share of production industries in non-agricultural employment, USA and UK

Notes: HistStat: Historical Statistics of the United States from Colonial Times to 1970; BLS: **ww.bls.gov**; Feinstein: Feinstein (1972); OECDLFS: OECD Labour Force Statistics, ONS: Office of National Statistics.

2.3 The rise of non-manual work, part 1: skill substitution

Could this great change be driven entirely by changes in labour supply? Such changes have, of course, taken place. Most types of non-manual work require more advanced education than manual work, and as Chapter 11 shows, the British labour force was much better educated by the end of the century than at the beginning. This improvement accelerated in the second half of the century. The increase in women's participation in the labour market was also more marked in the second half of the century. Highly educated workers and women are both groups who tend more to occupy non-manual jobs, so it could be that changes in the structure of labour supply have forced all of the change in employment. Evidence on this question comes from the behaviour of wages.

To understand this evidence we need to accept the proposition that if the rise in skilled/non-manual[1] labour supply were the sole cause of their greater employment, then we would expect to find a fall in their relative wages. This will be the case as long as skilled and unskilled workers are not perfectly substitutable in production.

However there are no long-term falls in the relative wages of skilled workers. In fact the trend is quite the opposite, at least after 1980. Since 1980, the rise in skilled non-manual labour supply went hand in hand with *rising* relative wages (see Chapter 4). Katz and Murphy (1992) develop a formal test of the labour supply hypothesis. They find strong evidence for the existence of demand shifts in favour of skilled workers in the United States in the 1980s. Similar evidence is given for the UK in Machin (1996).

The shift towards non-manual work reflects changes in the types of goods and services produced by British workers as well as changes in methods of production. The changing skill mix within industries is the topic of this section, while the next section contains a discussion of industrial changes. Table 2.6 illustrates the shift to non-manual employment within manufacturing. An analysis of the data given in Tables 2.1, 2.2, and 2.6 allows us to estimate that of the 24 percentage points increase in the non-manual share of classified employment in Britain 1950–2000, just over one-third (9 percentage points) was due to the rise of employment in the service sector (which is historically more non-manual intensive). The other two-thirds of the shift was due to changes in the skill mix within industry groups. Fourteen and a half percentage points were due to an increased non-manual share of employment in the production sector and 0.5 percentage points were due to an increased non-manual share of employment in services.

The rest of this section is devoted to explaining this skill substitution within the manufacturing sector. The trend away from production work took place

Table 2.6. The share of administrative, technical, and clerical staff in manufacturing, 1948–2003

	Men	Women	All
December 1948	15.2	17.9	
June 1963			22.8
June 1973			27.0
June 1983			28.8
November 2003			44.4

Sources: 1948: BLSHA, table 144; 1963, 1973, 1983: OECD Labour Force Statistics; 2003, author's calculations from the Labour Force Survey, November 2003.

[1] In the economics literature the words 'skilled', 'educated', and 'non-manual' tend to be used interchangeably. This practice is followed here, for brevity.

throughout the century, but accelerated in the last four decades of the century and especially after 1980. Again it is an international phenomenon. Table 2.7 shows distinct falls in the share of production workers in manufacturing for four countries, 1973–89. Most economists consider this to have mainly occurred due to the impact of technological change, though there is a school of thought that argues that the lowering of barriers to trade with developing countries has also had an effect. These two arguments are explained and evaluated in what follows.

On technical change, Goldin and Katz (1998: 695) argue that the twentieth century can be characterized as a period in which there was swift advance in batch and continuous process technologies, which use fewer production workers and more machines and technicians. The technicians are complementary to the machines, in the sense of being required to monitor and maintain the production process. These technologies are common in food and chemical manufacture, but have advanced into other fields, for instance, 'robotized assembly lines . . . [use] relatively fewer less-skilled operators and more skilled machine crewmen' (1998: 696). Goldin and Katz contrast this to the dominant technological production shift of the nineteenth century, which was a period of replacement of skill by capital as factory production superseded the workshops of artisans.

Many researchers have sought to test the hypothesis that in the late twentieth century technological change has been associated with increased demand for skilled workers. Evidence for Britain is given in Machin (1996) and Machin and Van Reenen (1998), for instance. Economists became interested in the question because of the rise, during the 1980s in UK and USA especially, in the gap between the wages of skilled and less-skilled workers: see Chapter 4 for a fuller discussion. Most studies find in favour of the hypothesis. A good example is Machin and Van Reenen (1998), who demonstrate how the demand for skilled workers increases in companies that devote more resources to research and development and/or companies with high levels of investment in digital technology.

Table 2.7. The percentage share of production workers in manufacturing, four countries, 1973 and 1989

	1973	1989
Denmark	75	68
Sweden	73	70
UK	74	67
USA	75	70

Source: Machin and Van Reenen (1998).

An alternative, or perhaps additional, hypothesis is that changes in the patterns of international trade have made Britain more specialist in producing skill-intensive goods. The argument is most fully articulated by Wood (1994, 1998). The underlying logic behind the hypothesis derives from the theory of comparative advantage, which is a fundamental theory of international trade patterns. Here is a simplified version.

Suppose two countries are endowed with different abundances of factors of production (labour, capital, geographical features). In the absence of international trade the patterns of costs of production among goods that require these inputs in different proportions will vary with these abundances. In other words, countries abundant in some factor will be able to produce goods that rely on that factor *relatively* cheaply. This variety of costs of production makes international trade potentially profitable. If trade is allowed, countries will tend to specialize in producing the goods that they produce relatively cheaply.

Now we can grasp the Wood argument about trade and skills. In Wood's thesis, increased trade with developing countries will lead the advanced, skill-abundant economies to specialize in skill-intensive goods, while the developing countries would specialize in less-skilled or manual-intensive goods. There has been an enormous volume of research into this trade hypothesis, and though the argument is plausible, the results find quite strongly against it. See Neary (2002) for a brief summary and Machin and Van Reenen (1998) for an example of study which fails to find an association between skill mix and involvement in international trade among British and other firms.

One needs to be careful here. If a researcher finds technology to be important in changing the demand for skill, but finds measures of trade not to be important, should we infer that internationalization is unimportant? Certainly not. For instance, the threat of international competition might be enough for producers to adopt new technologies, which in turn lead to altered skill demand. Indeed, to reinforce this point, new technology is often transferred between countries via trade.

One other aspect of internationalization has been found to be important, though. Feenstra and Hanson (1999) argue that there have been major changes in the degree of spatial integration of production. In particular, increased international trade flows partly reflect the splitting of the stages of production by multinational companies across countries. This is often called *outsourcing*. For many manufacturing industries, from aerospace to shoes and clothing production, this became commonplace at the end of the century and it is exactly the process usually referred to as 'globalization'.

Feenstra and Hanson (1999) among others show that outsourcing was an important source of skill-based technical change in US manufacturing in the late part of the century. In other words outsourcing, initially at least, usually took the form of moving routine production to low-income countries. What remained in the richer countries were higher-skill managerial, design, and research work.

It may be that attempting to separate the employment impacts of globalization on the one hand and technology on the other is at least partially impossible. An example illustrates this. Some contemporary multinational car producers use different technologies when producing in countries at different stages of development, so they might use robot streets where production labour is expensive, but more labour-intensive assembly lines where labour is cheaper.

Why has outsourcing expanded? This is a big question but clearly the two main effects are from trade policy changes on the one hand and technological change on the other hand. The impact of trade policy is vividly illustrated by the economic history of China and India since 1990. On the other hand, the information technology revolution made geographically remote production much easier, even feasible. This revolution accelerated after 1990.[2]

2.4 The rise of non-manual work, part 2: the increase in service sector work

Why did service sector employment rise? Let us eliminate one tempting theory. Two of the largest service sectors are education and health care. In Britain, both sectors have expanded since 1950 and both have been dominantly in the public sector. Is the rise in services partly due to government policy? There is no doubt these services expanded while within the public sector in the UK. However, other services not in the public sector such as the hotel and restaurant industries and financial services have also expanded greatly (see Table 2.1). Additionally, in other countries where parts of the health care and education industries are privately provided, the USA most obviously, there has been even greater expansion of these sectors than in the UK. These observations suggest that ultimately and somehow, education, especially tertiary education, and health care would have expanded even if they had been mostly outside the public sector. Post-1950 trends in public sector employment (see Table 2.8) show little expansion in the share of the public sector in UK employment.

Schettkat and Yocarini (2003) lay out two main theories of the shift to services in the richer countries in the latter part of the twentieth century. First, it might be that demand for services may have increased, either because people changed their pattern of expenditures, or because advanced countries have become specialist service providers on world markets. This theory does not fit the facts for Britain. Consumers of British output stayed constant in the relative quantities of manufactures and services demanded in the latter half of the century (see Figures 2.3 and 2.4).

---

[2] See Bhagwati et al. (2004) for a good discussion of outsourcing and Egger and Egger (2002, 2003) for Central European evidence.

Table 2.8. Public sector employment 1953–2003 (000s, mid-year estimates)

	Public sector	Public corporations	Total employment	Share of the public sector (%)	Share of corporations within public sector (%)
1953	6,282	2,836	23,709	26.5	45.1
1963	5,933	2,136	26,266	22.5	36.0
1973	6,805	1,890	26,732	25.5	27.8
1983	6,952	1,663	25,285	27.5	23.9
1993	5,477	530	27,154	20.2	9.7
2003	5,454	386	30,125	18.1	7.1

Sources: Public sector employment: 1953: BLSHA, table 152, p. 298; all other years ONS Labour Market Trends, July 2004. Total employment: 1953: Feinstein (1972); all other years: Workforce jobs data from **www.statistics.gov.uk/ STATBASE/**.

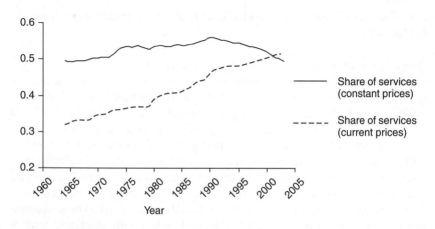

Figure 2.3 The share of services in consumer expenditure, 1964–2003
Source: **www.statistics.gov.uk/STATBASE/**

The second and remaining theory is that the increase in service employment is related to a sectoral bias in productivity growth. This was first hypothesized by Baumol (1967), who pointed out that the rise in service employment is a consequence of the long-run facts of trends in productivity and demand. First, productivity growth was faster in the production industries than the rest of the economy throughout the century (see Figure 2.5). This is a well-known 'stylized fact' in the analysis of economic growth, recognized at least since Clark (1940). Data from Feinstein (1972) show that from 1900 to 1965 output per worker grew 1.01 per cent per annum across the whole economy, and at 1.6 per cent per annum in the production industries. Though productivity growth sped up after 1980, this gap remains. Official data for 1979 to 2003 show that productivity growth in the whole economy was about 1.8 per cent per annum, whereas in the production industries it was much higher, at 3.8 per cent per annum. If this is combined with the fact, already established, that relative demand for British goods and services remains roughly constant, then a falling share of production workers in employment is a logical consequence. To see this, write the productivity growth rates in production and services as the differences between output growth rates and employment growth rates; then if productivity growth is faster in production we will have, in obvious notation: $g_{op} - g_{ep} > g_{os} - g_{es}$. But if $g_{op} = g_{os}$ then we have $g_{es} > g_{ep}$.

The question 'what happens to the redundant production sector workers?' emerges. In the frictionless world of textbook economics, rising productivity in

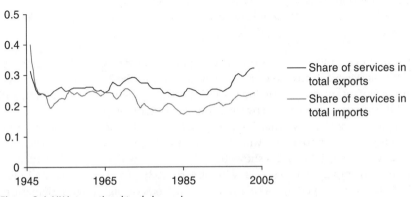

Figure 2.4 UK international trade in services
Source: **www.statistics.gov.uk/STATBASE/**

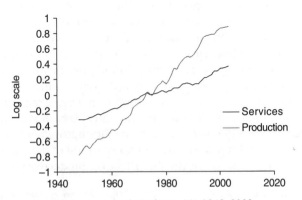

Figure 2.5 Gross value added per worker by industry, UK, 1948–2003
Source: **www.statistics.gov.uk/STATBASE/**

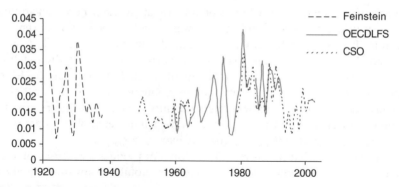

Figure 2.6 Industrial change indices

Notes: Each index is constructed from data on shares of employment by industry. Let Δs_i be the annual change in share of industry *i* in total employment, then the index $I = \sum_i |\Delta s_i|$.

Sources: Feinstein (1972); OECD Labour Force Statistics, various issues; **www.statistics.gov.uk/STATBASE/**

the production sector lowers the price of goods against services, making households better off. Households raise their demand for both goods and services. Some workers in the production sector leave their jobs, voluntarily or not, and fill the job vacancies created by the extra demand for services.

This is *very* roughly what happened. Of course the shift of workers from goods production to service work has been anything but smooth and continuous. As Figures 2.2 and 2.6 show, there have been periods of rapid structural change in employment, especially in the early 1930s, the 1970s, and the 1980s. Not surprisingly, perhaps, these were also periods of high unemployment in the UK. The extent to which structural change was responsible for these periods of high unemployment is discussed in Chapter 10.

The two stylized facts of the relative productivity theory need explaining. First, why was productivity growth faster in the production industries, especially manufacturing, than services? Secondly, why didn't the demand for goods versus services shift? On relative productivity, it is clear that the technological revolutions of the first seventy years of the twentieth century (see the introduction to this chapter) primarily led to improvements in the manufacturing of goods and to new manufactured goods, which met consumer demand in a superior way, rather than to improvements in services.

In principle, productivity in many services can also be improved, though in some, especially personal services, the scope for improvement seems intrinsically limited. The information technology revolution of the latter part of the century famously[3] had no measurable effect on productivity until the late

---

[3] Robert Solow's often-quoted remark, made in 1987, that 'we can see the computer age everywhere except in the productivity statistics' encapsulated what became known as the Solow paradox, or the computer paradox.

Table 2.9. Price changes, 1964–2001

	Factor by which prices rose between 1964 and 2001
All goods and services	11.6
Food	8.5
Restaurants	15.6
Clothing and footwear	4.4
Cleaning clothes	13.2
Household electrical appliances	3.4
Appliance repairs	21.7
Cars	8.7
Rail fares	23.3
Post	19.2
Telephone services	5.4
Audio-visual recording	0.7
Information processing	0.6
Hairdressing	25.0
Average earnings	24.9

Source: Implied deflators for consumption expenditure and average earning index from ONS website, **www.statistics.gov.uk/**.

1990s. For the United States, though, Triplett and Bosworth (forthcoming) find a new spurt of productivity growth in US services from 1995 onwards, which they relate to new technology.

The question of why relative demand did not move is perhaps harder to answer. For instance part of Britain's story could have been a shift to producing more services, perhaps because of emerging international comparative advantage. But most services are not traded. Indeed net imports of travel and tourism on the one hand and net exports of financial and business services on the other are the major elements of Britain's service trade and have accounted for no more than 30 per cent of trade (see Figure 2.4). But the more telling fact illustrated in Figure 2.4 is that the service share of exports has not risen, so the country did not become more specialized as a service provider to the rest of the world.

What of demand from domestic agents? The prices of physical goods relative to services declines as relative productivity grows (see Table 2.9), so one might imagine consumers substituting away from services. On the other hand there could be an offsetting effect from rising real incomes, if demand for services relative to goods increased with income.

The shares of consumer spending on goods and services are plotted in Figure 2.3, which shows the share of services in UK consumer's expenditure 1964–2003 at current prices and at constant (2001) prices. In the mid-1960s consumers spent a little over 30 per cent of their budget on services. By 2003, this had risen to over 50 per cent. However, if goods and service expenditures are recalculated at 2001 prices, the share of services takes no decisive trend. It moves from just under 50 per cent in 1960 to about 56 per cent in 1990 and then returns to the initial level by 2003. So, the share of services in real terms has been roughly constant, implying that the rise in money terms is almost all due to the rise in the prices of services relative to goods. This price movement was particularly strong after about 1990.

From a theoretical point of view, consumers would only keep goods and services in a roughly constant ratio if (a) they could not substitute between these broad categories or (b), as above, there were roughly offsetting trends in components of the set of goods and services. Clearly (a) is unlikely. What are the offsetting trends in goods and service use? A full answer to this question is not possible within this chapter, but Newell (2005) shows that there are offsetting trends in different components of consumer spending. Two examples illustrate this.

First, the demand for services in food consumption rose. Despite a large rise in the relative price of eating at restaurants versus home production (see Table 2.9), British consumers turned away from cooking and towards eating out in the second half of the twentieth century. Why? One might simply argue this demonstrates that demand for restaurant meals is sufficiently income elastic to offset the adverse price changes. It may be this income elasticity is due to changing time allocation. Cooking takes time, so eating out is time-saving. If, as real wages rise, households want to increase leisure time, one way of doing that is reducing housework time.

Secondly, the demand for services in overland transport trended downward in the second part of the twentieth century. Department of the Environment data show that self-provided overland transport increased from around 40 per cent of all passenger miles in 1952 to around 87 per cent of passenger miles in 1998. Why? The price of self-provided transport services (that is, mostly, running a car) fell on trend relative to public transport services, because of the fall in the relative price of cars. In the case of transport, it is clear that the income effect did not offset the price effect, in other words public transport seems not to have been an income-elastic good. Why not? Newell (2005) argues that for most journeys, there is no time saving in using the public service, in fact the opposite is often the case, and this is the critical reason for the different trend in transport service spending when compared to food.

This time-saving argument, though elegant, cannot account for all of the persistence in service demand, because many services cannot be described as time-saving. Nevertheless it is a useful way of thinking about some of the social changes of the second half of the century.

To recap, the rise in service employment seems to reflect two main facts of the demand for labour. First, productivity growth was much faster in goods production and, secondly, the share of services in consumer demand stayed roughly constant. On the supply side, the entry of women into the workforce and increased education levels provided the corresponding shift in the workforce.

2.5 Structural change before 1950

It has already been noted that structural change, in terms of shifts between one-digit (i.e. major) occupational and industrial categories of employment was much smaller in Britain in the first half of the century than the second half. Managerial, professional, technical, personal service, sales and clerical workers were about 34 per cent of the British workers in 1921, rising to 39 per cent in 1950 and 69 per cent in 2001. Similarly the production industries accounted for about 57 per cent of jobs in 1900, 51.5 per cent in 1950, and 22.4 per cent in 2001. Nevertheless there was notable structural change in Britain between the two world wars, but it was within the production sector. Many scholars, for instance Magee (2004) and Bowden and Higgins (2004), have noted and analysed how production switched during the period from the old 'staple' industries, coal, iron and steel, shipbuilding, and textiles, to new industries such as vehicle manufacture and electrical consumer appliances.

Figure 2.7 plots employment during the inter-war years for the staples industries on the one hand and the non-staples on the other. It is immediately clear that the rising underlying trend in employment over the period after 1921 is entirely due to employment in the non-staple industries. Indeed employment in those industries barely fell at all in the downturn of the 1930s. This contrasts sharply with the staple industries. In 1920 these accounted for about 35 per cent of all employment. By 1938, this share had fallen to 17.8 per cent. In the 1920/21 depression and in 1930/01, the falls in employment were disproportionately in the staple industries. In 1920/01 1.258 million jobs, or 59 per cent of the total fall of employment, were lost from the staple industries. Similarly in 1930/01 356,000 jobs, 79 per cent of the total fall of employment, were lost from the staple industries.

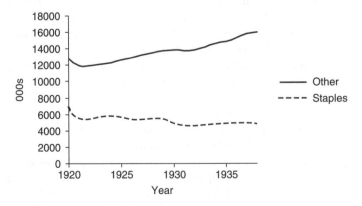

Figure 2.7 British employment in the inter-war years
Source: Feinstein (1972).

Why did the staple industries fare so badly over the period? Knick Harley (2004: 180) argues that part of the answer was the loss of export markets due to the building of rival capacity, in Japan and India, for instance, during the First World War, while the war itself was keeping British factories busy. Indeed this export shock is part of the explanation for the severe recession of 1920/21. Knick Harley's (2004) other argument is that this shift in the global location of production was a longer-term phenomenon. By 'the early twentieth century, the technology in these industries had stabilised and had been transferred around the world by British machine-making firms which sold complete factories to foreign competitors and provided advice to get them operating'.

In addition, the staple industries, which disproportionally relied on exports, were the most vulnerable to adverse shocks to demand in the Great Depression of the early 1930s. The Great Depression was initially an export shock for the UK, as trading partners were afflicted by financial and banking crises. This inevitably affected the staple industries more than the rest of the economy. The unemployment consequences of these structural shocks, which were strongly concentrated in regions heavily reliant on staple industries, are discussed in Chapter 10.

2.6 Timing and conclusions

Lastly, there should be a brief discussion of why the structural change took place *when* it did. With the decline of the staple industries between the wars it seems that macroeconomic events and structural changes coincided, in 1920/21 and 1930/31. There were similar surges of structural change in the macroeconomic depressions of 1980–82 and 1990–92. Figure 2.6 demonstrates increased industrial turbulence at times of recessions. Causality could be either way. That is, macroeconomic depressions could sometimes be caused by major structural shifts, or it might be that macroeconomic downturns lead to the disproportionately large squeezes on vulnerable, contracting industries. These two hypotheses have never been separated.

On longer-term timing issues, Figure 2.2 shows how the decline of production industries in the UK lagged behind the USA, especially through the 1950s and 1960s, and then subsequently caught up rapidly. Why was this? There are two hypotheses. First, post-Second World War reconstruction in much of mainland Europe and Japan, and damaged capacity of those countries, combined to create high levels of worldwide demand worldwide for UK capital goods, plant, and machinery through the immediate post-war decades. Because of this, the decline in employment in the production sector in Britain, a more open economy, was slowed down relative to the USA over the period. Once capacity was rebuilt, by the early 1960s, say, then the economy reverted to trend. This story seems consistent with some aspects of the decline of manufacturing in the 1960s and 1970s. In many industries, it was competition from much higher-productivity new factories in Japan and Germany which delivered the final blow to British production.

The second theory is that industrial policy, in the form of nationalization, locked Britain into an increasingly outdated industrial structure for over thirty years, until the waves of privatizations in the 1980s. One might argue that without the nationalizations of the 1940s and later, the old staple industries especially might have either disappeared or completely transformed themselves with more modern technologies. Either way the level of employment in these industries would have been much lower much earlier.

References

Baumol, W. J. (1967). 'Macroeconomics of Unbalanced Growth: An Anatomy of Urban Crisis'. *American Economic Review*, 57: 415–26.

Bhagwati, J., Panagariya, A., and Srinivasan, T. N. (2004). 'The Muddles over Outsourcing'. *Journal of Economic Perspectives*, 18/4, Fall: 93–114.

Bowden, S., and Higgins, D. M. (2004). 'British Industry in the Inter-War Years', in R. Floud and P. Johnson (eds.), *The Cambridge Economic History of Modern Britain*, ii: *Economic Maturity 1860–1939*. Cambridge: Cambridge University Press.

Clark, C. (1940, revised and reprinted in 1951). *The Conditions of Economic Progress*. London: Macmillan.

DeLong, J. B., and Summers, L. H. (1991). 'Equipment Investment and Economic Growth'. *Quarterly Journal of Economics*, 106: 445–502.

Egger, H., and Egger, P. (2002). 'How International Outsourcing Drives up Eastern European Wages'. *Weltwirtschaftliches Archiv*, 138/1: 83–96.

—— —— (2003). 'Outsourcing and Skill-Specific Employment in a Small Economy: Austria and the Fall of the Iron Curtain'. *Oxford Economic Papers*, 55: 625–43.

Feenstra, R. C., and Hanson, G. H. (1999). 'The Impact of Outsourcing and High Technology Capital on Wages: Estimates for the United States, 1979–1990'. *Quarterly Journal of Economics*, 114/3: 907–40.

Feinstein, C. H. (1972). *National Income, Expenditure and Output in the UK, 1855–1965*. Cambridge: Cambridge University Press.

Goldin, C., and Katz, L. F. (1998). 'The Origins of Technology–Skill Complementarity'. *Quarterly Journal of Economics*, 113: 693–732.

Katz, L. F., and Murphy, K. M. (1992). 'Changes in Relative Wages, 1963–1987: Supply and Demand Factors'. *Quarterly Journal of Economics*, 107: 35–78.

Knick Harley, C. (2004). 'Trade 1970–1939: From Globalisation to Fragmentation', in R. Floud and P. Johnson (eds.), *The Cambridge Economic History of Modern Britain*, ii: *Economic Maturity 1860–1939*. Cambridge: Cambridge University Press.

Lucas, R. E., Jr. (2000). 'Some Macroeconomics of the 21st Century'. *Journal of Economic Perspectives*, 14/1, Winter: 159–68.

Machin, S. (1996). 'Wage Inequality in the UK'. *Oxford Review of Economic Policy*, 12/1, Spring: 47–64.

—— and Van Reenen, J. (1998). 'Technology and Changes in Skill Structure: Evidence from Seven OECD Countries'. *Quarterly Journal of Economics*, 113: 1215–44.

Magee, G. B. (2004). 'Manufacturing and Technological Change', in R. Floud and P. Johnson (eds.), *The Cambridge Economic History of Modern Britain*, ii: *Economic Maturity 1860–1939*. Cambridge: Cambridge University Press.

Mitchell, B. R., and Deane, P. (1962). *Abstract of British Historical Statistics*. Cambridge: Cambridge University Press.

Mowery, D. C., and Rosenberg, N. (1998). *Paths of Innovation*. Cambridge: Cambridge University Press.

Neary, J. P. (2002). 'Competition, Trade and Wages', in D. Greenaway, R. Upward, and K. Wakelin (eds.), *Trade, Investment, Migration and Labour Market Adjustment*. Basingstoke: Palgrave Macmillan.

Newell, A. T. (2005). 'The Rise of Service Employment, the Demand for Services and Household Production in the UK'. Mimeo, University of Sussex.

Schettkat, R., and Yocarini, L. (2003). 'The Shift to Services: A Review of the Literature'. IZA Discussion Paper 964, Dec.

Triplett, J., and Bosworth, B. (Forthcoming). ' "Baumol's Disease" Has Been Cured: IT and Multifactor Productivity in U.S. Services Industries', in Dennis W. Jansen, (ed.), *The New Economy. How New? How Resilient?* Chicago: University of Chicago Press. Available from: **www.brookings.edu/dybdocroot/views/papers/triplett/20020419.pdf**

Wood, A. J. B. (1994). *North–South Trade, Employment and Inequality*. Oxford: Oxford University Press.

—— (1998). 'Globalisation and the Rise of Labour Market Inequalities'. *Economic Journal*, 108/450: 1463–82.

3

Manual Work and Pay, 1900–70

Ian Gazeley

3.1 Introduction

This chapter examines changes in the nature of waged work and pay in the first seventy years of the twentieth century. At the beginning of the century the vast majority of adult men and only one in three adult women worked. By 1970 nearly half of all adult women were in paid employment and the proportion of economically inactive adult men had increased to about one in ten. In 1901, nearly one in three men was employed in metal, mining, or building. By mid-century, the proportion had declined a little, but not by as much as might be imagined given the rise of new industries. The reason for this is the distorting impact of two world wars, which expanded capacity in industries required for the production of war munitions. Female employment remained concentrated in very few industrial sectors during the first half of the century.

National pay bargaining became the norm across a swath of British industry during the First World War and wage differentials by skill started to level up; a process that continued across the Second World War. These changes in pay inequality marked the end of a period of stable skill differentials at the end of the nineteenth century. There was also a reduction in the extent of gender pay inequality; especially across the Second World War and limited to those industries that were crucial for the war effort, though this process was a slow one and gender pay inequality remained a feature of the pay structure even after anti-discriminatory legislation in the early 1970s. Workers in the post-Second World War period worked fewer hours than their Victorian forebears and were paid significantly more, even allowing for price increases during the century. For all groups of workers, the growth in earnings outstripped wages and the disparity between them grew steadily, accelerating in the 1950s and 1960s.

3.2 Work

Changes in the industrial composition of the workforce can be ascertained from the decennial population censuses. The enumeration of occupation was not always straightforward because of dual employment and the tendency for late nineteenth- and early twentieth-century censuses to under-record paid work carried out by women (Roberts 1995: 6–13). As Table 3.1 shows, adult men's labour market participation remained fairly stable until the last third of the twentieth century, when it started to decline. In 1901, 84 per cent of adult men were economically active; slightly less than the proportion economically active in 1951 and 1961. The long-term pattern of women's paid employment is probably best described as a U-shape, with participation around 42–3 per cent in the mid-nineteenth century, falling to about 32 per cent by 1881, where it remained until the Second World War, before increasing again in the post-war period, reaching 44 per cent by 1971. The fall in participation in the late nineteenth century is partly the result of under-enumeration of women's paid work and partly genuine (Hakim 2004: 61). In the early part of the century, recorded female labour market participation was concentrated among young single women. In the period before marriage, nearly three-quarters of early twentieth-century young women aged 14–24 were in paid work (Gittins 1982: 70). Much of the increase in female participation in the immediate post-First World War era was due to an increase in the number of older, married women in work. The abolition of marriage bars meant that women typically continued to work until the birth of their first child. As women's labour force participation increased, men's rates fell—from a high point of 91 per cent in 1931 to 81 per cent in 1971. In the mid-1970s less than 8 per cent of men aged 16–64 were economically inactive, whereas by 1998 the proportion had grown to 13 per cent (due mainly to sickness and to a less extent earlier retirement among older workers). In

Table 3.1. Economic activity rates

	Adult men	Adult women	Men 16–64	Women 16–59
1901	84	32	96	38
1911	84	32	96	38
1921	87	32	94	38
1931	91	34	96	38
1941	n./a.	n./a.	n./a.	n./a.
1951	88	35	96	43
1961	86	38	95	47
1971	81	44	91	57

Notes: Rates refer to England and Wales from the Population Census returns 1901–61 and Great Britain for 1971. The definition of adult changes in the census: 1901–11 people aged 10 and over, 1921 people aged 12 and over; 1931 people aged 14 and over; 1951–71 people aged 15 and over. They related to the 'occupied' population 1901–51 and 'economically active' population 1961–71. Table adapted from Hakim (2004: 62, table 3.1).

contrast, women's economic inactivity fell from 37 per cent to 27 per cent over the same period (Gregg and Wadsworth 1999: 49–50).

Decennial census summary data by industry for the period 1901–61 are given in Tables 3.2*a*, 3.2*b*, 3.3*a*, and 3.3*b*. There was no census in 1941 due to the war. It is not always possible to directly compare changes in the occupational distribution of the labour force over time, because enumerator categories were subject to periodic revision, although, between 1901 and 1951 these changes were fairly minor. In the first twenty years of the century male employment was heavily concentrated in five industrial groups: transport and communications; agriculture, horticulture, and forestry; mining and quarrying; metals manufacture; and building and construction. These categories accounted for over half of all occupied men 1901–21, using 1911 census categories. After 1921 these categories remained important collectively, but they accounted for a progressively smaller proportion of the occupied male labour force. This fall was primarily the

Table 3.2*a*. Employment by industry, 1901–21 (males) (000s)

Occupied (based on 1911 classification)	1901 Male	1901 Male (%)	1911 Male	1911 Male (%)	1921 Male	1921 Male (%)
Public administration	191.0	1.7	271.0	2.1	383.0	2.8
Armed forces	176.0	1.5	221.0	1.7	236.0	1.7
Professional occupations	348.0	3.0	413.0	3.2	415.0	3.1
Domestic offices and personal services	341.0	3.0	456.0	3.5	371.0	2.7
Commercial occupations	597.0	5.2	739.0	5.7	904.0	6.6
Transport and communications	1,409.0	12.2	1,571.0	12.1	1,530.0	11.3
Agriculture, horticulture, and forestry	1,339.0	11.6	1,436.0	11.1	1,344.0	9.9
Fishing	51.0	0.4	53.0	0.4	51.0	0.4
Mining and quarrying	931.0	8.1	1,202.0	9.3	1,240.0	9.1
Metals manufacture, machines, vehicles, etc.	1,485.0	12.9	1,795.0	13.9	2,125.0	15.6
Building and construction	1,216.0	10.5	1,140.0	8.8	894.0	6.6
Wood, furniture, fittings, and Decorations	267.0	2.3	287.0	2.2	511.0	3.8
Bricks, cement, pottery, and glass	152.0	1.3	145.0	1.1	100.0	0.7
Chemicals, oil, soap, resin, etc	116.0	1.0	155.0	1.2	93.0	0.7
Skins, leather, hair, and feathers	87.0	0.8	90.0	0.7	72.0	0.5
Paper, printing, books, and stationery	212.0	1.8	253.0	2.0	193.0	1.4
Textiles	557.0	4.8	639.0	4.9	409.0	3.0
Clothing	423.0	3.7	432.0	3.3	315.0	2.3
Food, drink, and tobacco	701.0	6.1	806.0	6.2	228.0	1.7
Gas, water, and electricity supply	62.0	0.5	86.0	0.7	n./a.	
Others occupied	887.0	7.7	741.0	5.7	2,186.0	16.1
Total occupied	11,548.0	100.0	12,927.0	100.0	13,656.0	100.0

result of a reduction in the number and proportion of men employed in agriculture and mining. There was also a modest growth of some male tertiary sector employment during the first half of the century. As Table 3.2*a* reveals, using 1921 census categories, the proportion of men occupied in professional and technical industries showed a marked increase by 1951, but for other occupations within the tertiary sector this was not so (for example, personal services, commercial, financial, and insurance industries).

At the beginning of the twentieth century, women's employment was concentrated in just three industrial groups: domestic offices and personal services, textiles, and clothing. Fully three-quarters of all women in the labour force in 1901 were occupied in these three sectors. By 1921, concentration in these three industrial groups had declined to just over half of all occupied women, partly as a consequence of the fall in the number and proportion of women occupied in domestic services. The pattern of female employment exhibited significant local variation depending on the industrial structure of

Table 3.2*b*. Employment by industry, 1901–21 (females)

Occupied (based on 1911 classification) (000s)	1901 Female	1901 Female (%)	1911 Female	1911 Female (%)	1921 Female	1921 Female (%)
Public administration	29.0	0.6	50.0	0.9	81.0	1.4
Armed forces	n./a.		n./a.		n./a.	
Professional occupations	326.0	6.9	383.0	7.1	441.0	7.7
Domestic offices and personal services	2,003.0	42.1	2,127.0	39.3	1,845.0	32.4
Commercial occupations	76.0	1.6	157.0	2.9	587.0	10.3
Transport and communications	27.0	0.6	38.0	0.7	72.0	1.3
Agriculture, horticulture, and forestry	86.0	1.8	117.0	2.2	105.0	1.8
Fishing	n./a.		n./a.		n./a.	
Mining and quarrying	6.0	0.1	8.0	0.1	9.0	0.2
Metals manufacture, machines, vehicles, etc.	84.0	1.8	128.0	2.4	175.0	3.1
Building and construction	3.0	0.1	5.0	0.1	5.0	0.1
Wood, furniture, fittings, and decorations	30.0	0.6	35.0	0.6	31.0	0.5
Bricks, cement, pottery, and glass	37.0	0.8	42.0	0.8	45.0	0.8
Chemicals, oil, soap, resin, etc.	31.0	0.7	46.0	0.8	35.0	0.6
Skins, leather, hair, and feathers	27.0	0.6	32.0	0.6	33.0	0.6
Paper, printing, books, and stationery	111.0	2.3	144.0	2.7	121.0	2.1
Textiles	795.0	16.7	870.0	16.1	701.0	12.3
Clothing	792.0	16.7	825.0	15.2	602.0	10.6
Food, drink, and tobacco	216.0	4.5	308.0	5.7	123.0	2.2
Gas, water, and electricity supply	n./a.		n./a.		n./a.	
Others occupied	75.0	1.6	98.0	1.8	688.0	12.1
Total occupied	4,751.0	100.0	5,413.0	100.0	5,699.0	100.0

Source: Mitchell and Deane (1962: Occupations 1911–51, pp. 60–1).

the area and the job opportunities available for women (Lewis 1984: 149). Between 1921 and 1951 female employment remained heavily concentrated in a small number of industrial groups. In 1921, more than 7 out of every 10 women were occupied in one of five industrial groups: personal services; commercial, financial, and insurance occupations; clerks, typists, etc.; textiles and textile goods and clothing. By 1951, the collective importance of these five industrial groups had declined a little—reflecting the continued contraction of employment in personal services and, to some extent, textiles and clothing. The decline in the importance of these three industries in the early post-Second World War years was almost entirely offset by an increase in the

Table 3.3a. Employment by industry, 1921–51 (males)

Occupied (based on 1931 census classification) (000s)	1921 Male	1921 Male (%)	1931 Male	1931 Male (%)	1951 Male	1951 Male (%)
Public administration	261.0	1.9	141.0	1.0	214.0	1.4
Armed forces	221.0	1.6	189.0	1.3	560.0	3.6
Professional and technical occupations	378.0	2.8	490.0	3.3	788.0	5.0
Professional entertainers and sportsmen	74.0	0.5	100.0	0.7	90.0	0.6
Personal services	372.0	2.7	516.0	3.5	512.0	3.3
Commercial, financial, and insurance occupations	1,180.0	8.6	1,621.0	10.9	1,357.0	8.7
Clerks, typists, etc.	581.0	4.2	778.0	5.2	932.0	6.0
Transport and communications	1,591.0	11.6	1,748.0	11.8	1,569.0	10.0
Agriculture, horticulture, and forestry	1,341.0	9.8	1,282.0	8.6	1,105.0	7.1
Fishing	51.0	0.4	40.0	0.3	26.0	0.2
Mining and quarrying	1,204.0	8.8	1,083.0	7.3	675.0	4.3
Metals manufacture, machines, vehicles, etc.	1,888.0	13.8	1,765.0	11.9	2,517.0	16.1
Building and construction	738.0	5.4	970.0	6.5	1,268.0	8.1
Wood and furniture	453.0	3.3	497.0	3.4	492.0	3.1
Treatment non-metalliferous mining products	69.0	0.5	82.0	0.6	86.0	0.5
Coal, gas, coke, chemicals, and allied trades	41.0	0.3	52.0	0.4	102.0	0.7
Leather, leather goods, and fur	178.0	1.3	178.0	1.2	125.0	0.8
Paper, books, and printing	155.0	1.1	178.0	1.2	178.0	1.1
Textiles	314.0	2.3	324.0	2.2	220.0	1.4
Textile goods and clothing	155.0	1.1	164.0	1.1	135.0	0.9
Food, drink, and tobacco	147.0	1.1	161.0	1.1	175.0	1.1
Administrators and managers in executive or manufacturing	287.0	2.1	350.0	2.4	347.0	2.2
Warehousemen, storekeepers, packers, bottlers, etc.	243.0	1.8	268.0	1.8	379.0	2.4
All others occupied	1,749.0	12.8	1,851.0	12.5	1,794.0	11.5
Total occupied	13,656.0	100.0	14,790.0	100.0	15,649.0	100.0

Table 3.3b. Employment by industry, 1921–51 (females)

Occupied (based on 1931 census classification) (000s)	1921 Female	1921 Female (%)	1931 Female	1931 Female (%)	1951 Female	1951 Female (%)
Public administration	78.0	1.4	3.0	0.0	21.0	0.3
Armed forces	n./a.		n./a.		18.0	0.3
Professional and technical occupations	408.0	7.2	443.0	7.0	588.0	8.4
Professional entertainers and sportsmen	30.0	0.5	24.0	0.4	23.0	0.3
Personal services	1,845.0	32.4	2,129.0	33.9	1,610.0	23.1
Commercial, financial, and insurance occupations	579.0	10.2	701.0	11.1	856.0	12.3
Clerks, typists, etc.	492.0	8.6	648.0	10.3	1,409.0	20.2
Transport and communications	75.0	1.3	82.0	1.3	149.0	2.1
Agriculture, horticulture, and forestry	107.0	1.9	71.0	1.1	114.0	1.6
Fishing	n./a.		n./a.		n./a.	
Mining and quarrying	7.0	0.1	4.0	0.1	2.0	0.0
Metals manufacture, machines, vehicles, etc.	123.0	2.2	147.0	2.3	208.0	3.0
Building and construction	10.0	0.2	17.0	0.3	14.0	0.2
Wood and furniture	10.0	0.2	8.0	0.1	15.0	0.2
Treatment non-metalliferous mining products	36.0	0.6	46.0	0.7	48.0	0.7
Coal, gas, coke, chemicals, and allied trades	4.0	0.1	5.0	0.1	14.0	0.2
Leather, leather goods, and fur	59.0	1.0	66.0	1.0	67.0	1.0
Paper, books, and printing	97.0	1.7	108.0	1.7	93.0	1.3
Textiles	634.0	11.1	663.0	10.5	413.0	5.9
Textile goods and clothing	544.0	9.5	544.0	8.7	474.0	6.8
Food, drink, and tobacco	77.0	1.4	73.0	1.2	97.0	1.4
Administrators and managers in executive or manufacturing	25.0	0.4	26.0	0.4	30.0	0.4
Warehousemen, storekeepers, packers, bottlers, etc.	141.0	2.5	162.0	2.6	199.0	2.9
All others occupied	319.0	5.6	317.0	5.0	497.0	7.1
Total occupied	5,701.0	100.0	6,265.0	100.0	6,961.0	100.0

Source: Mitchell and Deane (1962: Occupations 1911–51, pp. 60–1).

proportion of females employed as clerks and typists (so-called white-blouse work). Outside of these industries, the proportion of women employed in metal manufacture, machines, and vehicles, etc. remained very low. As Table 3.3b shows, in 1951 this industrial group only accounted for 3 per cent of female employment.

The reasons for the sex segregation of employment in the first half of the century can be traced to the way in which work and home were separated by nineteenth-century industrialization. The dominant nineteenth-century ideology of the household was based upon a separation between a male breadwinner and female engaged in unpaid domestic work. Within this patriarchal framework, adult male work was thought of as being remunerated by a 'family' wage', while for those women who combined paid work with unpaid domestic work, their wages were seen as making only a contribution to the household economy (Todd 2005). At the beginning of the twentieth century, the tension between women's reproductive and productive roles gave rise to debate surrounding the forms of paid employment that were suitable for women (Harris 1993: 23–32; Lewis 1984: 146–61). Within the working class, male-dominated trade unions, especially craft unions, are often seen as having reinforced the segregation of women into low-paid repetitious work (Lewenhak 1977; Boston 1987). In addition, Savage (1988) argues that state intervention in the labour market (via factory legislation and the role of labour exchanges) also tended to enforce a gendered segregation of labour. Historians are divided on the question of whether the two periods of war had a lasting impact on sex segregation of employment. During the wars women workers were directed to work in industries that had been traditionally male dominated, such as metals and chemicals, which reduced segregation significantly, but with demobilization many of these women withdrew from this type of industrial work. This was either through choice or because agreement concerning their employment in these male-dominated sectors was for the duration of the war only. Nevertheless, as Summerfield (1985: 187) argues, a greater proportion of workers were female in industries such as engineering in 1950 than they had been in 1939 (women's share of employment in engineering was 21 per cent in 1950 compared with 34 per cent in 1943 and 10 per cent in 1939).

3.3 Pay

3.3.1 Hours of work and methods of payment

In the first half of the century, the normal working week for full-time workers was progressively shortened. The exact length of the working week varied by industry, but a working week of about 54 hours was fairly typical in many manufacturing industries in 1914. In 1919–20 normal hours were cut to about 47 or 48 per week as the 'eight-hour day' became widespread. Across all industries for which the Ministry of Labour collected wage rate data, Dowie (1975) reckons that the reduction in hours in 1919–20 was about 13 per cent.[1] This reduction in the normal working week was not usually accompanied by corresponding reductions in wage rates (Broadberry 1986). In some industries, hours worked were further reduced at the end of the 1930s, but in most cases, further reductions in the length of the normal working week occurred after the Second World War. Between 1946 and 1948 the standard working week was reduced to

---

[1] According to Dowie, 97% of all decal changes in hours worked occurred in these two years, with 95% taking place in 1919.

Table 3.4. Normal and actual hours worked, 1924–1968

	Normal men	Normal women	Normal all	Actual men	Actual women	Actual all
1924			47.0			45.8
1935			47.3			47.8
1938			47.1	47.7	43.5	46.5
1945			47.1	49.6	43.2	47.2
1950	44.4	45.1	44.6	47.3	41.7	45.9
1955	44.4	45.1	44.6	48.9	41.7	47.0
1960	43.4	44.4	43.7	48.0	40.7	46.2
1965	41.2	42.1	41.4	47.3	38.9	45.3
1968	40.2	41.0	40.5	46.3	38.4	44.5

Source: Historical Abstract of Labour Statistics, table 84. Normal weekly hours refer to all industries and services; whereas actual weekly hours only refer to those industries covered by regular earnings inquiries. Where data exist, normal weekly hours for those industries covered by regular earnings inquiries are not significantly different from those reported here.

about 44 hours in the vast majority of manufacturing industries. By 1968, about 40 hours was standard in most industries, as normal hours were reduced again in the early 1960s.[2]

Actual hours worked varied because of short time or overtime working and part-time working. During the worst of the inter-war depression, there is some empirical evidence on the extent of short-time working and its likely impact on average earnings. According to Bowley, short-time working depressed average earnings by 2.5 per cent in 1924, by nearly 4 per cent in 1931, and by 3 per cent in 1935.[3] Table 3.4 makes clear that in the period after the Second World War, men's average actual hours always exceeded men's average normal hours, because of overtime working in the prosperous conditions of the post-war boom. In contrast, women's average actual hours were less than average normal hours because of the large proportion of women part-time workers.

Payment for work could be by time (weekly or hourly) or by results (typically piecework). Before the First World War, time rates were customarily negotiated locally. The 'district rate' was jealously guarded by the old craft unions. Over the first half of the century, however, the result of statutory wage fixing and national wage bargaining was to diminish the extent of regional wage variation. During the First World War, many groups of workers entered into collective bargains over wages and working conditions with the state. As Sells (1939: 26) points out, during 1917 there was a move to national wage agreements in many manufacturing industries as 'wages of a large proportion of British workers were prescribed by government decree'. In most industries, this

[2] Historical Abstract of Labour Statistics, table 84.
[3] According to Bowley (1937), short-time working depressed average earnings by 2.5% in 1924, nearly 4% in 1931, and 3% in 1935.

move signalled a more formal shift to national bargaining and settlement, as wages were indexed to prices. At that time, plain time rates were generally composed of a basic rate (that varied by district) and a national bonus. Although different district rates still applied for much of the inter-war period, uniform changes to the basic rate and the national bonus had the effect, over time, of reducing the extent of regional wage diversity for the same occupation, or grade of worker. Although regional wage variation had become fairly insignificant by 1950, some regional diversity in earnings was still apparent in some industries (Robertson 1961: 64–70).

This process of wage equalization was augmented by the action of statutory authorities that specified minimum wages under the Whitley councils and trade boards in the immediate post-First World War period. Gradually, during the inter-war years, statutory authorities would regulate increasing numbers of workers' wages, especially for the very low paid, through Whitley councils. At their peak there were 106 Whitley councils covering about 3 million workers The Ministry was, however, opposed to a national minimum wage (Lowe 1986: 92). In the mid-1930s, the Ministry of Labour estimated that 2.7 million workers were in trades covered by statutory wage-fixing machinery and about 11 million workers were covered by voluntary or quasi-voluntary wage-fixing agreements. Allowing for double counting, Sells (1939) reckons that in total approximately 11 million industrial and agricultural workers, from a total of about 15 million, were covered by wage fixing in one form or another in the mid-1930s.[4]

Payments by results took a wide variety of forms, with specific formulae that were often bespoke to the industry concerned. (see Cole 1928; Robertson 1960). In some industries like textiles and steel melting, wage adjustment was by means of a uniform percentage change to a standard list of piecework prices (Cole 1928: 33). In most metal industries, piece rates tended to be fixed in relation to time rates, though some group or squad work existed, especially among riveting gangs in shipbuilding.[5] During wartime, pieceworkers also received national bonuses of similar (though not usually the same) amounts to time workers and these also tended to be uniform across regions.

Information on the proportion of workers paid by time or piece in particular industries is patchy before 1938, but for the whole of the manufacturing sector, the Ministry of Labour's earnings inquiries provide data on the proportions paid by time and by results for 1938, 1947, and 1961. The results of these inquiries are reported in Tables 3.5 and 3.6. Across all the industries covered by the Ministry of Labour's surveys, the usual method of payment for men and

---

[4] The 2.7m workers covered by statutory wage fixing were estimated as 1.136m trade board workers (Ministry of Labour *Gazette* (1935) 127), 0.742m agricultural workers, 0.2m road haulage, 0.615m underground coal miners (Ministry of Labour *Gazette* (Oct. 1923: 383). A full list of trade boards industries is given in Sells (1939: 188).

[5] So called 'black squads', see Cole (1928: 34).

Table 3.5. Methods of payment, 1938 and 1947

Percentage on time work, October 1938, April 1947	Men 1938	Men 1947	Youths and boys 1938	Youths and boys 1947	Women 1938	Women 1947	Girls 1938	Girls 1947
Mining and quarrying (not coal)	73	72	91	93				
Treatment of non-metallic quarry products	85	84	91	89	70	77	60	
Brick, pottery, glass	66	68	76	77	49	56	71	67
Chemicals, paint, oil, etc.	95	92	95	94	76	85	85	86
Metals, engineering, shipbuilding	61	54	61	62	45	48	58	54
Textiles	71	73	86	87	36	42	65	56
Leather, fur, etc.	66	66	88	83	77	77	86	80
Clothing	64	73	87	86	59	64	78	71
Food, drink, tobacco	92	94	95	95	73	81	83	84
Woodworking	87	82	91	90	74	78	81	82
Paper, printing, stationery	95	96	97	99	71	80	86	86
Building, contracting, etc.	100	98	99	100		93		
Miscellaneous manufacturing	73	65	77	75	58	58	66	66
Transport, storage, etc.	97	98	99	100	97	98		
Public utility services	99	99	99	100	99	100	100	100
Government industrial establishments	81	90	72	92	76	79		90
All above	82	77	79	82	54	62	73	69

Source: Ministry of Labour *Gazette* (Oct. 1947: 325).

boys as late as 1947 was a time rate. As Table 3.5 makes clear, about four out of every five men were paid in this way in 1938 and 1947. By contrast only just over half of adult women were paid by time in 1938, though this proportion increased to just less than two-thirds by 1947. The 1961 earnings inquiry was based on a different industrial classification, but it is clear from Table 3.6 that in most industries, time work remained the predominant method of pay-ment—especially for men—though in some industries piece rates had revived. In comparison with 1947, the proportion of adult men paid by time declined considerably in shipbuilding, engineering, and vehicles. As few as one in three men in shipbuilding were paid by plain time rates in 1961. Among women workers in 1938, payment by result was more commonplace. In textiles, 36 per cent were paid by time and in many industries the proportion was nearly 50 per cent. Nevertheless, among all wage earners for all the industries included in the 1961 inquiry, two out of every three were still paid by time rather than payment by result.

In addition to a basic rate or piecework price and a national bonus (price indexed during both wars), some workers also received additional special bonuses. Many firms rewarded reliable labour with 'time-keeping bonuses' and some operated bonuses in the form of collective output premiums. Bonuses

Table 3.6. Methods of payment, 1961

Percentage on time work, April 1961 (1958 industrial classification)	Men	Youths and boys	Women	Girls	All wage earners
Food, drink, and tobacco	86	89	72	74	80
Chemicals	78	94	80	76	79
Metal manufacture	38	59	56	42	41
Engineering and electrical	54	67	44	41	53
Shipbuilding and marine engineering	33	46	76	n./a.	35
Vehicles	48	49	46	30	48
Metal goods not elsewhere specified	60	70	54	53	59
Textiles	61	75	39	44	49
Leather, leather goods, and fur	61	76	70	79	67
Clothing and footwear	66	68	50	52	53
Bricks, pottery, glass, cement, etc.	61	69	53	58	60
Timber, furniture, etc.	73	85	66	73	74
Paper, printing, publishing	83	90	75	78	81
Other manufacturing	55	73	49	45	53
All manufacturing industries	59	70	53	65	58
Mining and quarrying (except coal)	77	89	57	n./a.	77
Construction	85	93	93	84	86
Gas, electricity, and water	98	100	100	n./a.	98
Transport and communication	93	97	98	n./a.	93
Miscellaneous industries	91	95	75	78	87
Public administration	98	98	100	100	98
All above	70	78	56	56	67

Source: British Labour Statistics: Historical Abstract, table 80.

could also be negative: deductions for poor time keeping and spoilt work were widespread in the first half of the century (Cole 1928: 44). The existence of special bonuses, or supplementary payments, is an important factor in explaining the growing divergence between wage rates and earnings at a time when wage bargaining was increasingly at a national rather than local level (Thomas 1997). The earnings gap is the difference between total weekly earnings and negotiated wage rates and earnings drift as the rate of increase of that gap (Hart and MacKay 1975: 38). Table 3.7 reports indices of earnings and comparable wage rates, for the period 1935–68.[6] Notice that for both men and women, weekly earnings grew significantly faster than weekly wage rates and hourly earnings faster than hourly wage rates. This is especially true from the late 1950s onwards (Flanagan et al. 1983). The extent of this earnings drift is greater for men than women. This is because these data include part-time workers, who were predominantly female, and it is likely that men benefited from 'supplementary bonuses' to a greater extent than women and worked more overtime at higher rates. These last two factors also help explain why for both men

[6] *British Labour Statistics: Historical Abstract*, table 85. These data are based upon earnings and wage rates from industries covered by the Ministry of Labour earnings inquiries, using the 1948 industrial classification.

Table 3.7. Indices of average earnings and comparable wage rates, 1935–68 (all industries, average 1956 = 100)

.	Weekly earnings		Hourly earnings		Weekly wage rates		Hourly wage rates	
	Men	Women	Men	Women	Men	Women	Men	Women
1935 October	27.3	25.7						
1938 October	29.2	26.7	29.7	25.5				
1943 July	51.3	51.2	47.0	46.2				
1947 October	54.1	57.1	56.4	56.9	61.9	59.6	61.3	59.1
1950 October	63.6	67.8	64.8	66.9	67.5	66.3	67.4	66.2
1955 October	94.2	95.0	93.5	94.3	94.2	94.2	94.2	94.3
1960 October	122.7	121.9	124.1	124.6	114.4	116.3	118.4	119.5
1965 October	165.4	157.7	170.7	168.6	139.1	144.9	151.3	156.8
1968 October	194.0	185.6	202.8	200.6	161.0	168.5	178.0	186.0

Source: British Labour Statistics: Historical Abstract, table 85.

and women, the growth in hourly earnings (and hourly wage rates) is greater than the growth in weekly earnings (and weekly wage rates).

3.3.2 Earnings by occupation, age, and gender

The Board of Trade conducted the first wage census in Britain in 1886. This was followed by a similar inquiry by the Labour Department in 1906. After the First World War, the Ministry of Labour undertook a number of surveys of earnings and hours. There were four inquires conducted in the inter-war period (October 1924, October 1928, October 1931, and October 1935), the results of which were published in the *Gazette*, under the title *Average Earnings and Hours Enquiries*. In addition, the Ministry carried out another survey in 1938, but the results were not published until 1943 (see below). This was followed by annual inquires in July 1940 and 1941 and biannual surveys from 1942. These inquiries differ in size and scope and the system of industrial classification was changed at a number of points during the century. All the twentieth-century enquiries were based on a set of industries which were mainly, though not exclusively, drawn from the manufacturing sector and were generally restricted to data relating to one week in the month of the survey (see Bowley 1937: 100–6 for a full discussion).

Estimates of average earnings derived from these inquiries for 1906, 1924, 1931, 1935, and 1938, taken from Bowley (1937), are given in Table 3.8. With the important exceptions of coal mining and agriculture, mean male earnings more than doubled between 1906 and 1924. Coal miners are the best paid of male manual workers in 1906, but they lose this position after the First World War. Notice, too, that throughout this period agricultural earnings were consistently low when compared with men's mean earnings in industry. This would have been only partly offset by agricultural workers' payments in kind.

Table 3.8. Average earnings, 1906–35 (s/week)

Industries	1906 Men and boys	1906 Women and girls	1924 Men and boys	1924 Women and girls	1931 Men and boys	1931 Women and girls	1935 Men and boys	1935 Women and girls
Textiles	22.9	13.4	51.0	28.6	48.0	26.9	49.2	27.5
Clothing	24.2	11.2	54.8	26.9	53.6	26.9	54.3	27.8
Food, drink, tobacco	23.4	9.7	58.0	27.9	57.5	28.0	56.6	26.6
Paper, printing	27.2	9.9	70.7	28.0	71.8	28.3	75.4	28.1
Gas, water, electricity	26.4	13.1	62.0	28.6	62.8	26.8	62.5	26.6
Coal mining	31.5		53.0		45.2		44.8	
Metal manufacture			59.9	24.5	54.7	24.8	61.5	28.0
Engineering			51.1	26.3	50.4	26.8	55.0	28.0
Railway works			69.3		64.0		68.4	
Vehicles			57.2	26.9	57.2	28.6	65.9	31.8
Shipbuilding			54.3		51.8		54.2	
Metal industries			53.3	24.6	52.8	24.7	55.5	26.0
Total metals	28.1	10.7	56.4	25.2	53.8	25.6	58.8	26.9
Coke, cement			61.8		65.2		54.9	
Bricks, pottery, glass			55.1	23.3	51.7	22.4	52.5	23.9
Chemicals			59.0	25.8	58.8	27.7	60.6	26.5
Building, contracting			59.9		58.2		56.2	
Wood, furniture			54.8	26.3	52.0	27.4	53.8	28.1
Other mining			51.0		51.3		51.7	
Leather			54.6	25.7	52.7	25.4	53.7	25.4
Transport			69.4	30.8	66.3	24.9	65.1	28.3
Local government			51.6	27.8	52.7	26.2	52.7	28.0
Others			59.2	28.5	58.1	26.0	55.4	26.5
Total actual earnings	27.0	11.8	57.6	27.5	55.7	26.9	56.9	27.3
Total full-time earnings	26.7	11.8	58.9	28.4	57.3	28.0	56.6	27.2
Agriculture	18.3		31.5		35.0		35.7	
Gender pay ratio (all industries)	0.44		0.48		0.49		0.48	
Gender pay ratio (metal industries)	0.38		0.45		0.48		0.46	

Source: Bowley (1937: 51) (pay ratios calculated by author from total actual earnings data).

Women's earnings also increase markedly across the First World War, but average women's earnings were still less than half of those of men in 1924. For all industries covered by these inquiries, the reduction in gender inequality was fairly modest across the First World War (a narrowing of 4 percentage points in the pay ratio between 1906 and 1924—about 10 per cent), though there was some variance around this average figure. In metal industries the reduction in inequality was greater (7 percentage points, or about 18 per cent).

More information about the shape of the wage distribution, and how it changed over the course of the inter-war period, is provided by Rottier's estimates of average and interquartile ranges in earnings given in Table 3.9. Notice that Rottier's (1966) figures are median data and differ from the mean estimates given by Bowley (1937: 51) using the same data from these inquiries. It can be

Table 3.9. Earnings dispersion, 1924–38

Average earnings (s/week)	1924	1931	1935	1938
All industries				
Median male earnings	52.9	52.5	61.5	61.2
Interquartile range	6.0	13.0	14.6	15.0
Coefficient of dispersion	0.11	0.25	0.24	0.25
Mean male earnings (Bowley)	57.6	55.7	56.9	n./a.
All industries				
Median female earnings	28.2	27.3	31.3	31.8
Interquartile range	2.0	3.2	4.6	3.2
Coefficient of dispersion	0.07	0.12	0.15	0.1
Mean female earnings (Bowley)	27.5	27.3	27.3	n./a.
Staple industries				
Median male earnings	52.3	45.3	47.7	57.9
Interquartile range	3.2	4.6	21.2	14.4
Coefficient of dispersion	0.06	0.1	0.44	0.25
New industries				
Median male earnings	58.2	57.4	61.5	61.3
Interquartile range	1.2	3.8	8.2	8.8
Coefficient of dispersion	0.02	0.07	0.13	0.14

Source: Adapted from Rottier (1966) and Bowley (1937).

seen from Table 3.9 that the dispersion of earnings increased markedly between the 1920s and 1930s. For men, the interquartile range more than doubled, and only a small part of this is due to the growth in median earnings as there is a similar increase in magnitude of the coefficient of dispersion (interquartile range/median). Rottier also analysed the difference in earnings behaviour between sectors. The dispersion of male earnings around the median increased markedly in staples during the depression. The coefficient of dispersion in male earnings quadruples between 1931 and 1935, compared with a doubling in new industries.[7] Generally, median male earnings were lower in staples than they were in new industries and exhibited greater volatility.

Table 3.10 reports the summary statistics by age and gender for several benchmarks from 1938 to 1968. The first key feature evident from this table was the increase in mean nominal earnings for all classes of worker in the first half of the Second World War.[8] This was true for all industries and for all workers, irrespective of age and gender, though real earnings increased significantly less. This was partly a function of increased wage rates (see below), but was also due to longer hours (including a large amount of overtime), increasing numbers of workers in relatively highly paid industries (especially munitions), and

[7] Rottier's group of staple industries is coal mining, wool and cotton spinning and weaving, general engineering, and shipbuilding. New industries are chemicals, vehicles, non-ferrous metals, electrical engineering, and building (1966: 239–41).

[8] The 1938 survey is the first survey that reports details of both earnings and hours worked disaggregated by industry, gender, and age.

Table 3.10. Earnings and hours by gender and age, 1938–68 (all industries; average earnings and hours)

	Men s/week	Men hours	Men s/hour	Youths and boys s/week	Youths and boys hours	Youths and boys s/hour
October 1938	69	47.7	1.45	26.08	46.2	0.56
July 1943	121.25	52.9	2.29	47.2	48	0.98
July 1945	121.33	49.7	2.44	45.5	45.6	1.00
October 1947	128.08	46.6	33.0	51.84	44.1	14.08
October 1950	150.42	47.6	37.9	63.75	44.4	17.16
October 1955	222.92	48.9	54.7	94.16	45.0	25.08
October 1960	290.67	48.0	72.7	130.0	44.3	35.16
October 1965	391.75	47.0	100.0	179.84	39.6	50.33
October 1968	459.92	46.4	118.9	214.5	41.9	61.33
	Women s/week	Women hours	Women s/hour	Girls s/week	Girls hours	Girls s/hour
October 1938	32.5	43.2	0.75	18.5	44.6	0.41
July 1943	62.17	45.9	1.35	33.84	45.1	0.75
July 1945	63.17	43.3	1.46	35.08	43.5	0.81
October 1947	69.42	41.4	20.08	43.75	42.1	12.42
October 1950	82.33	41.8	23.6	53.42	42.6	15.0
October 1955	115.42	41.6	33.3	75.67	42.7	21.25
October 1960	148.33	40.5	44.0	96.84	41.4	28.16
October 1965	191.92	38.7	59.5	129.5	39.6	39.16
October 1968	225.92	38.3	70.8	151.33	38.8	46.8

Source: *Gazette* (various issues), *British Labour Statistics: Historical Abstract*, tables 42, 43, 44, 45, 46, 47, 48, and 49. Women are full time and aged over 18 years; men are full time and aged over 21 years. October 1938 to October 1947 uses pre-1948 industrial classification, October 1950 to October 1955 uses 1948 classification, and post-October 1960 uses 1958 classification.

possibly also to an extension of the use of payment by results. Mean adult male earnings increased 75 per cent between October 1938 and July 1943, mean female earnings by about 90 per cent, and mean juvenile earnings by about 80 per cent over the same period.[9] Of course, these are nominal increases and because of price inflation real earnings increased significantly more modestly.

It is also clear that the trend towards increased dispersion in earnings (evident in the inter-war data) was reversed during the Second World War period. Rottier's analysis of the data for earnings and hourly earnings, for men and women, suggests that there was a substantial convergence of earnings across all

[9] The increase in earnings varied widely by industry from less than 40% to over 80% for men and between 50% and 100% for women. For all industries, the average increase for men was 76%, 81% for youths, 91% for women, and 83% for girls. Women's earnings increased more than men's on average due partly to the increased number of women working in munitions on work previously undertaken by men. Women who continued to work in industries where their jobs were defined as 'women's work' did not experience such large percentage increases in earnings. Ministry of Labour *Gazette* (Feb. 1944), 27.

Table 3.11. Earnings dispersion, 1938–51

	Oct. 1938	July 1943	July 1945	Oct. 1946	Oct. 1947	Oct. 1948	Oct. 1949	Oct. 1950	Oct. 1951
Male: weekly earnings	0.25	0.27	0.21	0.265	0.245	0.175	0.19	0.17	0.135
Female: weekly earnings	0.1	0.27	0.3	0.2	0.15	0.125	0.13	0.12	0.11
Male: hourly earnings	n./a.	0.305	0.29	0.22	0.28	0.21	0.19	0.185	0.165
Female: hourly earnings	n./a.	0.26	0.215	0.165	0.15	0.14	0.125	0.125	0.11

Source: Rottier (1966).

industries from 1943 onwards (1966: 243).[10] His evidence is set out in Table 3.11, which reports the coefficient of dispersion for selected earnings inquires between July 1943 and October 1951. It is clear that the variance of male weekly earnings was similar in the last two years of the war to what it had been in the 1930s, although the variance may have been a little lower in 1945 than in 1938. In the immediate post-war years, dispersion fell steadily. In the case of female weekly earnings, wartime dispersion was markedly greater than during the 1930s, but when the war was over, female weekly earnings also converged. Similar trends are evident in the time path of hourly earnings dispersion.

The second key feature of Table 3.10 is the dramatic increase in earnings for most groups during the 'golden age'. There was a near tripling in male average earnings and earnings per hour between October 1950 and October 1968. Of course, price inflation eroded the purchasing power of these gains, but even allowing for the change in prices, real earnings increased by over 40 per cent between 1950 and 1965 (see Table 3.14 below). This was achieved on the basis of slightly reduced hours. Gains of similar proportions are evident in these data for youths and boys. The proportionate advance in women's average earnings and earnings per hour in the 1950s and 1960s was slightly less than for men, suggesting a small widening of the gender pay gap, which eroded some of the gains made by women during the Second World War.

3.3.3 The inequality of pay, 1914–65

Knowles and Robertson (1951) provide estimates of wage-rate differentials between adult male skilled and unskilled workers, based on representative grades of workers in building, shipbuilding, engineering, railways, and the police. In later work they explored earnings inequality, but this was restricted to a study of engineering and shipbuilding. As Table 3.12 shows, in all the industries they studied, the unskilled/skilled wage rate ratio narrowed considerably between 1914 and 1950. Most of this levelling occurred during periods

[10] The coefficient of dispersion reported here is interquartile range/median. Rottier prefers to report (interquartile range/median) 100.

Table 3.12. Adult male time rate wages pay differentials, 1880–1950

Year	Building	Shipbuilding	Engineering	Railways	Police
1880	63.9	54	60		
1885	63.6	54	60	50.5	81.6
1890	65.6	51	59		
1895	67.1	53	60		
1900	66.7	52	58		
1904	65.6	53	59		
1910	65.2			50.9	
1914	66.5	55.2	58.6	54.3	
1918	80.1	73.6	75.7	74.8	
1920	81.0	77.2	78.9	81.2	70.0
1924	75.6	68.8	70.9	68.1	70.0
1929	74.7	68.0	71.3	65.2	70
1932	74.6	68.3	71.2	61.6	62.0
1935	74.9	68.3	71.9	61.1	62.0
1939	76.3	73.4	75.6	61.5	62.0
1943	79.2	79.2	80.9	74.1	67.7
1945	80.8	81.0	81.9	76.0	70.3
1948	80.4	81.8	84.4	74.6	70.0
1950	84.1	81.7	84.7	77.4	75.6

Source: Adapted from Knowles and Robertson (1951).

of war when wages were generally indexed to changes in the cost of living and the war bonuses paid were mainly flat-rate lump sums. Because price inflation was significantly greater in the First World War than the Second World War the flat-rate indexation of wages to changes in the cost of living during the Great War had a more pronounced effect on adult male pay ratios than it did during the Second World War. Knowles and Robertson did not find a strong positive correlation between movements in pay ratios and levels of employment 1920–39. In shipbuilding, engineering, and building, they found pay ratios stable in the depression. Only in the case of railway workers and the police was there a 'decided trough in the 1930s', as wage rate differentials widened again. By the middle of the twentieth century there was a considerable convergence in the unskilled/skilled pay across the industries they studied. In all five industries, the unskilled worker earned about four-fifths of the skilled worker's wage in 1950. This represented a major break with past experience for male unskilled workers.

Their conclusions were limited to wage rate inequality for adult male manual workers in a small selection of industries. Routh's (1965 and 1980) work on earnings inequality attempted to evaluate the changes in the relative pay of men and women in all socio-economic classes. It should be noted, however, that he included only a relatively small number of examples drawn from manufacturing industry. Furthermore, his analysis was restricted to benchmark estimates for 1913–14, 1922–24, 1935–36, 1955–56, and 1960 (and in later

Table 3.13. Earnings pay ratios (occupational class averages as percentages of the mean for all occupational classes)

	1913–14	1922–24	1935–36	1955–56	1960	1970	1978
Men							
1. Professional							
A. Higher	405	372	392	290	289	211	209
B. Lower	191	204	190	115	120	136	137
2B. Managers etc.	247	307	272	279	263	245	203
3. Clerks	122	116	119	98	97	97	93
4. Foremen	152	171	169	148	144	121	118
Manual							
5. Skilled	131	115	121	117	113	104	110
6. Semi-skilled	85	80	83	88	83	93	97
7. Unskilled	78	82	80	82	76	83	86
Men's average (current weights)	116	114	115	119	120	123	121
% mean deviation	68	73	70	48	47	35	30
Women							
1. Professional							
A. Higher	—	—	—	(218)	(217)	178	169
B. Lower	110	137	130	82	86	88	98
2B. Managers etc.	99	102	104	151	142	135	128
3. Clerks	56	68	61	60	61	61	69
4. Forewomen	70	98	96	90	86	73	81
Manual							
5. Skilled	54	56	53	60	56	49	57
6. Semi-skilled	62	63	62	51	48	47	59
7. Unskilled	35	47	45	43	40	44	57
Women's average (current weights)	62	66	64	60	59	59	68
% mean deviation	31	37	38	67	67	59	43

Source: Routh (1980).

editions 1970 and 1978). Routh's (1980) results are reported in Table 3.13. The most obvious feature of this table is the halving of the earnings of male professional workers relative to the average of all male workers between 1913–14 and 1978 and the more modest reduction in the relative earnings of managers, foremen, and clerks over the same period. Only the earnings of the male unskilled and semi-skilled showed an improvement relative to the earnings of all classes.

The First World War stands out as a period in which there was significant levelling in earnings within the manual working class. Unskilled male workers' earnings were 78 per cent of the mean of all classes in 1913–14 and skilled workers' earnings were 131 per cent of the mean of all classes. By 1922–24, they were 82 and 117 per cent respectively (of a slightly reduced mean earnings). Although there appears to be little movement in earnings differentials over the period of the Second World War in Routh's data, there is reliable industry-level evidence that shows that male adult earnings per hour differentials did compress across the Second World War (Gazeley 2006). In shipbuilding, wartime levelling is most apparent when unskilled time workers' earnings per hour are compared with skilled pieceworkers' earnings per hour, though also evident in a straightforward comparison of time rates by grade of skill. Unskilled time workers' earnings per hour were little over a half of skilled pieceworkers' earnings per hour in 1940, but had improved by about 10 percentage points by the end of the war.[11] Similar data are available for the engineering industry. Hart and MacKay (1975: 39) provide earnings and hours worked data for fitters and labourers, for 1934–42 and 1948, derived from the Engineering Employers' Federation records. These data are weighted means of twenty-eight engineering regions. In terms of earnings per hour pay ratios, their data show a picture of wartime differential narrowing similar to the one revealed by the shipbuilding data. Prior to 1942, differentials in engineering widen slightly, but by 1948 earnings per hour pay ratios narrow by about 7 percentage points, compared with 1938.

Routh's results indicate that women did make some advances (relative to the average of all men and women) during the First World War, though the improvement is restricted to unskilled women.[12] Over the Second World War period, the position of skilled women improved (relative to the average of all men and women), while the position of semi-skilled and unskilled women deteriorated. Routh does not give a benchmark estimate for 1938–50, so it is not possible to comment on the short-term impact of the Second World War on women's relative pay. Routh (1980: 123) provides calculations of female/male earnings ratios, which appear to show that on average, across all classes of women, pay ratios actually deteriorate relative to all classes of men between 1935–36 and 1955–60. This conclusion is somewhat misleading, however, and is the product of Routh's choice of denominator and his use of earnings rather than earnings per hour data. Men work significantly longer hours than women during the war, which masks the reduction in gender pay inequality evident in earnings per hour data. As Gazeley (2005) shows, on the basis of earnings per hour data derived from the wartime Ministry of

[11] This may seem odd in view of the well-known disparity of earnings and wartime earnings growth of skilled pieceworkers' earnings. Two points need to be made in this context. First, there are significant differences in hours worked between these groups at the beginning of the war, but by the end of the Second World War they converge. In 1940, time workers work longer hours than pieceworkers and the hours of unskilled workers are greater than skilled workers, but by 1948 hours worked for all three groups are much closer. As a consequence the pay ratio of skilled time workers' earnings per hour relative to skilled pieceworkers' earnings per hour shows significant levelling between 1940 and 1948.

[12] On the basis of Bowley's (1937) data, the female/male pay ratio increases somewhat in the trans-First World War period, from 0.44 to 0.48 across all industries, but much more in metals than elsewhere. The female/male pay ratio increases from 0.38 in 1906 to about 0.45–0.48 in the inter-war period, though it is possible that this increase is actually due to age effects, changes in skill composition, or changes in the method of payment affecting men and women unequally.

Labour inquiries, there was a significant reduction in average gender pay inequality across the Second World War period, from 0.52 in October 1938 to 0.61 in October 1947. Furthermore, this levelling in pay inequality was heavily concentrated in male-dominated industries, such as metals and chemicals, while inequality in traditional female sectors of manufacturing, such as clothing and textiles, did not change significantly between 1938 and 1947.

The evidence suggests that most levelling occurred in the first half of the century during the two periods of wartime and all writers agree that 'proximate cause' of levelling between unskilled men and skilled men and between women and men was the granting of flat-rate bonuses. However, the underlying causes remain in dispute. In the 1950s the debate was polarized between those who argued that changes in relative pay were the result of changes in conditions in the labour market, in particular, the supply and demand of particular classes of labour, and those who stressed an institutional explanation based on changes in trade union bargaining strategies (see Reder 1955 and Turner 1957, for opposing views). Over the last fifty years the relationship between relative earnings and employment has been picked over fairly extensively. Routh noted, in common with Knowles and Robertson, that during the first half of the twentieth century, changes in relative pay are not associated with aggregate indicators of excess demand or supply of labour.[13]

Instead, most writers explain levelling in Britain by pointing to developments in the wartime labour market itself. Knowles and Robertson (1951: 121) place great emphasis on the role of trade union wage bargaining in the process of narrowing pay ratios. During the first half of the century, as the unionization of unskilled workers quickened, many new amalgamations and federations were formed and wage bargaining shifted to a national level. One feature of these national agreements was the 'freezing' of differentials. There were very few industries where workers were represented solely by one union, so centralized bargaining required separate unions to reach agreement by a common formula which appeared fair to members of all groups (Turner 1957: 232–3). Such formulae could take the form of a flat-rate or a percentage addition. In the former case, the money value (in nominal terms) of the differential between skilled and unskilled workers would remain unchanged, but the relative differential would compress. In the latter case, the money value of the differential would widen and the relative differential would remain constant. It is likely that the preponderance of flat-rate claims was due to the relative strength of

[13] Routh (1980: 200–1) argues that changes in relative pay were associated with changes in retail prices. When prices were increasing, differentials narrowed, and vice versa when prices were falling. Similar conclusions have been reached from the study for engineering (Hart and MacKay 1975: 42). However, Gazeley (2005) found that the narrowing in the gender pay during the Second World War was positively correlated with changes in the employment share of women.

unskilled workers in an industry (or because of the necessity of attracting unskilled members in the exceptional circumstances of wartime). Examples cited by Turner (1957: 241–2) include metals and woodworking trades, with engineering the 'outstanding example', where the nominal cash value of the difference between fitters' and labourers' standard rates was constant between 1926 and 1948. This point is amplified by Penn (1983: 81), who claims that the adoption of flat-rate increases in pay was one of the unintended outcomes of a union wage-bargaining strategy that had its roots in the period before the First World War. During the Second World War, general unions approved of such increases on egalitarian grounds and the craft unions accepted the rough justice of flat-rate advances. At the same time, burgeoning union membership and the institutionalization of unions in wartime production, through Joint Production Committees, strengthened the role of shop stewards. Union national officers who negotiated basic time rates had a preference for the simplicity afforded by flat-rate claims, whereas district officials (and factory shop stewards) determined local piece rates, merit, and bonus systems. As a consequence, there is more levelling apparent in comparisons of wage rates than in comparison of earnings (Penn 1983: 82).

3.4 Conclusion

During the first half of the twentieth century, the material well-being of manual workers improved significantly. In terms of real incomes, the broad trends are apparent from Feinstein's (1972) data. His figures for average weekly wages, average weekly earnings, and retail prices are reproduced in Table 3.14, for the period 1913–65.

Table 3.14. Average income, 1913–65 (1913 = 100)

	Average weekly wages	Average weekly earnings	Retail prices	Average real wages	Average real earnings
1913	100	100	100	100	100
1920	257	278	244	105	114
1924	178	196	172	103	114
1929	176	195	161	109	121
1938	185	207	153	121	135
1945	280	368	226	124	163
1950	344	490	283	122	173
1956	507	771	389	130	198
1961	606	978	437	139	224
1965	711	1240	503	141	247

Source: Columns 1–3 taken from Feinstein (1972: T141). Columns 4 and 5 are author's own calculations.

From Table 3.14, it can be seen that average weekly wages increased steadily during the First World War and short post-war boom, so that by 1920 they were on average about 2.5 times higher than they had been in 1913. During the inter-war period, wages fell back somewhat in the early 1920s and then remained pretty flat until the late 1930s when they started on an upward path that quickened during the Second World War and continued during the late 1940s through to the mid-1960s. By the end of the Second World War, average weekly wages were about three times higher than they were in 1913 and more than double again by the early 1960s. Earnings drift (the growth in disparity between the weekly wages and weekly earnings) is an important feature of these data.[14] The time path of average weekly earnings displayed a similar trend, but earnings growth outstripped wage rate growth in every period. Earnings grew slightly faster than wages during the First World War and remained in advance of wages throughout the inter-war period. By 1950, average earnings were nearly five times higher than in 1913, and by the early 1960s, earnings had increased by more than tenfold their 1913 value. This impressive increase in average income was based upon substantial growth in productivity, as outlined in Chapter 1.

Feinstein's index of retail prices has been used to calculate the indices of average real wages and average real earnings reported in Table 3.14. Notice that Feinstein's index of retail prices did not grow as fast as wages or earnings by 1920, indicating some real wage and earnings gains relative to 1913. During the war years themselves, prices actually grew somewhat faster than wages, resulting in a small decline in average real wages (Clegg 1994: 178). Conversely, over the course of the inter-war depression, prices fell faster than wages, producing modest real wage and earnings growth. From the mid-1930s until 1965, prices generally rose less quickly than either wages or earnings, though price inflation during the early 1950s briefly reversed the gains in wage rates of the mid- and late 1940s. Nevertheless, by the end of the period real wages were about 40 per cent higher than 1913, but real earnings were 140 per cent higher. About half of this increase in real earnings occurs in the fifteen years after 1950.

Another key feature of the labour market that stands out is the change in pay inequality that took place during the first half of the twentieth century. As Phelps-Brown (1977: 65) records, the ratio of wages between craftsmen and labourers had been stable in southern England for about 500 years, from about the end of the Black Death until the onset of the First World War. In 1412 craftsmen's wages in the building trade were 6d. per day and labourers' 4d. per

---

[14] Earnings gap is the difference between total weekly earnings and minimum wage rates; earnings drift is the rate of increase of the gap; wage gap and drift exclude overtime earnings from total earnings.

day. This ratio of 3:2 still pertained in 1914, when craftsmen's wages were 10.5*d*. and labourers' 7*d*. per day. Phelps-Brown suggests that this 'rule of thumb' was 'accepted as fair and reasonable mainly because it was customary'. Evidence for other industries suggests a similar and fairly stable relationship between skilled and unskilled wages during the late nineteenth century, with unskilled workers receiving a little over half of skilled workers' wages (Williamson 1985). During the first half of the twentieth century, skill differentials were compressed quite sharply, so that by 1950 an unskilled worker could expect to be paid about four-fifths of the skilled wage. Less dramatic, but equally important, was the gradual levelling in pay by gender. The relative pay of women workers gradually increased, so as to be just under two-thirds of the average for adult men by the late 1940s. Indeed, women's average earnings per hour remained at about this level until gender pay inequality was sharply reduced in the mid-1970s, following the imposition of anti-discriminatory legislation (Zabalza and Tzannatos 1985).

The periods of war stand out as being important in this context. From 1917, there was a move towards national pay bargaining across British industry as workers, employers, and the state became embroiled in corporatist wage-fixing arrangements (Middlemass 1979). As the twentieth century progressed, the state increasingly directed labour, most obviously in wartime, but also through labour exchanges and institutional arrangements designed to guarantee a social minimum wage. These arrangements included legislation on paid holidays and regulations governing the length of the working week for juveniles. Many of the institutional mechanisms for the direction of labour in the First World War were used as templates during the Second World War, when the corporatist nature of the labour market reached its zenith. This framework conditioned relations in the labour market for a generation after the end of the war, until it gradually broke down in the 1960s and early 1970s, as fissures became increasingly evident between the policies followed by trade union leaders and the attitude of many of the membership (Wrigley 1996).

Important shifts in the industrial and occupational distribution of the labour force accompanied these changes in average and relative pay. Despite the decline in domestic service, women's employment remained segregated in a small number of industries for the entire period, though temporarily during both world wars large numbers of women were engaged in war work in industries that were dominated by men. Male employment became increasingly diversified during the first half of the twentieth century. This is due to both a shift from primary sector employment to secondary and tertiary sector employment, as relatively fewer men work in agriculture and mining, coupled with a significantly reduced concentration of male employment in staple and building industries. This was accompanied by a gradual reduction in the proportion of men who were economically active and corresponding increases in the proportion of women in paid work.

References

Boston, S. (1987). *Women Workers and the Trade Unions*. London: Lawrence and Wishart.

Bowley, A. L. (1937). *Wages and Income since 1860*. Cambridge: Cambridge University Press.

Broadberry, S. N. (1986). 'Aggregate Supply in Inter-War Britain'. *Economic Journal*, 96: 467–81.

Clegg, H. A. (1994). *A History of British Trade Unions since 1889*, iii: *1934–51*. Oxford: Oxford University Press.

Cole, G. D. H. (1928). *The Payment of Wages*. London: G. Allen and Unwin.

Dowie, J. A. (1975). '1919–20 is in Need of Attention'. *Economic History Review*, 28/3: 429–50.

Feinstein, C. H. (1972) *National Income, Output and Expenditure of the U.K since 1870*. Cambridge: Cambridge University Press.

Flanagan, R., Soskice, D., and Ulman, L. (1983). *Unionism, Economic Stabilization and Incomes Policies: European Experience*. Washington: The Brookings Institution.

Gazeley, I. (2003). *Poverty in Britain 1900–1965*. Basingstoke: Palgrave Macmillan.

—— (2005). 'Women's Pay in British Industry during World War Two'. Mimeo.

—— (2006). 'The Levelling of Pay in Britain during the Second World War'. *European Review of Economic History*, August.

Gittins, D. (1982). *Fair Sex: Family Size and Structure 1900–39*. London: Hutchinson.

Gregg, P., and Wadsworth, J. (1999). 'Economic Activity', in P. Gregg and J. Wadsworth, *The State of Working Britain*. Manchester: Manchester University Press.

Hakim, C. (2004). *Key Issues in Women's Work*. London: GlassHouse.

Harris, J. (1993). *Private Lives, Public Spirit: Britain 1870–1914*. London: Penguin.

Hart, R. A., and MacKay, D. I. (1975). 'Engineering Earnings in Britain, 1914–68'. *Journal of the Royal Statistical Society*, 138: 32–50.

Knowles, K. G. J. C., and Robertson, D. J. (1951). 'Differences between the Wages of Skilled and Unskilled Workers, 1880–1950'. *Bulletin of the Oxford University Institute of Statistics*, April: 109–27.

Lewenhak, S. (1977). *Women and Trade Unions*. London: Benn.

Lewis, J. (1984). *Women in England, 1870–1950*. Brighton: Wheatsheaf.

Lowe, R. (1986). *Adjusting to Democracy: The Role of the Ministry of Labour in Britsh Politics, 1916–1939*. Oxford: Clarendon Press.

Middlemas, K. (1979). *Politics in Industrial Society*. London: A. Deutsch.

Mitchell, B. R., and Deane, P. (1962). *Abstract of British Historical Statistics*. Cambridge: Cambridge University Press.

Penn, R. (1983). 'The Course of Wage Differentials between Skilled and Non-Skilled Manual Workers in Britain between 1856 and 1964'. *British Journal of Industrial Relations*, March: 69–90.

Phelps-Brown, H. (1977). *The Inequality of Pay*. Oxford: Oxford University Press.

Reder, M. W. (1955). 'The Theory of Occupational Wage Differentials'. *American Economic Review*, 45: 833–52.

Roberts, E. (1995). *Women's Work, 1840–1940*. Cambridge: Cambridge University Press.

Robertson, D. J. (1960). *Factory Wage Structures and National Agreements*. Cambridge: Cambridge University Press.

—— (1961). *The Economics of Wages and the Distribution of Income*. London: Macmillan.

Rottier, G. (1966). 'The Evolution of Wage Differentials: A Study of British Data', in J. T. Dunlop (ed.), *The Theory of Wage Determination*. London: Macmillan.

Routh, G. (1965). *Occupation and Pay in Great Britain, 1906–1960*. Cambridge: Cambridge University Press.

—— (1980). *Occupation and Pay in Great Britain 1906–1978*. London: Macmillan.

Savage, M. (1988). 'Trade Unionism, Sex Segregation and the State: Women's Employment in "New Industries" in Inter-War Britain'. *Social History*, 13/2: 209–29.

Sells, D. (1939). *British Wage Boards*. Washington: The Brookings Institution.

Summerfield, P. (1985). *Women Workers and the Second World War*. London: Croom Helm.

Thomas, M. (1997). 'Wage Behaviour in Inter-War Britain: A Sceptical Enquiry', in G. Grantham and M. Mackinnon (eds.), *Labour Market Evolution*. London: Routledge.

Todd, S. (2005). *Young Women, Work, and Family in England 1918–50*. Oxford: Oxford University Press.

Turner, H. A. (1957). 'Inflation and Wage Differentials in Great Britain', in J. T. Dunlop (ed.), *The Theory of Wage Determination*. London: Macmillan.

Williamson, J. G. (1985). *Did British Capitalism Breed Inequality?* Boston: Allen and Unwin.

Wrigley, C. (1996). *A History of British Industrial Relations, 1939–1979*. Cheltenham: Elgar.

Zabalza, A., and Tzannatos, Z. (1985). 'The Effect of Britain's Anti-Discriminatory Legislation on Relative Pay and Employment'. *Economic Journal*, 95: 839–43.

4

Wages and Wage Inequality, 1970–2000

Florence Kondylis and Jonathan Wadsworth

4.1 Introduction

Most people of working age rely on wages as their primary source of income. As such, knowing how the rewards to work are determined and how these rewards evolve over time is fundamental to an understanding of a modern industrial society. In what follows we concentrate on one of the most important labour market developments of the last quarter of a century, namely the explosion in wage inequality that began in the early 1980s and the subsequent rise, albeit at a slower pace, into the first decade of the new century. Why is this so important a development, even exempting the debate about why inequality matters? First, according to the best estimates available (see Gregg and Machin 1994), wage inequality in Britain had remained relatively stable in the hundred years prior to the 1980s. This suggests then that the current level of inequality in pay is now higher than at any time since the 1920s. Second, widening wage inequality was experienced only in Britain and one or two other industrialized countries, notably the United States (see OECD 1996). Explaining why this happened is one of the most important issues facing economists today.

In what follows we track the development of wages and wage inequality in Britain since the 1970s, focusing on the principal differences why wages differ across individuals and on which of these factors seem to explain the rise in wage inequality. In so doing we document the evolution of the main institutional features of wage determination and discuss the evolution of these features across governments of various political hues over the period. Section 4.2 begins with a discussion of the principal data sources used to track the evolution of wages over time. Section 4.3 gives some facts and figures on the extent of wage inequality across groups and over time, while section 4.4 outlines and evaluates the main hypotheses put forward to explain rising wage inequality. Section 4.5 offers some concluding observations.

4.2 Measuring wages

In order to study changes in wages it is necessary to have access to data that are consistent, that cover a concerted period of time, and that will also allow researchers a degree of disaggregation in order to try to understand the issues that shape aggregate events. Even though what matters to most people is weekly or monthly take-home pay, most researchers choose to work with real hourly wage data, the weekly wage divided by the number of hours worked during the week, adjusted for the general rise in prices over time. Comparing the hourly wage over time avoids the distortions that might arise from a comparison of the weekly wage if part-time working became more prevalent, as it has over the past forty years. However use of the hourly wage is not without problems and there is scope for mis-measurement if the hours data do not correspond directly to the nature of the wage payment. For example, most people are not paid by the hour and so weekly wage data could include any overtime worked but the hours data may not.

The largest consistent survey of hourly wage rates of individuals available in Britain is the New Earnings Survey (NES). The NES is a 1 per cent sample of all employees in Great Britain sponsored by the Department of Trade and Industry (and its various incarnations) since 1970[1]. The employers of those selected are surveyed rather than the individuals themselves. Unfortunately there are misgivings over the NES coverage of low-paid workers and the NES lacks information on many of the socio-economic characteristics of the individuals, for example education, which, as we show below, is necessary if we are to begin to understand the factors which help explain rising wage inequality.

A consistent wage series from the late 1960s onward can be gleaned from the individual responses contained in the Family Expenditure Survey. However this survey again does not contain adequate accompanying information on the educational attainment of the individuals surveyed. In what follows we draw on the individual wage data contained within the annual General Household Survey (GHS). This yearly, government-sponsored survey of around 10,000 randomly selected households going back to 1972 does contain information on the gross pay and the socio-economic characteristics of the individuals surveyed. However the hourly wage series is not consistent over time, since the weekly wage data include overtime payments, but the weekly hours worked data exclude overtime before 1997 and include it after that

---

[1] In practice, all those whose National Insurance number ends with a specific two-digit combination are surveyed.

point. We therefore use the GHS between 1972 and 1996 and continue after that with wage data from the larger Labour Force Survey (LFS). The LFS began in 1975, as a requirement of European Union entry, primarily as a means of establishing consistent regional unemployment rates across the Union, which were then used as one of the criteria with which to allocate funding. Since then the sample survey of around 60,000 households has grown in scope over the years and is now the primary source for labour market information in the UK. Since 1997, the LFS has contained wage data on around 15,000 employees each quarter. It also provides gross weekly wage data including overtime pay, and contains hours data both excluding and excluding overtime.[2] To make the LFS and GHS series as consistent as possible we use LFS hours excluding overtime as the denominator to construct an hourly wage series from the period 1997 to the present.[3] Readers should however note that the wage series that appears in the subsequent figures and tables is discontinuous around this point.

The measures of wage inequality that we use in the chapter are based around comparisons of wage levels at points toward the top and bottom of the pay distribution, (the 90th and 10th percentiles respectively) and wages at the middle of the distribution, the median or 50th percentile. It is common to measure inequality by looking at either the difference in or the ratio of these percentiles of the wage distribution (see Appendix 4.1 for more details). We also report a summary measure of inequality in the pay distribution as a whole, commonly used in the inequality literature, namely the standard deviation of log of hourly wages.

4.3 Wages, institutions, and governments

4.3.1 *The 1970s*

Back in the 1950s, Kuznets (1955) had promoted the idea that (income) inequality would rise during the early stages of industrialization and fall during the more mature stages of growth. It had been generally assumed that economic growth would bring benefits for all, rich and poor. The wage data available for Britain over the 1970s do not appear to contradict this view, though in truth there were many institutional features in play over this period that helped confirm Kuznets's hypothesis.

---

[2] For more information on the history and structure of the GHS and LFS see the descriptions given under the Major Studies link at the UK Data Archive website at the University of Essex, **www.data-archive.ac.uk.**

[3] The two series give similar estimates in the years they overlap. For example, in 1996 the median real weekly wage for men in the GHS was £359.96 and in the LFS £359.25. The median hourly wages were £8.85 and £8.06 respectively. Machin (2003) provides a comparison of wage levels and inequality over time using all four wage sources.

Attempts to influence the outcomes of wage determination at the beginning of the 1970s followed on from the consensual wage-setting arrangements between employers, employees, and government put into practice increasingly during the 1960s when concerns over cost-driven price inflation began to emerge. Outside the confines of incomes policies, private sector pay determination was increasingly set at the level of the firm, rather than within sub-groups at the firm, sometimes subject to industry-wide recommendations. In the public sector, pay remained the product of negotiations at industry or, what amounts to the same thing, national level (Flanagan et al. 1983).

Given the perceived continued presence of cost-driven factors, the attempts at consensual wage determination were revived with varied degrees of success in the 1970s under both Conservative and Labour governments. In the first two years of the Conservative regime of 1970–4, there were no formal incomes policies. Instead, restrictions on wage increases in the public sector were sought out, with the private sector left to bargain freely with unions subject to more stringent industrial relations legislation and a more deflationary macro-economic regime (Flanagan et al. 1983). When the government failed to persuade several unions to adhere to the strategy of gradual reductions in nominal wage increases and with the deflationary macro-regime also failing to have much effect on the growth in real wages of those still in work,[4] the Conservatives re-introduced pay (and price, rent, and dividend) freezes in November 1972, a policy regime which lasted for around six months. When this freeze was relaxed, stages 2 and 3 of the policy imposed both relative and absolute ceilings on all subsequent pay increases along with a minimum settlement duration of twelve months (Blackaby 1978). This policy continued when Labour assumed power in 1974, following the failure of the Conservatives in the elections of that year, campaigning under the slogan 'Who Governs Britain?'; the electorate decided that the Conservatives did not.

The wage regimes favoured by the Labour government of 1974–79 can be divided into three periods (Flanagan et al. 1983). The first period 1974–75 sought to maintain zero real wage growth based on consensus agreements of the unions and employers without imposing implicit incomes policies. Faced with accelerating inflation and real wages in the private sector, Labour imposed an incomes and prices policy in July 1975. The policy imposed flat-rate increases, of £6 a week, and an annual upper income limit, of £8,500, beyond which no wage increases were allowed. Phase 2 of the policy, in July 1976, reduced the nominal increase maximum to £4 a week. However, by 1978, the TUC was unable to get its member unions to continue adhering to the policy and a return to free collective bargaining ensued. The phase 2 government-recommended nominal pay increase norm of 5 per cent was not rescinded, but in the main it was not adhered to.

---

[4] Unemployment grew from 2.6% in 1970 to 3.9% by the end of 1972, the highest rate since 1940.

Table 4.1. Real hourly wages and wage inequality by gender

	Hourly wage at given percentile of wage distribution			Percentile ratios			Standard deviation of log wage
	90th	50th	10th	90/10	50/10	90/50	
Men							
1972	9.7	5.6	3.3	3.0	1.7	1.7	0.476
1980	11.5	6.8	4.0	2.9	1.7	1.7	0.448
1990	15.5	8.4	4.2	3.7	2.0	1.9	0.552
1996	16.2	8.4	4.1	3.9	2.0	1.9	0.559
1997	16.0	8.2	4.1	3.9	2.0	2.0	0.564
2004	18.5	9.2	4.9	3.8	1.9	2.0	0.535
Change							
1972–80	1.8	1.2	0.7	−0.1	0	0	−0.028
1980–90	4.0	1.6	0.2	0.8	0.3	0.2	0.104
1990–6	0.7	0.0	−0.1	0.2	0	0	0.007
1997–2004	2.5	1.0	0.8	−0.1	−0.1	0	−0.029
Women							
1972	5.8	3.1	1.9	3.0	1.6	1.9	0.477
1980	7.2	4.1	2.7	2.7	1.5	1.8	0.418
1990	10.8	5.2	3.0	3.6	1.7	2.1	0.528
1996	11.7	5.8	3.4	3.5	1.7	2.0	0.511
1997	11.6	5.9	3.4	3.4	1.7	2.0	0.516
2004	13.8	7.1	4.3	3.2	1.9	2.1	0.486
Change							
1972–80	1.4	1.0	0.8	−0.3	−0.1	−0.1	−0.059
1980–90	3.6	1.1	0.7	0.9	0.2	0.3	0.110
1990–6	0.9	0.6	0.4	−0.1	0	−0.1	−0.017
1997–2004	2.2	1.2	0.9	−0.2	0.2	0.1	−0.030

Note: Hourly wages in 2004 prices.
Source: GHS 1972–96; LFS 1997–2004.

Against this background, average nominal wages, that is wages for workers in the middle of the pay distribution, broadly kept pace with (rising) inflation throughout the first half of the 1970s but rose faster than inflation during the second half of the decade. As a result, Table 4.1 shows that average (median) real wages were some 20 per cent higher at the end of the decade than in 1972.

The other main result of the implicit and explicit incomes policy regimes that held sway throughout (Blackaby 1978) was that wage inequality remained stable or even declined. Pay grew at much the same rate throughout the distribution, aided by the recommendations of the wages councils which continued to protect the low paid across several industrial sectors. The imposition of absolute limits on weekly wages over the last two years of the Conservative administration and over the period 1975–78 under the Labour administration (Peden 1985) helps explain why wages of those at the top of the pay distribution fell somewhat relative to other workers over this period, as shown in

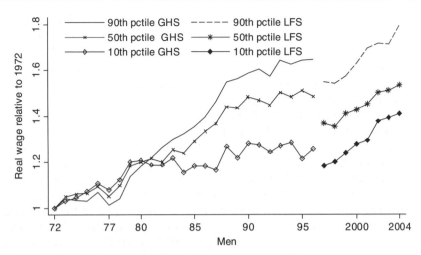

Figure 4.1 Changes in value of real hourly wages relative to 1972

Figure 4.1 and Table 4.1. Indeed this was often one of the stated aims of the various incomes policies in play, though the overall effects were not great. By and large, therefore, the distribution of pay at the end of the decade remained pretty much as it had at the start of the decade and probably as it had for much of the earlier part of the twentieth century.

4.3.2 Wages under the Conservatives, 1979–97

The tripartite arrangement that sustained prices and incomes policies broke down in 1978, and was never used again. When the Conservatives were elected in 1979 with a professed priority of bringing down inflation, a policy of targeting money supply growth rates through interest rate movements—also used by Labour governments in 1967 and 1976—replaced incomes policies as the principal means of managing inflationary expectations and hence, it was believed, wage settlements. At the same time, Keynesian demand management policies were abandoned, public sector borrowing was reduced, and sterling was allowed to appreciate as part of the counter-inflationary strategy. Any attempts at a consensus approach to wage determination were abandoned. Firms were to be allowed 'the right to manage', subject to the constraints imposed by the new macroeconomic order. Attempts were made to entrench the trend toward local (firm-level) bargaining seen in earlier decades, rather than encourage national or industry-wide agreements. Significantly, trade unions were perceived as part of the problem rather than part of the solution to wage outcomes. The 1980 and 1982 Employment Acts were explicitly aimed at curbing their influence. The closed shop was outlawed, ballots became compulsory before strike action could be taken, secondary strike action was outlawed, and unions could now be sued if found to be in breach of the legislation (Metcalf 2003). In a series of high-profile strikes, notably the steelworkers in 1981 and the miners in 1984, the government faced down the unions in a deliberate attempt to 'encourage the others'.

At the same time, the combined effect of the new government's macroeconomic policies contributed to the deepest recession Britain had experienced for fifty years. Unemployment tripled between 1979 and 1984, with the manufacturing sector particularly affected by the high interest rates and the high value of sterling policies adopted in the government's deflationary stance. Trade union membership fell by 3 million members over the decade. Somewhat surprisingly given the severity of the recession and the onslaught on the unions, throughout the recessionary period of the early 1980s, the real value of average wages was constant. Significantly, as Figure 4.1 and Table 4.1 show, it is at this time that real wages for those toward the top of the earnings distribution began to grow faster than among the rest of the population, a trend that has continued until the present. After 1984 there were no other major labour market interventions by the Conservatives until their defeat in the 1997 election, with the exception of the overhaul of the unemployment benefit regime. Beginning in 1983, eligibility and job search criteria were both gradually tightened and the means-tested arm of the benefit system promoted at the expense of the National Insurance-based contributions. More competition for jobs among the unemployed was intended to encourage wage restraint.

Between 1979 and 1996, real hourly wages at the 90th percentile of the male wage distribution grew by 46 per cent, while real hourly wages at the 10th percentile grew by only 5 per cent over the same period. As a result the ratio of hourly pay for those at the top 10th relative to those at the bottom 10th percentile increased from 3 times larger to 4 times larger. The absolute hourly pay gap grew from £7.50 an hour to £12 an hour (in 2004 prices).[5]

The trends in pay for women are almost as dramatic. Wages at the top pulled away from wages at the bottom. However the widening inequality here was accompanied by non-negligible real increase in hourly wages of women at the bottom of the pay distribution, continuing the boost to real levels of pay of many women, particularly toward the bottom of the pay distribution, generated by the introduction of the Equal Pay and Sex Discrimination Acts of 1975 (see Chapter 7).

---

[5] Atkinson (2003) suggests that the real incomes of those at the very top, i.e. the top 1% of all earners, grew by much more than 40% over the same period.

4.3.3 *Wages under New Labour, 1997–present*

With Labour elected on the back of 1997 manifesto promises of 'fairness' and governing 'for the many, not the few', it was widely believed that this would include a serious attempt to tackle rising wage inequality. The government began immediately implementing a significant three-pronged strategy intended to raise the gain from working relative to not working, 'making work pay', by reducing income taxes for the low paid, introducing generous government supplements to those in work (the Working Families Tax Credits), and, for the first time in Britain, establishing a national minimum wage. All three of these policies benefited those toward the bottom of the wage distribution and not those at the top.[6] The introduction of the national minimum wage in 1999 undoubtedly shored up gross pay levels at the very bottom of the wage distribution, but this covered at most 5 per cent of employees (Low Pay Commission 2003),[7] and so made little impact on the aggregate inequality measures. Over the period real pay levels of those at the top have risen more, in absolute terms, than for those at the bottom. In relative terms wages at the bottom have risen more. Hence the overall impact of these changes on inequality during this later period is somewhat ambiguous. During the Labour administration inequality did not increase at anything like the rate observed in the 1980s. Yet, as Table 4.1 and Figure 4.1 show, wage inequality did not fall back. At the end of the sample period, a man at the 90th percentile of the gross hourly wage distribution earned around four times as much as a man at the 10th percentile of the distribution. Back in the early 1970s, pay at the 90th percentile exceeded that at the 10th percentiles by a factor of three. It is true, however, that the *level* of the real wage at the bottom of the pay distribution rose perceptibly over the years after Labour was elected, unlike under the preceding regime. So even if inequality was not changing, some aspects of Kuznets's law appear to have re-emerged, in that the working poor were also benefiting from the 3 per cent average annual growth rate that held throughout the New Labour administration.

4.4 Why did wage inequality rise?

If the rewards to working in Britain are now so much more unequal, it seems natural to ask why this has happened. One feature that many economists have focused on as the basis for building explanatory theories is the observation that the rewards to different levels of educational attainment became increasingly

[6] Dickens and Manning (2004) find that spillover effects from the minimum wage—due to workers away from the bottom attempting to restore differentials—were negligible.

[7] The other two main policy tools affect net, take-home, wages and so will not show up in the gross wage data used here.

Table 4.2. Changes in the relative wage returns to education

	1972	1980	1990	1996	1997	2004
Men						
Degree	2.1	1.7	2.0	1.9	1.8	1.9
Intermediate	1.5	1.4	1.6	1.5	1.5	1.5
Low	1.2	1.2	1.3	1.2	1.2	1.2
Women						
Degree	2.8	2.1	2.4	2.1	2.0	1.9
Intermediate	2.0	1.7	1.8	1.7	1.6	1.4
Low	1.3	1.2	1.3	1.2	1.2	1.2

Note: Intermediate category is any qualification, academic or vocational, above GCSE but below degree level. Low category is GCSE and under. Reference category is those with no formal qualifications. Relative wage differentials based on a regression of the log hourly wage on three qualification dummies controlling for age, age squared, and region. Numbers in the table give the ratio of the average hourly wage for each category relative to the average hourly wage of those with no qualifications.
Source: GHS and LFS.

dispersed over this period. As Table 4.2 shows, during the 1980s and 1990s, average earnings of graduates rose more than among the rest of the population.

Moreover, graduate wage differentials relative to others grew over a period when the share of graduates in the population also grew rapidly, helped by the Conservative administration's decision to expand the tertiary education sector, a policy which continued under the subsequent Labour administration (see Table 4.3). Among women the relative increase in the supply of 'skilled' workers was boosted by increased participation rates among graduates. According to the GHS, the female employment rate grew from around 57 per cent in 1972 to around 71 per cent in 2004. Wadsworth (1999) shows that over much of this period, participation rates were both higher and rose faster among the more highly qualified than among the less qualified. Among men participation rates fell much more among the less skilled than among the more highly skilled. This relative increase in the supply of skilled workers might have been expected to dampen both the rise and dispersion in real wages among graduates. Since relative graduate wages rose when the supply of graduates was rising, this has led economists to conclude that the demand for what are loosely described as 'skills' must have risen faster than the supply of skills. If supply had kept pace with demand then wages of skilled workers would not have risen as much. There is, however, a suggestion from Table 4.4 that the pace of growth of relative earnings of graduates has slowed over the past decade as the supply of graduates continues to expand, so that supply-side stories may have become more important recently.

The search for a reason for rising wage inequality based around rising demand for skills has thrown up two main explanations. One is that increased trade with the developing world has reduced demand for less-skilled workers in

Table 4.3. Changes in population shares by educational attainment

	1972	1980	1990	1996	1997	2004	Change			
							1972–80	1980–90	1990–96	1997–2004
Men										
Degree	3.2	7.3	11.4	13.3	13.9	17.9	4.2	4.1	1.9	4.0
A level and equivalent	10.4	11.1	16.9	18.3	14.7	17.6	0.7	5.8	1.4	2.9
GCSE and equivalent	27.4	38.4	40.7	44.2	45.7	42.5	10.9	2.3	3.5	−3.2
None	59.0	43.2	31.1	24.2	25.7	22.0	−15.8	−12.2	−6.8	−3.7
Women										
Degree	1.2	3.1	6.1	9.5	10.2	15.8	1.9	3.1	3.4	5.6
A level and equivalent	7.5	10.3	14.8	16.4	17.1	20.9	2.8	4.5	1.5	3.8
GCSE and equivalent	24.4	34.4	44.6	46.7	43.7	40.0	10.0	10.2	2.1	−3.6
None	67.0	52.2	34.4	27.4	29.1	23.3	−14.8	−17.8	−7.0	−5.8

Note: Sample is population of working age. Numbers in the table give the percentage of the relevant population with given level of educational attainment.
Source: GHS and LFS.

the West, replaced by cheaper labour elsewhere, which has kept down wages toward the bottom of the UK pay distribution and allowed the rest of the distribution to pull away from the bottom (Wood 1994; Freeman 1995). While quite plausible, the received wisdom now seems to conclude that the share of trade between the UK and the developing world is neither large enough, nor has it risen fast enough, to account for most of the rise in inequality. Moreover, this is a story about the traded sector, where costs may be more sensitive to international influences than among the non-traded goods sector. It is therefore harder for this hypothesis to explain why, as Table 4.4 shows, wage inequality has also risen in the service sector.

The other main demand-based explanation is that innovation and development of information technology has generated increased demand for skilled labour that complements high-tech capital and reduced demand for less-skilled labour that can be more easily replaced by capital. Certainly technological upgrading appears to be more highly correlated with changes in wage inequality than do changes in trade with the developing world (Machin and Van Reenan 1998). However, as DiNardo and Card (2002) note, the pace of technological innovation has been faster over the past decade when the growth of wage inequality has been slower. It is also hard to argue that the rate of technical innovation was so much different in countries like the United Kingdom and the United States, where inequality rose perceptibly, than in other industrialized countries where inequality did not rise as much. It seems that additional explanatory factors are required.

Table 4.4. Changes in wage inequality by education age and sector

	1972	1980	1996	1998	2002	Change 1972–80	Change 1980–96	Change 1998–2002
Men								
Production	.414	.394	.483	.475	.478	−0.020	0.089	0.003
Services	.523	.536	.581	.547	.554	0.013	0.045	−0.007
Age 50–9	.422	.403	.493	.478	.493	−0.019	0.090	0.015
Age 35–49	.411	.394	.482	.468	.490	−0.017	0.088	0.022
Age 20–34	.364	.367	.457	.464	.469	0.003	0.090	0.005
Degree	.460	.414	.451	.459	.475	−0.046	0.037	0.016
Intermediate	.483	.441	.479	.479	.495	−0.042	0.038	0.016
Low	.478	.451	.527	.488	.478	−0.027	0.076	0.010
None	.388	.380	.444	.446	.426	−0.008	0.064	−0.020
Age 35–49 low quals.	.390	.344	.453	.390	.441	−0.046	0.109	0.051
Women								
Production	.355	.348	.475	.472	.475	−0.007	0.127	0.003
Services	.488	.448	.507	.515	.503	−0.040	0.059	−0.012
Age 50–9	.433	.418	.462	.495	.466	−0.015	0.044	−0.029
Age 35–49	.446	.420	.499	.502	.518	−0.026	0.079	0.016
Age 20–34	.429	.405	.474	.474	.460	−0.024	0.069	−0.014
Degree	.464	.453	.474	.408	.478	−0.011	0.021	0.070
Intermediate	.509	.455	.494	.494	.469	−0.054	0.039	−0.025
Low	.451	.391	.449	.441	.432	−0.060	0.058	−0.009
None	.360	.321	.376	.379	.399	−0.039	0.055	0.020
Age 35–49 low quals.	.435	.359	.428	.407	.434	−0.076	0.069	0.027

Note: Two year moving averages. Numbers in table are standard deviations of log hourly wages for each group.
Source: GHS.

4.4.1 *Within-group inequality*

The demand-based explanations above are said to be *between-group* explanations of rising wage inequality, because, as the phrase suggests, they attempt to explain changes in wage inequality by looking at differences in pay trends between readily identifiable groups. The idea that new technology or trade has displaced all unskilled jobs is not borne out by the findings of Goos and Manning (2003). They show that employment has risen both at the top *and* at the bottom of the pay distribution. They argue that new technology has replaced routine jobs but that non-routine jobs, including many 'unskilled' jobs that require things like hand–eye coordination, are, as yet, difficult to perform with machines. In other words, there may be differential employment and wage trends *within* broadly defined skill groups. Some unskilled workers lose out to new technology while others do not.

This idea is given some support in Table 4.4 which reports the level of and changes in the dispersion of wages within different sub-groups of the population over time. The dispersion of pay is typically larger in the service sector than in the production sector, greater among older workers than younger workers, and larger among graduates than those with lower levels of educational attainment. Over time however, the dispersion of pay within all these groups has risen, albeit more among production workers and the less skilled.[8]

The table also shows how inequality has risen across several other dimensions, notably by age—more so among younger women. Often, a combination of factors known to be associated with the increased dispersion of pay, such as age and low qualifications, has led to larger increases in inequality than the average. Since it is harder to reconcile rising wage inequality within groups with stories about differential demand conditions between groups, explanations for this trend have instead focused on institutional changes in the British labour market that were not observed elsewhere.

4.4.2 Trade unions

One obvious institutional feature that appears to be correlated with rising wage inequality is the decline in unionization in Britain over this period. Union membership peaked at 13 million in 1979, some 55 per cent of the employed. Thereafter membership fell by around 5.5 million over the next twenty-five years (Metcalf 2003). This matters for pay inequality because union presence at the workplace is known to reduce the dispersion of wages (Metcalf 2003). Table 4.5 confirms this. The dispersion of pay is lower among unionized workers.

Since, as Table 4.5 shows, there were many more union members in 1983 than in 2004, a declining union presence over time can explain some of the rise in wage inequality. Union membership has fallen more among men and so

Table 4.5. Union membership and wage dispersion, 1983–2004

	Men			Women		
	1983	2004	Change	1983	2004	Change
Union						
Standard deviation	0.384	0.453	0.069	0.412	0.436	0.024
% share	56.9	31.6	−25.3	42.2	30.0	−12.8
Non-union						
Standard deviation	0.554	0.597	0.043	0.453	0.508	0.055
% share	43.1	68.4	25.3	57.8	70.0	12.8

Source: GHS 1983, LFS 2004.

[8] This observation is consistent with Goos and Manning's hypothesis of differential demand among the less skilled.

the impact of unionization on pay inequality is greater among men than among women. Gosling and Lemieux (2003) estimate that around one-third of the rise in wage inequality over this period is due to declining union presence but only 5 per cent of the rise in female dispersion in pay is due to falling unionization. It is also true that inequality within the union sector rose more, at least among men, than in the non-union sector over the period. Again, this calls for a more nuanced within-group explanation of why this is so.

4.4.3 Minimum wages

Another important institutional feature of pay determination that changed noticeably over the period was the floor on low pay imposed by the wages councils and their successor, the national minimum wage. Introduced by Churchill in 1909, the wages councils set minimum wages on a sectoral basis for many low-paid workers. Throughout the 1980s the powers of the wages councils were gradually eroded. In 1993 they were abolished by the Conservative government of the time. Some 2.5 million workers, about 10 per cent of employees, were covered at the time of their abolition (Dickens et al. 1999). In 1999, the Labour government introduced a national minimum wage to take the place of the industry-level minimum wages that were set by the wages councils. The level of the national minimum was such that it covered around 5 per cent of employees at its inception. Table 4.6 reports the real value of the 5th percentile relative to the median (50th percentile) over time alongside a measure of overall wage dispersion. The 50/5 wage gap rises over the period when the powers of the wages councils eroded and remains stable after 1999 when the national minimum wage was introduced. Since more women receive low pay than men, further evidence that the minimum

Table 4.6. Wages at the bottom

	1988	1993	Change	1999	2004	Change
Men						
5th percentile	3.40	3.40	0	3.60	4.10	+0.5
50th percentile	8.60	9.00	+0.4	8.40	9.20	+0.8
50/5	2.5	2.6	+0.1	2.3	2.2	−0.1
Standard deviation	0.551	0.569	+0.018	0.544	0.535	−0.009
Women						
5th percentile	2.50	2.80	+0.3	3.10	3.70	+0.6
50th percentile	5.30	6.00	+0.7	6.20	7.10	+0.9
50/5	2.1	2.1	0	2.0	1.9	−0.1
Standard deviation	0.509	0.544	+0.043	0.499	0.486	−0.013

Source: GHS 1988–93, LFS 1999–2004.

wage has some effect can be seen by the observation in Table 4.6 that the gender pay gap at the 5th percentile does appear to have narrowed a little over the period when the minimum wage has been in place. Moreover the real value of wage levels at the 5th percentile rose much more in the latter five-year period. These trends do suggest then that official policy and attitudes toward the minimum wage can influence the level of wages at the bottom of the pay distribution and hence the distribution of earnings.

4.4.4 Privatization and contracting out

Throughout the past twenty-five years successive government policies have been aimed at reducing the role of the public sector in economic life. This was initiated at the start of the 1980s under the Conservatives with a series of 'privatizations'—the policy of selling off many state-owned industries that had been nationalized over the previous two decades, starting with British Aerospace in 1981 (see Parker 2004 for a history of privatization). The mass privatization process ended with the advent of the Labour government in 1997, but Labour has continued the process, also begun under the Conservatives, of the contracting out, or opening up to competitive tender, of many services originally carried out by the public sector. These policies, as Table 4.7 shows, have been associated with a fall in the public sector share of male employees from around 35 to 25 per cent, though the share of women working in the public sector rose over the same period. Wage inequality for men is much greater in the private sector. As a result the falling share of public sector workers in male employment will have contributed to the rising wage inequality. Conversely a rising share of public sector workers among women will have offset the trend toward more dispersion in pay somewhat.

Table 4.7. Wages by public/private sector status

	Men			Women		
	1983	1994	2004	1983	1994	2004
Public sector						
% share	35	29	25	37	39	44
10th percentile	5.10	5.10	5.90	3.60	4.30	5.00
50th percentile	8.40	9.70	10.60	5.50	7.50	8.50
90th percentile	14.70	16.50	19.00	11.10	13.30	14.50
Standard deviation	0.424	0.522	0.463	0.445	0.488	0.444
Private sector						
10th percentile	3.90	3.90	4.70	2.60	3.20	4.00
50th percentile	7.00	7.80	8.70	4.10	5.30	6.20
90th percentile	12.50	18.00	18.40	6.90	10.10	12.70
Standard deviation	0.491	0.565	0.550	0.417	0.480	0.492

Source: GHS 1983, LFS 1993, 2004.

4.5 Conclusion

For most people in work, the period since 1970 can be characterized as one which delivered continuous, if somewhat erratic, growth in real wages. What makes this period stand out is the extent to which the wages of the (working) rich grew much more than the wages of the (working) poor. Such trends had not been observed prior to this for at least fifty years, nor were they observed contemporaneously in many other industrialized countries. Increased capital substitution away from less-skilled workers, increased trade with the developing world, falling unionization, and the lack of an effective floor on wages at the bottom from an absence of minimum wages all contributed to some degree to the unprecedented widening of pay levels that began in the early 1980s. The combination of global shifts in demand away from less-skilled workers in the industrialized West and institutional changes in the British labour market, which were not observed elsewhere, probably explains why Britain experienced much more growth in inequality.

These trends, with the exception of the minimum wage, look set to continue so that downward pressure on wages at the bottom will persist, as it has throughout the history of industrial Britain. To some extent, the increase in the average skill level of the workforce that is currently in progress will work to offset some of the between-group influences on inequality, reducing skill shortages and hence wage pressure at the top. This will take many years to become effective, however. Increased immigration aimed at boosting the supply of skilled workers is one possible complementary action that looks set to become part of the political debate. The challenge for the next decade is whether governments will be willing to open up debates about how much inequality is to be tolerated and the consequences of inaction and whether they will be willing to effect policies that might offset these trends.

Appendix 4.1: Measuring wage inequality

There is a vast literature on defining and measuring inequality (ably summarized in Cowell 1995). The idea of inequality implies that there is a spread or distribution in the values of any particular variable of economic interest. This can be seen quite easily if the entire distribution of, say, wages is simply graphed (as below for the 2004 UK gross hourly wage distribution), with the lowest wage at the left-hand side of the graph and the highest wage at the right-hand limit of the graph. The rest of the population are observed between these two limits. In these 'frequency distributions', the height of the graph at any given wage corresponds to the share of the population with that wage. Typically the hourly wage distribution is 'skewed to the right', which means that most individuals are observed with wages quite close to each other, with a relatively small number of high earners a long way away from the rest.

In order to quantify the extent of inequality and to make comparisons across time or across groups, it is necessary to use summary statistical measures of distributions such as that above.

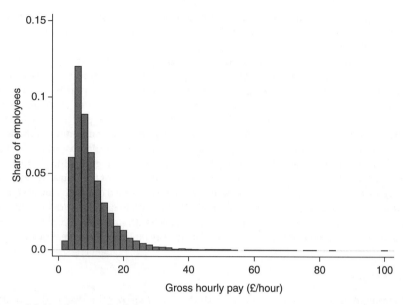

Figure 4.2 Hourly wage distribution
Source: LFS 2004.

An extremely popular measure of inequality which can be calculated given any distribution is the *Gini coefficient*. Based on a comparison of the actual wage distribution with that which would occur if everyone were paid the same, a Gini coefficient of 1 indicates complete inequality, a Gini value of zero indicates perfect equality. The closer a Gini coefficient is to zero, the more equal the distribution. While this measure of inequality does satisfy several of the criteria that social scientists deem worthy, comparisons of Gini coefficients over time can be quite sensitive to *where* in the distribution income changes take place. Nor can the aggregate Gini coefficient be calculated by aggregating up the Gini values for various sub-groups in the population.

A similar method to the Gini involves comparing the distance between an individual's wage and the average (mean) wage. If we square this deviation and average over the whole N members of the population, we get the *variance*

$$V = \frac{1}{N}\sum_{i=1}^{N}(w_i - \overline{w})^2$$

One problem with this measure is that if we double everyone's income—moving the wage distribution rightwards, but leaving the spread unchanged—we quadruple the variance, despite the fact that inequality has not changed. To get round this problem we can look at the variation in the logarithm of the wage around its mean

$$LV = \frac{1}{N}\sum_{i=1}^{N}[\log(w_i - \overline{w})]^2$$

or its square root, the *standard deviation of log wages*. Again the higher this value the greater the degree of inequality. Like the Gini coefficient, comparisons in this measure across time or across groups can be sensitive to where in the distribution differences in wages arise (so changes in wages at the bottom can give different values from changes in wages at the top).

Measures of inequality which avoid this 'sensitivity' problem are the *percentile ratios* which simply compare the wages of individuals at specified percentile in the wage distribution. The most common percentiles on which to base comparison is the 50th (or median)—which gives the wage level in the middle; 50 per cent of observations are above this wage and 50 per cent are below. The other two common percentiles—the 90th and the 10th—capture wage levels toward, but not at, the top and bottom of the wage distribution respectively. Comparing the values of these percentiles over time, or their ratios, can help pinpoint *where* in the wage distribution changes in inequality have occurred. For example, all a comparison of the Gini coefficient or the standard deviation of log wages over time can do is say whether inequality has risen or fallen. However if the 90/50 ratio has stayed constant over this period but the 50/10 ratio has widened, then we know that wages of those in the middle have kept pace with wages of those at the top and that the wages of those at the bottom have fallen away (at least in relative terms).

References

Atkinson, A. (2003). 'Top Incomes in the United Kingdom over the Twentieth Century'. Working Paper, Nuffield College, Oxford.

Blackaby, F. (1978). 'Incomes Policy', in F. Blackaby (ed.), *British Economic Policy 1960–74*. Cambridge: Cambridge University Press.

Cowell, F. (1995). *Measuring Inequality*. London: Prentice Hall.

Dickens, R., and Manning, A. (2004). 'Has the National Minimum Wage Reduced UK Wage Inequality?' *Journal of the Royal Statistical Society*, Series A/167: 623–6.

—— Machin, S., and Manning, A. (1999). 'The Effect of Minimum Wages on Employment: Theory and Evidence from Britain'. *Journal of Labor Economics*, 17: 1–23.

DiNardo, J., and Card, D. (2002). 'Skill-Biased Technical Change and Rising Wage Inequality: Some Problems and Puzzles'. NBER (National Bureau of Economic Research) Working Paper 8769.

Flanagan, R., Soskice, D., and Ulman, L. (1983). *Unionism, Economic Stabilization and Incomes Policies: European Experience*. Washington: The Brookings Institution.

Freeman, R. (1995). 'Are your Wages Set in Beijing?' *Journal of Economic Perspectives*, 9/3, Summer: 15–32.

Goos, M., and Manning, A. (2003). 'Lousy and Lovely Jobs: The Rising Polarisation of Jobs in Britain'. Centre for Economic Performance Discussion Paper 604.

Gosling, A., and Lemieux, T. (2004). 'Labor Market Reforms and Changes in Wage Inequality in the United Kingdom and the United States', in R. Blundell, D. Card, and R. Freeman (eds.), *Seeking a Premier League Economy: The Economic Effects of British Economic Reforms 1980–2000*. Chicago: University of Chicago Press.

Gregg, P., and Machin, S. (1994). 'Is the UK Rise in Inequality Different?', in R. Barrell (ed.), *The UK Labour Market*. Cambridge: Cambridge University Press.

Kuznets, S. (1955). 'Economic Growth and Income Inequality'. *American Economic Review*, 49: 1–28.

Low Pay Commission (2003). *The National Minimum Wage: Fourth Report of the Low Pay Commission*. London: Her Majesty's Stationery Office.

Machin, S. (2003). 'Wage Inequality since 1975', in R. Dickens, P. Gregg, and J. Wadsworth (eds.), *The Labour Market under New Labour: The State of Working Britain*. London: Palgrave-Macmillan Press.

—— and Van Reenan, J. (1998). 'Technology and Changes in Skill Structure: Evidence from 7 countries'. *Quarterly Journal of Economics*, 113: 1215–44.

Metcalf, D. (2003). 'Trade Unions', in R. Dickens, P. Gregg, and J. Wadsworth (eds.), *The Labour Market under New Labour: The State of Working Britain*. London: Palgrave-Macmillan Press.

OECD (Organization for Economic Cooperation and Development) (1996). *Employment Outlook*. Paris: OECD.

Parker, D. (2004). 'The UK's Privatisation Experiment: The Passage of Time Permits a Sober Assessment'. February, CESifo Working Paper Series 1126.

Peden, G. (1985). *British Economic and Social Policy*. Oxford: Phillip Allen.

Pencavel, J. (2004). 'The Surprising Retreat of Union Britain', in R. Blundell, D. Card, and R. Freeman (eds.), *Seeking a Premier League Economy: The Economic Effects of British Economic Reforms 1980–2000*. Chicago: University of Chicago Press.

Wadsworth, J. (1999). 'Economic Inactivity', in P. Gregg and J. Wadsworth (eds.), *The State of Working Britain*. Manchester: Manchester University Press.

Wood, A. (1994). *North–South Trade, Employment and Inequality*. Oxford: Clarendon Press.

5

Work over the Life Course

Paul Johnson and Asghar Zaidi

For every individual the experience of employment and non-employment occurs in a continuum across the whole of the life course: the juvenile has to negotiate labour market entry; the prime age worker strives for career mobility; the older worker manages exit into unemployment, inactivity, or retirement. The individual supply-side characteristics of each person—their age, health, education, skills, family and household circumstances, and so on—interact with structural, cyclical, and stochastic changes to labour demand to create dynamic life-course employment trajectories. Yet the majority of labour market studies pay little attention to the pattern of employment over the life course, and how this has changed over time for successive birth cohorts. There is often good reason for this. Many labour market questions—for instance about the level of employment or rate of pay for different groups of workers in different places—can best be addressed by using cross-sectional evidence from a single year. Even when the focus of analysis is change over time, a great deal of useful information can be derived from comparison of the experience of particular categories of workers between certain years—for example the employment rate of 30-year-olds between 1970 and 1990, or changes in the relative wage rate of this same group over the same period.

Most time series analysis of labour market categories, however, contains a degree of hidden bias because it does not compare like with like. The 30-year-old worker in 1970 was very different from the 30-year-old worker in 1990. Although born only two decades apart their labour market experience will have been conditioned by very different life-course trajectories. Barely 4 per cent of persons born in 1940 gained a university qualification before entering the labour force; instead the great majority of this birth cohort started work at age 15, during the middle of the post-war economic 'golden age' which was characterized by low unemployment and uninterrupted wage growth. Among the 1960 birth cohort, by contrast, roughly 13 per cent progressed from secondary school to study at university, and they subsequently entered the graduate labour market with relatively high salaries (Halsey 1988: tables 7.2 and 7.5; Blundell et al. 1997). However, their less academically successful peers entered the labour market in 1976 (the school leaving age was raised from 15 to 16 in 1973) at just the point when the long post-war boom was terminating in the oil shock, 'stagflation', and rising unemployment. We can immediately see that a simple comparison across time of the circumstances of a given age group may fail to identify both compositional differences within the group, and ways in which these compositional differences have been forged by, and have interacted with, the economic and social environment. Thus a comparison of the labour market status of 30-year-olds in 1970 and 1990, which at first sight appears to be comparing like with like, in fact can be seen to be muddling together in an indistinct way the impact of chronological age, of timing of birth, and of life-course experience.

In addition to the significant differences between birth cohorts in average employment experience over the life course, there exists substantial life-course variation within birth cohorts. Educational opportunity, for example, is not equally distributed, and the level of educational attainment can have an important impact on subsequent labour market experience. Among boys born in the period 1913–22 only 1.8 per cent entered higher education, but within this cohort over 7 per cent of boys from professional and managerial backgrounds went to university, compared to less than 1 per cent from households where the father was a manual worker. Thirty years later, 8.5 per cent of boys from the 1943–52 birth cohort went to university, but the relative chances for children from professional backgrounds had improved, such that more than 1 in 4 of them (26.4 per cent) entered higher education, compared to fewer than 1 in 30 boys (3.1 per cent) from manual backgrounds (Halsey et al. 1980: table 10.8). These differences matter, because, as we will show below, education is a key determinant of both employability and earnings across the rest of the life course.

The manner in which employment patterns develop over the life course can be studied both at the individual level and, if the experience of a birth cohort is pooled, at the group level. In this chapter we examine both individual and group characteristics of work experience over the life course, with the level of analysis being determined by the availability of relevant data. The first section examines long-run changes across the twentieth century in employment rates by birth cohort, and this is followed by a parallel examination of long-run changes in life-course patterns of earnings. Section 5.3 then turns to look in more detail at individual longitudinal data from the 1990s in order to trace the impact of individual characteristics and experience on life-course employment trajectories, and section 5.4 follows this with a longitudinal analysis for the 1990s of earnings over the life course; the concluding section summarizes the findings.

5.1 Long-run trends in employment over the life course

In order to trace employment characteristics over the life course, it is necessary to have data from different time periods in which the experience of individuals at different ages (preferably the same individuals) can be linked together. Modern longitudinal surveys which re-interview each respondent on a regular basis provide just this sort of data. The British Household Panel Survey (BHPS) provides a continuous record since 1991 of the employment, income, health, housing, and household status of roughly 10,000 individuals living in over 5,000 households in the UK. For earlier periods, however, no equivalent individual longitudinal data are available. The General Household Survey (GHS), which commenced in 1971, annually surveys around 9,000 households about their education, employment, health, housing, and family status, but each annual sample of respondents consists of different individuals, so there is no possibility of linking personal characteristics from one year to the next in order to reveal individual employment trajectories. Similar constraints apply to data collected by the Labour Force Survey (LFS). From inception in 1973 until 1992 this survey operated on an annual or biennial basis, with no continuity of respondents between successive waves of the survey. Since 1992 respondents have been interviewed across five successive quarters, and this can provide useful longitudinal information about short-run changes in labour market status for individuals.

For any period prior to 1971, the UK lacks any annual household or individual survey data which might shed light on employment trajectories, and this means that researchers have to rely on patchy data produced as a by-product of administrative processes—such as unemployment rates derived from National Insurance returns—or on occasional, and possibly unrepresentative, local surveys, or on the decennial population census. There have been few attempts to use these sources to extract longitudinal data, but in this and the following section we make use of both the census and local surveys to sketch a picture of life-course employment and earning trajectories over the twentieth century.

We should make it clear that the inferences we draw from these data are tentative, because the sources we use are far from ideal for our purposes. Furthermore, the definitions of employment or labour market status that were used in past censuses and surveys are often ambiguous, and quite possibly inconsistent with current definitions. Even carefully designed modern surveys can suffer from problems of internal inconsistency; in the case of the LFS, data for the period 1973–79 are now considered not to be of usable quality, and those for the period 1979–92 are inconsistent with data for the post-1992 period (ONS 2003b). Furthermore, regulatory developments such as increases in the school leaving age in 1947 and 1973, or conscription during the two world wars, or a periodic widening or narrowing of eligibility for unemployment benefit, can have important effects on the working of the labour market, and thus on individual employment status (ONS 2003*a*). However, these regulatory changes are not always easy to identify, and thus their impact on employment trajectories may be mis-identified.

Despite these difficulties, it is possible to make some headway with a long-run analysis of employment trajectories over the life course. Here we turn to data drawn from the decennial censuses. A census of the entire population of Britain has been conducted once every ten years since 1801, with the exception of the wartime year of 1941. The quality of the data before 1841 is poor, and the classification of employment status prior to 1881 is unreliable, because persons who were not in work for reasons of unemployment or retirement were typically returned under their previous occupational category. From 1881, however, the census data are good enough to provide a plausible account of the structure of the British labour market.

A census conducted once every ten years provides a repeated snapshot of the structure of employment, and at first sight this offers little scope for analysis of employment trajectories over the life course. However, since the 30-year-olds in one census constitute the 40-year-olds in the next census and the 50-year-olds in the census after that (minus those who have died or emigrated in the intervening period, plus those who have arrived through immigration), a general sense of the life-course employment trajectory of different birth cohorts can be extracted from successive censuses. Furthermore, because the censuses since 1881 report occupations for males and females separately by five-year age groups, it is possible, with a degree of interpolation between census years, to trace the employment rates of each five-year birth cohort over time (for details of the way in which these data are derived from the census reports see Appendix 5.1).

Figures 5.1 and 5.2 report the average life-course employment trajectories for males and females respectively of twelve five-year birth cohorts beginning with those born in 1862–66, and finishing with those born in 1972–76 (the intervening cohorts born 1867–71 through to 1967–71 have been omitted simply to improve the clarity of the graphs). Each line represents the average employment rate at given ages for a single five-year birth cohort as the members of that cohort progressed through life. What inferences can be drawn from these graphs about the way in which the experience of work over the life course has changed through the course of the twentieth century?

Figure 5.1 shows that for men born between 1862 and 1902 there was a more or less unchanging pattern of employment between the ages of 15 and 64. As juveniles they had a greater than 90 per cent chance of being in work, and between the ages of 20 and 59 barely 2 per cent of them were not active in the labour market. It was only as they approached pension age that their experience of employment differed (public old age pensions were first paid to persons aged 70 and above in 1909, and to insured persons aged 65 and above in 1928).

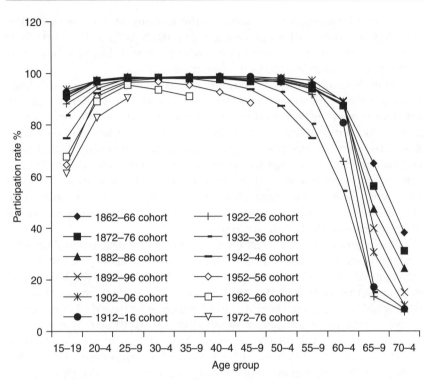

Figure 5.1 Cohort participation rates: males

The 1862–66 cohort reached pension age in the late 1920s, and although their engagement in the labour force declined as they moved beyond age 60, two-thirds of them were still in employment when aged 65–9, even though most of them were by then eligible to collect an old age pension. For this birth cohort, therefore, access to a public pension did not determine labour market status; almost 40 per cent of them continued to be in employment at the age of 70. Subsequent birth cohorts displayed ever lower participation rates beyond age 65, so that by the time the 1902–06 cohort reached pension age in the late 1960s, this event triggered a mass exodus from work; only 30 per cent of them continued in employment beyond age 65.

In the mid-1970s the long post-war 'golden age' of sustained economic growth came to an end and the unemployment rate began to drift upwards from 4.3 per cent in 1975 to reach 11.9 per cent in 1984. This change in macro-economic conditions coincided with, and was partly responsible for, a clear change in the life-course employment pattern for adult males. By the time the 1922–26 cohort reached the age of 60–4, only two-thirds of them were in employment; the tight labour market conditions of the mid-1980s seemed to bear heavily on this cohort of older workers, and fewer than 15 per cent of them continued to work beyond state pension age. However, what is clear from Figure 5.1 is that changes in the aggregate level of labour demand cannot fully account for changes in life-course employment patterns since the 1970s, because the secular decline in unemployment rates from a second peak in 1993 has not been associated with any increase in older age employment rates. Each birth cohort from 1922–26 through to 1972–76 displays significantly lower adult male participation rates than its immediate predecessor.

This downward drift began at older ages, and represents the development and embedding of the practice of 'early retirement', which is commonly defined as permanent withdrawal from the labour force before state pension age. Early retirement was widely adopted by employers in the 1970s as a low-cost way of restructuring their labour force; low cost because the government provided substantial income replacement for early-retired workers through the unemployment and disability benefit systems. There has been much academic debate about the extent to which early retirement is the result of worker choice, employer inducement, or the incentives embodied in a variety of public policy initiatives (Johnson 1998), but there is no dispute that it has become an important feature of the late twentieth-century labour market. It should be noted, however, that a general decline over time in participation rates is not confined to older workers, but can now be observed across the entire age range. Thus we can see that for males aged 35–9—prime working age—employment rates were around 98 per cent for all cohorts from 1862–66 through to 1942–46. For the 1952–56 cohort the rate fell to 95 per cent, and this might be accounted for by the relatively high unemployment rate of the late 1980s and early 1990s. However, by 2001 the economy-wide unemployment rate had fallen below 6 per cent, yet participation among 35–9-year-olds, born 1962–66, had declined to just 91 per cent.

There have also been important changes in employment rates at younger ages for successive birth cohorts, which reflect increases in the school leaving age, and the expansion of further and higher education over the course of the twentieth century. Figure 5.1 shows that prior to the increase in the school leaving age to 15, which first affected the 1932–36 birth cohort, employment rates for the 15–19 age group were at or above 90 per cent. But it is striking that this 'education effect' appears now to have an impact even on the 25–9 age group (born 1972–76), whose participation rate, at 90 per cent, is lower than the rate for 15–19-year-olds for cohorts born prior to 1922–26.

There seems, therefore, to have been significant change in the life-course employment pattern for males in Britain over the course of the twentieth century. Males born before the First World War could expect to enter the labour market in their teens, work consistently through to age 65, and then reduce their labour effort. More recent birth cohorts have experienced delayed entry into the labour force, lower prime age employment rates, and a pronounced reduction in the probability of employment from their early fifties or late forties. Education

103

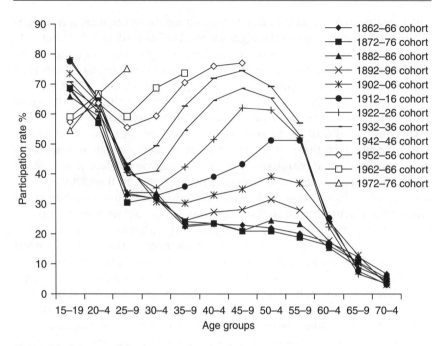

Figure 5.2 Cohort participation rates: females

clearly accounts for some of the changes at lower ages, pension rules for some of the changes at higher ages, and the general state of the labour market for some of the developments in the intermediate age groups. But we should be cautious about making casual inferences from the data represented in Figure 5.1 because, as Figure 5.2 shows, the experience of women has been very different.

Figure 5.2 shows that the labour force experience of successive birth cohorts of 15–19-year-old women has been very similar to that of men of the same age, although with slightly lower overall participation rates. Thereafter, however, the female experience diverges markedly from the male. For women born before the Second World War the employment trajectory was more or less invariant through their twenties: around two-thirds worked at ages 20–4 but this proportion fell to around one-third by ages 25–9 as married women withdrew from the labour market to provide full-time childcare. For the mid-Victorian birth cohorts (1862–76) participation rates continued to decline as these women aged, touching just 10 per cent by age 65–9. For each subsequent cohort, however, the initial decline in participation from age 20–4 was reversed at later ages. This effect was very marginal for women born 1882–86, whose participation rose slightly as they moved into their fifties (in the mid-1930s), but by the time the 1912–16 cohort reached their fifties (in the mid-1960s), over half these women were engaged in paid employment. For the 1962–66 birth cohort the decline in participation rates from age 20–4 to age 25–9 was slight (just 8 percentage points) and temporary, with more of these women in employment in their early thirties than in their early twenties. For the most recent birth cohort (1972–76) there appears to be no decline in participation at all, with this generation of women exhibiting an attachment to the labour market almost as strong as that of their male peers.

Figure 5.2 shows that the life-course employment trajectory of women has been completely transformed over the course of the twentieth century. The changes have occurred incrementally: each successive birth cohort has spent more time in paid employment, with the changes coming initially as women reached their fifties. These developments coincide with a decline in fertility from the 1870s to the 1930s. However, the trends revealed in Figure 5.2 cannot be explained simply by reference to demographic events, because there is no reversal in this pattern for the 1922–26 cohort of women who experienced higher fertility (the 1940s 'baby boom') than the immediately preceding cohorts.

One possible explanation of the change over time seen in Figure 5.2 is that it reflects improvements in data collection as much as a change in experience. There is clear evidence that female labour force participation was under-enumerated in the nineteenth-century censuses, particularly among female homeworkers and those who engaged in part-time work (Higgs 1987). Female part-time workers appear to have been under-recorded even as late as the 1981 census (Joshi and Owen 1987). However, a careful comparison between labour force participation estimates independently derived from censuses and social surveys between 1911 and 1931 confirms that the census under-counted part-time workers, but shows also that it over-counted the participation of middle-aged women (Hatton and Bailey 2001). Overall the hypothesis that the census significantly under-counted female employment is not supported by contemporaneous social survey data. Thus it seems reasonable to believe that the changes over time revealed in Figure 5.2 reflect real changes in behaviour, even though the censuses undoubtedly exhibit some measurement error.

Many factors may have contributed to this transformation, but it is difficult to determine their relative significance. Throughout the inter-war period female employment in the civil service, teaching, and many other white-collar occupations was curtailed by a 'marriage bar' which required female employees to resign upon marriage. The civil service dropped this restriction in 1946, but it endured in many businesses until well into the 1950s. The relative pay of women also rose throughout the post-war period, thereby making (re)employment more attractive. The 1946 Royal Commission on Equal Pay had found that the pay gap between men and women could not be explained in terms of productivity differences, and appeared to be based largely on 'sociological' factors, but it was not until 1970 that legislation was introduced to prevent discrimination in pay between men and women. At this date the earnings of full-time working women were, on average, 30 per cent less than those of equivalent male workers; by the end of the twentieth century this pay gap had fallen to 20 per cent (Thane 1994; DTI 2003). Social expectations have also changed over time. Social surveys conducted during and immediately after the Second World War indicated that a majority of women believed that married women (with or without children) should not 'go out to work' (Thane 1994), but, as Figure 5.2 indicates, by 2001, 73 per cent of women aged 16–59 were economically active, and over half of all mothers with children under 5 were in employment.

The highly aggregated nature of census data means that the comparative birth cohort analysis offered in Figures 5.1 and 5.2 can describe changes over time in the life-course employment trajectory, but cannot directly explain these changes. In order to gain a sense of the relative importance of the potential causal factors we need to look in much more detail at the characteristics of individual workers, and this can only be achieved with longitudinal data derived from the 1990s. We will turn to this task in section 5.3, but for the moment we will continue to examine long-run changes in work over the life course through an analysis of age-specific earnings across the twentieth century.

5.2 Long-run trends in earnings over the life course

Data on earnings over the life course are even more patchy than data on employment; the nineteenth- and twentieth-century UK censuses did not record any information on income or earnings. Business archives sometimes contain wage books, and in a few cases the pay of specific workers can be tracked throughout their careers. However, lifetime employment with the same company has never been common in the UK, and seems to have been concentrated in a small number of sectors, such as railways and banking, where employers consciously constructed and operated internal labour markets (Howlett 2004). For the majority of workers who moved between jobs a number of times in their careers we lack any representative longitudinal data.

A second-best approach is to examine successive cross-sectional surveys of earnings for specific occupations collected at different dates. Again there is a paucity of data until the later twentieth century; here we make use of three historical earnings surveys, together with some additional data from 2000. Figure 5.3 reports cross-sectional earnings profiles by age for males employed in manual jobs derived from historical wage surveys for the 1830s, 1880s, 1930s, and from the government's New Earnings Survey for 2000 (for details of the historical datasets, see Appendix 5.2). In each case the earnings at a given age have been reported as a percentage of the average earnings for the age group 30–9. Even the youngest workers in the 1830s dataset would have left the workforce by the beginning of the twentieth century, though men in their early twenties in the 1880s data correspond to the 1862–66 birth cohort in

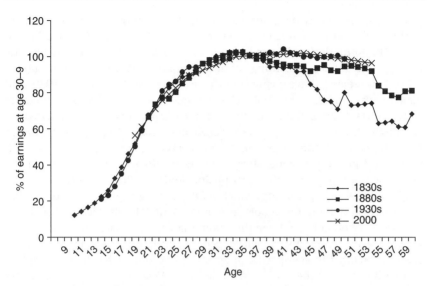

Figure 5.3 Male manual earnings by age: 1830s, 1880s, 1930s, 2000

Figure 5.1. Likewise, men in their early twenties in the 1930s dataset correspond to the 1912–16 birth cohort, while men in their late twenties in 2000
correspond to the 1972–76 birth cohort. It should be pointed out that the data
reported in Figure 5.3 do not include any element of economy-wide growth of
real wages over time. If real wages grow by an average of, say, 2 per cent a year,
then the real income of a worker will continue to grow over time even if his
earnings fall relative to those of a 30–9-year-old, as long as this relative age-
specific decline is at a rate less than the rate of growth of real earnings.

Cross-sectional data on earnings by age (that is, data collected at one point
in time on individuals of different ages) do not provide a good indication of
the pattern of earnings over the life course unless it can be shown that there is
considerable similarity between successive cross-sectional datasets. It might be
expected that the shape of the age–earnings profile would have changed
significantly since the 1830s as education, technology, management processes,
unionization, and wage payment systems have evolved. For example, an
increase over time in the number of years of formal education might be
expected to increase the human capital of younger workers relative to their
older co-workers, and thus raise juvenile wages relative to those of adults.
Similarly, increasing mechanization of the production process might be
expected to have reduced the relative utility of, and financial return to, physical strength, and thus to have reduced the wage of prime age adults relative to
their older and younger peers. In fact, as Figure 5.3 shows, from ages between
the late teens and mid-thirties, there appears to have been no change in

relative age-specific earnings for male manual workers over the past 170 years. In the 1830s and 1880s relative wages began to decline from about age 35, and in the 1830s this decline became pronounced from age 45, which may indicate the negative impact on earnings of declining physical strength or outmoded skills. This seems to have changed in the twentieth century: for the 1930s and 2000 the data indicate that male relative wages reached a plateau at about age 35 which was then sustained for at least fifteen years. This constancy across the twentieth century in the pattern of average male manual age-specific earnings from the point of entry into the labour market right through to their mid-fifties (and possibly beyond—but there are insufficient observations in the 1930s dataset to confirm this) is surprising, and it indicates the presence of a rigidity of age-specific earnings which produces a high degree of predictability of life-course income for people in employment. The implication of this is that, once a worker has entered the labour market and established his position in an earnings hierarchy, he will experience little earnings mobility—other than that related to age-specific progression—as long as he stays in employment; this is confirmed by modern studies (Dickens 1999). Unfortunately there are insufficient historical data to determine whether similar long-run predictability of age-specific relative earnings applies to female workers, or to males in non-manual occupations.

5.3 Recent trends in employment over the life course

For the period since 1991 the British Household Panel Survey (BHPS) provides much more detailed information on the pattern of employment and earnings over the life course. Not only can the employment and earnings of survey respondents be traced from year to year, but they can also be related to other characteristics of the respondents. Here we focus on two of the most important characteristics: education and dependent children.

Figure 5.4 shows the age-specific employment probabilities for BHPS males over the period 1991–2001 by birth cohort; Figure 5.5 presents the equivalent data for females. These graphs differ from those in Figures 5.1 and 5.2, which traced the average life-course employment trajectories of single birth cohorts over several decades. For the BHPS we have only eleven years of data for each birth cohort, and so Figures 5.4 and 5.5 present a series of overlapping eleven-year-long cohort employment trajectories, together with a summary measure which presents age-specific totals. There is some minor variance of the cohort-specific data around the age-specific average, but in general the fit is good. The shape of the profile for males in Figure 5.4 is similar to that represented by the historical data in Figure 5.1, thereby confirming the stability of prime age male life-course employment trajectories over time, although Figure 5.4 also confirms that by the 1990s there was an established practice of lower labour

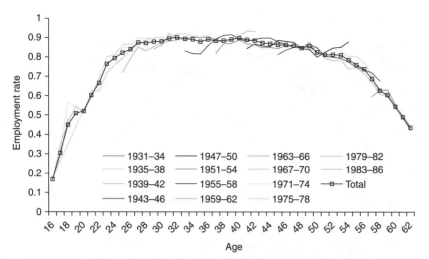

Figure 5.4 Age-specific employment probabilities for men, BHPS 1991–2001

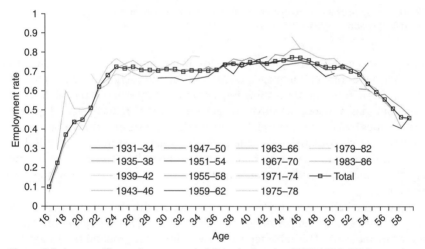

Figure 5.5 Age-specific employment probabilities for females, BHPS 1991–2001

force participation for males at both ends of the age spectrum. For females, the shape of the profile in Figure 5.5 is very different from the historical data in Figure 5.2. This shows clearly that women at the end of the twentieth century had very different lifetime employment experiences from those of their mothers and grandmothers.

The richness of the BHPS data allows us to disaggregate these employment probabilities according to various characteristics. Figure 5.6 reports the

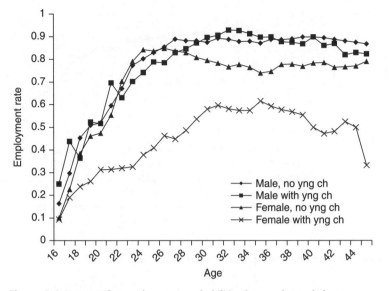

Figure 5.6 Age-specific employment probabilities by gender and the presence of young (aged 0–4) children, BHPS 1991–2001

age-specific employment probabilities for males and females, according to whether there were children aged under 5 in their household. The presence of young children has no discernible impact on the employment probabilities of men, but has a major negative impact on women, reducing employment probabilities by between 20 and 40 per cent. It is noticeable also that although employment probabilities for women without young children are identical to those of men up to age 28, they then decline markedly. This may reflect the unpaid caring responsibilities borne by these women as mothers of school age children.

A more detailed representation of the impact of educational and household characteristics on the employment probabilities of the BHPS population is presented in Table 5.1. This table reports the employment probabilities by age for males and females according to their level of education and the presence of young children in the household. In each case the employment probabilities are compared with those of a highly educated (i.e. with degree) male with no young children. In every case, lower educational attainment is associated with a lower relative employment probability. The presence of young children, however, marginally increases the employment probabilities of men with high and medium education levels, though it reduces the probability for men with no formal qualifications. For women, the presence of young children significantly reduces employment probabilities, but it does so to an increasing extent as educational attainment declines. This is unsurprising, since the cost

Table 5.1. Relative employment probabilities

	16–22	23–9	30–9	40–9	50–9	60–4
Highly educated, no young children						
Male	1.00	1.00	1.00	1.00	1.00	1.00
Female	0.94	0.95	0.94	0.93	0.90	
Highly educated, with young children						
Male	1.04	1.01	1.01	1.01	a	a
Female	0.51	0.72	0.76	0.73	a	
Medium level of education, no young children						
Male	0.74	0.96	0.95	0.96	0.95	1.12
Female	0.68	0.90	0.84	0.87	0.83	
Medium level of education, with young children						
Male	0.79	0.98	0.96	0.98	0.97	a
Female	0.31	0.64	0.59	0.63	0.51	
No education, no young children						
Male	0.53	0.72	0.81	0.85	0.79	0.94
Female	0.48	0.62	0.63	0.71	0.63	
No education, with young children						
Male	0.51	0.70	0.79	0.84	0.77	0.90
Female	0.17	0.28	0.30	0.37	0.28	

Notes: Medium level of education refers to those who have attained 'school leaving certificate', 'O level or equivalent', or 'A level or equivalent' level of education. High educated persons are those who attained higher than A level or equivalent education. Young children are those aged 0–4 years.

The employment probabilities were predicted on the basis of a logistic regression, which included age groups, education, and the presence of young children as explanatory factors.

[a] The results are omitted because cell size is smaller than 20 observations.

of paid childcare is more likely to exceed earned income for women with no formal qualifications who will be concentrated in the lowest-paid sectors of the labour market.

If we draw together the historical data in Figure 5.2 with the employment probabilities reported in Table 5.1, we can see that the life-course employment trajectory for women has become increasingly segmented by educational attainment over the twentieth century. For all women born before the Second World War (1932–36 cohort) it was normal to withdraw from the workforce on the birth of the first child, and to re-enter employment only when children were well established in school. Table 5.1 shows that this pattern still holds for women with no educational qualifications, but it is now exceptional for women with degree-level qualifications, who exhibit a continuing attachment to the labour market even when they have pre-school children.

5.4 Recent trends in earnings over the life course

Figure 5.7 presents a summary of age-specific earnings data for the 1990s derived from the BHPS, together with equivalent data from the 1930s. In both cases data are reported for males and females separately, and are set relative to

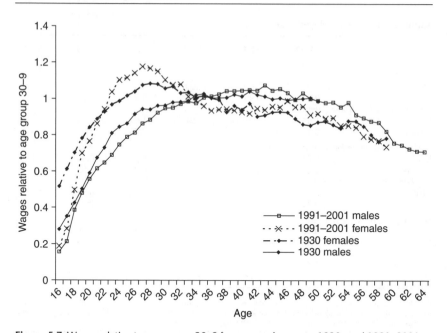

Figure 5.7 Wages relative to age group 30–9 for men and women, 1930s and 1991–2001

Note: Earnings data for 1991–2001 are derived from an estimated earnings equation, using age groups, education, and presence of young children as explanatory factors.

the average earnings of 30–9-year-old males and females respectively. The absolute level of earnings of males was significantly higher than that for females in both the 1930s and the 1990s; for example the reference wage for males aged 30–9 in the BHPS was £1,139 per month (in January 2001 prices) compared to a reference wage of only £680 per month for females.

It is clear that there are some strong similarities between the age-specific earnings patterns of the 1930s and the 1990s. Female earnings peak between the ages of 27 and 29, whereas male earnings peak between the ages of 41 and 43. Two factors seem to drive the hump-shaped pattern for females. First, there is a tendency for women with dependent children to work fewer hours than their male counterparts, even in full-time jobs. In 1998 the majority of full-time women worked between 30 and 39 hours per week, including paid over-time, whereas the majority of men worked between 40 and 49 hours (Harkness 1999). This means that the total work effort delivered by full-time female workers on average is lower for women in their thirties than in their twenties. Secondly, there is a 'scarring effect' on persons who take time out of the labour force for whatever reason, whereby they find it difficult to regain their previous position on a career ladder; thus their life-course earnings progression is retarded. This effect is more prevalent for women than men, because women

Table 5.2. Predicted earnings (£ per month)

	16–22	23–9	30–9	40–9	50–9	60–4
Highly educated, no young children						
Male	608	1,038	1,414	1,543	1,344	585
Female	506	859	969	895	841	
Highly educated, with young children						
Male	751	1,164	1,587	1,715	a	a
Female	443	627	782	707	a	
Medium level of education, no young children						
Male	448	841	1,019	1,128	996	750
Female	344	661	560	567	533	
Medium level of education, with young children						
Male	528	908	1,079	1,169	1,063	
Female	314	442	456	521	716	
No education, no young children						
Male	394	713	782	895	841	672
Female	288	512	389	436	420	
No education, with young children						
Male	473	753	807	930	897	a
Female	282	347	352	413	417	

Notes: These results are based on an estimated earnings equation, using age groups, education, and presence of young children as explanatory factors.

Earnings variable refers to 'net monthly pay', recorded for the month of September in the survey year.

[a] The results are omitted because cell size is smaller than 20 observations.

are much more likely to interrupt their employment for a number of years in order to care for children.

The impact of education and children on earnings in the 1990s is revealed in more detail in Table 5.2, which reports estimated monthly earnings. In all cases women earn less than men, and for all education levels the presence of young children is associated with marginally higher earnings for males and lower earnings for females. The relative impact of young children on female earnings across the different education levels is much less than the relative impact of young children on female participation reported in Table 5.1. The costs, in terms of forgone income, of having children fall almost entirely on women, and this cost is mainly the consequence of time out of the labour market (both fewer working years, and fewer hours when in work), rather than lower earnings when in work. Estimates made by Davies and Joshi (1999) of the total forgone earnings of women due to child rearing indicate that for low- and medium-education couples the total lifetime cost is around £155,000 for one child and £250,000 for two children.

5.5 Conclusion

The analysis presented in this chapter reveals that there has been both huge change and remarkable continuity in the experience of paid work over the life course for men and women in twentieth-century Britain. For men, the major change has been a substantial reduction in total number of years spent in paid employment, particularly at older ages. Men born in the early 1860s on average worked for fifty years between the ages of 15 and 69, whereas men born in the early 1970s are likely to work for no more than 41 years between these ages, assuming that current age-specific participation rates continue into the future. For women, the change has been in the opposite direction: the 1860s cohort worked on average for only sixteen years between the ages of 15 and 69, whereas the 1970s cohort can expect to work for at least thirty-two years. The transformation for women has come from the gradual combination of marriage/motherhood with paid employment, though much of this employment is on a part-time basis. Despite the scale of these changes, their occurrence has been gradual rather than dramatic, as each cohort has followed an employment pathway slightly different from that of its immediate prede-cessor. Throughout the twentieth century, therefore, sons and daughters could expect to follow an employment life course which was distinctly different from that of their fathers and mothers, but which was very similar to that of their elder or younger siblings.

When we look at the pattern of earnings over the life course, however, the picture is one of continuity rather than change across the twentieth century. Peak earnings have consistently been received by women in their late twenties, and by men in their early forties. The reason for this stability is unclear; long-run changes in the structure of the labour market, the nature of work, and the level and quality of human capital might have been expected to alter relative age-specific earnings. What this stability does indicate is that, for persons in employment, the trajectory of life-course earnings has been fairly predictable.

Overall, a life-course view of work over the twentieth century gives a clear sense of the dynamic of the employment experience, and how this has changed in very different ways for men and for women. Figure 5.6 also shows, for the 1990s, the very large effect of young children on women's participation rates, while Table 5.1 reveals the differential impact according to the education level of the mother. The absence of comparable data precludes a more precise analysis for earlier periods, and we should be cautious about drawing strong inferences from aggregated historical data. Nevertheless, when used in con-junction with other historical labour market data, the life-course analysis pre-sented here can contribute towards a fuller, more rounded view of work in Britain in the twentieth century.

Appendix 5.1

The censuses provide a snapshot once every ten years of labour force participation by five-year age groups. In order to provide estimates of participation rates for each five-year birth cohort across the years of normal working life it is necessary to find some method of filling gaps in the data. For example, the 1882–86 birth cohort was aged between 15 and 19 years at the 1901 census, and was aged between 25 and 29 years at the 1911 census, and thus we can directly determine the participation of this birth cohort at these ages. However, we do not have any information about the participation of this birth cohort when aged 20–4 in 1906. The procedure adopted has simply been to interpolate missing age-specific participation rates from the age-specific data of the immediately preceding and succeeding cohorts. So, to estimate the participation rate for the 1882–86 cohort when aged 20–4, the actual rates for 20–4-year-olds from the 1877–81 cohort (recorded in the 1901 census) and the 1887–91 cohort (recorded in the 1911 census) have been averaged. For further details of the process and the underlying data see Johnson (1994).

Appendix 5.2

Three historical datasets relating to the earnings of workers have been used in this analysis. The earliest data were collected in 1833 by Dr James Mitchell, who was appointed by the Royal Commission on the Employment of Children in Factories to conduct an extensive survey of the conditions of employment in a large number of factories. He collected data on the earnings of 21,483 males and 30,301 female workers employed in almost 300 separate factories, primarily in the textile trades. The data used in this chapter relate solely to 3,769 male workers employed in the Lancashire cotton textile trade, which was widely perceived to be the most modern and mechanized industrial sector of the age. Data for the late 1880s come from a survey of 1,024 British working-class household budgets undertaken by the US Bureau of Labor, as part of a Europe-wide study of working-class living costs. The earnings data cover just over 1,000 male workers in coal, iron and steel, textiles, and glass. Data for the early 1930s come from a random sample of 28,000 working-class households in London who participated in the New Survey of London Life and Labour; the earnings of over 25,000 male and 10,000 female workers were recorded. More information on these sources, and on the reliability of the data, can be found in Johnson (2003).

References

Blundell, R., Dearden, L., Goodman, A., and Reed, H. (1997). *Higher Education, Employment and Earnings in Britain*. London: Institute for Fiscal Studies.

Davies, H., and Joshi, H. (1999). 'Who Bears the Cost of Britain's Children in the 1990s?' Birkbeck College Dept of Economics working paper, September 1999.

Dickens, R. (1999). 'Wage Mobility in Britain', in P. Gregg and J. Wadsworth (eds.), *The State of Working Britain*. Manchester: Manchester University Press.

DTI (Department for Trade and Industry) Women and Equality Unit (2003). *Towards a Closing of the Gender Pay Gap*. London: DTI.

Halsey, A. H. (1988). 'Higher Education', in A. H. Halsey (ed.), *British Social Trends since 1900*. Basingstoke: Macmillan.

—— Heath, A., and Ridge, J. (1980). *Origins and Destinations*. Oxford: Oxford University Press.

Harkness, S. (1999). 'Working 9 to 5?', in P. Gregg and J. Wadsworth (eds.), *The State of Working Britain*. Manchester: Manchester University Press.

Hatton, T. J., and Bailey, R. E. (2001). 'Women's Work in Census and Survey, 1911–1931'. *Economic History Review*, 54: 87–107.

Higgs, E. (1987). 'Women, Occupation and Work in the Nineteenth Century Censuses'. *History Workshop Journal*, 23: 59–80.

Howlett, P. (2004). 'The Internal Labour Dynamic of the Great Eastern Railway Company, 1870–1913'. *Economic History Review*, 57: 396–422.

Johnson, P. (1994). 'The Employment and Retirement of Older Men in England and Wales, 1881–1981'. *Economic History Review*, 47: 106–28.

—— (1998). 'Parallel Histories of Retirement in Modern Britain', in P. Johnson and P. Thane (eds.), *Old Age from Antiquity to Post-Modernity*. London: Routledge.

—— (2003). 'Age, Gender and the Wage in Britain, 1830–1930', in P. Scholliers and L. Schwarz (eds.), *Experiencing Wages*. London: Berghahn.

Joshi, H., and Owen, S. (1987). 'How Long is a Piece of Elastic? The Measurement of Female Activity Rates in British Censuses, 1951–81'. *Cambridge Journal of Economics*, 11: 55–74.

ONS (Office for National Statistics) (2003*a*). 'A Century of Labour Market Change: 1900 to 2000', *Labour Market Trends*, March: 133–44.

—— (2003*b*). 'Experimental Consistent Time Series of Historical Labour Force Survey Data'. *Labour Market Trends*, September: 467–75.

Thane, P. (1994). 'Women since 1945', in P. Johnson (ed.), *Twentieth Century Britain: Economic, Social and Cultural Change*. London: Longman.

6

The Household and the Labour Market

Sara Horrell

The twentieth century has seen dramatic changes in the household and the labour market. The millennium family with two children aged between 8 and 15 supplied some 62 hours of paid work time to the labour market. Sixty-eight per cent of this was done by the father, 28 per cent by the mother, and less than 4 per cent was contributed by the children. The children each worked for less than ten minutes per day; they spent the majority of their time studying (28 hours per week) or watching television (16 hours).[1] A century earlier a typical family would have over three children, of all ages, would do a very similar number of total hours of paid work, 63 per week, but would be more reliant on the work of the husband. He was responsible for providing 81 per cent of the total work time. The children provided the majority of the remainder, 13 per cent or 9 hours per week.[2] Indeed, some 21 per cent of boys and 12 per cent of girls aged 10–14 were working in 1901 (Lavalette 1999: p.124). The mother worked only 4 hours per week compared with her counterpart in 2000 who worked 17.5 hours per week. This shift in the household's relationship to the labour market is perhaps best illustrated through the changed labour force participation rates of men and women (Figure 6.1). Male participation rates have declined. In 1901 96 per cent of British males aged 15 and over were economically active; by 2002 this was true for only 71 per cent of adult men. Conversely, the participation rates for women have risen from 36 per cent in 1901 to 56 per cent by 2002.[3] What underlies these changes?

---

[1] UK 2000 Time Use Survey.

[2] The labour market participation of this average family was computed from analysis of household budgets collected around the turn of the century. For a detailed discussion of these budgets see section 6.1 and n. 8 below. The budgets detailed total income and the earnings of women and children. Applying an hourly earnings rate of 53% of male wages for women (taken from Mitchell 1988: 173–4) and an assumed 50% for children enables shares of total work time to be calculated. Men's full-time hours are known to be 56.4 per week in 1913 (Mitchell 1988: 147).

[3] 1901 figures computed for GB from Mitchell (1988: 15–17, 104). Equal Opportunities Commission publications. (EOC (1993, 2003).

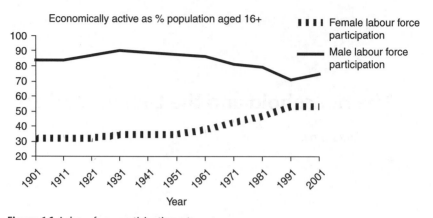

Figure 6.1 Labour force participation rates
Note: GB untill 1951, England and Wales 1961, 1971. UK thereafter.
Sources: Mitchell (1988: 104–7); Annual Abstract of Statistics (1994: tables 2.3, 6.1; 2003: table 7.1).

Increases in the statutory school leaving age and greater access to and import-ance of training and education have reduced the number of young people found working (Figure 6.2). The role of older children in the household eco-nomy has changed from one where they made significant financial contribu-tion from their paid work to a more dependent role. Additionally, improved life expectancies mean that more people expect to retire and enjoy leisure in their later years. These effects will decrease participation rates for both men and women. Against this backdrop the rise in the numbers of women working is even more remarkable. This rise has mainly occurred in the second half of the century and is attributable to increased proportions of married women working. In 1911 maybe only 10 per cent of married women had regular paid jobs, by 1971 49 per cent of married women of working age were economically active, and this had risen to 71 per cent by 1990.[4] Such a noticeable change across most Western societies prompted the *Wall Street Journal* to describe it as 'the social revolution of our time'.

Why has married women's participation changed over this century? Changes in the demand for labour offer a partial explanation. For instance, marriage bars requiring women to leave certain occupations on marriage were removed in the 1940s and 1950s so enabling some increase in numbers work-ing. Increases in the numbers of 'women's jobs', often to be found in the ser-vice sector, has increased demand for female labour, and reconciling this demand with family life has meant that many are offered on a part-time basis.

[4] EOC (1992).

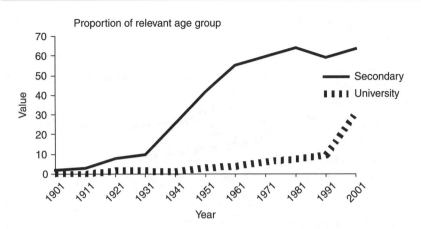

Figure 6.2 Proportions in full-time education

Notes: England, Wales, and Scotland till 1981, UK thereafter. Pupils at secondary school excludes 6th form colleges in England and Wales in 2001. Numbers taking university courses as % aged 20–4, GB 1901–71, UK 1981–91. Full-time students in higher education for first or other undergraduate degree, all ages, UK 2001/02. This includes the Open University and the former polytechnics and central institutions which obtained university status in 1992.

Sources: Mitchell (1988: 15, 799–815); Annual Abstract of Statistics (2003: tables 5.3, 6.2, 6.8).

But changes have also occurred on the supply side. These have stemmed from the increased availability of women for work, altered attitudes towards women's role, and increased uncertainty about marital stability and the security of income from a male breadwinner. Arguably, running the home requires less time, leaving women with time at their disposal which can be used in remunerated activity. Crucial to this change has been improved domestic technology: labour-saving machinery has reduced the time input required to maintain the family. Additionally, changed fertility patterns have reduced the amount of time women spend childbearing and rearing, again allowing this time to be reallocated elsewhere (Figure 6.3). But it is not just greater availability for work that underpins married women's increased participation. There has been an increased likelihood of women with dependent children working. Young dependent children do affect the probability of the mother undertaking paid employment, but the effect is much less pronounced than in the past.[5] A number of factors may have contributed to this change. Increased female wages will make the opportunity cost of staying at home higher, and changes in the availability and cost of childcare can help facilitate the move into the

[5] In 1987–9 the activity rates of women aged 16–59 in Great Britain were 78% for those with no dependent children, 77% for those whose youngest child was over 10, 69% for those whose youngest was aged 5–9, and 43% for those with 0–4 year olds. EOC (1992).

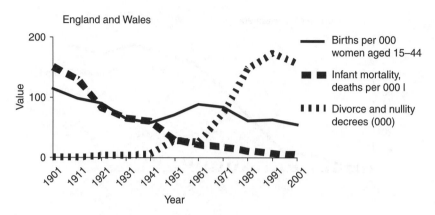

Figure 6.3 Birth, mortality, and divorce rates
Sources: Mitchell (1988: 45, 53–4, 73–6); Annual Abstract of Statistics (2003: tables 5.15, 5.20, 5.12, 5.13).

labour market. Recent evidence for the USA suggests that these are indeed important determinants of women's altered life-cycle participation patterns (Attanasio et al. 2004). But women, particularly those with skills and qualifications, may also fear the effect on career progression and lifetime earnings that would be occasioned by spells out of the labour market. One study has shown the £285,000 loss in lifetime earnings a low-skilled woman can expect from taking time out of the labour market followed by part-time work. For a high-skilled woman who continues to work full time with the exception of one year the loss can be reduced to £19,000.[6] The importance of continuous working for women is also underlined by increased marital instability (Figure 6.3). From negligible numbers of people obtaining divorces in the first half of the century, 30 per cent of marriages were terminated by divorce by 1975 and this had risen to 43 per cent by 1995 (Smith 2002: 213). Having a paid job may make it easier for women to opt out of unsatisfactory marriages but the loss of income and extent of poverty after divorce may also act to encourage women to ensure they have their own resources in case marital breakdown occurs.

Changes in household structure, fertility rates, and domestic technology all have consequences for labour market behaviour. This chapter explores these links. It starts by describing household structure and the role of children at the start and end of the century. The next section considers the impact of domestic technology on women's availability for work and the final section considers the interrelationship between work, fertility decisions, and divorce.

---

[6] Women's Incomes over a Lifetime (2000) study conducted by the London School of Economics for the government's Women's Unit.

6.1 Household structure and the role of children, 1900 and 2000

Household structure has changed considerably over the century. Average household size was around 4.6 people at the start of the last century but this had declined to less than 3 people by 1971 and reduced further to 2.4 people per household in 2002. Declining household size has fed into an increase in the number of households. Alongside this change is a decline in the 'traditional' family household: a couple with dependent children. In 1971, 35 per cent of families fell into this category, by 2002 they represented only 23 per cent of family types (Table 6.1). Instead there has been an increase in the number of lone parent families and one-person households, particularly under state pension age. A decline in the proportion of households with non-dependent children can also be observed.[7]

How does this compare with the household in 1900? Information on household structure is hard to find but estimates suggest considerable continuity in household size, at around 4.6 people per household, throughout the nineteenth century and consider the vast majority to have been of 'nuclear' family form (Laslett 1972). However, household size began to decline from 1901; by 1931 it had reached 4.1 (Gazeley 2003: 160). Falling fertility rates underpin some of this decline. The average family had 2.2 children in 1921–25, this had fallen to two children by 1936–40 (Coleman 2000: 36, table 2.3), and now stands at 1.8. Certainly there were one million more children aged 14 or under in the population in 1901 than in 1997 (EOC (1993)). Marital dissolution and the increase in single-person households have also added to the trend towards declining household size as the century has progressed.

More detail on the membership of households and their labour market participation in 1900 can be gained from contemporary survey evidence. Using data on seventy-four geographically dispersed households where there are both a husband and a wife and the husband is employed in one of a variety of occupations for the period 1889–1905 affords some insight into the nuclear family at this time.[8] Household size ranged from 3 to 10 people with two-thirds

Table 6.1. Household composition (% all households)

	1971	2002
% households headed by a couple	70%	58%
% with no children	27%	29%
% with dependent children	35%	23%
% with non-dependent children only	8%	6%

Source: EOC (2003), table 2.2.

[7] EOC (2003), table 2.2.
[8] The data came from the following sources: Rowntree (1901) (16 cases), Booth (1889) (22 cases), Cadbury et al. (1908) (5 cases), and Board of Trade (1889) (31 cases).

of households having 3, 4, or 5 people. Around 35 per cent of the wives earned an income either from paid employment or taking in lodgers but the amount they contributed to family income in these households amounted to 11 per cent on average. The mean number of children was 3.28 per household and 16 per cent of these children were also working.[9] In fact 22 of these families had at least one child working. The average age of these working children was 13.4 years old with the youngest at age 6 and the eldest at age 19.[10] On average these children contributed 24 per cent of the income to their households. Thus women and children could make quite substantial contributions to the household's income, contributions which could be crucial in seeing the family through expensive phases of the life cycle.[11]

Horrell and Oxley's (2000) analysis of late nineteenth-century industrial workers' households demonstrates the importance of children's earnings over the family life cycle for keeping families out of poverty even in normal circumstances. Children had to work to ensure stable life-cycle consumption patterns. The husband's/father's earnings were relatively invariant to the needs placed upon them. In times of distress, too, family earning was important. Membership of friendly societies and other self-help insurance groups did little to protect against protracted unemployment, lengthy illness, the defraying of medical expenses, or the losses associated with the death of a family member. Instead, in these unfortunate, but not unusual, circumstances, reliance was again placed on the income earning and labour market participation of women and children. Wives might take in lodgers to make ends meet, children might curtail training or education to earn a wage.

A detailed family case study of a London cabinetmaker shows that even the illness of a secondary worker, the wife, can throw the household finances into turmoil and necessitate a variety of crisis responses (Horrell and Oxley 2000). As a young man the illness and death of his first wife left the cabinetmaker seriously indebted and this debt took five years to clear. The absence of any other resources to draw on at this point in his life meant that borrowing and going into debt were the only strategies open to him. His second wife too had a serious bout of illness later on in life. She and her daughter made a significant contribution to the household finances by taking in lodgers and through this helped support both themselves and the three sons of the family. With the wife's illness the children were forced into labour market participation. The daughter, aged about 20, and the two eldest sons, aged 14 and 11, all went out to work. The family also adopted other, informal strategies. They

---

[9] A similar participation rate is found from the census for 10–14-year-olds in England and Wales. This was 16.9% in 1901, but had declined to 14.3% by 1911 (Nardinelli 1990: 119).

[10] The dispersion of working children across age ranges was: 6–9 13%, 10–13 21%, 14–17 53%, 18–19 13%.

[11] Averaged across all households, the contribution of women and children to household income amounted to 10% of the total.

moved to a smaller house to economize on rent and reduced their expenditure on food.

These analyses highlight an important feature of household change over the twentieth century. In the early years of the century cohabiting children were often working and were vital resources to the family economy. Indeed it has been suggested that parents might take an instrumental attitude to their children which ensured reasonable treatment in their early years in the expectation of recouping benefits later (Anderson 1971). In the inter-war period children were still making significant contributions to their households and often handed over their wages to their mothers to be returned a small portion as spending money. In the 1920s male earnings remained insufficient to support a family and children's earnings were necessary to maintain the family above the poverty line (Bowley and Hogg 1925: 12–17, 92–3). By the 1930s incomes for families in work were better but even in 1936 young workers' earnings remained important to the household and were needed for any expenditures beyond the basic necessities (Bowley 1937: 39). Towards the end of the twentieth century many children were to be found in full-time education until their late teens or early twenties instead of earning. The trend in increased educational uptake is evident through the century. People born in 1913–22 had an average school leaving age of 14.5; this had risen to 15.8 years for those born in 1943–52. Less than 12 per cent of those born in the early part of the century left with GCSE equivalents and only 2 per cent with A levels; only 1.8 per cent went on to university. For the mid-century cohort these percentages had risen to 34 per cent, 14 per cent, and 8.4 per cent (Halsey et al. 1980: 197). Subsequent cohorts have seen further impressive rises (see Figure 6.2). Children thus represent a financial cost rather than a monetary benefit to their parents. Parents may only rarely recoup the earlier costs. This is a dramatic change in household structure and the role of children. Why does this change occur?

The human capital model explains the change in terms of the costs and benefits of acquiring education or training.[12] Under this model individuals decide the extent to which they will invest in their education on the basis of the costs of education and the expected returns from the additional education over their working life. For instance, the costs of acquiring a university degree would be the fees payable, the costs of the course, rent, books and so on, and the opportunity cost of not earning a wage for the three years the course takes. The gross benefits would be the extra earnings the successful graduate might expect for the rest of his working life above those he would have earned had he

---

[12] Although the analysis for both education and training is similar, the focus here is on education as training is discussed in detail in Chapter 11. Furthermore, if training is on the job it will not necessarily affect participation rates and it is the change in these which we are keen to explain.

started work after leaving school. The net benefit from a degree is obviously the gross benefits less the costs. However, these net benefits need to be discounted to reflect the lengthy time over which the benefits will accrue. Most individuals might be expected to prefer income now to later so the returns are discounted to reflect the lower desirability of deferred gratification. If the rate of return thus calculated represents an adequate rate of return from the individual's perspective they will make the educational investment.[13]

How does this help explain changes in children's education and labour force participation? A number of factors will have influenced the human capital acquisition decision over the twentieth century. The costs of education have been reduced. The 1944 Education Act made secondary education free for all and bursaries and grants increased the financial accessibility of university places. The opportunity cost of undertaking secondary education was also reduced. At the turn of the century the minimum age of child workers was 12; although the hours that over 12s were able to work were restricted secondary schooling entailed the cost of forgoing work. The competition between the two forms of activity is witnessed by the fact that many children continued to work at 'half-time' or 'out-of-school jobs' and that an estimated 1 million out of 5.75 million children on the registers of schools were absent every day in 1903 (Lavalette 1999). The statutory school leaving age was raised from 12 to 14 in 1921, to 15 in 1947, and to 16 in 1972–73. This increasingly restricted the availability of work for children and made the choice to attend school easier. Additionally changes in technology may have reduced the number of jobs typically done by children and so decreased demand for child labourers. Higher incomes for male workers have reduced the necessity of children's work to the family economy (see Table 6.2). Equally importantly, the development of the welfare state has reduced the likelihood of children having to work and forgo human capital development in times of family crisis. Throughout the first half of the twentieth century the disastrous financial implications of eventualities such as unemployment, ill health, old age, and widowhood were progressively reduced. The state started to provide financial benefits to offset some income loss under these circumstances and it bore the costs of medical attention.

The direct cost of higher education has also changed. The discount rate faced by individuals varies according to their circumstances. Innate abilities play a role but so too does the availability of finance to defray the costs of education. A person from a poorer household may have to borrow to finance a university education, one from a wealthier household may rely on the family's savings

---

[13] The decision to invest in human capital will be made if the discounted income gains appear better than alternative returns, such as investing the money for fees in the stock market. The income gains can be formally described as:

$$Sum\ (E_t - N_t)/(1 + i)^t$$

Where E is income with education, N is expected income without the extra education, t is year, i is the discount rate, and the whole is summed over the expected years of working life.

Table 6.2. Hourly wages (£ real, 1900 = 100, full-time workers in manual jobs)

	Male	Female	Female:male ratio
1900	0.029	0.015	0.52
1905	0.026	0.014	0.54
1910	0.028	0.014	0.50
1915	0.022	0.011	0.50
1920	0.037	0.020	0.54
1925	0.035	0.019	0.54
1930	0.037	0.020	0.54
1935	0.039	0.020	0.51
1940	0.045	0.022	0.49
1945	0.054	0.032	0.59
1950	0.061	0.038	0.62
1955	0.068	0.041	0.60
1960	0.078	0.048	0.62
1965	0.091	0.054	0.59
1970	0.107	0.064	0.60
1975	0.129	0.087	0.67
1980	0.127	0.089	0.70
1985	0.134	0.093	0.69
1990	0.149	0.110	0.74
1995	0.152	0.116	0.76
1998	0.164	0.124	0.76

Source: See Horrell (2000: appendix).

and accumulated assets. The difference in financing costs will affect the amount of investment undertaken. Over time wealth has increased and more families are able to bear the costs of their children's education. Estimates of real wealth per capita in 1900 prices for the UK suggest levels of £151 in 1920, £330 in 1950, and £752 in 1995 (Horrell 2000). Furthermore government loans have overcome a capital market distortion. Typically formal capital markets have been unwilling to lend for educational purposes as it represents an unsecurable asset: the human capital is embodied in the borrower and the bank cannot repossess it in the event of default. Increasing the accessibility of loans for education has increased the numbers who can now finance their degrees.

The importance and benefit of education has also increased. There has been a trend rise in returns to skills and the wage gap has widened between those with and those without training and education. Returns to education are consistently higher than the returns on most alternative investments. Returns to literacy in 1870 have been estimated at 19 per cent for men and 9 per cent for women (Mitch 1984: 563). Returns to post-compulsory schooling may have been as high as 15 per cent per annum for working aged men in the early 1980s (Harmon and Walker 1995). Men born in 1958 were receiving a return of around 15 per cent per annum at age 33 (in 1991) for getting A level qualifications, and a further 9 per cent per annum for a degree. The corresponding figures were 15 and 12 per cent for women. Vocational qualifications returned about 12 per cent per annum (Deardon 1998). However, declines over time can be observed in the returns to a degree. In 1955 graduates earned 17.5 per cent on their degree; by 1985 this had fallen to 8.5 per cent. Engineers too saw smaller returns: in 1967–8 returns were 14.5 per cent per annum but had fallen to 9 per cent per annum by 1978–79 (Bosworth et al. 1996: 226). These declines can be explained by the greater numbers staying on at school and taking degrees, so increasing the supply of educated people, without a fully compensating increase in the demand for qualified labour having occurred. Even so rates of return remain respectable and the widening gap between those with and without higher levels of education has helped drive increased uptake.

The human capital model undoubtedly highlights factors important in increasing the numbers of young people in full-time education over the twentieth century. However, the analysis is conducted at the level of the individual. Considering the education decision as one made by parents in the context of the family may point up other aspects which have fed into the change in children's role over the last hundred years.

Analysing the decision within a household framework demonstrates additional factors which impact on the labour force participation and education of children. In particular, increasing adult incomes have an effect beyond reducing the financial necessity of children's work at certain points in the life cycle or at times of crisis. Real per capita incomes have increased over the century. If children are viewed as 'consumption' goods to their parents a rise in income will lead parents to demand both more and better-'quality' children, where quality relates to the children's education, health, training, and other factors that will improve the child's lifetime standard of living. The effect on quality is expected to be more noticeable than that on quantity.[14] Indeed one of the explanations of the decline in child labour has been this effect of rising incomes (Nardinelli 1990). Instead of reaping immediate financial rewards from the labour of children families could afford to invest in human capital so allowing the children to obtain better jobs and rewards later on in life and, consequently a better standard of living. This represented intergenerational advance for the family. This investment may reflect paternalistic attitudes on the part of parents but it could also be consistent with an expectation that higher-earning children would be better placed to support their parents in old age. Whether such an expectation has been realized at the individual level is, of course, difficult to ascertain. Declining infant and child mortality (Figure 6.3) too has reduced the cost to parents of investing in quality children. As there is a greater likelihood of each child surviving, the rate of return on investment increases thus helping to increase the level of human capital investment.

[14] The effect on quantity is discussed in detail when fertility is considered.

Thus a multiplicity of factors underlie the changed role of children within the household with the effect that they have ceased to be earners and are instead dependent learners. This has had significant consequences for the numbers and quality of entrants to the labour market.

6.2 Housework, domestic technology, and women's work

The improvement in domestic technology over the twentieth century is probably unprecedented. This improvement would be expected to reduce the time spent in housework by married women and thus increase the time available for their labour market participation. Since the advent of electricity and domestic gas there have been increased numbers of durables available which have altered the nature of housework. Keeping the house warm and water heated can be done through the medium of central heating rather than making up, stoking, and cleaning out open fires. Cooking utlilizes gas or electric cookers and microwave ovens and is done 'at the touch of a button' rather than on the old, high-maintenance range, open fire, or stove. The washing machine and tumble drier have replaced coppers and mangles. The vacuum cleaner has superseded the broom and mop and even hand washing up has become obsolete as kitchens are increasingly equipped with dishwashers. The increased ownership of selected durables over the century is evident, although the low levels of ownership of most appliances until the 1960s should be noted (Table 6.3). Indeed, only 6 per cent of households in Britain were wired for electricity at the end of the First World War. The Electricity (Supply) Act of 1926 standardized generation, rationalized distribution, and created a national grid, with the result that prices fell. Thirty-two per cent of households were wired for electricity in 1931 and this had reached 86 per cent by 1949. In the same year 79 per cent of households had a gas supply and only 3 per cent had neither

Table 6.3. Household durable ownership (% households having)

	1933	1946	1950	1960	1964	1970	1980	1990	1994/95	2000
Washing machine	1	5	8	36	53	65	79	86		92
Refrigerator		1	3	18	34	58	75			
Vacuum cleaner	24		51	75		85	93			
Central heating					7	30	59	79		91
Car					37	52	60	67		72
Tumble dryer									50	53
Dishwasher									18	25
Microwave									67	84

Sources: 1933, 1946, 1950, 1960, refrigerator 1970, 1980 and vacuum cleaner 1970: Bowden and Offer (1994). 1964: *Family Expenditure Survey*. 1970, 1980, 1990, 1994/95, 2000: *Family Spending* (2002)

(Davidson 1982: 38–9). However the availability of supply did not necessarily mean that all appliances were readily adopted. Although gas cooking was popular, only 19 per cent of families used an electric cooker in 1948. Furthermore 75 per cent of the fuel used for domestic heating purposes in Britain at the outbreak of the Second World War was solid fuel. Heating was still a major part of housework. In 1948 only 4 per cent of families had an electric washing machine; most still heated the water in pans and washed by hand.

Probably one of the least lauded but most important changes has been easily accessible water. Without piped water the water for all household needs had to be collected from streams, wells, and public standpipes. This was arduous and time consuming and clearly placed limits on the frequency with which household tasks, such as laundry, washing up, cleaning, and even cooking, were conducted. Although some urban areas had provided internal water supplies for the majority of their population by 1900 this was not universal and rural areas lagged behind. In 1917 Maud Pember Reeves reported that fetching water was still a heavy task for women in Lambeth and the weekly clothes wash would take a whole, tiring day. Even in 1934 a survey of working-class London showed that half the households studied still had to fetch water from outside their accommodation. In 1913, 62 per cent of rural households in England lacked piped water. Even in 1951 this was still true for one-fifth of all households and in 1961 22 per cent of the population did not have a hot tap in their home. Indeed in 1951 45 per cent of households in England and Wales did not have a fixed bath, 21 per cent had no water closet, and 12 per cent no kitchen sink (Davidson 1982: 16, 20, 36). But by mid-century it could be said that the 'most fundamental revolution in the working lives of British women was thus almost complete. Soon the centuries-old sight of women bearing water—on their heads, by their hands, and from their shoulders—was to disappear altogether' (Davidson 1982: 32). But it is noteworthy how late into the twentieth century this fundamental revolution occurred.

Such changes in technology would be expected to have their corollary in reduced housework time for women over the century. A report on electricity in working-class homes in 1934 showed that women spent 26.25 hours per week tending lamps, stoves, and fires, washing, ironing, and cleaning and demonstrated that this could be reduced to 7 hours if the home was fully electrified as many of these tasks would be removed or reduced (Davidson 1982: 43). However, in 1948 a study of London working-class women found they were still doing around 8 to 9 hours of housework per day. Certainly in the first half of the twentieth century the conclusion that 'the spread of utilities and time-saving appliances did not have any discernible long-term effect on the average housewife's working hours' (Davidson 1982: 192) seems reasonable. However, a decline in housework time since the 1960s is supported by the data (Table 6.4). But the decline is maybe not as great as might be expected given the revolutionary changes in domestic technology that occurred. Furthermore, it

Table 6.4. Housework time per day—includes domestic work, childcare, and shopping (all women aged 16+)

	Housework hours per day	Source
1920	6.64	a
1935	6.32	c
1937	5.90	b
1955	6.55	c
1960	6.78	c
1961	6.0	b
1974/75	5.1	b
1984	5.3	b
1990/01	5.3	d
2000/01	4.1	e

Notes: 1920: assumed same as 1960. Vanek (1974) finds this to be true for American women. 1900–41: assumed 30% women work of which 40% work part-time, the rest are assumed housewives when aggregating to get average housework time. 1951–2001, between one-third and more than half women work, assumed 40% work part time when aggregating to get average housework time.
1920, 1937: assumed time ratio of housework time of 1.24:1 for housewife:part-time worker, 1.64:1 for full-time worker:part-time worker. Based on ratio in other years. Average time = (housewife time * 0.30 * 0.40/1.24) + (housewife time * 0.70) + (housewife time * 0.30 * 0.60/1.24/1.64)
1935, 1955, 1960: average time = (housewife and part-time worker's housework time * 0.18/1.04/1.64) + (housewife + part-time workers' time * 0.82).

Sources: *a* Vanek (1974); *b* Bowden and Offer (1994); *c* Gershuny (1983: 151); *d* EOC (1992, table 10.2) (less 27% time quoted for personal care); *e* EOC (2003: 224–5) from UK 2000 Time Use Survey.

should be noted that these surveys report time used in housework, shopping, and childcare as one category; as will be seen, subdivision can alter the conclusion of declining housework time.

The correspondence between the increased availability of domestic appliances and married women's increased labour force participation has led economists to seek explanations related to the effect on housework time. An early proponent, Jacob Mincer (1962), pointed out that the availability of substitutes for women's labour time in the home and changes in the degree of substitutability would affect the woman's productivity in the home and so affect the responsiveness of her labour allocation between competing activities—paid work, housework, and leisure—to changes in the wage rate. Put simply, the ownership of household durable goods has enabled women to reduce the time they spend in domestic work and put more time into paid work as wages have risen. A more sophisticated analysis of this effect is provided by Gary Becker (1965) in his New Household Economics. His starting point is that time is in short supply and its allocation between different activities will be determined by market-determined variables, that is, wages and incomes. Furthermore, the household's desire is to consume 'commodities'; these commodities are produced from a combination of time and market good inputs and there are a variety of ways in which they can be produced. For instance, the commodity 'having a meal' will require time and goods in preparation and consumption. Obviously food will need to be bought, and utensils, pots, a cooker, electricity, and time will be needed in preparation and a table and chair, cutlery, china, and time needed to eat it. But the way the meal can be produced can be varied. The meal could be cooked from scratch using the basic ingredients (time intensive, goods saving) or it could be purchased as a ready-prepared meal (time saving, goods intensive). The implication is that time allocated to different activities will be affected by the cost of time, as measured by the wage rate in paid work, as will the types of goods consumed and the way these goods are produced. Because women spend more time in domestic commodity production than men their time allocation will be more responsive to a change in the wage than men's because they have more options for substitution. If the wage offered increases, women's time at home becomes more expensive so less will be used here (the compensated wage effect) and the way this will be achieved is by consuming fewer time-intensive and more goods-intensive commodities and using less time-intensive methods in the production of each commodity. Equally, improvements in domestic technology allow greater substitution of market goods for time in the production of commodities resulting in changes in the way commodities are produced, which commodities are consumed, and the time spent in consumption and market work activities. For instance, changes in the availability of market-provided childcare increase the opportunity for substitution of the woman's own time and allow an increased labour supply elasticity, the responsiveness of time at work to the wage, to be predicted (Juster and Stafford 1991).

Becker's framework implies that housework and paid work time will be responsive to wages, incomes, and production technology. But empirical evidence has questioned some of these relationships. Time budget study data have been used to ascertain the responsiveness of different time uses to the wage rate. Some studies do find a relationship. Gronau (1977) finds working women's housework time and leisure both decrease with increases in the female wage, although the decrease in leisure is four times that of the decrease in housework.[15] Other studies show that the wage has a clear effect on time spent at work but that it has no impact on the amount of time used in either housework or leisure. Instead traditional divisions of labour, household composition, and cultural norms seem to have greater explanatory power for the time spent in home production (Gershuny 1983; Morgensen 1990; Pedersen 1990; Horrell 1994). Comparisons of the time spent in housework by working and non-working women do indicate that those in paid work appear to be saving time in household activities but closer analysis reveals the saving largely occurs from reducing the amount of time spent in childcare. Pure

---

[15] Housework time was not clearly defined in the survey used for this analysis and respondents may have included childcare.

'housework' and shopping time is relatively invariant to the women's work status (Vanek 1974; Vickery 1979; Piachaud 1982; Brown and Preece 1987; Horrell 1994). Indeed the UK 2000 Time Use Survey shows average hours of housework for women with children in the household to be fairly invariant to the age of the youngest child and to stand at about 3.5 hours per day. Childcare time is on top of this and this reduces from 2.9 hours for those with a youngest child aged 0–2 to none for those with a youngest child 16–17 years old. Also there is little evidence of any differences in frequency or method of meal preparation between working and non-working women once factors such as income and life-cycle phase have been accounted for (Strober and Weinberg 1980). Generally empirical studies show very little substitution occurs between women's time and market goods in housework (Brown and Preece 1987). Indeed, far from women engaging in paid work being able to reallocate time saved from housework, longitudinal studies reveal women's total work time increasing until relatively recently (Gershuny 1983; Horrell 2000). Total work time is only now equalized at 7 hours 50 minutes per day for men and women who undertake any paid work. Of course, women spend more of this total time in housework chores while men spend more time in the labour market (UK 2000 Time Use Survey).

That empirical studies reveal women's time in the home to be unresponsive to the market wage rate offered may not be that surprising. Feminist studies of domestic technology have challenged the notion that changes have been time saving. They have pointed out that new tasks have replaced old ones and have highlighted the role that improved standards have played in increasing the frequency with which tasks are done so offsetting time savings from technical improvements. The vacuum cleaner may have made lighter work of sweeping but an expectation arose that carpets, curtains, and furniture would be cleaned more often. Washing machines reduced the physical labour associated with the wash but norms changed so that the laundry was done more frequently (Schwartz Cowan 1976; Davidson 1982). Indeed, many machines have been developed with built, in obsolescence and additional functions which involve an increased use of time (Hardyment 1988). A recent study concludes that new technology has done little to reduce the burden of housework; hours remain relatively unaffected although the physical labour required has been reduced (Bowden and Offer 1994).[16] Advertising and marketing campaigns have been identified as the culprits in creating the anomaly that labour-saving durables do not economize on time. Many appliances were marketed as ways to improve standards and advertising put a new emphasis on cleanliness, hygiene, and efficiency. This created new behavioural patterns and wants and ensured continued expansion of the market. In addition to keeping one's home and family clean, clothed, and well fed, the housewife

---

[16] For a detailed review of the impact of the technology see Wajcman (1991).

also had to become a discerning consumer and 'shopping and shopping wisely were occupying increasing amounts of housewives' time' (Schwartz Cowan 1976: 14).

Significant changes in domestic technology have occurred over the twentieth century. However, the extent to which these changes have been time saving as well as labour saving is debatable and the prediction of the neoclassical model that women would be able to reduce home production time to enable increased labour market participation in response to a rising wage is rarely supported empirically. Indeed, time budget studies suggest that time savings in the areas of child rearing and own leisure time may be more important in enabling married women to take on paid work.

6.3 Fertility, marital breakdown, and women's work

Fertility rates in most Western societies have declined over the twentieth century. The fertility rate per thousand women aged 15–44 in Britain has nearly halved from 115 in 1900–02 to 60 in 1997.[17] In the 1900s 25 per cent of women had five or more children; as early as the 1940s only 5 per cent of women had this many (D'Cruze 1995). Although the percentage of women who had any children increased from about 80 per cent of those born in 1920 to 90 per cent of women born in 1945 it has since fallen. It is estimated that 17 per cent of women born in 1955 will not have any children and proportions who remain childless look likely to increase.[18]

Women have become less constrained to spending most of their lives child rearing but the reasons hypothesized to underlie this decline in fertility are controversial. Some argue that it is intimately related to opportunities in the labour market. Responsiveness to rising female wages manifests itself as a desire for 'quality' rather than quantity of children. Others point to changed relationships between parents and children brought about by economic change. Alternatively, bargaining models of the household suggest that fertility is declining because of the impact child rearing has on women's lifetime earnings and thus on their bargaining position and threat point within marriage. To avoid weakened positions women may continue to work and opt to have fewer or no children. Increased marital instability too is likely to reinforce trends towards greater labour market participation by married women. Here we consider the interrelationship between fertility decline and the observed increase in married women's labour force participation.

Under Becker's New Household Economics framework decisions to have children form one part of the household's time allocation and consumption decisions. Children have roles as 'consumption' goods to their parents,

---

[17] EOC (1992).   [18] EOC (1992), p. 47.

consumers in their own right, and producers who contribute their time to paid work and household tasks to increase the amount of consumption available to the household. Parents have to weigh up the costs and benefits of children in each of these roles when deciding how many children to have. But the decision is slightly more complex: parents also have to decide the quality (education) of the children they have and, given fixed resources, there will be a trade-off between quality and quantity.

Children take both time and goods to rear so fertility decisions will be taken alongside decisions about competing uses of time—work, leisure, and consumption activities—and the consumption of other commodities, and will be subject to the usual constraints of the total amount of time available and money income, as determined by the wage rate offered and the amount of time spent working. The net cost of a child will then be the goods and services required by the child, the time spent by family members looking after the child, less any earnings the child contributes to the family's resources. Clearly if the child is considered in the same way as any other commodity, the decision to have a child will be affected by changes in the prices of the inputs; goods and time; changes in his or her contribution to the household; and changes in income. Thus a reduction in child labour opportunities will probably reduce the demand for children. Similarly, as the opportunity cost of a mother's time rises, the price of bringing up a child will rise and fertility will fall. Conversely a reduction in the price of childcare substitutes, such as nurseries, can reduce the cost of child rearing and increase the numbers born. The decline in children's work and the rise in female wages in the labour market both help to explain secular declines in fertility rates over the twentieth century. It is more difficult to estimate the effect of childcare substitutes. This may not be particularly important in the UK: childcare expenditure is not tax deductible, nursery places are few and expensive, and other forms, such as childminders, are often deemed poor substitutes for a mother. For nearly 5 million children under the age of 8 in the UK in 2000 there were only 726,000 places in a day nursery, with a registered childminder, or at an out of school club. That is childcare for only one in seven children.[19] In any case, we don't know the extent to which availability has changed over time. Formal care may only have served to replace the informal care of networks of siblings and grandparents of the past. Changes in income too have an effect on fertility. Incomes have risen over the twentieth century. Theoretically this should have increased the demand for children but an unprecedented decline in fertility is actually observed. To explain this phenomenon child quality needs to be considered.

In Becker's model the interaction between quantity and quality of children is explored. Here the price of quantity of children to the household is partly determined by their quality and the price of quality partly determined by

---

[19] EOC (2000).

quantity. Because of these interactions many fewer children will be born but their quality will be higher in response to a small increase in the cost of having a child. These price effects are assumed to dominate the effect of rising incomes over time. Thus rising female wages (see Table 6.2) represent an increasing cost to having children in terms of forgone earnings, so, despite the resultant higher incomes, the number of children born will be reduced. Furthermore, rising incomes will increase demand for quality and this too will reinforce the tendency to declining quantity.

Under this scenario the rise in wages offered to married women over the twentieth century is the driving force behind their increased labour market participation. This has also been a cause of the decline in childbearing. Indeed empirical tests of the influence of the wage, costs of children, and incomes on fertility using British data support this interpretation (Ermisch 2003: 121–2).[20]

More radical interpretations suggest that the changing nature of relations between parents and children may be as important as economic variables in explaining the fertility decline. In particular, Folbre (1982) points out that the neoclassical school assumes that net child costs will be increased by the reduction in child labour and increased investment in education but, she says, this may not necessarily be the case. Well-educated children have the potential for higher earnings and therefore can make a greater contribution to the household than those sent into the labour market at an early age. However, the outcome on net cost is uncertain as it depends on the reciprocity of the child: an adult child has greater control over his or her earnings and contributions to the parents will be voluntary rather than required. It is this reciprocity, not changes in prices, that determines their cost, and reciprocity will be determined by culture, attitude, affection, and other unquantifiable factors. The development of the economy diminishes parental power as their control of productive assets, such as land, is reduced and because the timing of intergenerational transfers changes. Instead of, say, inheriting land on the death of a father as in pre-industrial society, the development of labour markets increases the requirement for early investment in children through education. The return on this education to the parent is less certain than the labour power of children on the family farm prior to inheritance. Indeed the development of state involvement in support for old age can be interpreted as a response to the reduced responsibility children are obliged to feel for ageing parents, but it could also be seen as a rationale for the continued decline in intergenerational transfers. How then does this affect fertility? The net benefits of children are reduced because the returns are more uncertain so fertility will decline. But as fertility declines

---

[20] The decline in fertility is also facilitated by the increased ease and reduced cost of fertility regulation. Contraception has developed from 'natural' methods in the early twentieth century to barrier methods which were available cheaply after the First World War to the contraceptive pill available from the 1960s. See Easterlin (1980) for an account of how such changes might have influenced the secular decline in fertility.

women will necessarily allocate less time to child rearing. As the time in reproduction is reduced the justification for support from an earning male is also reduced and more time in paid employment for women will result. This interpretation suggests a reverse causation to that of the New Household Economics. The changed nature of relations within the home, brought about by the developing economy, led to reduced fertility and women finding work outside the home, rather than higher wages enticing women into the labour market as an alternative to having children. Other work lends support to the centrality of reciprocal relationships. Adult children remained an important source of support to ageing parents throughout the inter-war period and it has been argued that it was in parents' interests to develop a reciprocal economic and emotional relationship with their children (Thane 2000; Todd 2004).

The impact of relationships between members of the household in determining fertility and labour market decisions has been developed theoretically in bargaining models of the household (Ott 1995). In a standard neoclassical, joint utility maximizing household, having a child benefits the couple by increasing their joint welfare. Although the wife may lose out on future earnings because she takes time out of the labour market to rear the child, the assumption of shared gains means that both husband and wife are better off from the birth of a child so they will decide to reproduce. Under a bargaining framework the outcome is less certain. Here gains are not equally shared but are determined for each partner by their bargaining, or threat, points. These, in turn, are based on factors such as each individual's waged income. Stopping work to have a child may adversely affect the wife's lifetime earnings and thus her threat point and bargaining position so that she ends up with a reduced share of the gains to the marriage, even though the total gain has been increased by having a child. If her position is worsened sufficiently she will opt not to have a child despite the addition to welfare to the household that the child would create. Thus the loss of earnings from engaging in child rearing and the consequent weakened position of women within the household may deter some women from having children. Declining fertility rates across Europe can be interpreted in this way. Again it is the relationships within the household that are central to the fertility and labour market outcomes observed.

These theories offer explanations for the secular decline in fertility, but the decline has not been linear. Britain, along with many other developed countries, witnessed a post-Second World War 'baby boom' lasting over a decade. This was followed by a 'baby bust' (Figure 6.3). Such cyclical variation needs closer examination. The fluctuations over boom and bust are hard to interpret using only price and income effects. Relative movements in male and female wages do not fit easily with the growth then decline in fertility rates. In periods of rising male and stagnant female wages a baby boom might be predicted as rising incomes raise the demand for children whilst children become relatively cheaper to the woman. If both male and female wages are rising or women gain on men then the opportunity cost of the woman's time will rise, this will dominate fertility decisions, and a decline in births will result. Data on male wages show them to be rising throughout, as were women's wages. Women's wages relative to men's made significant progress during the boom, but were static during the bust (Table 6.2). Thus wages do not seem to be the driving force behind the cyclical movements in fertility.

One explanation for the cyclical behaviour has relied on the impact of generational relative incomes (Easterlin 1980). Fertility is determined by the extent to which a generation's labour market experience exceeds or falls short of their expectations, which themselves are based on living standards in childhood. Although appealing, evidence suggests that this cannot provide a comprehensive explanation for the movements observed. Instead elements of both relative income and female wage models are needed to explain the cyclical behaviour (Macunovich 2003).

Women may have saved time from child rearing to work. Time budget data is supportive of this view. But whether the declining fertility response is solely, or even largely, brought about by changes in the available wages for women is much more debatable. Causation could run the other way. Women may have decided to spend less time child rearing, have gained more qualifications and labour market experience, and so have earned higher wages in the labour market. Fertility decline may even be due to factors outside the labour market, such as changed bargaining power between generations or between the sexes within the home. One indicator of the importance of these more cultural types of effect is the increase in participation in the UK among younger cohorts of women even when education, labour market experience, and domestic responsibilities are accounted for (Joshi et al. 1985). The increase in participation is attributed to changing tastes and attitudes to work. Indeed a detailed study of attitudes shows that women have become more committed to the labour force and more oriented towards working through their adult years and that they are more likely to work when their children are young than their mothers or grandmothers (Dex 1988). However, this change in attitudes towards work does not translate into changed views about the domestic division of labour and responsibilities for various domestic tasks. Many attitudes of younger and older women are still very traditional. A factor that might have altered women's attitudes and view of paid work is the increased instability of marriage as a source of lifetime income.

Across most Western countries there was increased permissiveness in divorce laws from the 1960s which transformed marriage by considerably easing access to divorce. In England and Wales the Divorce Reform Act that was implemented in 1971 introduced new grounds for divorce. Adultery and desertion remained but separation and unreasonable behaviour were added. Subsequently quick divorces were permitted which obviated courts from investigating the grounds for divorce and allowed divorce on weak fault grounds. The change was typical: a switch from fault towards no-fault divorces.

This changed the power to divorce from the person least wanting the divorce to the spouse most wanting a divorce and thus reduced the protection offered by marriage. No longer protected by fault divorce laws, we might expect people to find other ways to protect their position in the event of marital breakdown; in particular it is argued that women may alter their labour force participation behaviour. Women make family-specific investments when they stay at home and look after the children with obvious costs in terms of labour market experience and worth. If these investments are not accounted for or human capital depreciation not compensated for in divorce settlements then the woman will be worse off after divorce. She may try to prevent this impoverished situation occurring by working during marriage and child rearing, particularly if she is likely to experience large declines in human capital from being out of the labour force.

However, to the economist, causation could operate in the reverse direction. In a neoclassical model, there are gains to be achieved from specialization within marriage and both partners share in these gains. Specialization would be in housework or market work. As women's labour force participation increases, mainly in response to the higher wages on offer, the gains from specialization are reduced. Declining fertility has also reduced the total benefit of the marriage-specific good—children—to the marriage. The incentive to remain married is commensurately reduced and where the expected utility from remaining married is less than the expected utility from becoming single again a divorce will occur. Women's increased financial independence lies at the root of this; women's labour market work is one of the reasons for increased marital instability (Becker 1981). But even with this view of the world it is acknowledged that as divorce becomes more likely women will want to ensure they have the skills that would allow them to earn respectable incomes in the event that they have to support themselves after a divorce, and this will raise female participation rates. This feedback effect of women insuring themselves against divorce is evident in empirical work (Johnson and Skinner 1986).

If women are working to protect themselves financially in the event of divorce the change of regime to no-fault divorce should increase the labour force participation rates of married women and the hours they supply to the labour market. The USA provides fertile ground for testing this hypothesis as divorce laws differ across states. The results are likely to understate true magnitudes as changes have occurred over time and the line between fault and no-fault divorce is blurred in some states. Even so, the evidence shows the labour force participation rates of married women is 2 per cent higher in no-fault divorce states and they work on average four hours more per week than their sisters working in fault divorce states (Allen 2002). Of course, it is possible that higher participation and greater divorce rates occur not because women are trying to insure their future income against divorce but because the woman working is destabilizing to the marriage. However, an empirical test suggests that working has no real impact on divorce probabilities but anticipated divorce has a significant impact on working (Johnson and Skinner 1986).

Thus women's increased participation and the concomitant effects on fertility can be seen as a response to more available divorce and changed bargaining positions within the household, rather than increased working being a response to higher wages and, through this mechanism, causing lower fertility and more divorce.

6.4 Conclusion

The twentieth century has seen dramatic changes in the household and its relationship to the labour market. Children have become learners not earners, their financial contribution to the household has probably reduced, and it is definitely less certain. The welfare state has developed to take on many aspects of support that would previously have fallen to family members. Higher incomes and improved access to and returns from education explain much of this transformation. Women's role too has undergone change. Married women are no longer primarily engaged in housework and child rearing; they are nearly as likely to be working in paid employment as their husbands. But explaining this change is not easy. Domestic technology has certainly reduced the physical burden of housework but it has had relatively little impact on its time requirements. Thus women's paid work has not been facilitated by reduced housework requirements. They are, however, having fewer children and this time has been reallocated to the labour market. But, whilst labour market and fertility decisions appear intimately related, the mechanism proves elusive. Higher wages are offered as one explanation but changed family relations and reduced economic worth of children are equally plausible. Indeed the state of marriage itself has also been transformed. It is no longer a stable institution, for better or worse, but a partnership nearly as likely to end in dissolution as to remain intact. Women's work opportunities may have enabled them to opt out of unsatisfactory marriages, but it is just as likely that women continue to work during marriage and child rearing to ensure they have adequate earning power to protect themselves in the event of divorce. The increase in marital instability itself might underpin the increased labour force participation of married women and have increased the opportunity cost to women of taking time out of the labour market to rear children.

References

Allen, D. W. (2002). 'The Impact of Legal Reforms on Marriage and Divorce' in A. W. Dnes and R. Rowthorn (eds.), *The Law and Economics of Marriage and Divorce*. Cambridge: Cambridge University Press: 191–209.

Anderson, M. (1971). *Family Structure in Nineteenth Century Lancashire*. Cambridge: Cambridge University Press.

Attansio, O., Low, H., and Sanchez-Marcos, V. (2004). 'Explaining Changes in Female Labour Supply in a Life-Cycle Model'. Mimeo. Working Paper, UCL (University College London), IFS (Institute for Fiscal Studies).

Becker, G. S. (1965). 'A Theory of the Allocation of Time'. *Economic Journal*, 80: 493–517.

—— (1981). *A Treatise on the Family*. Cambridge, Mass.: Harvard University Press.

Board of Trade (1889). *Labour Statistics: Returns of Expenditure by Working Men*. Cd. 5861. London: HMSO.

Booth, C. (1889). *Life and Labour of the People in London*, vol. i. London: Williams and Norgate.

Bosworth, D., Dawkins, P., and Stromback, T. (1996). *The Economics of the Labour Market*. Harlow: Pearson Education Ltd.

Bowden, S., and Offer, A. (1994). 'Household Appliances and the Use of Time: The United States and Britain since the 1920s'. *Economic History Review*, 47, November: 725–48.

Bowley, A. L. (1937). *Wages and Income in the United Kingdom since 1860*. Cambridge: Cambridge University Press.

—— and Hogg, M. H. (1925). *Has Poverty Diminished?* London: P. S. King and Son.

Brown, C., and Preece, A. (1987). 'Housework', in *The New Palgrave*. London: Macmillan, 678–80.

Cadbury, E., Matheson, M. C., and Shann, G. (1908). *Women's Work and Wages*. London: T. Fisher Unwin.

Coleman, D. (2000). 'Population and Family', in A. H. Halsey and J. Webb (eds.), *Twentieth-Century British Social Trends*. Basingstoke: Palgrave Macmillan, 36, table 2.3.

Davidson, C. (1982). *A Woman's Work is Never Done: A History of Housework in the British Isles 1650–1950*. London: Chatto and Windus.

D'Cruze, S. (1995). 'Women and the Family', in J. Purvis (ed.), *Women's History: Britain 1850–1945*. London: University College London Press, 51–83.

Deardon, L. (1998). 'Ability, Families, Education and Earnings in Britain'. Institute for Fiscal Studies working paper, July WP98/14.

Dex, S. (1988). *Women's Attitudes towards Work*. Basingstoke: Macmillan.

Easterlin, R. A. (1980). *Birth and Fortune*. New York: Basic Books.

EOC (Equal Opportunities Commission) (1992). 'At the Millennium'. *Social Trends*, 22: 71. Available at: **eoc.org.uk**

—— (2000). 'Facts about Men and Women in Britain 2000'. *Social Trends*. Available at: **eoc.org.uk**

—— (2003). 'Facts about Men and Women in Great Britain'. *Social Trends*. Available at: **eoc.org.uk**

Ermisch, J. (2003). *An Economic Analysis of the Family*. Princeton: Princeton University Press.

Folbre, N. (1982). 'Exploitation comes Home: A Critique of the Marxian Theory of Family Labour'. *Cambridge Journal of Economics*, 6: 317–29.

Gazeley, I. (2003). *Poverty in Britain, 1900–1965*. Basingstoke: Palgrave Macmillan.

Gershuny, J. (1983). *Social Innovation and the Division of Labour*. Oxford: Oxford University Press.

Gronau, R. (1977). 'Leisure, Home Production and Work: The Theory of the Allocation of Time Revisited'. *Journal of Political Economy*, 85: 1099–123.

Halsey, A. H., Heath, A., and Ridge, J. (1980). *Family, Class and Education in Modern Britain*. Oxford: Clarendon Press.

Hardyment, C. (1988). *From Mangle to Microwave: The Mechanization of Household Work*. Cambridge: Polity Press.

Harmon, C., and Walker, I. (1995). 'Estimates of the Economic Return to Schooling for the United Kingdom'. *American Economic Review*, 85, December: 1278–87.

Horrell, S. (1994). 'Household Time Allocation and Women's Labour Force Participation', in M. Anderson, F. Bechhofer, and J. Gershuny (eds.), *The Social and Political Economy of the Household*. Oxford: Oxford University Press, 198–224.

—— (2000). 'Living Standards in Britain 1900–2000: Women's Century?' *National Institute Economic Review*, 172, April: 62–77.

—— and Oxley, D. (2000). 'Work and Prudence: Household Responses to Income Variation in Nineteenth-Century Britain'. *European Review of Economic History*, 4: 27–57.

Johnson, W., and Skinner, J. (1986). 'Labor Supply and Marital Separation'. *American Economic Review*, 76: 455–69.

Joshi, H., Layard, R., and Owen, S. (1985). 'Why are More Women Working in Britain?' *Journal of Labour Economics*, 3, January, supplement: 147–76.

Juster, F. T., and Stafford, F. P. (1991). 'The Allocation of Time: Empirical Findings, Behavioral Models, and Problems of Measurement'. *Journal of Economic Literature*, 29, June: 471–522.

Laslett, P., with Wall, R. (eds.) (1972). *Household and Family in Past Time*. Cambridge: Cambridge University Press.

Lavalette, M. (ed.) (1999). *A Thing of the Past? Child Labour in Britain in the Nineteenth and Twentieth Centuries*. Liverpool: Liverpool University Press.

Macunovich, D. (2003). 'Economic Theories of Fertility', in K. S. Moe (ed.), *Women, Family and Work: Writings on the Economics of Gender*. Oxford: Blackwell Publishing, 105–24.

Mincer, J. (1962). 'Labor Force Participation of Married Women: A Study of Labor Supply', in *Aspects of Economics*, a report of the National Bureau of Economic Research. Princeton: Princeton University Press.

Mitch, D. (1984). 'Underinvestment in Literacy? The Potential Contribution of Government Involvement in Elementary Education to Economic Growth in Nineteenth-Century England'. *Journal of Economic History*, 44, June: 557–66.

Mitchell, B. R. (1988). *British Historical Statistics*. Cambridge: Cambridge University Press.

Morgensen, G. V. (1990). *Time and Consumption*. Copenhagen: Danmarks Statistik.

Nardinelli, C. (1990). *Child Labor and the Industrial Revolution*. Bloomington: Indiana University Press.

Ott, N. (1995). 'Fertility and Division of Work in the Family', in E. Kuiper and J. Sap (eds.), *Out of the Margin: Feminist Perspectives on Economics*. New York: Routledge, 80–99.

Pedersen, L. (1990). 'Determinants of Time Use Patterns for Men and Women in the Workforce', in G. V. Morgensen (ed.), *Time and Consumption*. Copenhagen: Danmarks Statistik, 95–122.

Pember Reeves, M. S. (1980). *Round about a Pound a Week*. London: Garland Publishing.

Piachaud, D. (1982). 'Patterns of Income and Expenditure within Families'. *Journal of Social Policy*, 11/4: 469–82.

Psacharopoulas, G. (1981). 'Returns to Education: An Updated International Comparison'. *Comparative Education*, 17: 321–41.

Rowntree, B. S. (1901). *Poverty: A Study of Town Life*. London: Macmillan.

Schwartz Cowan, R. (1976). 'The "Industrial Revolution" in the Home: Household Technology and Social Change in the 20th Century'. *Technology and Culture*, 17 January: 1–24.

Smith, I. (2002). 'European Divorce Laws, Divorce Rates and their Consequences', in A. W. Dnes and R. Rowthorn (eds.), *The Law and Economics of Marriage and Divorce*. Cambridge: Cambridge University Press, 212–29.

Smith, S. (2003). *Labour Economics*, 2nd edn. London: Routledge.

Strober, M. H., and Weinberg, C. B. (1980). 'Strategies Used by Working and Non-Working Wives to Reduce Time Pressures'. *Journal of Consumer Research*: 337–48.

Thane, P. (2000). *Old Age in English History: Past Experiences, Present Issues*. Oxford: Oxford University Press.

Todd, S. (2004). 'Young Women, Work and Leisure in Inter-War England'. Mimeo, Institute for Historical Research, London, forthcoming *Historical Journal*.

Vanek, J. (1974). 'Time Spent in Housework'. *Scientific American*, 231, November: 116–20.

Vickery, C. (1979). 'Women's Economic Contribution to the Family', in R. E. Smith (ed.), *The Subtle Revolution: Women at Work*. Washington: The Urban Institute, 159–200.

Wajcman, J. (1991). *Feminism Confronts Technology*. Cambridge: Polity Press.

7

Women and Work since 1970

Sara Connolly and Mary Gregory

7.1 The issues

The increased role of women in paid work has been one of the most sustained and significant economic trends of the second half of the twentieth century. In the UK the number of women in the labour force has risen from 7 million in the immediate post-war years to approaching 13 million. The male labour force, on the other hand, has been broadly static, even tending to decline. As a result, the expansion of employment in the UK is now accounted for entirely by the rising numbers of women in work. As the upward trend in women at work shows no sign of abating the new millennium brings the prospect of near parity of numbers between men and women in the labour force for the first time within the span of modern statistics.

While the experience of the UK has its individual features, the growing number of women in work[1] broadly parallels developments in the rest of the industrialized world. The most striking instance is the USA, where the number of women in work has doubled over the past generation at a time when the 'great American jobs machine' was expanding employment by 60 per cent overall. In Japan women's employment has increased by one-third over the same period. Across the European Union women are not only in work in record numbers, but, as in the UK, they are making up most, sometimes all, of the growth in employment.

Moreover, worldwide, women are now entering occupations and industries from which they were previously absent, or are entering these in increasing numbers. This development is particularly marked for managerial positions and in the professions. This progressive shift of women's economic activity from household to market place has brought an unprecedented degree of

[1] Throughout this chapter we will use 'work' to mean paid work. Unpaid work, as in the home, will be referred to as such.

financial independence for women, and has been a key element in the transformation of their economic and social status.

But while working women have made, and continue to make, major economic gains the position of women in employment does not parallel their
numerical role. On average they receive lower pay, occupy a much smaller share
of 'top jobs', and are much more likely to work part time. Gender segregation
in jobs remains marked, with women's employment concentrated into a
relatively narrow range of activities. Women predominate in part-time work,
where the types of jobs available, and the opportunities for career advancement, are limited. Most conspicuously in Britain, women are by far the largest
category of the low paid. In the EU generally, although not in Britain, unemployment rates for women are higher than for men. It is clear that equality of
outcomes in the labour market has not been achieved. Largely unmeasured in
economic statistics, but of great practical importance, outside the labour market women still provide the bulk of childcare and other non-market services.

These persistent differences in gender roles and circumstances can be presented as evidence of continuing unequal treatment for women. For some, the
persistence of unequal outcomes, with the restricted individual opportunities
and underutilization of female abilities which it implies, is economically
inefficient and socially inequitable. A generation after the introduction of
comprehensive anti-discrimination legislation in most countries, and after
several decades of massive social change, discrimination or 'unequal treatment' is still seen as a major issue. For others, unequal outcomes should not be
unexpected and need not be unacceptable. If the labour market position of
women is freely chosen in the face of equal opportunities then there is no
cause for concern at its 'inferiority' and intervention would be distortionary.
For others again, there is the uneasy feeling that genuinely equal opportunities
are not on offer, but that the issue of parity in the labour market is secondary to
issues of parity in the home and in non-market work. The role of women in
childbearing and child rearing poses a basic difference or inequality to which
there are no simple counters; but it should not lead to a lifetime's difference in
economic status.

Yet others, however, voice an opposing concern. As the demand for low-
skilled manual labour declines it is male jobs which are being lost.
Simultaneously, the declining role of traditional skilled and semi-skilled jobs,
notably in manufacturing, has been eroding employment in traditional male
heartlands. Not only are women already taking a disproportionate share of
new jobs, but this trend is likely to accentuate with the emphasis on 'soft' skills
in the increasingly dominant service sector. Natural advantage now seems to
be favouring women, with men the disadvantaged group. The fact that a
minority, but a significant and growing one, of complaints to the Equal
Opportunities Commission are now made by men may be seen as a straw in
the wind on this.

This chapter assesses the changing position of women in the labour market against the background of these conflicting attitudes. Our primary focus will be the UK, but other advanced economies will be used to provide a perspective against which to assess British experience and performance. In reviewing the evidence our basic criteria will be the efficiency and equity of the present and prospective position of women in the labour market. But this is an area where the interaction of economic with social factors is also of central importance. Women increasingly engage in paid work because social attitudes are changing; social attitudes change because more women are in work. In a rapidly changing economic and social environment any assessment of gender roles and gender discrimination has to aim at a moving target.

Section 7.2 reviews the changing position of women in the labour force. Section 7.3 outlines the legal context of women's work, involving equal pay, equal opportunities, and maternity rights. Section 7.4 looks at the jobs that women do, tracing the trends in activity rates, occupational structure, and gender segregation. Section 7.5 confronts the issue of the gender pay gap, analysing the changing characteristics which women bring to work, such as educational attainment and work experience, and the rewards which these earn in the labour market. For women in full-time work we find evidence of significant progress over recent decades. But in the extremely important area of part-time work we find a very different picture. In many respects women in part-time work constitute a new underclass in the labour market. Section 7.6, on work and the family, looks at the ways in which women combine employment with domestic responsibilities. Section 7.7 concludes by considering present problems and future prospects for women in the labour market.

7.2. Women into paid work

The number of women in work in the UK has risen virtually without interruption over the past half-century, from 7 million in 1951, to 9 million in 1971, to just over 13 million in 2000, an average growth rate of 1.3 per cent per year. Figure 7.1a illustrates the record over recent decades. Over 70 per cent of women between the ages of 16 and 59 are now classified as economically active, against 56 per cent in 1971 and around 40 per cent in 1951. Since the number of men in the labour force has remained static, women have made up the entire net expansion of the UK workforce over this period (Figure 7.1b).

This record on women's participation in paid work gives the UK an intermediate position among the advanced economies (see Table 7.1). The highest participation rates occur in the Scandinavian countries, followed by the USA and Canada. The activity rate in the UK is markedly higher than in Germany or France, while rates are lowest in the southern European countries, Italy

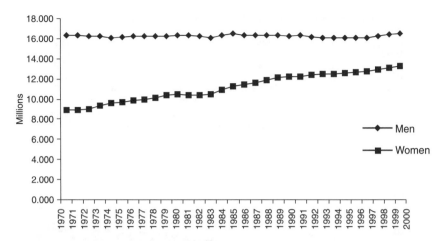

Figure 7.1a Men and women in the labour force
Source: OECD Labour Force Statistics, various years (1970–90, 1980–2001).

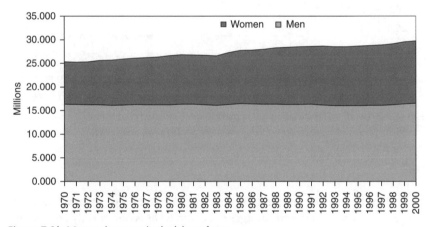

Figure 7.1b Men and women in the labour force
Source: OECD Labour Force Statistics, various years (1970–90, 1980–2001).

and Spain. While diversity remains, there has been a marked trend towards convergence over the past thirty years, with women's participation growing particularly strongly in those countries where it is still lowest, while remaining static, or even declining, in the Scandinavian countries, where it is already established at high levels (Figure 7.2).

These activity rates are in sharp contrast to the rates of around 30 per cent which prevailed widely over the 100 years prior to the Second World War. The

Table 7.1. Female labour force participation rates, selected countries, 2000 (%)

Norway	73.4	Australia	66.8	Germany	58.1
Sweden	72.1	UK	65.2	France	53.1
Poland	72.0	Canada	65.1	Ireland	52.2
Denmark	71.2	Japan	62.7	Spain	40.3
USA	68.0	The Netherlands	62.1	Italy	39.7

Notes: Women aged 15–64; minimum school leaving and pensionable ages differ across countries.
Source: Social Situation in Europe. Eurostat 2003 and Society at a Glance and Employment Outlook OECD, 2002.

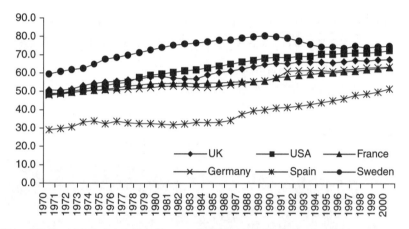

Figure 7.2 Trends in female labour force participation, selected countries
Source: OECD Labour Force Statistics, various years (1970–90, 1976–96, 1990–2004).

1931 Population Census for Great Britain, for example, reported only 26 per cent of women between the ages of 25 and 64 as economically active. This comprised 61 per cent of single, widowed, and divorced women, and 10 per cent of married women.[2] The first major impetus to the expansion of women's employment, through the 1950s and 1960s, was the erosion of the marriage bar, the convention (sometimes compulsory) of resignation from paid work on marriage. This brought a doubling of the proportion of married women who were in work, from 23 per cent in 1951 to 46 per cent in 1971. In the course of the 1960s, for the first time for many generations, marriage ceased to be the most frequent reason for women leaving employment.[3]

[2] Further figures, for this and other years, are given in *British Labour Statistics: Historical Abstract*, 1886–1968, especially table 109.   [3] See Hakim (1979) and Joshi et al. (1985).

Most married women are also mothers, and this changing employment status for married women was soon transformed into a growing labour market presence by mothers. Over recent decades the next wave of change has been carried forward by mothers remaining in, or returning to, work, in increasing numbers in the childbearing and child caring years. While women of all ages are now more likely to be in paid work than in previous generations, much the biggest change has been among women in their late twenties and early thirties. In 1971 participation dipped sharply in this age group. Over the 1970s it increased, but only at a rate similar to other age groups; in the 1980s it rose sharply, such that by 1991 only a minor dip was still evident; by 2001 the dip had been filled in completely (Figure 7.3).

A similar pattern of change in the activity rates of younger women has occurred across the advanced economies (Figure 7.4). The upward trend has been strong everywhere except recently in Sweden, where it has declined somewhat from an earlier rate of almost 90 per cent. As with activity rates as a whole, the trend towards international convergence is striking, with participation rates for young women, widely spread in the early 1970s, now remarkably similar across the developed countries.

Most notably in Britain, this expansion of women's employment has taken the form of a growth in part-time work (Figure 7.5). Full-time employment for women has risen only marginally, from 5.5 million in 1971 to just over 6 million in 2000. In spite of this relatively flat trend full-time employment remains

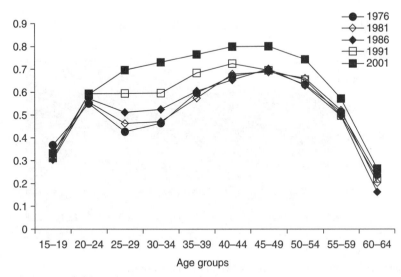

Figure 7.3 Female labour force participation by age group, UK

Source: ILO Yearbook of Labour Statistics, various years (1945–89, 1993, 2003).

the most common type of activity among working women. Part-time employment, by contrast, has almost doubled, from 2.8 to 5.8 million. This expansion of part-time work has dominated the growth of women's employment over this period. Motherhood has replaced marriage as the major influence on a

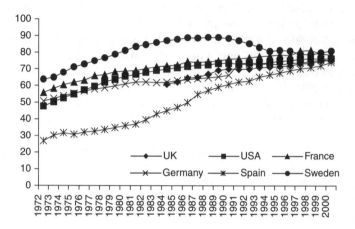

Figure 7.4 Labour force participation by women aged 25–34, selected countries
Source: OECD Labour Force Statistics, various years (1970–90, 1976–96) and ILO statistics, various years (1990–2005).

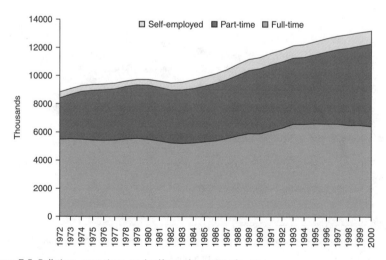

Figure 7.5 Full-time, part-time, and self-employment of women
Source: Employment Gazette, Historical Supplement 4, various years (1971–93), and Annual Abstract of Statistics, Labour Market Trends, various years (1992–2003).

woman's employment status, as part-time employment has increasingly established itself as one of the major routes through which women combine paid work with responsibilities for child rearing.

The assessment of this record on women in employment and its implications for the position of women will be the focus of the remainder of the chapter.

7.3 Women and discrimination

The legal framework for the position of women in employment was set in three complementary pieces of legislation enacted in the first half of 1970s, the Equal Pay Act, the Sex Discrimination Act, and the Employment Protection Act. These three areas—equal pay, equal opportunities, and maternity rights in employment—are still those which are central to women's position in the labour market and the debates on discrimination.

7.3.1 *Equal pay and pay discrimination*

The Equal Pay Act, passed in 1970, has as its central provision equal pay for men and women doing 'the same or broadly similar work'. By 1975, after the five-year transition period allowed, separate pay scales for men and women, now illegal, had disappeared as women's rates were integrated with men's. In establishing the legal commitment to equal pay the UK was following a widespread trend, although as a relative laggard. The Treaty of Rome, establishing the European Economic Community with its original six members in 1957, had already committed each member state to 'maintain the principle of equal remuneration for equal work as between men and women workers' (art. 119).

The issue of equality in pay was not, however, to be settled so easily. Men and women often perform different jobs, giving rise to marked gender segregation across occupations. Where this horizontal segregation prevails, the requirement to pay men and women on the same pay scales can be largely irrelevant. Men and women employed in 'female occupations' are often observed paid at equal, but equally low, rates; a preponderance of women in the workforce may bring lower pay for men there. To counter this, 'equal pay for equal work' has now been replaced by the requirement of 'equal pay for work of equal value'. This redefinition was reluctantly adopted by the UK government in 1983 following an EC Directive (later confirmed by the European Court of Justice) extending article 119 to 'comparable worth'—one of a number of instances where developments within the European Union have set the pace for the UK in advancing women's rights in employment.[4]

---

[4] Formally, the UK had already been committed to this for many years. The International Labour Office (ILO) in its Convention 100 of 1951 had pledged its signatory states, which

Implementing 'equal value' provisions is an altogether more complex matter than outlawing discrimination in the form of separate pay scales for men and women. Where men and women do different jobs, it requires detailed evaluation of the skills and responsibilities involved, along with the relative desirability of the jobs (their net advantages, following Adam Smith's famous discussion). This may at least in principle be attainable where the jobs are with a single employer. It can certainly be successfully contested, as in the landmark ruling which found the work of a female cook in a shipyard canteen to be of equal value with that of her more highly paid male colleagues, a painter, an insulation engineer, and a joiner.[5] It has also led to pre-emptive revisions to company pay structures in line with equal value assessments, as when Marks and Spencer plc raised the pay of 44,000 sales assistants by an average of 26.5 per cent to bring them into line with warehouse workers.[6] But to establish on an economy-wide basis how far the stipulation of equal pay for work of equal value is met in practice, and how far unequal treatment persists, requires a more general approach.

7.3.2 Equal opportunities

The Sex Discrimination Act of 1975 outlawed unequal treatment in other aspects of employment, including hiring, promotion opportunities, job transfer, provision of training, and dismissal procedures. This was seen as complementary to the right to equal pay, which becomes nugatory if access to jobs and rights in employment are restricted. The Act also established the Equal Opportunities Commission, with the tasks of monitoring the implementation of the law, advising on the promotion of equal opportunities, and assisting complainants. This legislation was influenced by the US Civil Rights Act of 1964, Title VII of which outlaws discrimination; the immediate motivation in the US case was to counter racial discrimination, but the Act was to give a major impetus to addressing gender discrimination.[7]

Traditionally women's lower levels of education have brought unequal opportunities in access to jobs—'discrimination before the market'. The reduced demand for education by women could derive from expected career breaks shortening the expected working life over which the return would be gained. Alternatively, it could derive from the lower wage return which it would earn—anticipated discrimination. In either case the predictions tend to

included the UK, to 'ensure the application to all workers of the principle of equal remuneration for men and women workers for work of equal value'. Unlike EC Directives, compliance with the terms of ILO Conventions is voluntary and in this case was not honoured.

[5] *Hayward* v. *Cammell Laird* 5979/84. The pay rise she was awarded following the ruling was 31%.　　　　　　　　　　　　　　　　[6] For further details see Perlman and Pike (1994: ch. 5).

[7] For a detailed review of these developments for the USA and the UK see Dex and Shaw (1986).

be self-fulfilling, as lower earnings weaken attachment to paid work. When anticipated discrimination leads to underinvestment in education differences in attributes are themselves the outcomes of discrimination. Similarly the anticipated return to the investment in employer-provided training will be lower if early termination or any break in employment is expected. When women receive less training their opportunities for career advancement and salary gains are reduced, in turn making continuing employment a less attractive option. For these reasons equal pay must be set in the context of equal opportunities.

7.3.3 Maternity rights

For women with family responsibilities the commitment to equal opportunities may be ineffective if domestic circumstances prevent their participation in paid work. The first step towards recognition of this was the Employment Protection Act of 1975 which introduced statutory maternity pay, payable for fourteen weeks, and job protection during maternity leave. Mothers were given the right to reinstatement in their previous job for up to twenty-nine weeks after the birth of a child, provided they had been working for their employer on a full-time basis for two years or for five years part time. In 1994 the European Court of Justice, on grounds of equal treatment, forced the extension of maternity rights to all working women, regardless of tenure and full-time or part-time status. All women who have worked during pregnancy now have the right to job-protected maternity leave, extended in 2005 to twenty-six weeks.[8]

Childbirth is only the start of a substantial period in which labour market participation is made more difficult, overwhelmingly for women, by responsibilities for childcare. While unequal treatment may not be the most useful way of characterizing this issue, a potential interaction with discrimination is clear. When women face low wages in paid work they are more likely to accept, and be expected to accept, the main burden of domestic responsibilities. To the extent that this domestic orientation implies reduced commitment to paid employment, the result will be continuing lower wages. On the view that unequal treatment in the labour market is the primary source for this sequence of events, this is not only inequitable but inefficient. Women are induced to

---

[8] 'Pregnant employees are entitled to 26 weeks' ordinary maternity leave, regardless of how long they have worked for their employer. Most mothers will usually qualify to be paid Statutory Maternity Pay or Maternity Allowance during ordinary maternity leave. (For more information see below). Women who have completed 26 weeks' continuous service with their employer by the beginning of the 14th week before their EWC can take additional maternity leave. Additional maternity leave starts immediately after ordinary maternity leave and continues for a further 26 weeks. Additional maternity leave is usually unpaid although a woman may have contractual rights to pay during her period of additional maternity leave.' DTI (2005). **www.dti.gov.uk/er/individual/mat-pl958.htm**

substitute domesticity for paid employment, bringing less development of their skills and productive potential than if equal rewards had been available.

This interpretation of unequal labour market outcomes in terms of discrimination does not go unchallenged. Where men and women differ systematically in their preferences between paid work and its attributes, and the rewards of the domestic environment, equal outcomes are not to be expected, even if the labour market meted out only equal treatment. Differing and complementary lifestyles for men and women can be both efficient and equitable.[9] This issue of differing tastes and its relationship to discrimination is addressed further below.

7.4 The jobs that women do

7.4.1 *Personal characteristics of working women*

Women now comprise 44.5 per cent of the UK labour force. They are one-third of the full-time workforce, making them still clearly a minority, although a substantial one. This minority status contrasts sharply with their dominant position in part-time work, where they are 85 per cent of the workforce. While the number of women in full-time employment has been rising only marginally, the characteristics which they bring to work and the jobs which they do have been changing in important ways. Equally, the strong growth of part-time work has shaped, and been shaped by, the changing types of jobs in the economy. This section reviews the jobs which women do in full-time and part-time work, and compares these with the jobs performed by the (overwhelmingly full-time) male workforce. The jobs performed by women in full-time and part-time work differ at least as significantly from each other as each does from the jobs performed by men.

For both men and women economic activity rates[10] peak at ages 25–49, normally regarded as the prime working years. Almost all men in this age group are economically active, as are a substantial majority of women (Table 7.2). The gap between men's and women's activity rates is, however, also at its widest then. Whereas almost all economically active men of prime age are in full-time employment, only half of the women are working full time. Part-time work is an important activity for women in all age groups, most notably for women over the age of 40. By contrast, fewer than 8 per cent of men engage in part-time work. Looking after the family or home, of negligible importance as a main activity for men, features for women in all age groups, most markedly between the ages of 25 and 39.

---

[9] Authors at least partially sympathetic to this view include Mincer and Polachek (1974), Becker (1981), and Hakim (1996).

[10] These include the self-employed, the unemployed, and those on government training and employment programmes as well as those in employment.

Table 7.2. Employment status of men and women, 2000 (%)

Age group	Men		Women			
	Economically active	In full-time work	Economically active	In full-time work	In part-time work	Looking after family/home
16–24	72.4	52.4	65.3	42.0	30.4	8.0
25–39	93.8	93.0	75.4	52.0	37.7	17.9
40–9	91.6	92.0	79.2	47.1	40.2	10.4
50–9/64[a]	72.4	81.4	65.9	41.9	40.2	9.9
All ages	83.8	82.9	72.5	47.0	37.6	12.8

Note: 7.7% of men work part-time, 0.9% are looking after family/home (all ages).

[a] Men to age 64, women to age 59.

Source: Labour Force Survey 2000.

Table 7.3. Women's employment status by marriage and dependent children, 2000 (%)

	Full-time employment	Part-time employment	Looking after family/home
Married or living together	36.8	40.1	14.1
Not married or living together[a]	46.4	25.6	9.4
With dependent children	28.8	43.5	23.6
Without dependent children	54.4	27.4	4.9

[a] Includes single, widowed, divorced, and separated women if not cohabiting.

Source: Labour Force Survey 2000.

Marriage historically marked a major divide between women who took paid work and those who stayed at home, a divide never relevant for men. The main influence on women's employment status is now parenthood (although marriage partially overlaps with this) (Table 7.3). The presence of dependent children sharply reduces women's participation in full-time work, mothers (of any marital status) being only half as likely to be in full-time work as women without dependent children. Conversely, mothers are substantially more likely to work part time than women without dependent children (44 against 27 per cent). For women without dependent children looking after family or home has almost disappeared as the major activity. Among mothers, however, the numbers of full-time homemakers are only marginally smaller than the numbers in full-time employment. Motherhood is now clearly the dominant influence on women's employment status.

A further restriction on women's labour market status has for long been their lower levels of educational attainment. The past twenty years have witnessed a substantial rise in the average levels of qualification among the UK workforce as a whole due to greatly increased rates of enrolment in post-compulsory

Table 7.4. Educational attainment of men and women (%)

	1981			1991			2000		
	Men	Women		Men	Women		Men	Women	
		Full time	Part time		Full time	Part time		Full time	Part time
All aged 16–59	100	100	100	100	100	100	100	100	100
Degree/higher	11	11	4	16	14	6	21	25	11
A levels or equiv.	39	18	12	19	20	12	41	31	29
O levels/GCSEs	15	34	22	36	43	39	28	35	43
No qualifications	35	38	61	30	23	42	10	9	18
Aged 16–24									
Degree/higher	4	4	2	5	5	2	10	18	4
A levels or equiv.	46	21	14	22	25	16	41	48	40
O levels/GCSEs	28	55	58	52	58	63	41	32	46
No qualifications	23	20	26	22	11	19	8	3	10
Aged 25–34									
Degree/higher	16	20	6	19	18	6	25	32	11
A levels or equiv.	42	21	16	23	26	17	39	32	31
O levels/GCSEs	14	30	27	37	45	51	30	32	49
No qualifications	28	29	51	20	12	26	6	4	9
Aged 35–49									
Degree/higher	14	13	4	20	19	8	23	25	13
A levels or equiv.	37	14	12	17	15	11	43	27	28
O levels/GCSEs	11	21	20	30	34	35	25	37	42
No qualifications	39	52	64	32	32	46	9	11	17
Aged 50–9									
Degree/higher	10	8	2	13	12	4	19	21	11
A levels or equiv.	30	12	9	11	11	7	42	22	20
O levels/GCSEs	8	15	12	27	30	23	23	36	36
No qualifications	52	65	77	49	47	65	16	21	33

Note: Percentages sum to 100 across qualification levels within each age/gender group.
Source: LFS 1981, 1991, and 2000.

education. Women have been particularly to the fore in this development. In 2003 59 per cent of girls gained five or more GCSE passes at grades A*–C, against 48 per cent of boys. At A level women, having surpassed men for the first time in 1989, continue to pull ahead, 43 per cent of girls obtaining two or more passes compared with 34 per cent of boys and 47 per cent of girls obtaining one or more passes compared with 38 per cent of boys. Enrolments by men in first-level degree programmes are around 80 per cent higher than in 1970, while enrolments by women have increased fourfold; women students now outnumber men 54 to 46 per cent.[11]

But this rise in educational attainment by women predominantly involves the younger age groups, in spite of the growing numbers of mature students in

---

[11] See *Social Trends*, annual issues, for further details.

further and higher education. Although it is a powerful force for change it has not yet eliminated the historically lower levels of education and qualification among women in the labour force as a whole.

The gender gap in qualifications has, however, largely disappeared when women who work full time are compared with men. While both groups have moved strongly away from the position in the 1970s when 'no qualifications' was the norm, the change by women has been the most emphatic. By the early 1990s the proportion of women in full-time work who had no qualifications, 23 per cent, was already well below the 30 per cent among men; this gap continues to widen as girls increasingly outperform boys at school. Equally strikingly, at the other end of the qualifications scale, the proportion of women working full time who are qualified to degree level or equivalent now matches that for men. The younger age cohorts are the spearhead in this development, with women under the age of 35 in full-time work more likely than men to be qualified to degree level or equivalent.

However, the major area of employment growth for women is in part-time work, and here the improvement in women's educational status is much less marked. While the proportion of part-time women holding qualifications has increased substantially at each level, almost halving the number without qualifications, women working part time remain the least qualified group, as they were in the early 1980s, and significantly less qualified than both women working full time and men.

Part of the dynamic behind the differing educational status of women in full-time as against part-time employment is that the incentive for labour market participation, and the response to it, rise with educational attainment, particularly for women. In 2000, 86 per cent of women with tertiary-level education were economically active compared with 50 per cent of women with less than secondary-level qualifications (OECD, *Employment Outlook* 2002). Women with qualifications, particularly at higher educational levels, have access to better-paid jobs. They are therefore more able to afford childcare, particularly if they work full time. Moreover, absence from the labour market is most costly in terms of future career advancement for these women, creating a higher opportunity cost of a career break. As a consequence, women with higher qualifications are more likely to be in full-time employment and to take shorter breaks from it.

7.4.2 Occupational structure, segregation, and the 'glass ceiling'

What jobs do women do, and how far are there specifically 'female' jobs in the modern economy? Table 7.5 shows that, while men are evenly divided between manual and non-manual jobs, women are heavily concentrated in non-manual occupations. This is particularly the case among women in full-time work. Many men and few women work in craft or machine operative jobs, while the

Table 7.5. The distribution of occupations, 2000 (%)

	Men	Women	
		Full-time employment	Part-time employment
Managers and administrators	19.8	17.4	5.1
Professionals	11.8	12.7	6.2
of which			
Science and engineering	4.5	1.1	0.3
Health professionals	0.9	0.9	0.6
Teaching	2.9	7.7	4.3
Associate professional and technical occupations	9.0	13.9	9.3
of which			
Health associate	0.7	5.7	5.3
Teaching associate	4.9	6.6	3.6
Clerical and secretarial	6.7	27.0	21.5
Craft and related	20.3	2.4	1.2
Personal and protective services	6.5	12.3	21.8
Sales occupations	5.3	6.4	18.5
Plant and machine operatives	13.3	4.8	2.2
Other occupations	7.3	3.2	14.2
Total	100	100	100

Source: Labour Force Survey 2000. Occupations are at the level of the Major and Sub-Major Groups of the Standard Occupational Classification.

reverse is the case in clerical and secretarial jobs. Beyond that, however, the differences between men's and women's jobs are less significant than the differences between the jobs held by women working full time and those working part time. Among women working full time the top occupations, managers and administrators, and professionals, feature almost as prominently as among men—more prominently if associate professionals are included. Within these, men are more strongly represented in science and engineering, women in teaching and health. Women in part-time work, on the other hand, are severely under-represented in the top occupations, particularly as managers and administrators. Their employment is disproportionately concentrated in sales and 'other' low-skill occupations (catering assistants, cleaners). To contrast 'men's' and 'women's' jobs is therefore to miss key dimensions. Women working full time, who are increasingly the equal of men in education and qualifications, do rather different jobs from men, in different professions and in offices rather than factories, but at broadly the same occupational level. Women who work part time, on the other hand, remain significantly less well qualified, are under-represented in the higher-level occupations, and are concentrated into a relatively narrow range of lower-level jobs.

The claim is sometimes made that women hold lower-status jobs than men. While this would be consistent with their lower levels of qualification, the

Table 7.6. Employment of men and women by social class (%)

		1981			1991			2000		
		Men	Women		Men	Women		Men	Women	
			Full time	Part time		Full time	Part time		Full time	Part time
I	Professional	5.8	1.4	0.4	8.0	4.4	1.6	9.1	4.5	1.8
II	Managerial and technical	20.7	23.3	12.0	27.2	32.1	15.8	31.2	40.4	19.4
III	Skilled: non-manual	12.7	44.7	35.4	12.8	39.2	39.7	11.9	33.6	40.1
III	Skilled: manual	37.6	10.2	6.1	32.5	9.2	6.9	29.7	8.0	6.9
IV	Partly skilled	17.6	18.4	29.4	14.4	12.8	20.2	13.4	12.0	21.9
V	Unskilled	5.6	2.0	16.7	4.1	2.0	15.8	4.0	1.4	10.0
	Armed forces				1.0	0.3	0.1	0.7	0.1	0.0
All		100	100	100	100	100	100	100	100	100

Source: LFS 1981, 1991, and 2000.

sharper thrust of the assertion is in terms of the reverse causality: jobs are accorded lower status because they are held predominantly by women. The social class structure of employment, shown in Table 7.6, in part rejects and in part supports this view. As with the occupational structure, the main divide is between women working full time and those working part time. Social Class I, top professional jobs, has traditionally been a male preserve, and men's presence there continues to grow. Women in full-time work are beginning to establish themselves there, although still at only half the rate for men. Social Class II, managerial and technical occupations, has been a major growth area for both men and women, particularly for women working full time. It includes a wide range of newer managerial positions, such as building society branch managers, alongside the traditional female professions of teaching and nursing. In a highly significant development, more women in full-time work are now in Class II jobs than in Class III (non-manual) which includes most secretarial jobs. Among women working part time, however, although Class II jobs are again growing in importance, Class III secretarial jobs remain the dominant category. The main area where male jobs have been lost, skilled manual jobs in Class III, is not an important area of employment for women; in this respect segregation has been an advantage. The view that women are crowded into low-status jobs is strongly supported in the case of part-timers, one-third of whom hold partly skilled and unskilled jobs in Classes IV and V, twice the rate among those working full time and among men.

The greater occupational concentration of female, particularly part-time, jobs is easily confirmed. In Figure 7.6 Lorenz curves are constructed from the 371 occupations at the Unit Group level of the Standard Occupational Classification (SOC90) ranked in ascending order of employment size. The

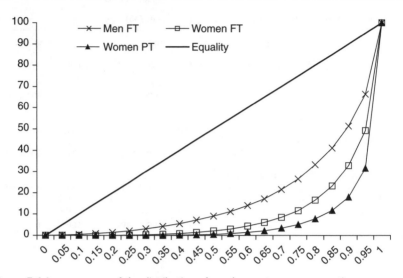

Figure 7.6 Lorenz curves of the distribution of employment across occupations: men, and women in full- and part-time work, LFS 2000

least occupationally concentrated pattern of employment is for men working full time.[12] Female employment in full-time jobs is more concentrated, and part-time employment for women more concentrated still.

All 371 occupations feature in the distribution of male employment; women working full time are present in 290, and women working part time in only 235. Among the male workforce the five largest occupational groups employ 15 per cent of men in employment (goods vehicle drivers; sales managers; production managers; fitters; storekeepers). Among women in full-time work the corresponding figure is 23 per cent (general clerks; accounts clerks; general secretarial; nurses; primary teachers) and among women working part time this rises to 38 per cent (sales assistants; cleaners; care assistants; general clerks; nurses). Similarly the top ten occupations for men employ 24 per cent of men in work; among women working full time 37 per cent, and among women working part time 53 per cent.

The pattern of gender segregation in the UK is broadly in line with experience internationally. A study of seven countries (OECD 1998) using a set of 50–80 occupational groups shows that between 60 and 80 per cent of women are employed in the 'top ten' largest occupations. The top ten, which include clerical work, sales, teaching, nursing, and cleaning, are remarkably similar across countries, although in the USA and Canada managerial occupations also

[12] Only full-time employment for men is used since the numbers working part time are small and concentrated towards the ends of the age range.

feature. The study finds no clear trend towards reduced concentration of women's employment in female jobs, although they note some evidence for this in the UK, and in the USA and Norway. Rubery et al. (1996), who examine indices of segregation and dissimilarity, conclude that European labour markets are highly segregated and that little change has occurred, a conclusion shared by Jonung and Persson (1998).

These measures of segregation by occupation, however, fail to measure the status of women *within* individual occupations. The failure of women to achieve career advancement comparable to men's in management and the professions is recognized as the 'glass ceiling'. Women, who are 44 per cent of the labour force and 33 per cent of full-time workers, hold 24 per cent of the jobs in Social Class I. In the mid-2000s there is only one woman chief executive among the FTSE 100 leading companies, and fewer than 5 per cent of main board directors of public companies are women. Women are 6 per cent of QCs and 7 per cent of judges, with only one female High Court judge. Only 30 per cent of heads and deputy heads of secondary schools are female, although women make up more than half of the teaching staff. The list can be extended across occupations at all levels.[13] Segregation, in a vertical sense, persists even within mixed occupations as long as promoted positions remain male dominated.

The evidence that men and women do different jobs is not sufficient to establish discrimination or unequal treatment, although it may provide pointers. The key issue is not how far segregation exists, but how it affects women's well-being in the labour market. Horizontal segregation, with men and women holding different jobs at the same level, may reflect differing preferences and choices, without necessary disadvantage to women. It is notable that horizontal segregation occurs in occupations at all levels, professional (teachers), intermediate (secretaries), and low skilled (counter assistants). However, where women are concentrated in certain occupations because of restricted opportunities elsewhere, or where this concentration depresses their earnings, this is unequal treatment. Where women are unduly restricted in their access to promoted positions, depriving them of career advancement with the satisfaction, prestige, and remuneration which go with it, this vertical discrimination is both inequitable and inefficient. Much of this can be measured through the gender earnings gap. This gap and its sources are examined in the next section.

7.5 Assessing discrimination against women in employment

Women earn less than men. This statement has almost universal validity, going back to Old Testament times.[14] But it is not immutable. Over recent years

---

[13] For further instances see *Social Focus on Men and Women*, annual issues.

[14] 'the valuation shall be for the male . . . fifty sheikels of silver . . . and if it be a female then the valuation shall be thirty sheikels', Leviticus 27: 1–4.

the gender pay gap in Britain has been changing in significant and sometimes subtle ways. First we review these developments. We then assess how far the gap can be explained by differing relevant characteristics of men and women, and how far it is attributable to unequal treatment, implying discrimination.

7.5.1 *The gender gap in pay*

Women's pay remains clearly and systematically below men's on each of the three measures shown in Figure 7.7—weekly and hourly pay for men and women in full-time work, and hourly pay between men in full-time work and women working part time. The earnings gap between women and men in full-time work is greater when measured by weekly earnings than by hourly earnings, with women receiving 85 per cent of men's hourly earnings against 76 per cent of their weekly earnings in 2000. This difference reflects the shorter weekly hours typically worked by women, and has remained virtually constant at around 10 percentage points over the past thirty years. The basis chosen for measuring the gender pay gap therefore has a significant impact on its size although not on the trend.

The relative pay of women in full-time work has shown a clear upward trend on both measures, from 54 to 76 per cent of men's in the case of weekly earnings, and from 62 to 85 per cent for hourly earnings. The most rapid gains were made in the mid-1970s, with the gap narrowing by 8 percentage points

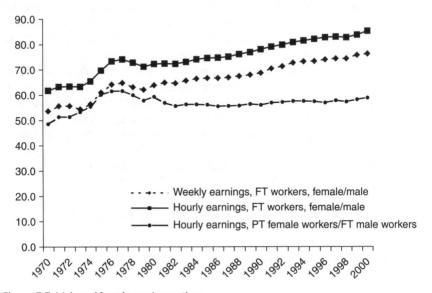

Figure 7.7 Male and female earnings ratios
Source: NES published tables.

between 1974 and 1976, coinciding with the implementation of the Equal Pay Act and the passing of the Sex Discrimination Act.[15] After levelling off briefly in the immediate aftermath, the pay of women in full-time work relative to men has risen steadily but slowly since the early 1980s, narrowing the gender gap by around a half percentage point per year. Women who work part time, on the other hand, are not sharing in these gains. They too experienced a sharp, but brief, gain in the mid-1970s, but over more than twenty years since that time their hourly earnings have shown a marginal decline relative to those of men working full time. At their peak in 1976–7 they were 62 per cent of men's; throughout the 1990s the ratio was steady at 57 per cent, rising to 59 per cent by 2000.[16] A further implication of these developments is that the two groups of working women, in full-time and part-time work, have moved further apart as the relative pay gains realized by women in full-time work have not been matched by part-timers. The average hourly earnings of women in part-time work have declined from 85 per cent of those for full-time women in the mid-1970s to under 70 per cent in 2000. These trends in the gender pay gap reiterate the point already made from various perspectives: women in employment are two separate populations, those who work full time and those who work part time, with sharply differing labour market outcomes.

The pay disadvantage for women is repeated in each of the nine major occupational groups as shown in Figure 7.8. Professional occupations (Group 2) give women the highest earnings in absolute terms and relative to their male counterparts; women professionals who work full time receive on average 93 per cent of men's pay, with those who work part time actually earning a slight premium over those working full time. Women managers (Group 1) are well paid relative to women in other occupations, but face the widest gender gap, receiving 71 per cent of men's earnings in full-time work and only 62 per cent in part-time work. For both full- and part-time work the gender gap is conspicuously wider in manual jobs, Groups 5–9, than in non-manual occupations. Within individual occupations the hourly pay of women working part time is typically between 75 and 95 per cent of women who work full time (except professionals). This is less than half of the size of the gap in the aggregate in Figure 7.7. The pay disadvantage experienced by women in part-time work derives more importantly from their concentration into lower-wage occupations than from lower pay within each occupation.

Differences in national definitions and coverage mean that earnings statistics cannot be compared exactly across countries, but 'no matter how the gender wage gap is measured, women's hourly earnings are below those

---

[15] The Equal Pay Act was passed in 1970 but a five-year notice period was allowed before full implementation of its provisions.

[16] This small recovery, already detectable in 1999, reflects the introduction of the national minimum wage in April 1999, from which women working part time were the largest group of beneficiaries.

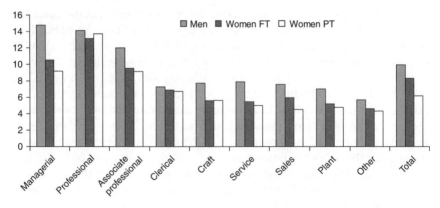

Figure 7.8 Male and female hourly earnings by occupations, 2000
Source: LFS 2000.

received by men in all countries', with an average wage gap of 16 per cent in recent years, down by one-quarter over the preceding twenty years (OECD 2002). For women working full time the gender pay gap in the UK, measured at 20 per cent, is one of the widest in the OECD group of nineteen advanced economies. Women in part-time jobs appear not to suffer any additional penalty in many of the OECD countries, including the Netherlands, where the incidence of part-time work is the highest; the UK, however, is one of the small group of exceptions to this.

7.5.2 *The gender pay gap across the distribution*

Most of the analysis of the gender pay gap is based on a comparison of the average female wage with the average male wage. A further question we might pose is: does the average provide an accurate reflection of the pay gap experienced at the top and bottom ends of the earnings distribution, and in different parts of the country? Table 7.7 shows that the gender pay gap is often wider at the top of the distribution and narrower at the bottom decile, and also shows significant regional variation. The gender gap at the lower end of the pay distribution has narrowed significantly since the introduction of the national minimum wage in 1999—so significantly that its main impact may already have been achieved. In their analysis of the impact of the NMW the Low Pay Commission (2005) state that:

We found clear evidence suggesting that the minimum wage has had a major impact in narrowing the gap between women workers and that of men at the lower end of the earnings distribution . . . . The minimum wage has now had such a marked effect at the bottom of the distribution that only a very large uprating in relation to average earnings would have much further effect.

Table 7.7. The gender pay gap for low- and high-paid workers; gross hourly earnings of full-time workers by region (April 2003)

Country/region	Lowest decile %	Highest decile %
England	10.2	20.5
Wales	8.4	5.2
Scotland	9.4	20.7
Great Britain	10.4	19.9
North-east	10.5	5.6
North-west	9.8	14.6
Yorkshire and the Humber	14.2	12.8
East Midlands	12.7	15.8
West Midlands	14.7	13.3
South-west	10.9	22.0
East	11.6	25.8
London	2.3	27.0
South-east	10.3	30.3

Source: New Earnings Survey 2003, vol. ii; Corby et al. (2005).

Whilst women's lower qualifications and experience and the type of jobs which they do might provide an explanation for a gender pay gap at the lower end of the distribution, in specialist job markets such as the professions a narrower gender gap may be expected. With professional qualifications clearly defined, all of those employed in the sector have made the same high levels of investment in human capital and typically have a strong career commitment (female graduates tend to have much shorter breaks for family formation); within individual professions men and women are employed in similar jobs. But gender gaps in terms of pay and promotion are nonetheless frequently substantial. McNabb and Wass (2005) report that the earnings of female solicitors are on average only 56 per cent of those of male solicitors. Ward (2001) for academics and Blackaby et al. (2005) for economists conclude that influences on pay, including productivity, seniority, and tenure, explain only part of the gender pay gap. Blackaby et al. (2005) note that male economists are more likely to receive outside offers of employment, and their employers respond with more generous counter-offers than they do for women in the same circumstances. It appears that men and women are behaving differently in the market, and being treated differently by their employers, possibly because employers find it less credible that women will leave, which Blackaby et al. (2005) refer to as the 'loyal servant' hypothesis.[17]

---

[17] A range of studies have examined the position of highly qualified women in the USA: MIT (1999) for science; McDowell et al. (1999, 2001) for economics; Ginther and Hayes (1999, 2003) for humanities. The MIT report 'A Study on the Status of Women Faculty in Science at MIT' provided a high-profile case study of the different experiences of men and women in academe. Its findings included that across the six departments within the science faculty at MIT in 1994 there were only 15 women in tenured faculty positions compared with 194 men,

7.5.3 *Measuring discrimination*

However pervasive and suggestive, the measured pay gap between men and women just described does not give a measure of discrimination. Not only do men and women often perform different jobs, offering varying non-wage advantages and disadvantages, but individuals differ in a wide range of attributes, such as educational attainment and work experience, which affect their productivity. Part of the pay differential observed between workers will reflect differences in their productive characteristics and in the net advantages of their jobs and workplaces. Discrimination in pay occurs where individuals receive differing rewards on the basis of a characteristic such as gender, when it does not affect their productivity in the job. Discrimination arises only in the part of the pay gap due to unequal treatment for like characteristics, or unequal treatment due to unlike characteristics which are irrelevant to performance in the job. Discrimination is then inequitable; unequal reward for equally productive work violates horizontal equity between individuals. It is also economically inefficient; rewards which do not reflect the value of marginal product delivered distort the efficient allocation of resources.

Measuring discrimination is not straightforward. To find pure discrimination we need to identify the extent to which individuals receive differing rewards for the same characteristics when working in equally desirable jobs. The standard approach to this is to disaggregate the differential observed between men's and women's pay into two components: the part which reflects differing characteristics relevant to productivity in work, and the part reflecting the differing rewards which they receive for the same characteristics.[18]

Denoting men's and women's pay as w_M and w_F respectively, and their productive characteristics as C_M and C_F, (the logarithm of) pay for each group can be written:

$$logw_M = a_M + b_M C_M$$
$$logw_F = a_F + b_F C_F$$

where b_M and b_F denote the pay reward per unit of productive characteristics received by men and women respectively. The gender pay gap, $logw_M - logw_F$, can be written as:

$$logw_M - logw_F = (a_M - a_F) + b_F(C_M - C_F) + (b_M - b_F) C_M$$

numbers which had been stable over the previous two decades. The study also reported that the marginalization of women in terms of numbers and roles within departments was 'often accompanied by differences in salary, space, awards, resources, and response to outside offers between men and women faculty, with women receiving less despite professional accomplishments equal to those of male colleagues'.

[18] These are often referred to as 'Oaxaca decompositions' after their originator, Oaxaca (1973). There have been further developments to the literature on measuring and decomposing gender pay gaps with key contributions being made by Juhn et al. (1993) and Oaxaca and Ransom (1994, 1999).

$(C_M - C_F)$ gives the differences in the productive characteristics which men and women bring to the job, and any differences in the net advantages of their jobs. The differing rewards to these attributes are measured by $(b_M - b_F)$. This formulation allows us to decompose the observed pay gap into the part attributable to the differing characteristics of men and women and their respective jobs, $(C_M - C_F)$, and the part due to the different pay rewards which they receive for these attributes. The latter part of the pay gap, $(a_M - a_F)$ and $(b_M - b_F)C_M$, can be attributed to pure discrimination.[19] A similar decomposition can be applied to the pay gap between women in full- and part-time work.

7.5.4 Decomposition studies

A number of major studies have recently examined women's pay in the UK, applying this methodology to different but complementary datasets. Harkness (1996), Lissenburgh (2000), Swaffield (2000), and Anderson et al. (2001) analyse earnings for women of all ages; Joshi and Paci (1998) give a detailed assessment for the age cohort of women born in 1958; Black et al. (1999) analyse the earnings of married women.[20] The results are summarized in

Table 7.8. Estimates from decomposition studies of the gender pay gap, 1974–98 (%)

	All	Full time	Part time
Total pay gap	19–29	17–20	35–45
Explained	4–18	1–9	21–23
Human capital	5–16	1–9	6–21
Qualifications	2	0	2
Experience	5–12	2–3	5–9
Training	0	0–1	2
Occupation	2–4	1–3	0–6
Employer	1	0–1	2
Sector	0	0	0
Size	1	1	2
Unexplained	8–16	9–18	13–22

[19] The gender pay gap can also be written

$$logw_M - logw_W = (a_M - a_W) + b_M(C_M - C_W) + (b_M - b_W)C_W$$

The expression in the main text evaluates the differences in characteristics between men and women at the women's rate of reward b_W, while the differences in reward rates are evaluated at the levels of men's characteristics. The expression here reverses these. Since C_M is generally greater than C_F and C_W is less than C_M the reversed formulation gives a larger 'explained' component to the pay gap and a lower estimate of discrimination. The differences are not necessarily large, and both or an average are often quoted. There is no uniquely correct answer to this index number problem.

[20] Harkness uses data from the General Household Survey (GHS) for 1974 and 1983, and from the British Household Panel Survey (BHPS) for 1992–93. Swaffield also uses the BHPS but

Table 7.8. Harkness (1996) examines the wage gap between men and women in full-time work in 1974, 1983, and 1992–93, estimating the extent of wage discrimination at each point and how this changed over these twenty years. She reports that the overall pay gap narrowed by half, from 50 per cent in 1974 to 25 per cent in 1992–93.[21] This narrowing was due both to the increasing similarity of men and women in terms of characteristics, and to a reduction in discrimination. Harkness (1996) summarizes her interpretation of her findings:

falling 'discrimination' was the most important factor in reducing the gender wage gap between 1974 and 1992–93. It remains the case, however, that in 1992–93, the majority of the full-time gender wage gap (85 per cent or over under all specifications) resulted from differences in returns to characteristics by gender (or 'discrimination').

These findings are stark. However, they relate to women of all ages in full-time work. Since the position of older women to some extent reflects the economic and social environment prevailing when they first entered employment, the position of younger women is a more precise gauge of current conditions. Joshi and Paci's (1998) analysis is based on the earnings experience of women aged 33 in 1991. However, their findings on the trends in the pay gap and its sources for these younger women are in line with those of Harkness; in 1991 unequal treatment, although much reduced, was still the dominant source of women's pay disadvantage in the full-time labour market. The results obtained by Anderson et al. (2001) using data from 1998 are broadly in line with these earlier studies; they are able to explain 10 per cent of the gender pay leaving the remaining 11 per cent unexplained and attributable to discrimination.

The occupational structure, including segregation, emerges as a significant source of the gender pay gap for full-time work. Vertical segregation—the 'glass ceiling'—is measured by ranking the individual's occupation hierarchically, and horizontal segregation by its degree of 'feminization' (women's share in employment). Vertical segregation appears to be the more important, although the distinction becomes blurred in a detailed horizontal classification, where, for example, teachers and head teachers are distinguished as separate occupations.[22] While the differing occupations followed by men and women clearly

over the more extended period 1991–97. Lissenburgh used the 1992 Employment in Britain Survey. Anderson et al. use the Workplace and Industrial Relations Survey 1998. Joshi and Paci use the National Child Development Survey (NCDS), following a 1958 birth cohort. They also use as comparators the age cohort born in 1946 from the MRC National Survey of Health and Development. Black et al. used a 1989 sample of married women.

[21] Harkness reports log differences, $logw_M - logw_F$. These have been converted into percentages, expressed relative to the smaller number, women's pay.

[22] These results are in line with the more detailed findings for an earlier period by Sloane (1990): 'It seems that differences in pay within existing occupations are much more significant than differences in occupational distribution [in explaining differences between the pay of men and women]. Therefore, occupational segregation in so far as it is related to pay is vertical rather than horizontal in nature. That is, women earn less than men not so much because they

contribute to the gender pay gap, how far this represents discrimination is a matter of debate. If men and women are seen as choosing freely from a range of occupations with differing pay levels, then occupational choices 'explain' part of the pay gap, and discrimination involves only the gender pay differences occurring within occupations. The alternative view is that the association of 'women's occupations' with lower pay should be regarded as part of discrimination itself, one of the channels through which their human capital is less well rewarded.

For women in part-time work the picture is very different, bleak both overall and in its key trends. While the gender pay gap for women in full-time work continues to narrow, women in part-time work, already seriously disadvantaged, are tending to lose further ground. Women working full time have made pay gains from improved educational attainment as well as better rewards to it. Women working part time, on the other hand, have experienced deteriorating relative pay on both counts. Moreover, the pay gap between women working full time and those working part time is now significantly wider than the gender gap between men and women for full-time work.

The role of motherhood is a further central element which has to be addressed in any analysis of women's position in the labour market and gender discrimination. Mothers with dependent children are now returning to work more frequently and after shorter spells out of the labour force. The presence of children is a major motivation for women to take part-time rather than full-time work. The 1958 birth cohort analysed by Joshi and Paci were amongst the first for whom statutory maternity rights were in place when they entered the labour market and began family formation. At age 33 their family responsibilities would be at their height. For mothers working, with or without career breaks, there is no evidence of a 'penalty to motherhood'. Given their levels of education, occupation, and other relevant characteristics, the pay received by mothers is not significantly different from the pay of non-mothers. Mothers who take only standard maternity leave and then return to work lose no ground in pay terms relative to childless women. The mothers for whom there is a pay gap are those who have taken a longer break from employment. The size of the pay gap, however, is commensurate with their reduced time in work.

While there is no direct 'penalty to motherhood' when mothers and non-mothers in full-time (or part-time) work are compared, the indirect penalty is nonetheless clear. The presence of dependent children induces many mothers to take up part-time work, and women in part-time work are poorly paid. This important interaction between work and the family will be examined further in the next section.

enter occupations which are particularly low paid but because they fail to advance as fast as men within particular occupations' (p. 167).

7.6 Work and the family

As we have seen, women have accounted for the entire growth in the UK labour force over the past thirty years. Whilst participation has increased for women of all ages, the most significant change has occurred amongst the 25–35 age group—women of childbearing and child caring age. A key element in the increasing number of younger women in work is the change in fertility. The availability of reliable forms of contraception has meant that since the 1960s women have been able to exercise choice and control over the number and timing of births. This now provides an important part of the context in which decisions on employment are made.

7.6.1 *Trends in family formation*

After the baby boom of the mid-1960s the overall fertility rate for women declined until the late 1970s and has remained stable since then. Women are having smaller families, including choosing not to have children at all. Cohort analyses for England and Wales show that while women born in 1936 had had an average of 1.9 children by their 30th birthday, women born in 1966 had had only 1.3 children by this age. Among women born in 1946 just 9 per cent were childless by the age of 45; of those born in 1951 15 per cent were childless at the same age, and it is predicted that 20 per cent of women born in 1966 will be childless when they reach 45.

Childbearing now occurs later. Fertility rates amongst younger women have been falling whereas those for women over 30 have tended to rise. The highest fertility rate remains among women in their late twenties, but since 1992 women in their early thirties have had a higher fertility rate than women in their early twenties. This trend is confirmed in the rising mean age of mothers at childbirth, which in England and Wales has risen from 24.4 in 1977 to 26.8 in 1997. This delay in embarking on family formation allows women a longer initial span of earning years and the opportunity to establish a career.

These are international trends. In 1960 the number of children per completed family in the countries of the EU-15 varied from 2.2 in Sweden to 3.8 in Ireland, with the EU average at 2.6. By 2000 the highest rate was 1.9, in Ireland and France, while the average had fallen to 1.5. In spite of the dwindling family size the average age of mothers at childbirth has been rising (Figure 7.9) and now exceeds 30 in a number of countries including the Netherlands and Ireland.

7.6.2 *Combining work and family*

Now that they can choose the extent and timing of their family responsibilities, women are increasingly choosing greater involvement in the labour market.

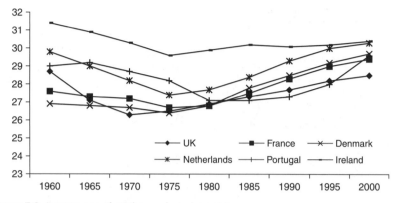

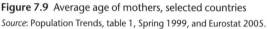

Figure 7.9 Average age of mothers, selected countries
Source: Population Trends, table 1, Spring 1999, and Eurostat 2005.

This shifting balance between the home and the market place comes through two changes in mothers' behaviour. Completed career breaks are becoming shorter as women return to work earlier after formation of the (now smaller) family is complete, typically while children are still at school. Increasingly, they are also returning to work after the birth of each child; one out of two new mothers now returns to the labour force before the baby's first birthday.

Even with these changes the most important influence on a mother's labour market status remains the age of the youngest child. The pattern of participation in full- and part-time work is shown in Table 7.9. The 'typical' mother with dependent children is now in work. Even among those whose youngest child was under 5 exactly half were in work at the end of the 1990s, up from just over one in three ten years earlier. Only a small minority of mothers are now economically inactive looking after the family, and this proportion drops sharply once the youngest child is over 10 years of age. Participation in full-time work rises steeply as the age of the youngest child increases. Most strikingly, full-time work has been increasing markedly among mothers with children at all ages, notably including mothers whose youngest child is under 5. Part-time work, however, remains much the most common position for mothers as long as children are of school age, and particularly as long as the youngest child is under 10. Although full-time work is becoming more prevalent, the role of part-time work is not diminishing. It remains the predominant route through which British mothers with school age children combine work with childcare.

In spite of the trend towards convergence across the advanced economies in the timing and duration of family formation, significant international

169

Table 7.9. Full- and part-time work amongst women, by age of youngest child (%)

	Age of youngest child				No children
	0–4	5–10	11–15	16–18	
1988					
Full-time work	12	18	29	35	51
Part-time work	25	44	43	39	21
Looking after family	50	24	15	13	7
1998					
Full-time work	18	24	35	41	49
Part-time work	32	44	40	39	23
Looking after family	40	20	13	9	5

Source: Labour Force Survey 1998; reported in 'Women in the Labour Market: Results from the Spring LFS', *Labour Market Trends* (Mar. 1999).

Table 7.10. Employment rates for mothers, 2000, selected countries (%)

	No children		One child		Two or more children	
	Employment rate	Part-time employment	Employment rate	Part-time employment	Employment rate	Part-time employment
Sweden	81.9	14.6	80.6	16.7	81.8	22.2
UK	79.9	23.7	72.9	46.6	62.3	62.8
USA	78.6	10.1	75.6	15.8	64.7	23.6
France	73.5	20.0	74.1	23.7	58.8	31.8
Germany	77.3	24.0	70.4	45.3	56.3	60.2
Ireland	65.8	16.6	51.0	37.2	40.8	46.4
The Netherlands	75.3	38.3	69.9	72.6	63.3	82.7
Italy	52.8	20.0	52.1	27.2	42.4	34.4
Spain	54.6	13.7	47.6	17.4	43.3	18.6

Source: OECD, *Employment Outlook* 2002.

differences remain in the labour force participation of mothers, including the relative roles of full- and part-time work. Table 7.10 shows for selected countries the employment rates for non-mothers and for mothers with one, or two or more children. At one extreme is Sweden (and the other Scandinavian countries) where participation rates are extremely high, and mainly in full-time work. Mothers' employment is also high in France, and again concentrated into full-time work. Like the UK, the Netherlands and to some extent Germany have moderate participation rates but heavy concentration of working mothers in part-time work.

These differences across countries can be linked with the extent of state provision of childcare, shown in Table 7.11. In Scandinavia women's right to

Table 7.11. Public support for parents of young children, 1999–2001 (%)

	Duration of base maternity leave in weeks (1)	Maternity benefits % of average wages	Duration of optional parental leave in weeks (2)	Parental benefits during optional leave % of average wages	Total duration (1) + (2)	Paternity leave	% of children in formal day care	
							0–3	3–7
Denmark	28	100	22	83	50	10 days	64	80
France	16	100	132	42.4	148	3 days	20	95+
Italy	22	80	26	30	48	0	6	95
Spain	16	100	128	7.3	144	2 days	5	84
UK	18	90	24	15.3	42	0[a]	34	60

Source: OECD, Employment Outlook 1999/2000; MISSOC (2001); Boeri et al. (2005).
[a] Paid paternity leave was introduced in the UK in 2003; eligible employees are able to take up to two weeks leave, see www.dti.gov.uk/er/individual/paternity-pl514.htm for details.

work has long been accepted and supported by the state through the provision of publicly funded childcare places and extensive provisions for parental leave. In France kindergarten places are provided for all 3–6-year-olds. This leads to high employment rates for mothers, particularly in full-time work. The UK and the Netherlands both have high levels of part-time work by mothers but in rather different circumstances. In the Netherlands mothers have relatively strong rights to negotiate parental leave in a variety of flexible forms. In conjunction with the limited availability of state-funded childcare places and the resulting costs of childcare this gives mothers the opportunity and the strong incentive to work part time. In the UK mothers face the same limited supply of childcare places, and the high cost of childcare which this implies is reinforced by the limited entitlement to parental leave to deal with family events. As a result many mothers choose part-time work, which they can combine with informal arrangements for childcare through other family members and friends.

7.6.3 Lone parents

Among mothers with dependent children around one-quarter are now single parents, making this a major category relevant to any discussion of women and work. Again, this is a rising trend internationally.[23] The commonest cause of lone parenthood, affecting 60 per cent of cases, is marital breakdown (divorce rates increased sevenfold between the 1960s and 1990s) with a further third involving women who have never married (8 per cent of all births in the 1960s were outside marriage, 36 per cent in the 1990s) and the remainder widows. Women who are the head of a single parent family face particular problems in entering the labour market, especially when their children are at pre-school ages. With no partner to share childcare, income in employment is greater than income outside the market place only if earnings are high or very low-cost (often, in practical terms, unpaid) childcare is available. Lone mothers tend to be less well qualified than mothers with partners, confining the first route to a minority of high earners. For the remainder, childcare costs make full-time work impracticable while the withdrawal of benefits on entering paid work makes part-time work unattractive. Single mothers therefore have the lowest rates of participation in paid work, with two-thirds of them dependent upon income support.[24]

---

[23] Whilst these figures represent a high for the post-war period, the levels of lone parenthood in the late nineteenth and early twentieth century were also high. The factors leading to lone parenthood were generally different, for example death of main income earner.

[24] In the UK in 2000, 40% of lone parent households fell below the poverty line compared to 9% of two-parent households. Worklessness is the major cause with double the proportion of lone parent households being without work. The position of lone parent households is discussed in Glennerster (1995). On childcare arrangements and costs particularly as they affect lone parents, see Duncan et al. (1995).

7.7 Prospects and policies

Women have always faced a difficult balancing act between responsibilities towards home and family and opportunities in the labour market. In the past, this trade-off resulted in many women, particularly mothers, leaving the labour market. But the combination of demographic changes with family planning and smaller families, growing employment opportunities, including in part-time work, and changing social attitudes has meant that the balance has shifted, and continues to shift, towards greater involvement by women in paid work. The record on women's changing position in the labour market is, however, an uneven one. For many, it has brought a career outside the home and financial independence. For others, it has brought secondary earnings from low-quality jobs. Yet others find themselves largely excluded from paid work.

For women choosing full-time employment labour market status and prospects have improved significantly over the past thirty years. Typically they are now employed in similar jobs to men, and their levels of qualifications equal and may even exceed those of men. They are the group who have enjoyed the highest growth in earnings, and their levels of pay and conditions of employment continue to move closer to those of men. As a consequence, labour market discrimination is now much less of an issue for this group. Despite this, equality of opportunity remains to be achieved in two key areas. The first, affecting all women, is promotion structures. Women continue to be under-represented, relative to their qualifications, in promoted posts, and to be paid less than men at each rung on the promotion ladder. Younger women are making gains in this respect, but it remains unclear how far these gains will continue to accrue as they advance through their careers, or whether the glass ceiling remains in place. Women in full-time work who are also mothers are now re-timing births to allow their career position to be better established before taking on the burden of family responsibilities. Nonetheless, those who take career breaks remain at a disadvantage in career progression and pay.

In contrast, in part-time work, where women's employment growth has been concentrated, the prospects for women have deteriorated. Employment opportunities there have been crowded into poor-quality jobs, with low pay, limited training, and little advancement. These are areas where labour market deregulation has had its greatest adverse effects, as low union recognition has failed to counter poor pay and employment conditions. For many women the shift from full- to part-time work, particularly after a spell of non-employment, is also a move down the occupation ladder.

Finally, there is the group of women who are outside the labour market, although many would prefer to be in work. These are lone parents for whom the combination of the cost of childcare and the structure of the welfare provisions creates serious barriers to taking employment. These women and their children, dependent on income support, face a major risk of poverty.

Partly in recognition of women's growing involvement in the labour market, particularly in the childcare years, and partly in response to the EU's social agenda adopted at Lisbon in 2000 with its objectives for women's employment and labour market status, the UK government is developing a range of policy measures to facilitate the difficult balancing act between work and home. These policy developments include: extending maternity leave, introducing paternity leave, extending the provision of childcare, subsidizing the costs of childcare for working families, and supporting employment by parents through the shift of welfare support from income transfers to targeting employment directly, notably through the system of tax credits for working families. In addition, women (particularly those in part-time employment) have been major beneficiaries of the national minimum wage, introduced in 1999. The Low Pay Commission Reports (1998, 2000, 2001, 2003, and 2005) show that the majority (two-thirds) of the workers whose hourly pay was uprated by the minimum wage have been women and of these the majority have been part-timers.

In many respects the prospects for women's employment overall are bright. The sectors of activity where employment is growing most rapidly, predominantly in services, are those in which women form a disproportionate share of employees. Women have escaped the extensive job destruction which characterizes many male-dominated manual occupations. Across the economy as a whole the demand for skills is rising, at a time when women's gains in educational attainment are qualifying them to meet it. Women also tend to be well equipped with the 'soft' interpersonal skills which many of the newer jobs require. But for some women, particularly lone mothers with lower levels of skills, perhaps even more than for men, these developments contain a threat. The shift to skills is already establishing a degree of polarization across jobs. Those with education and skills face expanding opportunities in managerial and professional positions. But the labour market prospects for the low skilled are deteriorating. This is already reflected in the levels of unemployment among the low skilled and in the widening inequality in earnings. While educational attainment at school is rising for girls, many still leave school with at best limited qualifications and do not follow this with further training. They will be increasingly at risk.

Perhaps the biggest contribution to enhancing the position of women in work more generally would come from improved status for part-time jobs. At present women in part-time work constitute a new underclass. Given that part-time work is the route which many women choose, and will continue to choose, in order to combine their commitment to childcare with employment, part-time work should not have its present inferior status. And it need not. Professional women are already beginning to show that it is possible to engage in part-time work without occupational downgrading or loss of career advancement. The superior educational attainment of girls at school is more than redressing women's current disadvantage in qualifications. This represents achievement and potential which will call for proper recognition and reward in the labour market.

References

Anderson, T., Forth, J., Metcalf, H., and Kirby, S. (2001). *The Gender Pay Gap*. Final Report to the Women and Equality Unit. London: Cabinet Office.

Becker, G. (1957). *The Economics of Discrimination*. Chicago: University of Chicago Press.

—— (1981). *A Treatise on the Family*. Cambridge, Mass.: Harvard University Press.

—— (1985). 'Human Capital, Effort and the Sexual Division of Labour'. *Journal of Labor Economics*, 3: 553–8.

Black, B., Trainor, M., and Spencer, J. E. (1999). 'Wage Protection Systems, Segregation and Gender Pay Inequalities: West Germany, the Netherlands and Great Britain'. *Cambridge Journal of Economics*, 23: 449–64.

Blackaby, D., Booth, A. L., and Frank, J. (2005). 'Outside Offers and the Gender Pay Gap: Empirical Evidence from the UK Academic Labour Market'. *Economic Journal*, 115, February: 81–107.

Boeri, T., Del Boca, D., and Pissarides, C. (eds.) (2005). *Women at Work: An Economic Perspective*. Oxford: Oxford Economic Press.

Booth, A. L., Francesconi, M., and Franks, J. (2003). 'A Sticky Floors Model of Promotion, Pay, and Gender'. *European Economic Review*, 47: 295–322.

British Labour Statistics: Historical Abstract 1886–1968 (1971). London: Department of Employment and Productivity, Her Majesty's Stationery Office.

Connolly, S., and Gregory, M. (2002). 'The National Minimum Wage and Hours of Work Implications for Low Paid Women'. *Oxford Bulletin of Economics and Statistics*, 64, Supplement 1: 607–31.

Corby, S., Stanworth, C., Long, S., and Fox, M. (2005). *Gender and the Labour Market in South East England*. London: South East England Development Agency.

Dex, S., and Shaw, L. (1986). *British and American Women at Work: Do Equal Opportunities Policies Matter?* Basingstoke: Macmillan.

Dex, S., Joshi, H., and Macran, S. (1996). 'A Widening Gulf among Britain's Mothers'. *Oxford Review of Economic Policy*, 12/1, Spring: 65–75.

Duncan, A., Giles, C., and Webb, S. (1995). *The Impact of Subsidising Childcare*. Research Discussion Series No. 13. London: Equal Opportunities Commission.

Employment Gazette Historical Supplement No. 2, Employment Statistics, Employment Gazette, 97/11, November 1989.

George, V., and Taylor-Gooby, P. (1996). *European Welfare Policy: Squaring the Welfare Circle*. Basingstoke: Macmillan.

Ginther, D., and Hayes, K. (1999). 'Gender Differences in Salary and Promotion in the Humanities'. *American Economic Review*, 89, May Papers and Proceedings: 397–402.

—— —— (2003). 'Gender Differences in Salary and Promotion for Faculty in the Humanities, 1977–95'. *Journal of Human Resources*, 38/1: 34–73.

Glennerster, H. (1995). *Paying for Welfare*. Hemel Hempstead: Harvester Wheatsheaf.

Gregory, M. B., and Thomson, A. W. J. (eds.) (1990). *A Portrait of Pay, 1970–82: An Analysis of the New Earnings Survey*. Oxford: Clarendon Press.

Grimshaw, D., and Rubery, J. (2002). *The Adjusted Gender Pay Gap: A Critical Appraisal of Standard Decomposition Techniques*. Brussels: Prepared as part of the work by the co-ordinating Group of Experts on Gender and Employment commissioned by the Equal Opportunities Unit in the European Community.

Hakim, C. (1979). *Occupational Segregation: A Comparative Study of the Degree and Pattern of the Differentiation between Men and Women's Work in Britain, the United States and Other Countries*. Research Paper No. 9, London, Department of Employment.

—— (1996). *Key Issues in Women's Work: Female Heterogeneity and the Polarisation of Women's Employment*. Atlantic Highlands, NJ: The Athlone Press.

Harkness, S. (1996). 'The Gender Earnings Gap'. *Fiscal Studies*, 17/2: 1–36.

Humphries, J., and Rubery, J. (eds.) (1995). *The Economics of Equal Opportunities*. Manchester: Equal Opportunities Commission.

ILO (International Labour Office) (1990). *Yearbook of Labour Statistics 1945–89*. Geneva: ILO.

Jonung, C., and Persson, I. (eds.) (1998). *Women's Work and Wages*. London: Routledge.

Joshi, H., and Paci, P. (1998). *Unequal Pay for Women and Men: Evidence from the British Birth Cohort Studies*. Cambridge, Mass.: MIT Press.

—— Layard, R., and Owen, S. J. (1985). 'Why are More Women Working in Britain?' *Journal of Labor Economics*, 3, Supplement: S147–S176.

Juhn, C., Murphy, K. M., and Pierce, B. (1993). 'Wage Inequality and the Rise in the Return to Skill'. *Journal of Political Economy*, 101/3: 410–42.

Kahn, S. (1995). 'Women in the Economics Profession'. *Journal of Economic Perspectives*, 9/4: 193–205.

—— (2001). 'Gender Differences in Academic Career Paths of Economists'. *American Economic Review*, 83/2, May Papers and Proceedings: 52–6.

Labour Market Trends (1999). *Office for National Statistics*. Monthly. London: Her Majesty's Stationery Office.

Lissenburgh, S. (2000). *Gender Discrimination in the Labour Market: Evidence from the BHPS and EiB Surveys*. London: PSI Publishing.

Low Pay Commission (1998, 2000, 2001, 2003, 2005). *National Minimum Wage*. Various reports. London: Her Majesty's Stationery Office. **www.lowpay.gov.uk/lowpay/**

McDowell, J. M., Singell, L. D., and Ziliak, J. P. (1999). 'Cracks in the Glass Ceiling: Gender and Promotion in the Economics Profession'. *American Economic Review*, 89/2, May Papers and Proceedings: 392–6.

—— —— —— (2001). 'Gender and Promotion in the Economics Profession'. *Industrial and Labor Relations Review*, 54/2: 224–44.

McNabb, R., and Wass, V. (2005). 'Male–Female Earnings Differentials among Lawyers in Britain: A Legacy of the Law or a Current Practice?' *Labour Economics*, article forthcoming.

Manning, A., and Petrongolo, B. (2004). *The Part-Time Pay Penalty*. Report to the Women and Equality Unit. London.

Mincer, J., and Polachek, S. (1974). 'Family Investments in Human Capital: Earnings of Women'. *Journal of Political Economy*, 82/2: S76–S108.

MISSOC (Mutual Information System on Social Protection in the European Union) (2001). *Social Protection in the Member States in the EU*. Brussels: European Commission. Available from: **http://europa.eu.int/comm/employment_social/social_protection/index_en.htm**

MIT (Massachusetts Institute of Technology) (1999). 'A Study on the Status of Women Faculty in Science at MIT'. Available from: **http://web.mit.edu/fnl/women/women. html**

Oaxaca, R. (1973). 'Male–Female Wage Differentials in Urban Labour Markets'. *International Economic Review*, 14/3: 693–709.

—— and Ransom, M. (1994). 'On Discrimination and the Decomposition of Wage Differentials'. *Journal of Econometrics*, 61: 5–21.

—— —— (1999). 'Identification in Detailed Wage Decompositions'. *Review of Economics and Statistics*, 81/1: 154–7.

OECD (Organization for Economic Cooperation and Development) *Labour Force Statistics*, annual. Paris: OECD.

—— (1998). *The Future of Female-Dominated Occupations*. Paris: OECD.

—— (2002). 'Women at Work: Who are they and How are They Faring?' *Employment Outlook*. Paris: OECD.

Olsen, W., and Walby, S. (2004). *Modelling Gender Pay Gaps*. Manchester: Equal Opportunities Commission, Working Paper Series, No. 17.

Perlman, R., and Pike, M. (1994). *Sex Discrimination in the Labour Market: The Case for Comparable Worth*. Manchester: Manchester University Press.

Rubery, J., Fagan C., and Maier, F. (1996). 'Occupational Segregation, Discrimination and Equal Opportunity', in G. Schmid, J. O'Reilly, and K Schomann (eds.), *International Handbook of Labour Market Policy and Evaluation*. Cheltenham: Edward Elgar.

Schmid, G., O'Reilly, J., and Schomann, K. (eds.) (1996). *International Handbook of Labour Market Policy and Evaluation*. Cheltenham: Edward Elgar.

Sloane, P. J. (1990). 'Sex Differentials: Structure, Stability and Change', in M. B. Gregory and A. W. J. Thomson (eds.), *A Portrait of Pay, 1970–82: An Analysis of the New Earnings Survey*. Oxford: Clarendon Press.

Social Focus on Men and Women. Office for National Statistics, annually. London: Her Majesty's Stationery Office.

Social Trends. Office for National Statistics, annually. London: Her Majesty's Stationery Office.

Swaffield, J. (2000). *Gender, Motivation, Experience and Wages*. Centre for Economic Performance Discussion Paper No. 457, London: London School of Economics.

Walby, S., and Olsen, W. (2002). *The Impact of Women's Position in the Labour Market on Pay and Implications for UK Productivity*. London: Women and Equality Unit, Cabinet Office.

Ward, M. (2001). 'The Gender Salary Gap in British Academia'. *Applied Economics*, 33: 1669–81.

8

The 'Welfare State' and the Labour Market

Pat Thane

8.1 Introduction

State welfare expenditure has both direct and indirect impacts upon the labour market and on economic efficiency in general. The definition of what is, or is not, 'welfare' expenditure is broad and shifting. It may, for example, include subsidies to public transport or the costs arising from legal controls on wages and work conditions, as well as the costs of social services and other benefits funded from taxation. It certainly includes the social policies which have been most closely identified with the British 'welfare state'—social security, health, education, housing. Since the early twentieth century these have had a continuing, close, relationship with government perceptions of the needs of the labour market.

This chapter traces this relationship between government social policies and the labour market chronologically through the century.

8.2 The Labour Party and 'welfare to work'

Labour has been the political party most identified with the 'welfare state' (Thane 2000*b*). From the party's foundation in 1906 it believed that the most desirable means to maximize the 'welfare' of the population was full employment at adequate pay. Or, at least, full employment and adequate pay for men; the status of women in the labour market and in labour market policy has always been equivocal. As James Ramsay MacDonald, first secretary of the Labour Party and Labour's first Prime Minister in 1924 and 1929, the most effective and prolific propagandist of the party's early days, put it in 1911:

You can take your children, feed them, clothe them and house them at public expense, but that does not help you. That is simply patching up the old tin kettle. It does not help you to recreate society so that these poor things will disappear altogether . . . We must do better than that. What do we want? Increased incomes from labour—not doles in aid of low wages. We want wages boards applied to every industry . . . [these] . . . will immediately lift up the wages and then you will supply that reservoir of possession and economic power which is the source of working class liberty. (MacDonald 1912: 11; Speech in Italifax, 24 Nov.)

Labour's slogan at this time was 'The Right to Work or Full Maintenance'. The wording signified the party's order of priorities. It assumed that households dependent upon male breadwinners were the norm, as they were, though there were a substantial number of exceptions, including a proportion of households headed by single mothers as high as that a century later. This was due to widowhood rather than, as later, separation or divorce. Labour believed that fully employed men should and could provide for their own needs and those of their families. The role of welfare payments and services was to provide a safety net for those unable to work due to age, disability, failure of the labour market, or any other good cause. Even then, as MacDonald wrote in 1907: 'if this help is given as a mere palliative or as charity, the real conditions are only perpetuated . . . Unemployment schemes must therefore be educational; they must be in the form of training' (MacDonald 1907: 30–4). Social reform was secondary to economic reform, which alone could deliver lasting 'welfare'. Work and adequate wages were the best defences against poverty. Publicly funded welfare was for those who could not be supported by their own efforts or by their families. These were views from which no other mainstream party in early twentieth century Britain—or indeed for the remainder of the century—would seriously dissent, though, as we shall see, they varied among themselves and over time in the extent of their commitment to supporting the poorest people in society. The governing party at the time of MacDonald's comment of 1907 was the Liberal Party. Between its election in 1906 and the coming of war in 1914 the Liberals were responsible for a remarkable run of innovative welfare legislation. It was new not only for the nation but for the party. Traditionally the Liberals had been the party of minimal government and maximum self-help and voluntary action. Attachment to these beliefs remained a strong though diminishing strand of thought within the party. The main opposition party at this time, the Conservatives, was similarly divided between those who preferred low taxation and minimum state intervention in the economy or social life and those who believed that the better off had an obligation to help the worse off, not least in order to protect themselves from the anger of the dispossessed masses, and that such support was best mediated through central or, preferably, local government (Harris 1990, 1993; Thane 1990*a*).

8.3 The Liberal Party and the foundation of the 'welfare state', 1906–14

The Liberal Party was the first to combine practical measures to regulate the labour market with new, progressive, welfare legislation. From the time it won the general election in 1906, it introduced a run of new legislation which, for the first time in British history, provided services and/or benefits for poor people which were disconnected from the ancient and stigmatizing Poor Law.[1] They were designed, however, to be only minimally redistributive and, in general, they were as concerned with improving the health of the economy as with the alleviation of poverty. Among the first Liberal measures, the Education (Provision of Meals) Act 1906 provided free school meals for needy schoolchildren; the Notification of Births Act 1907 tightened up the requirement for the registration of new births to assist attempts to reduce the high infant mortality rate; the Education (Administrative Provisions) Act 1907 provided for free medical inspection of children in state-funded schools. Behind all three measures was a conscious determination to reduce infant mortality and the poor health and nutrition among children. This caused misery in itself and created when, or if, they grew up an unhealthy, insufficiently productive labour force (and armed force) in an increasingly competitive world, both economically and politically. Fears that Britain might be falling behind its economic rivals due to low levels of skill also lay behind increased expenditure on state education.

Even the innovative Old Age Pensions Act 1908, which was primarily designed to relieve the poverty of people aged 70 or above who were not physically able to work, required claimants to satisfy the pensions authority that he (or, in reality, more probably she, given the longer life expectancy and greater poverty of older women, who made up two-thirds of the first pensioners) had not been guilty of 'habitual failure to work according to his ability, opportunity or need, for his own maintenance or that of his legal relatives' (Thane 2000a: 223–6). This proved difficult to enforce, but it indicates that such pioneering state welfare measures were designed to reinforce the obligation to work as a condition of eligibility for benefits.

If people were expected to secure their own welfare and that of their dependants through paid work, it was essential that the financial returns for work were sufficient to meet predictable needs. The great poverty surveys at the turn of the century, by Charles Booth in London and J. S. Rowntree in York, suggested, as did A. L. Bowley shortly before the First World War, that all too often they were not (Booth 1889–1903; Rowntree 1915; Bowley and Burnett-Hurst 1915). All three researchers concluded that family size, old age, poor health, single motherhood due to death of the male earner, under- and unemployment were major causes of poverty. However, the greatest cause was low pay when in

---

[1] For more details see Thane (1996: 69–90).

work, though this might itself be related to one of the other causes, e.g. old, sick or disabled, and female workers were disadvantaged in the labour market.[2] The pay of female workers was generally much lower than that of males, but was vital to the economy of their households, whether they were living alone or with children, supporting elderly parents or sick or crippled husbands, or were young women contributing to the parental household. Hence the first tentative move of the British government towards a minimum wage was directed at women. The Trade Boards Act 1909 established 'trade boards', composed of representatives of workers and employers, to fix minimum wages in the largely un-unionized, largely female, 'sweated' industries, so named precisely because they worked people hard for minimal pay. The fact that they were not unionized was significant, since the government assumed that negotiation between trade unions and employers was the desirable path to improved pay and conditions at work. The Liberals facilitated this by means of the Trade Disputes Act 1906, which increased legal protection for unions, reversing the Taff Vale judgment which had crippled their bargaining capacities (see Chapter 9). Over the following years, arbitration machinery was established through the Board of Trade, designed to minimize tension between employers and increasingly unionized workers. Still, by 1914 only a minority of workers were unionized: among employed men in UK c.17 per cent in 1900, c.30 per cent in 1914, c.53 per cent by 1920; among employed women, c.3 per cent in 1900, c.8 per cent in 1914, c.22 per cent in 1920.[3] Low-paid workers, female and male, found it difficult to pay the regular dues required to keep unions in being. The Trade Boards Act was the outcome of demands from radical women, at a time of rising female militancy, male trade unionists, and philanthropists. In 1905 the women's section of the left-wing Fabian Society organized an exhibition in Westminster of reconstructions and photographs of the conditions in which thousands of women worked long hours for low pay, mainly in small workshops or as outworkers in their own homes. Press publicity, plus support from the trades council-based Anti-Sweating League, brought about the 1909 Act. It covered only four trades—tailoring, lace making, chain making, cardboard box making—but together they employed about 200,000 women. Even in these trades, old, infirm, or very young workers could be paid below the agreed minimum. The system was under-resourced and inadequately regulated.

In a period of unprecedented trade union militancy, in 1908 striking miners gained from a reluctant government a statutory eight-hour day and, in 1912, a minimum wage. In 1911 a long campaign by female trade unionists led to the Shops Act which reduced working hours by establishing a half-day closing each week. However the Liberals had wider-ranging plans to restructure the labour market, initiated by two figures who were to reach the height of their

---

[2] The best survey of these studies is Gazeley (2003).
[3] Halsey and Webb (2000: 310). For background to the statistics see Reid (2004: 159–276).

influence, in very different ways, during the Second World War: William Beveridge and Winston Churchill. In the 1900s Beveridge was a young Oxford graduate who had become acquainted with problems of poverty as a resident at the East London Settlement House, Toynbee Hall. He became recognized as an authority on unemployment, at a time when understanding of its extent and causes was scanty (Harris 1972). He was convinced that an important component of the problem was the oversupply of under-skilled, under-trained workers. This created the problem, particularly evident in East London, of a casualized, underemployed labour force, to whom employers had no incentive to give regular work or adequate wages. Beveridge believed that the solution was restructuring the labour market to ensure that all who wanted and needed work were in full-time, adequately paid work or, if unemployed for no fault of their own, received an adequate income from the state, assistance to find a job, and training where necessary. His proposals for unprecedented state intervention in the labour market were published as *Unemployment: A Problem of Industry* (1909) which was to become a classic text on unemployment for the next quarter-century (Harris 1997: 138–67). His ideas were shortly put into practice when they attracted the attention of Winston Churchill, then a Liberal, who became President of the Board of Trade in 1908 and responsible for labour market policy. Churchill appointed Beveridge to a post at the Board, with responsibility for putting into practice his ideas on unemployment policy. The first outcome of Beveridge's work was the establishment in 1909 of a nationwide network of labour exchanges (forerunners of present-day job centres). These were agencies, of a type already established by a few local authorities, to register vacancies and job seekers in order to maximize employment by improving information flows. Registration was also intended to improve the hazy information then available to the government about levels of unemployment and the size of the potential labour force. As Beveridge recognized, they were most helpful to the temporarily displaced skilled worker and made little difference to the major problem of the chronically underemployed.

The next step was to establish a system of social insurance to provide for the involuntarily unemployed while they sought work. Systems of social insurance—to which workers, employers, and the state make regular contributions to provide benefits for workers at times of risk, which they cannot afford to provide for themselves—for old age and sickness had been introduced in Germany and a number of other countries from the 1880s, but no state had previously extended the concept to the unemployed. The old age pensions introduced in Britain in 1908 were funded wholly from taxation, not through contributions. Regular contributions required regular wages, so the scheme was unlikely to help the casual underemployed, but, Beveridge believed, their problems should be solved by training and guidance provided through labour exchanges. An important feature of social insurance, in Beveridge's eyes, was that it encouraged workers in the virtue of regular saving; gave them a sense of ownership of their benefits rather than of dependence upon taxpayer hand-outs; and reminded employers of their social responsibilities by requiring them to contribute.

Unemployment Insurance was introduced in 1911. This innovative scheme began cautiously, covering only three trades: shipbuilding, engineering, and building and construction. These were chosen because they were liable to seasonal and cyclical fluctuations but not to heavy, and costly, levels of unemployment. Employers and workers made equal weekly contributions, but, for both, contributions were higher for casual than for regular workers in order to discourage casual working. The state contributed initially c.£1 million to the scheme, including providing the administrative infrastructure. After the first week of unemployment, the claimant received 7s. per week (barely enough for one person to survive on, their families had to resort to the Poor Law) for a maximum of fifteen weeks in any year, paid at a labour exchange, at which registration was compulsory for insured workers. Payment could be made only if unemployment was involuntary. Workers were allowed to refuse work where conditions were inferior to the norm for their occupation. By 1914 the scheme covered 2.3 million workers, overwhelmingly male. Almost no women worked in the insured occupations (Harris 1972: 295–333; 1997: 168–97). Textiles, for example,which employed a high proportion of women, was highly prone to cyclical fluctuations, but was not included in the scheme.

National Insurance, as it was called, was an innovation in British social policy and supplied the principle on which the British social security system has been based ever since. Unemployment Insurance formed only Part 2 of the National Insurance Act 1911. Part 1 was the equally innovative National Health Insurance. This was modelled on the German system and was open to all workers earning £160 per year or less (roughly the cut-off point between manual and white-collar earnings). It covered many more workers than Unemployment Insurance, but, again, contributions were relatively high for casual workers, who could in any case rarely afford them. Contributors received benefits for the first twenty-six weeks of sickness, long-term disability pension, access to free treatment by a general practitioner, and free treatment in a TB sanatorium—TB being a major scourge at this time—and wives of insured men received a 30s. maternity benefit. A major purpose of the scheme was to minimize working days lost due to sickness by improving the care and living conditions of sick workers; and to improve the survival rate of the next generation by improving maternity care.

8.4 The First World War and after

National Insurance was barely implemented when the First World War transformed the labour market in both the short and the long term. Unemployment rose in the first year of war. Thereafter, the combined demands of the armed services and the war economy created unprecedented levels of regular employment for men and women for the remainder of the war. The government, however, was concerned about the return of high unemployment after the war and the effects of this on a population who expected to be rewarded for the sacrifices of the war and whose expectations of work and wages had been enhanced by the wartime experience (Thane 1996: 119–54).

Beveridge remained at the Board of Trade until 1916 and seized the opportunity of closer wartime government control of industry to reduce casualization in essential industries and to achieve the upgrading and training of semi-skilled male and female workers, as demand outstripped the supply of skilled labour. He gave partial support to a minimum wage by, unsuccessfully, proposing its introduction for the largest low-paid group: women (Harris 1997: 196–227). The idea of a minimum wage was unpopular with both employers and trade unionists. Nevertheless, in the wartime emergency, it was introduced in 1916 for munitions workers and in 1917 for agricultural workers—a low-paid group who became vital to survival in wartime. Trade boards were extended to a wider range of better-paid, non-unionized industries. By 1920 they covered sixty-three industries and 3 million workers. Also, following the recommendations in 1917 of a government committee chaired by J. H. Whitley, MP, 'Whitley councils' were established in certain occupations (both manual and white collar) at which employers and workers could negotiate not only wages and conditions, but job security, training, and improvements in management. They were promoted with enthusiasm by the Ministry of Labour, as the Board of Trade became in 1917. This was not shared by employers or unions. The councils were most successful among white-collar workers, especially in central and local government, where some survive to the present (Lowe 1978; Middlemas 1979: 137–8).

From 1916 the government was planning post-war 'reconstruction'. During the war it acted further to improve infant and maternal care, aiming to improve the numbers and fitness of future generations of workers and soldiers. This was consolidated and extended in the Maternity and Child Welfare Act 1918, which increased government subsidies to local authority health and welfare services. Reconstruction was most fully worked out concerning education (see Sanderson, Chapter 11). Ministers and officials at the Board of Education and others, including Beveridge, thought it essential to increase access to and standards of education and training. Legislation planned during the war was introduced in 1918. It raised and standardized the school leaving age at 14, provided courses for children willing to stay at state elementary schools to later ages, abolished school fees, and introduced compulsory day-release education and technical training for workers aged 14–18. Technical education for children over the age of 11 was encouraged and teachers' salaries were increased to attract better-qualified people to the state system. State funding to universities (including 200 'state scholarships' for poorer students) and teacher training colleges was increased. The very expansion of education, and of other state services, impacted upon the labour market. It was becoming respectable for the first time for young middle-class women to enter paid employment. Many of them entered teaching or central and local government—at least until marriage, when they were removed by strict 'marriage bars' which survived until the Second World War. However, the onset of economic depression from late 1920 brought severe cuts in government expenditure, especially to post-14 education and training.

Wartime planning also led to a decisive increase in state expenditure on working-class housing. The main motive for seeking, at last, to improve the appalling state of housing in most cities was fear of the political effects of 'heroes' returning from privations of the front to the privations of urban squalor at home. But also important was the belief that good living conditions contributed to worker efficiency and that bad housing weakened the health of workers. Working-class women also campaigned for improvements in *their* primary workplaces: their homes. The result after the war was an unprecedented wave of state-subsidized house building. This also was cut, but not wholly extinguished, in 1921. By then, 252,000 houses had been built (Thane 1996: 135–7).

The government was less prepared for the return of servicemen and -women to the labour market. Beveridge left the Board of Trade in 1916 when his plans for further restructuring the labour market met opposition from civil servants and politicians. They also rejected his proposals for planned demobilization, designed to prevent unemployment and to enable businesses to plan the transition from war to peacetime production. When the war ended unexpectedly in November 1918 there were no plans in place. The government feared political revolt just a year after the Russian Revolution, fuelled by exaggerated reports from the Home Office of the revolutionary potential of the growing numbers of trade unionists and their possible incendiary effects upon ex-servicemen if they returned home to unemployment and poverty. Hurriedly, in November 1918, it responded by introducing a generous non-contributory, wholly state-funded 'out-of-work donation' for servicemen and -women, civilians thrown out of work by the transition, and for their dependants (Garside 1990: 35–7). Demobilization was staggered, but, since there was no clear plan in relation to labour market needs, its main effect was to incite mutiny among servicemen languishing in camps. The desire to cut the costly 'donation' without arousing political unrest led the government in 1920, this time with the advice of Beveridge, to replace it with an improved Unemployment Insurance scheme covering all workers earning £250 per year or less. This included many of the growing numbers of white-collar workers, but agricultural and domestic servants were excluded. In the latter case it was due to the difficulty of persuading employers to pay contributions. This was no small exclusion. Servants, who were overwhelmingly female, were the largest occupational group in the labour force. Agricultural workers, overwhelmingly male, were the third largest (Mitchell and Deane 1962: 61; Harris 1997: 196–227). Also excluded were employees normally regarded as free from the risk of unemployment, mainly public sector workers and railway workers. Insurance payments were available only for the first twenty-two weeks of unemployment, after which unemployed people had to apply to the stigmatizing Poor Law for relief. This had always been the case under the National Insurance legislation, but it afflicted increasing numbers of people as the numbers of long-term unemployed grew from 1921 (Garside 1990: 38 ff.).

The government retained the control over wages it had established during the war, maintaining wages at their wartime levels for a further eighteen months, to prevent what was feared would be a sharp fall, as returned servicemen flooded the labour market. When the period of control came to an end, the government rejected the opportunity to introduce a minimum wage, preferring to rely upon wage bargaining and the trade boards and Whitley councils. The two latter remained in place but their numbers and powers did not expand. As unemployment grew, employers resisted such controls on wages, trade unions were weakened, and the Treasury sought to cut costs by reducing the number of civil servants (Lowe 1978; Middlemas 1979).

8.5 The inter-war years: economic depression and welfare expansion

Despite the economic crisis and high unemployment, the inter-war years saw unprecedented expansion of expenditure on 'welfare' by central and local government. UK local plus central government expenditure on social services rose from 2.4 per cent of GNP in 1918 to 11.3 per cent in 1938 (Peacock and Wiseman 1961: 184–91). This was partly due to the costs of providing for the unemployed, but the level of provision was itself new. The stringency of administration of unemployment benefit between the wars was much criticized, often justly, but, for the first time in history, all unemployed men had a right to regular maintenance. Unemployed women had less security of entitlement. The rate of Unemployment Insurance benefit in 1920 was 15s. per week for men, 12s. for women, which, at post-war prices, was barely enough for survival. Nothing was provided for dependent spouses or children. Following protests, from 1921 payments were introduced for dependent wives and children, but not for dependent husbands or parents. It continued to be assumed that women were earning for their own needs alone or were supplementary earners, despite the abundant evidence that their earnings were often essential to their households (Todd 2003).

Unemployment Insurance had never been designed to provide for the mass, long-term unemployment experienced between the wars. Insurance benefit was available only for fifteen weeks in each year. Increasing numbers of people were unemployed for longer, many of them skilled workers whose unemployment could not be blamed on their indolence. The government could not take the political risk of abandoning them to the stigmatizing Poor Law, especially at a time when dispossessed workers were creating threats of revolution in Italy, Germany, Austria, and elsewhere, and strikes were frequent in Britain in 1920 and 1921. Men whose entitlement to insurance expired continued to receive equivalent benefits 'as if' still entitled, provided that they were judged to be 'genuinely seeking work', though these were strictly means tested and the system underwent constant adjustments through the inter-war years as governments strove to contain costs whilst avoiding political conflict.

Married women had especial difficulty in passing the 'genuinely seeking work' test, due either to official doubts about whether they needed paid work or to their unwillingness to work as domestic servants. Since these were always in demand, refusal, even by women with no experience of service, could be taken as evidence that their search for work was not 'genuine'. The Anomalies Act 1931 introduced consistency into the system by withdrawing recognition as 'unemployed' from all married women who were uninsured or whose entitlement to insurance benefit had expired. This caused particular hardship and resentment in areas of high unemployment, such as Lancashire textile towns, where married woman normally worked in factories and their families depended upon their incomes. Less consistently, the means test for unemployment benefit was extended in 1934 to include the incomes of all members of a claimant's household. This acknowledged that the wives and children, including daughters, of unemployed men were making an essential contribution to household income, as indeed they were (Todd 2003), despite the assertion of the Anomalies Act that they could not be unemployed because they did not need employment. Household possessions were also taken into account and benefit could be denied for ownership of, for example, 'excess' numbers of chairs. Such stringency especially contributed to the opprobrium with which the benefits system was later remembered. It was, however, the first time that a British government had acknowledged and subsidized involuntary unemployment on such a scale. In many households, regular, predictable benefit payments were an improvement on the irregular earnings from casual work to which they were accustomed, enabling unprecedented planning of family expenditure (Deacon 1976; Garside 1990).

The combination of falling prices and benefit increases created a real increase of 240 per cent in the value of benefit to a family of four between 1920 and 1931. The unprecedented level of payments helped to generate demand and employment, though this was not admitted to be a conscious policy objective. Governments and officials were always alert to the danger that, above a certain level, benefits would deter claimants from seeking work, though there was no evidence that such abuse occurred on a significant scale. An official investigation in 1937 found that average benefit rates for men, including dependants' allowances, were only two-fifths of the median wage and only 2.3 per cent of men and 5.2 per cent of women received more in benefit than they had earned when last employed. There is no evidence of labour shortage, or that lower, non-existent, or more stringently administered benefits would have benefited the economy (Thane 1996: 162–73; Harris 1997: 324–49).

Governments responded to the economic crisis in other ways. In September 1931 salaries in the public sector were cut: those of government ministers, judges, MPs, police, and the armed services were reduced by an average of 10 per cent, of teachers by 15 per cent. In the early 1930s interest rates were held down and food prices controlled and subsidized, with the establishment of marketing boards to regulate the price of agricultural products in order to restrict food imports and move the balance of trade in Britain's favour. From 1934 the government gave grants totalling £2 million to 'Special' (i.e. Depressed) Areas for building improved health and community services (such as hospitals, parks, swimming pools, sewerage schemes) to provide work, infrastructure conducive to inward investment, and facilities to improve the fitness and morale of the population. From 1937 remissions of rents, rates (local taxes), and income tax to firms willing to set up in Special Areas attracted mostly light industries employing chiefly low-paid women. Such work was welcome, but unhelpful to unemployed male miners and shipbuilders. The Ministry of Labour established training centres to keep the unemployed fit for work and, theoretically, to retrain them, but they focused upon low-skilled employment such as road making, stone breaking, or ditch digging, or, for women, domestic service. Attendance was voluntary, though often firmly encouraged, especially for single unemployed men. Increasingly, it became effectively compulsory for young men though it was never popular due to the small prospect that it would lead to regular employment (Garside 1990).

Other measures were designed to focus the available employment upon prime age male workers. The introduction of state widows' pensions in 1925 and, in the same legislation, the reduction to 65 of the qualifying age for the old age pension for members of the National Insurance scheme were partly designed to remove two large groups from the labour market. The International Labour Organization at this time was urging national governments to introduce or extend schemes of old age pensions to remove older workers and release jobs for younger people. The impact in Britain is hard to assess. The number of workers ceasing to be employed regularly from around age 65 increased, but this may have been due less to the attraction of the low pension of 10s. per week than to the fact that, once unemployed, older men and women found it more difficult than younger people to re-enter the labour market (Johnson 1994; Thane 2000a: 323–7).

This measure was, in fact, inconsistent with a growing concern in inter-war Britain about the effects on the labour market of the ageing population. This was due to the combination of the rapid fall in the birth rate and increasing life expectancy. From the mid-1920s through to the 1950s a range of, often conflicting, concerns were expressed. Keynes argued that it would be easier to improve living standards with a smaller population in which fewer people were competing for work (Keynes 1971–89: xix, 121). Increasingly, between the later 1930s and the 1950s, it was argued that efforts should be made to maximize national productivity by keeping older people in the workforce, and research demonstrated that the work capacities of people in their sixties was considerably greater than was generally believed.[4] Such pressures intensified during the labour shortage which followed the Second World War, though, as we will see, they did not succeed in persuading older people to remain in work beyond the state pensionable age (Thane 1990*b*).

The state pension age for women was reduced to 60 in 1940. This followed a campaign by the National Spinsters' Pensions Association which demanded a lower pensionable age for unmarried women on the grounds that, especially in clerical, secretarial, and shop-work, women were often forced into retirement in their fifties either by ill health or because employers preferred to employ younger women. A government inquiry claimed to be unpersuaded by these arguments. The government conceded a lower pensionable age for women on the different grounds that, on average, wives were five years younger than their husbands and men might be persuaded to retire at 65 if their wives received their pensions simultaneously (Thane 2000*a*: 330–2).

The participation of younger women in the workforce was restricted by the 'marriage bar', which excluded them from employment on marriage. This was not embodied in legislation but it became normal throughout the public sector, including in teaching and local government, in the 1920s and was also common in private sector clerical work, including in banks, and in some factories. This also died out under pressure of the post-Second World War labour shortage.

If pensions were designed to reduce the labour force participation of older people, and the 'marriage bar' that of women, education policy sought to raise the age of entry to work and the skills of new entrants. A succession of government and unofficial surveys between the wars pointed out how few, especially talented working-class, children remained at school beyond the official leaving age of 14. In 1923–24 only 12.6 per cent of all children were at school beyond age 14, by 1937 19.2 per cent. Increased investment in education achieved some, slow, improvement. Similarly increased public investment in house building and public health was in part designed to improve the fitness and productivity of the workforce in what was widely feared to be, in the language of the army medical service, an unfit 'C3 nation'. In the 1930s the Commissioner

---

[4] Including at least sixteen publications by F. Le Gros Clark for the Nuffield Foundation. These included Clark and Dunn (1955) and Clark (1955).

for Special Areas repeatedly stressed that the poor quality of 'human capital' (as it was not then termed), especially in the areas of high unemployment, was hindering economic development. The influential independent research agency, Political and Economic Planning, pointed out in 1937 that ill health was causing the diversion of capital investment from industry into health care. It calculated that the cost of ill health to the nation was £300 million per year: £120 million due to working days lost through illness, the remainder to the cost of treatment and prevention (Herbert 1939).

8.6 The Second World War and after

During the Second World War the government again took firm control of the labour market, this time directing middle-class as well as working-class labour as it had not in the First World War. Undergraduates studying subjects which were deemed to be war related, mainly in the sciences and medicine, received state grants (previously available only to a highly selected few) to study for their degrees in full. Males and females studying 'non-essential' subjects, including all arts subjects, were allowed to remain at university for only two years and then were required to enter prescribed, war-related jobs. From December 1941, when conscription was introduced for women over 18, female graduates might enter only the armed services, the civil service, teaching, nursing, medicine, the land army, or war-related factories. For some, this represented new opportunities. Others, who aspired to some of the new occupations opening up to women, for example in the law, journalism, or architecture, found their paths blocked, mostly forever since when the war ended they were married with families and/or deemed too old to retrain. The wartime direction of labour had a permanent effect on the labour force participation of some women. Men more readily regained their preferred career trajectory after the war.

Belief in the close relationship between high levels of 'welfare' and economic efficiency and productivity profoundly influenced the post-war reconstruction of the 'welfare state', as it began to be named during the war, in conscious opposition to a 'warfare state'. Nevertheless, the Labour government which was elected in 1945 saw its primary task as reconstructing the economy and achieving full employment. The needs of the economy had priority over welfare expenditure (Thane 2000b: 97–103). As in its early days, the Labour Party believed that work and wages were the primary guarantors of 'welfare'. And, as in the past, male workers took priority. In 1946, following a Royal Commission report on equal pay, and consistently until they were defeated in 1951, Labour refused to legislate for gender equality in pay, on the grounds that it would increase the costs of export industries. A Conservative government introduced equal pay in the public sector in 1955, following campaigning by professional women (Smith 1992).

Labour did encourage older women, whose children were grown, to be active in the labour market. With the effective abolition of the marriage bar, many more of them did so, in particular middle-class women, for whom paid work was now socially acceptable as it had not previously been. However, in the absence of opportunities for retraining, except in teaching in which there was a shortage, and in a continuing climate of low expectations of women's work capacities, their work tended to be low status, low paid, and often part time. Younger women were expected to remain at home caring for their children, with some assistance from the small family allowances which were introduced in 1945. Mothers of young children who wished to work were hampered, unless they were wealthy enough to buy childcare, by an acute shortage of nursery places and other forms of childcare, though these had been readily provided during the war when paid work, even by mothers, was regarded as a national necessity (Thane 1991: 183–4). Unwillingness to invest in childcare remained a feature of British 'welfare' policy for the remainder of the century.

The Labour government recognized that increased investment in education, health, and housing was necessary to improve the quality of human capital, but it was as concerned as its subsequent critics about the danger of burdening the economy with excessive welfare costs. Capital and materials for welfare purposes were strictly controlled and Britain spent less than neighbouring countries. In 1950, when much of the rest of Western Europe was only just emerging from economic collapse, Britain's spending on social security as a percentage of GDP was lower than that of West Germany, Austria, and Belgium. By 1952, Britain had fallen behind France and Denmark also (Harris 1991). In the eyes of Attlee's government, the needs of industry came first. In consequence, although the school leaving age was raised to 15 in 1947 and more teachers were trained, little was spent on school buildings. Not until 1950 did education expenditure exceed that before the war and then by only 4 per cent. Despite a promised 'housing drive', the shortage of housing, and the appalling state of much of it, worsened both by bombing and by the cessation of building during the war, investment in housing in 1945–51 was no higher than in 1925–37. Labour, raw materials, and investment were diverted where possible into industrial production rather than into development of the social infrastructure. Only in 1948 did Labour meet its promised target of 240,000 new houses per year. Nevertheless, the housing stock grew by 1,192,000 between 1945 and 1951, but this was far fewer than was needed. This was partly due to the laudable desire of the Minister of Health, Aneurin Bevan, to build high-quality, and hence expensive, working-class housing, but it was due also to strict expenditure controls imposed by the Treasury. Similarly, health services were reorganized and nationalized in 1948 but little was spent on hospitals or health centres. No new hospital was built until the late 1950s. Total government expenditure on social services rose only from 10 to 14 per cent of

GDP between 1945 and 1950, while total government expenditure fell by 20 per cent, mainly due to defence cuts (Thane 2000*b*: 97–193).

An important feature of the post-war reorganization of the welfare system was the overhaul of National Insurance, also implemented in 1948. This was based on the report written for the government in 1942 by William Beveridge, *Social Insurance and Allied Services* (Beveridge 1942). Beveridge retained the values of his earlier life, in particular the belief that regular work and adequate wages were the keys to personal welfare and that the state should provide no more than a safety net for those unable to provide for themselves; though he believed that it should also commit itself to achieving full employment and providing education and training, health care, and a minimum wage. He advocated pensions and other benefits to be set at no more than subsistence level. They should be supplemented by private saving, ideally through non-profit organizations such as friendly societies and trade unions.

Beveridge was aware of, and had long been concerned about, as his Report put it, 'The Problem of Age': the impending danger of a shrinking prime age population bearing the costs of increasing numbers of older people. He advocated building into the pension system incentives to remain at work past the pensionable age by raising the level of pension with each year of deferral. He also recommended that widows of working age without dependants should receive benefits for only thirteen weeks and that the payment of long-term disability benefit should be dependent upon retraining in appropriate cases. Beveridge recognized the problems of providing through a national insurance scheme for the needs of divorced and separated wives and unmarried women who were out of the labour force and recommended that they also should receive state benefits (Blackburn 1995; Harris 1997: 365–477).

All of these latter recommendations were among many to be rejected or watered down, either by the Treasury or by the Labour government. Beveridge's old ally Churchill, Conservative Prime Minister and war leader in 1942, opposed his proposals, for which he suffered at the polls in 1945. The Labour government set benefits at lower levels than Beveridge hoped and, in consequence, means testing was never reduced to the low levels he intended. Those who deferred retirement were granted higher pensions, but the premium was so small that it was not a significant incentive to stay at work. Labour claimed to be committed to discouraging earlier retirement especially in view of the labour shortage, and it made some efforts to persuade employers to keep older workers on. But this was at odds with the party's commitment to earlier retirement for working people after long working lives, which at this time had often begun at age 12 or 13. Earlier retirement was strongly advocated by the trade unions. In reality the numbers of men retiring at the pensionable age of 65 steadily increased. According to the censuses, in 1931 47.5 per cent of men were in employment past age 65; in 1951 31 per cent; 23 per cent in 1961; 19 per cent in 1971; 13 per cent in 1981. Through the 1950s

Conservative governments continued to express concern about the ageing of the population and a desire for workers to work to later ages, but, as the figures suggest, with no greater success. From the early 1960s, the effects of the wartime and post-war increases in the birth rate were beginning to impact on the labour market, together with the ending of National Service which released more young men into the labour force, the larger numbers of women working, and the arrival of migrant workers especially from the Caribbean and South Asia. In consequence, panic about an 'old age crisis' died away, only to revive in the 1980s. Meanwhile, for the first time in history, the mass of manual workers came to expect retirement as a normal phase of the life course, assisted by state pensions which, though less generous than in any other high-income country, were higher than ever before (Johnson 1994; Thane 1990b, 2000a: 333–54).

8.7 The legacy of the 1940s

Low benefits characterized the post-war British 'welfare state'. It was only minimally redistributive, but it provided a real safety net which, until the 1980s, prevented the poorest from falling seriously behind the rising living standards of the remainder. Far from recklessly diverting funds which could have been invested in reconstructing the economy, as some have claimed (notably Barnett 1986), 'the "welfare state" of the 1940s was an austere product of an age of austerity' (Tomlinson 1995). It can certainly be argued that full employment did more than social policies to promote post-war 'welfare' . The living standards of those unable to benefit from full employment and living on benefits due to old age, sickness, disability, etc. did fall behind those of the rest of the population in the post-war decades, though by less than they might have done in the absence of a 'welfare state'. They were protected from extreme poverty only by increasing and increasingly complex means testing. The proportion of the British population receiving means-tested benefits was just over 4 per cent in 1948, 8 per cent in 1974, 16 per cent in 1986, 20 per cent in 1994 (Johnson 2004: 24).

The principles on which the social security system was based, and the relatively low level of flat-rate benefits, hardly changed until the end of the century, despite a temporary rise in the relative value of benefits during the 1960s and 1970s. At the same time there was a steady fall in the threshold above which income tax was paid. In 1949–50 a married man with two children under the age of 11 began to pay income tax when his income exceeded 120 per cent of average manual earnings. By 1980–81 an identical household began to pay tax when its income exceeded only 50 per cent of average manual earnings (Johnson 2004: 221). This change occurred especially fast in the inflation of the mid-1970s. The lack of integration of the tax and social security systems created what were termed 'poverty traps' in which increasing numbers of households found that a slight increase in income simultaneously increased their tax liability and reduced their benefit entitlement, with a negative net impact on their incomes.[5] This created a disincentive even for those keen to work. The severity of these traps was gradually reduced from the late 1980s (Field and Piachaud 1971; Lowe 2005: 153, 298, 341).

8.8 The Conservatives and welfare, 1951–64

Conservative governments were in office from 1951 to 1964. They established a series of policy reviews designed to curtail the costs of health and welfare. Few cuts resulted, not least because the 'welfare state' was popular, including among middle-class voters. Many of them had struggled previously to pay the high costs of health care and education in particular, and they benefited disproportionately from the post-war changes since their children stayed longest in education and they were more likely than poorer people to live close to the best-equipped schools and hospitals.

The Conservatives implemented a notable programme of public sector house building, aware that the failure to tackle housing need had harmed Labour in the elections of 1950 and 1951, though the new housing was of poorer quality than that built between 1945 and 1951. From 1962 they embarked on the first hospital-building programme since the war. In other respects the ramshackle structure of the welfare state erected by Labour was little changed. Improvements in pensions, for example, were left to employers and the private market. The improvement in living standards during the period, due above all to near-full employment, and the real gains from improved welfare provision since 1945, whatever its inadequacies, muffled criticism (Lowe 2005: 174–272). Only in the early 1960s did research begin to measure the extent of continuing poverty especially among older people and working families with above average numbers of children (Abel-Smith and Townsend 1965; Townsend 1979; Gazeley 2003: 158–85).

8.9 The 1960s and 1970s: rising welfare expenditure

A belief, also, that the British economy was performing less well than its competitors contributed to the narrow defeat of the Conservatives in 1964. Labour's campaign gave primacy to the need to modernize the economy. Once in government again, Labour, led by Harold Wilson, aimed to put economic before social policy, though the two were seen to be closely related. The

[5] The term was coined and the problem defined by Field and Piachaud (1971).

Wilson government saw itself as carrying forward the agenda of the Attlee government. However, its immediate priorities were set by the combination of an unforeseen economic crisis and the slimness of its majority. It reacted to the latter with relatively generous improvements in welfare expenditure, with an eye to a speedy election. Pensions were raised to the highest level in their history, about 21 per cent of average male manual earnings, though still many pensioners could not survive on them without means-tested assistance. Means-tested benefits for pensioners were increased, renamed 'supplementary benefit', and administered more humanely to make them less stigmatizing and to increase the always incomplete uptake among the needy. Redundancy payments were introduced. Short-term unemployment benefits were increased and earnings-related supplements for short-term sickness and unemployment benefits were introduced in 1965, designed to promote flexibility in the labour market, where there was seen to be an over-concentration of workers in older industries. Labour also took steps to improve state education partly in response to a perceived shortage of skilled workers (Thane 2000b: 107–10).

Labour won the election of 1966 with a decisive majority after a campaign in which social policy was prominent. Almost immediately another economic crisis, followed by devaluation in 1967, led to its cutting back on its promises. Overall, however, by the time it was voted out of office in 1970, Labour had presided over a notably rapid expansion of social expenditure especially on housing, education, pensions, and child benefit. This, however, characterized all high-income countries at this time; the rate of growth of social expenditure in Britain was slower than in most other OECD countries, and was slower than before 1960 (Johnson 2004: 224).

A Conservative government led by Edward Heath followed from 1970 to 1974. Beset by growing international economic problems, it made no significant changes in the social welfare system. In February 1974, Wilson and Labour returned, again with a tiny majority in a mounting economic crisis. Again, expenditure on benefits and housing was significantly increased, mainly for electoral reasons. In a second election in October 1974 Labour gained a small increase in its majority. Amid worsening economic problems and rising unemployment it continued to increase expenditure on pensions, child, and other benefits, including introducing a lone parent benefit in response to a highly visible increase in low-income households headed by lone mothers due to a fast-rising divorce rate. In 1975 the Sex Discrimination Act gave women the right in principle to equal access to jobs and promotion and equal treatment at work with men. Statutory, paid, maternity leave was introduced in 1975. Government was now prepared to fund some assistance to working mothers, recognizing how vital women workers had become to the economy, and in response to pressure from women (Thane 2000b: 110–12). Nevertheless, in 1979 Labour lost another election, to be succeeded by a Conservative government, led, this time, by Margaret Thatcher.

In the 1960s and 1970s social and economic policy were less coherently linked than in 1945–51 and, as in the 1950s, government policy was often triggered by short-term electoral pressures. Social expenditure went through the fastest period of growth of the century, though slower in Britain and to a lower percentage of GDP than in any comparable country. For example, public expenditure on health rose between 1960 and 1980 from 3.3 per cent GDP to 5.2 per cent in the UK; 2.5 per cent to 6.1 per cent in France; from 3.2 per cent to 6.5 per cent in Germany. On pensions the percentage change was from 4 to 5.9 in the UK, 6 to 10.5 in France, 9.7 to 12.8 in Germany. From 1980 the growth of social expenditure slowed everywhere, but fastest in the UK. In 1960 the UK was close to the top among OECD countries in public spending on health and education; by the mid-1990s it was close to the bottom. Throughout the post-war period it was 'the most miserly provider' of pensions in the OECD (Johnson 2004: 224).

Successive accretions to a 'welfare state' which had been incoherent from its inception and had undergone no coordinated review since the Second World War had by the late 1970s created a structure which was failing to deliver support efficiently to many in real need. Throughout the century, up to the mid-1970s, it had been broadly accepted by all but a minority on the political right that state welfare helped to promote the efficiency of the labour force and hence the efficiency and growth of the economy as a whole. Since 1945 it had been broadly accepted that welfare expenditure could help to manage the economy out of short-term difficulties. Through the late 1970s and 1980s, by contrast, it was seen as a burden to be reduced in order to promote economic growth, a source of economic difficulties by diverting expenditure from savings and investment, creating disincentives to work and save rather than palliatives. In 1976, James Callaghan, who succeeded Wilson as Prime Minister in that year, signalled this change in the *Zeitgeist* by admitting that:

We used to think that you could just spend your way out of a recession, by cutting taxes and boosting government spending. I tell you in all candour that option no longer exists, and in so far as it ever did exist, it worked by injecting inflation into the economy. And each time that happened, the average level of unemployment has risen.[6]

8.10 Cutting back the 'welfare state'

Guided by similar beliefs, Conservative governments through the 1980s and early 1990s cut public expenditure on health, housing, education, and other benefits. The value of the pension was allowed to sink to its lowest post-war level. This differentially hurt older women who, at the end as at the beginning of the century, were more numerous and poorer in old age than men, with less

---

[6] Speech to the Labour Party Conference, *The Times*, 29 Sept. 1976.

access to occupational or other private sector pensions, and more dependent on the state pension and means-tested supplements. It was argued that measures to protect employees, for example against unfair dismissal, or benefits such as maternity leave, together with the power of trade unions to maintain rigid and excessive pay levels, were increasing the costs of employers and diminishing flexibility in the labour market. Deregulation followed, designed to minimize employee protection and encourage flexibility and to encourage individuals to shift from state-funded welfare to pensions and other benefits purchased in the private market. The post-war 'safety net' developed gaping holes and the income gap between rich and poor widened more rapidly than at any time since 1945. Total government social expenditure continued to rise, nonetheless, due to the rapid increase in unemployment. Unemployment benefits were cut. The earnings-related supplement was abolished in 1982, though still no government dared take the political risk of abandoning the unemployed entirely (Lowe 2005: 313–75).

The official statistics of unemployment rose from 5.4 per cent of insured workers in 1979 to 15.2 per cent in 1986. Thereafter it fell, only to rise again in the 1990s, remaining well above the pre-1979 level. This was despite the fact that there were more than thirty changes to the way that it was officially measured between 1979 and 1997, all in the direction of reducing the numbers, e.g. by excluding claimants with a working partner, or who refused work on grounds of being overqualified. The numbers 'genuinely seeking work' were further reduced by government encouragement of redundant workers (including many miners as the coal industry dwindled) to claim disability rather than unemployment benefit, or 'job seekers' allowance' as it became in 1996. 'Downsizing' firms were not discouraged from laying off older workers who could qualify for an occupational pension in place of unemployment benefit. By 1990 about one-third of all males reaching the age of 60 had retired, not all of them willingly (Thane 2000a: 489–90; Kohli et al. 1991). At the same time many more students were encouraged to enter higher education, thus deferring entry to the labour force until at least age 21.

The argument that welfare expenditure harms economic performance is, at best, unproven. In 1981 the OECD argued that rising social expenditure was a source of the current economic difficulties by correlating rising rates of social expenditure across the OECD countries from the late 1960s with the slowdown in economic activity. But if they had taken a longer view, taking in the even faster rates of growth of social expenditure from the 1950s to the mid-1960s, they would have found these to correlate with the strongest, most sustained period of boom ever experienced by the developed economies, as the OECD later acknowledged. Since for most of the period since 1945 Britain has spent less on welfare state transfers and services than most of its major competitors, it is difficult to see these as primarily responsible for any weaknesses in the performance of the economy. It is difficult to believe that performance would have been stronger if even less had been spent on improving the skills base or the health of workers (Johnson 2004: 226–7).

8.11 The Labour Party and 'Welfare to Work' 2

When New Labour came to power in 1997 it was as passionately committed as its Old Labour predecessors to the belief that work was the best route to welfare. When John Smith (decidedly 'Old' rather than 'New' Labour) became leader in 1992, he set about serious, long-term thinking about social policy, believing that, fifty years after the Beveridge Report, the 'welfare state' required rethinking. He established the Social Justice Commission for this purpose, but did not live to see its report in 1994. The first two propositions on which its recommendations rested were:

- We must transform the welfare state from a safety net in times of trouble to a springboard for economic opportunity. Paid work for a fair wage is the most secure and sustainable way out of poverty.
- We must radically improve access to education and training, and invest in the talent of all our people. (Commission on Social Justice 1994: 1–2)

The Report assumed that 'paid or unpaid work is central to our lives', so 'government must commit itself to a modern form of full employment' suited to what it recognized was now a labour market containing two sexes, operating in what it assumed to be a less stable, more flexible labour market than that of the 1940s. The long-term unemployed, including lone mothers of young children, should be reintegrated into the economy through access to education and training and help with childcare. A minimum wage, improved job security, and other rights at work, plus an integrated tax and benefit system designed to eliminate the 'poverty trap', would provide incentives to work. Government policy 'must offer a hand up, not a hand out' (Commission on Social Justice 1994: 7–8).

When New Labour came into office, the Treasury, under Gordon Brown, took an unprecedented lead in social policy development, on the lines advocated by the Social Justice Commission, once they had reassured what they assumed to be the conservative masses of 'middle England' by refusing for two years to exceed the limited spending plans of their predecessors (Toynbee and Walker 2001: 18–19). A minimum wage, which cost the government very little, was at last established in 1998. The government also began immediately to plan, as it had promised in its election manifesto, to implement what it called a New Deal, designed to get into the workforce those on benefit who were capable of work or training. This was much influenced by US 'Welfare to Work' schemes. It was financed by a £5 billion windfall tax on the privatized utilities. The scheme began in 1999 with the 250,000 18–25-year-olds who were neither in work nor education. They were summoned to meet advisers, who spent up to four months assessing each claimant and helping them to find jobs. If that failed, they had to accept one of four options: education for up a year, work with an employer paid £60 a week to take them on to give them experience of work; work on an environmental project or with a voluntary organization. For the first time unemployed people were given intensive personal advice and support. The scheme was later extended to single mothers. Work was never compulsory for them, but an interview, to demonstrate to them what was on offer, was obligatory from April 2001. Further schemes were then implemented for unemployed people over age 25, and for the over 50s who were involuntarily out of the workforce, though the problem remained of employer stereotyping of older people as far less capable and adaptable than they were. Finally it was extended to the most sensitive group, the 2.7 million (in 2005) on disability benefit who were assessed as capable of work, mildly at first, but more assertively in proposals issued in February 2005. In 2001 all the schemes were merged in the ONE gateway initiative.

By mid-2000 it was calculated that 75 per cent of under-25 graduates of the New Deal were in work within three months; the remainder vanished from the benefit system and were presumed to have been claiming fraudulently. Assessment of the effects of the New Deal was difficult because the economy was recovering and more jobs were becoming available, but even for the long-term unemployed over age 25, independent assessors estimated that the New Deal had doubled the number who found work. The percentage of lone parents (overwhelmingly mothers) in paid work rose between 1997 and 2005 from 45 to 55.8 (Toynbee and Walker 2003: 13–15; Dept. of Work and Pensions 2005; Lowe 2005: 403).

'If the New Deal was the Treasury's principal means for inducing people to work, tax credits were its principal means for ensuring that work paid' (Lowe 2005: 404) and for ensuring that the structure of benefits and taxation did not deter workers. The Working Families Tax Credit, introduced in 1999, was a major step to eliminating the 'poverty trap'. An array of further credits followed which were rationalized in April 2003 into three main schemes: Child Tax Credit, which amalgamated all tax allowances and benefits for children; Working Tax Credit which similarly amalgamated tax allowances and means-tested benefits for single people and childless couples, including disabled people; Pension Credit which provided a minimum income for pensioners. A fundamental change was beginning in the character of the post-war 'welfare state', de-emphasizing universal flat-rate benefits and giving primacy to means-tested (or 'targeted' as they were now termed) benefits adjusted to individual need.

The schemes were more generous than their predecessors. To reduce disincentives to work there was a reduction in the rate at which credits were withdrawn as working income rose (the 'taper'). To reduce disincentives to save, there was an increase in the level of savings disregarded in the calculation of entitlement. As ever, the main problem was less than optimal take-up, often because people were unaware of their entitlement. In 2004, one in five of the poorest pensioners were not receiving means-tested benefit for which they were eligible. Also the Treasury lacked the capacity to administer this new and very complex system efficiently and the accuracy and regularity of payments could not be guaranteed. In consequence, the Inland Revenue was severely criticized by the National Audit Office in 2003. The problems appeared to have been resolved by 2005 (Lowe 2005: 404–6).

Another strand of New Labour activity was influenced by renewed concern about the ageing of the population and the dwindling numbers of younger workers due to the steady fall in the birth rate since the late 1960s and continued rises in life expectancy. This had been evident internationally from the 1980s (World Bank 1994; Thane 2000a: 475–93). The chief response of the Conservative governments had been to cut state pensions. Labour were reluctant to restore the universal pension even to the real equivalent of its low pre-1979 levels, although, as we have seen, they substantially increased means-tested benefits for poorer pensioners. From 2004 they took more active measures than their predecessors in 1945–51 had done to prolong the working life of older people by means of the New Deal for over 50s and, from 2004, raising the retirement age in that part of the workforce they could easily control, the public sector, beginning with the civil service and the National Health Service. In much of the sector, it had been fixed at 60 since the mid-nineteenth century. Unquestionably, people were fit to work at later ages in the early twenty-first century than a century before, due in part to a century of state welfare (Thane 2000a: 475–93; Kirkwood 2001). In the private sector, also, the retirement age began to rise again, as employers realized that it had not been wholly wise to dispose of so many experienced and dependable older workers.

New Labour's welfare activities were centrally focused on the many facets of 'Welfare to Work', whilst they sought to minimize public expenditure on 'welfare' activities less clearly linked to the labour market, such as legal aid (introduced by Attlee's government in 1948) and housing. Under New Labour the 'welfare state' has been directed with particular vigour towards maximizing participation in the labour market, the full effects of which, in 2005, remain to be seen.

References

Abel-Smith, B., and Townsend, P. (1965). *The Poor and the Poorest*. London: Bell.

Barnett, C. (1986). *The Audit of War*. Basingstoke: Macmillan.

Beveridge, W. (1942). *Social Insurance and Allied Services: A Report*. Cmd. 6404. London: His Majesty's Stationery Office.

Blackburn, S. (1991). 'Ideology and Social Policy: The Origin of the Trade Boards Act'. *Historical Journal*, 34/1: 43–64.

—— (1995). 'How Useful are Feminist Theories of the Welfare State?' *Women's History Review*, 4/3: 369–94.

Booth, C. (1889–1903). *Life and Labour of the People of London*, 17 vols. London: Williams and Norgate.

Bowley, A. L., and Burnett-Hurst, A. R. (1915). *Livelihood and Poverty*. London: G. Bell and Sons.

Clark, F. Le Gros (1955). *Ageing Men in the Labour Force*. London: Nuffield Foundation.

—— and Dunn, A. (1955). *Ageing and Industry*. London: Nuffield Foundation.

Commission on Social Justice (1994). *Social Justice: Strategies for National Renewal*. London: Vintage.

Deacon, A. (1976). *In Search of the Scrounger*. London: Bell.

Field, F., and Piachaud, D. (1971). 'The Poverty Trap'. *New Statesman*, 3 December.

Garside, W. R. (1990). *British Unemployment, 1919–1939*. Cambridge: Cambridge University Press.

Gazeley, I. (2003). *Poverty in Britain, 1900–1965*. Basingstoke: Macmillan.

Halsey, A. H., and Webb, J. (2000). *Twentieth Century British Social Trends*. London: Macmillan.

Harris, J. (1972). *Unemployment and Politics: A Study in English Social Policy, 1886–1914*. Oxford: Oxford University Press.

—— (1990). 'Society and the State in Twentieth Century Britain', in F. M. L. Thompson (ed.), *The Cambridge Social History of Britain, 1750–1950*. Cambridge: Cambridge University Press, iii. 180–250.

—— (1991). 'Enterprise and the Welfare State: A Comparative Perspective', in T. Gourvish and A. O'Day (eds.), *Britain since 1945*. Basingstoke: Macmillan, 39–58.

—— (1993). *Private Lives, Public Spirit: A Social History of Britain, 1870–1914*. Oxford: Oxford University Press.

—— (1997). *William Beveridge. A Biography*, 2nd edn. Oxford: Oxford University Press.

Herbert, S. M. (1939). *Britain's Health*. Harmondsworth: Penguin.

Johnson, P. (1994). 'The Employment and Retirement of Older Men in England and Wales, 1881–1981'. *Economic History Review*, 47/1: 106–28.

—— (2004). 'The Welfare State, Income and Living Standards', in R. Floud and P. Johnson (eds.), *The Cambridge Economic History of Modern Britain*, vol. iii. Cambridge: Cambridge University Press, 213–37.

Keynes, J. M. (1971–89). *The Collected Writings of J. Maynard Keynes*, ed. D. Moggridge. London: Macmillan.

Kirkwood. T. (2001). *The End of Age: Why Everything about Ageing is Changing*. London: Profile Books.

Kohli, M., et al. (1991). *Time for Retirement: Comparative Studies of Early Exit from the Labour Force*. Cambridge: Cambridge University Press.

Lowe, R. (1978).'The Erosion of State Intervention in Britain, 1917–24'. *Economic History Review*, 31/2: 270–86.

—— (2005). *The Welfare State in Britain since 1945*, 3rd edn. Basingstoke: Macmillan.

MacDonald, J. R. (1907). *The New Unemployed Bill of the Labour Party*. London: ILP Publications.

—— (1912). *Labour Party's Policy*. London: ILP Publications.

Middlemas, K. (1979). *Politics in Industrial Society*. London: Deutsch.

Mitchell, B., and Deane, P. (1962). *Abstract of British Historical Statistics*. Cambridge: Cambridge University Press.

Peacock, A. T., and Wiseman, J. (1961). *The Growth of Public Expenditure in the UK*. Princeton: Princeton University Press.

Reid, A. J. (2004). *United We Stand: A History of Britain's Trade Unions*. London: Penguin.

Rowntree, B. S. (1915). *Poverty: A Study of Town Life*. London: Macmillan.

Smith, H. L. (1992). 'The Politics of Conservative Reform: The Equal Pay for Equal Work Issue, 1945–1955'. *Historical Journal*, 35/2: 401–15.

Thane, P. (1990*a*). 'Government and Society in England and Wales, 1750–1914', in F. M. L. Thompson (ed.), *The Cambridge Social History of Britain, 1750–1950*. Cambridge: Cambridge University Press, iii. 63–118.

—— (1990*b*). 'The Debate on the Declining Birth-Rate in Britain: The "Menace" of an Ageing Population, 1920s–1950s'. *Continuity and Change*, 5/2: 283–305.

—— (1991). 'Towards Equal Opportunities? Women in Britain since 1945', in T. Gourvish and A. O'Day (eds.), *Britain since 1945*. Basingstoke: Macmillan, 183–208.

—— (1996). *The Foundations of the Welfare State*, 2nd edn. London: Longman Pearson.

—— (2000*a*). *Old Age in English History: Past Experiences, Present Issues*. Oxford: Oxford University Press.

—— (2000*b*). 'Labour and Welfare', in D. Tanner, P. Thane, and N. Tiratsoo (eds.), *Labour's First Century*. Cambridge: Cambridge University Press.

Todd, S. (2003). 'Young Women, Employment, and the Family in Interwar England. D.Phil. thesis.

—— (2005). *Young Women, Work, and Family in England 1918–1950*. Oxford: Oxford University Press.

Tomlinson, J. (1995). 'Welfare and the Economy: The Economic Impact of the Welfare State, 1945–51'. *Twentieth Century British History*, 6: 220–43.

Townsend, P. (1979). *Poverty in the United Kingdom*. Harmondsworth: Penguin.

Toynbee, P., and Walker, D. (2001). *Did Things Get Better? An Audit of Labour's Successes and Failures*. London: Penguin.

World Bank (1994). *Averting the Old Age Crisis: Policies to Protect the Old and Promote Growth*. Oxford: Oxford University Press.

9

Industrial Relations

Chris Wrigley

British industrial relations changed very markedly during the twentieth century. The 'frontier of control' between managements and workforces oscillated greatly. Where the lines of demarcation lay was often affected by the changing role of the state, as in the two world wars, and by major changes in the international or national economies. There were often notably different conditions between the private and the public sectors, between large and small workplaces, between predominantly male and predominantly female workforces, as well as a myriad of variations between different industries and services.

Ways of looking at the development of British industrial relations have changed with changing circumstances. What had seemed to many commentators as inevitable in the three post-Second World War decades seemed less significant by the end of the century. Indeed, in some respects the history of British industrial relations has often had a distinctly Whiggish flavour to it. Part of Herbert Butterfield's (1931) definition of 'Whig history' was 'the tendency in many historians . . . to emphasise certain principles of progress in the past and to produce a story which is a ratification if not the glorification of the present'.[1] A feature of such accounts was the expression of considerable satisfaction at the British political system compared with the systems of France and other continental European nations.[2] These features are present in the dominant accounts of British industrial relations, to which Hugh Clegg was a major contributor, and their most influential outcome was the Donovan Report of 1968.[3]

In analysing the particular features of the British system of industrial relations Clegg and his colleagues were right to highlight its long evolution. In their preface to *The System of Industrial Relations in Great Britain* (1954) Allan

---

[1] For similar comments on 'the Whiggish flavour of inevitability' see Fox (1985: 167).

[2] For a discussion of the strong sense of British superiority over French and other nationalities in literature, see Collini (1991: 342–73).

[3] The Royal Commission on Trade Unions and Employers' Associations (1965–68) was chaired by Lord Donovan, its report being widely known as the Donovan Report.

Flanders and Hugh Clegg commented, 'The growth of our system of industrial relations has been inextricably intertwined with the growth of our entire social system', and they included in the book a chapter on the social background by Asa Briggs. The centrality of collective bargaining to the British system was clearly stated by Flanders and Clegg (1954: p. v):

Trade unions and employers' associations are the chief institutions of industrial relations. Their main relationship is through collective bargaining. The state supports and supplements collective bargaining in a number of ways, and the law of industrial relations therefore demands separate consideration. . . . More and more of the relationships between employers, trade unions and the state have come to be carried on through the method of joint consultation.

Otto Kahn-Freud in his chapter on the legal framework was notably explicit as to how the British system was a higher form of industrial relations than elsewhere. He observed,

The desire of both sides of industry to provide for, and to operate, an effective system of collective bargaining is a stronger guarantee of industrial peace and of smooth functioning of labour–management relations than any action legislators or courts or enforcement officers can ever hope to undertake . . . there exists something like an inverse correlation between the practical significance of legal sanctions and the degree to which industrial relations have reached a state of maturity . . . There is, perhaps, no major country in the world in which the law has played a less significant role in the shaping of these relations than in Great Britain and in which today the law and the legal profession have less to do with labour relations. (Flanders and Clegg 1954: 43–4)

Such were the dominant views of British industrial relations until at least the 1970s. This view was well summarized in the Ministry of Labour's written evidence to the Donovan Commission: 'The main feature of the British system of industrial relations is the voluntary machinery which has grown up over a wide area of employment for industry-wide collective bargaining and discussion between employers' associations and trade unions over terms and conditions of employment.'[4] The Donovan Report upheld the 'abstentionist attitude' of the state and 'voluntary collective bargaining' generally (Royal Commission 1968: 10).

Yet this long and uniquely British route to Otto Kahn-Freud's 'collective laissez-faire' could be seen as the explanation for various 'British diseases', ranging at various times from 'ca'canny' (restriction of output) to wildcat strikes and 'overmighty trade unions'. To some extent this was the antithesis of Whig history. Max Beloff (1979) made such links explicit for the post-Second World War period in 1979, when giving a paper on British history from the coming of the welfare state to then; he suggested that it was 'the Whig interpretation of

---

[4] Royal Commission (1965: 11). This evidence restated the Ministry of Labour's position as expounded in such publications as its *Industrial Relations Handbook* (1961).

history in reverse', showing things going from bad to worse since 1945 with industrial relations prominent in his account.

The critics of the trade unions and of the British system of industrial relations in the 1950s and 1960s believed that the 1906 Trades Disputes Act went too far in providing trade unions with legal immunity. In 1958 the Inns of Court Conservative and Unionist Society in a pamphlet entitled *A Giant's Strength* called for legal restrictions on trade union power and highlighted the closed shop, restrictive practices, secondary strikes, and demarcation disputes as problems needing remedies. In its evidence to the Donovan Commission the Inns of Court Conservative and Unionist Society observed,

There can be no doubt since 1906 trade unions have grown in stature. They are now among the most powerful and important bodies in the State. In the last twenty-five years there has been a seller's market for labour and the present power of the trade unions derives from this. It is likely to persist. Special legal privileges granted in the days of their weakness must be reviewed. (Conservative Political Centre 1966: 10)

The setting up of the Royal Commission in 1965 reflected a widely shared political recognition that the voluntarist system of industrial relations needed reform, whether mild or drastic. In spring 1964 Joseph Godber, the Conservative Minister of Labour, declared the intention of Sir Alec Douglas-Home's government to set up an inquiry into the law relating to trade unions and employers' associations. The Royal Commission was appointed in April 1965 when Harold Wilson's Labour government was in office. After the publication of the Donovan Report in 1968 both the Labour government, with its *In Place of Strife* proposals of early 1969, and its successor, Edward Heath's Conservative government, with the Industrial Relations Act 1971, moved further from voluntarism and towards greater legal provisions than the Donovan Report recommended. While the Labour legislation of 1974–75 returned to voluntarist approaches to industrial relations, this return was short-lived, with an array of laws curtailing trade unions' actions enacted under the Conservative governments of Margaret Thatcher (1979–90) and John Major (1990–97).

In understanding both the changes in British industrial relations and the way these have been understood it is necessary to review the growth and decline of at least national collective bargaining across the twentieth century and also the changing roles of the state and the law. The term 'collective bargaining' was coined and popularized by Beatrice and Sidney Webb in their 1890s writings on the cooperative and trade union movements. Allan Flanders, when discussing the term's origins and meaning, observed, 'Whatever else it may be, clearly it is a method of settling the terms and conditions of employment of employees', and added that it could be contrasted with individual bargaining and public regulation (Flanders 1954: 225–33).[5]

---

[5] For a recent discussion of the Webbs and their use of the term, see Lyddon (2003: 97–8).

In British writing on the history of industrial relations collective bargaining has frequently been linked intimately to the growth of trade unions and employers' associations and seen as spreading predominantly in the late nineteenth century. For the Webbs collective bargaining and trade unionism were linked together like a horse and carriage: 'the method of collective bargaining—in short Trade Unionism', as they once put it (quoted in Lyddon 2003: 98), and Flanders (1954: 262) commented that 'the history of collective bargaining during the nineteenth century is largely the history of trade unionism'. More recently, Jaffe (2000) has shown that local collective bargaining by workers concerned to regulate their work was widespread and well established earlier, in the first two-thirds of the nineteenth century.

Nevertheless, the growth of trade unions was the major reason in Britain for many employers or employers' organizations being prepared to negotiate. In 1892, roughly when the Webbs were initially writing on trade unions, British trade union membership was at about 1,468,000, a union density of just over 11 per cent, whereas in Germany trade union membership was about 295,000, a union density of a little over 2 per cent (Bain and Price 1980; Visser 1989).[6] German trade unionism grew rapidly in the early twentieth century, reaching 3,928,900 in 1913, a union density of 21.3 per cent, while British trade union membership reached 4,107,000, a density of 24.8 per cent, in 1913. See Table 9.1 for figures for these, the USA, and some other European countries.

Yet, the extent of collective bargaining in the two countries was very different. For Britain in 1910 the Board of Trade reported 1,696 collective agreements covering directly 2,400,000 industrial workers, under a quarter of the total. As this figure omitted single firms' agreements and public sector agreements with the local authorities, Clegg (1985: 548) suggested that near 3 million would be more accurate. In mining and quarrying there were fifty-six

Table 9.1. Trade unions, 1900–39

Year	Britain	France	Germany	Sweden	USA
1900	1,908 (13.1)	500	838.8 (5.7)	67.2 (4.8)	869 (5.5)
1914	4,117 (24.7)	1,000	2,436.3 (13.0)	159.1 (9.9)	2,566 (9/9)
1920	8,253 (48.2)	2,000	9,192.9 (45.2)	469.8 (27.7)	4,775 (16.7)
1931	4,569 (24.3)	884	6,888.0 (23.5)	740.0 (37.7)	3,142 (8.6)
1939	6,206 (31.9)	3,000[a]	—[b]	1,119.7 (53.6)	6,339 (14.9)

Note: The main figures are in thousands, the figures in brackets are trade union densities.

[a] The French figure for 1939 is very debatable. The CGT alone claimed 5,300,000 members in 1936, but this was too high and trade union membership fell by 1939.
[b] Suppressed by the Nazis.

Sources: Bain and Price (1980: 39, 88, 133, 142); Lorwin (1954: 23, 55, 74); Marquand (1939).

[6] The union density is the percentage of people in a trade union or trade unions out of those legally able to join.

agreements covering 900,000 workers (Board of Trade 1910). At the same time in Imperial Germany less than a hundred miners' conditions of employment were settled by collective bargaining. As well as local agreements between employers and unions, in Britain there were several regional or national agreements in such industries as cotton (the Brooklands Agreement, 1893), wool, lace, iron and steel, engineering, shipbuilding, boot and shoe, and printing. In Germany employers and the Kaiser's government were hostile to trade unions and to collective bargaining. Similarly, in tsarist Russia, where trade unions could be legal after the 1905 revolution, they were severely restricted within the law to acting mostly on welfare issues. In France, where there were 1,064,000 trade unionists affiliated to the General Confederation of Labour (CGT) in 1912, the dominant political and legal views of trade unions were also hostile, deeming them restrictions on individual liberty and free market forces (see Geary 1981; Magraw 1982; Swain 1983; Wrigley 2003b). So, while trade union growth and collective bargaining were linked in Britain before 1914, elsewhere—notably Germany—there could be rapid trade union growth but political and employer hostility to collective bargaining could be decisive.

For Britain, where, relative to other major European economies, trade unionism and collective bargaining were widespread, it has been debated as to whether such organization achieved much before 1914. Pollard (1965: 98–112) examined the British evidence for 1870–1914 and found some evidence in some industries of trade union power securing higher wages than would have been the case if their level had been left to market forces. He concluded that in the face of hostile pressures the unions 'did well to maintain the share of labour, while raising the absolute level of real wages'. Earlier, Clegg et al. (1964: 482) had observed, 'It is not difficult to establish an association between the development of collective bargaining and changes in the distribution of union membership, or in methods of union government; but the economic results of collective bargaining are not so evident.'

The First World War widened the coverage of collective bargaining. In Britain during the war 4,970,000 men were enlisted in the Army, 407,000 in the Navy, and 293,000 in the Air Force out of a total male labour force of under 15 million. This gave the remaining labour (including female and other replacement labour) a potentially very strong bargaining position which, in practice, was usually not used given the national emergency. Nevertheless, as shortages in the economy became increasingly evident, requiring ever wider state involvement, there was a powerful impetus for wage and other agreements to be settled nationally. The wartime economy encouraged the growth of both trade unions and employers' associations and greatly enlarged the area of British industry covered by national wage agreements (Wrigley 1987: 23–70). The government was the major purchaser of goods and services and indirectly employed huge numbers of people in production. It expected to deal with representatives of employers and workpeople at the national level and not to have the replicate negotiations at several levels. The establishment of Whitley committees (representing both sides of an industry) from 1917 brought collective bargaining to some sectors where trade unionism had previously been weak.

With the severe international recession of 1921–22 labour's position in the labour market was weakened. For instance, trade union membership in metals and engineering fell by over 47 per cent while in distribution membership fell by over 63 per cent between the 1920 peak and 1923. Overall, British trade union membership fell by nearly 35 per cent from its 1920 peak by 1923 (with the fall in numbers of female trade unionists being a little more severe at 38.5 per cent). With the weakening of labour in the traditionally poorly organized sectors, collective bargaining often ended. Many Whitley committees had collapsed by the late 1920s and even the relatively robust one in the wool industry faded out in 1930.[7] In wool, as in other industries, economic adversity encouraged some employers to go their own way, thereby weakening or even breaking employers' organizations. By 1936 the number of employers' associations had fallen to 1,550, from 2,403 in 1925.

Indeed, the changed economic conditions from 1921 gave employers the opportunity to challenge the trade unions over pay and various aspects of working conditions. In the case of engineering this led to a major lock-out in 1922, lasting from March to June, and ended with the Engineering Employers' Federation securing a return to work on its conditions, which focused on managerial prerogatives. There were similar assertions of the right to manage in other industries, most notably in coal (which led to the General Strike, 1926) and cotton. Generally, as Gospel (1996: 159–84) has commented of collective bargaining between the wars, 'though the employers sought to shift the balance within this system, they maintained the basic arrangement'.

In the Second World War the peak number of men in the armed forces was 4,653,000 in June 1945. In addition, in this war some women were also conscripted into the Women's Auxiliary Services, with the peak number of 467,500 occurring in December 1943. Together, the labour withdrawn amounted to 25 per cent of the total male and female labour force of 1940 (some 20,676,000). As in the First World War labour did not exercise the potential power arising from its scarcity in the labour market, largely for patriotic reasons but also because of wartime legislation. Strikes and lock-outs were illegal under Order 1305 (18 July 1940) while large sectors of industry were brought under control by the series of Essential Work Orders from 5 March 1941. With Ernest Bevin, the General Secretary of the Transport and General Workers' Union, as Minister of Labour and National Service, considerable impetus was given to the spread of collective bargaining. Bevin boosted joint committees of employers and trade unions wherever he could, explicitly stating his hope that 'by the time that hostilities cease, there will be not a single industry of any kind in the

[7] On the Whitley councils see Charles (1973: 77–226) and for wool, see Wrigley (1987).

country that has not wage-regulating machinery of some kind or another'. In the case of the catering trade, his endeavours in 1942 sparked off an unsuccessful Conservative backbench revolt in Parliament (Bullock 1967: 194; Wrigley 1996: 38–9).

While Britain suffered economic hardships after the Second World War, there was not an economic recession of the scale of 1921–22. Moreover, the Labour government of 1945–51 was eager to maintain collective bargaining in British industry. The Wages Council Act 1945 widened statutory regulation of wages beyond sectors of 'exceptionally low wages' (the criterion of the Trade Boards Act 1909) (Clegg 1994: 327).

From the early 1950s there was a long boom in the international economy for over twenty years. Hence, with the war and the post-war period of reconstruction, there was a high demand for labour for most of over thirty years (1940–73). Alongside the favourable international economic circumstances, British governments pursued policies which broadly accepted Keynesian economic ideas, notably maintaining a high aggregate level of demand and attempting to mitigate downturns in the economy in the interest of steady economic growth and near full employment. However, in the face of serious competition from other industrialized countries and increasing inflation, by the late 1960s some large firms were increasingly unhappy with national wage agreements, preferring to confine these to the lower-paid workers, and over the ensuing decade several left their employers' organizations. Many of the bigger firms moved to decentralized collective bargaining, negotiating at the plant level. Faced with the possibility of a Labour government or European Community measures, some 40 per cent of manufacturing plants had adopted worker representation in various consultative arrangements by the late 1970s. There was also a greater role for shop stewards with plant-level collective bargaining covering new technologies and new pay systems (Gospel 1996: 81–106; Terry 1995: 203–28).

The three post-war decades also saw increases in the numbers of workers covered by closed shop agreements (whereby only union members could be employed at a particular place of work). These arrangements spread as trade union densities rose, just as they diminished after 1979 as there were substantial job losses and trade union membership declined in steel, coal, and much of manufacturing. By the late 1970s some 27 per cent of trade unionists were in closed shops, with them prevalent in printing, shipbuilding, coal, and large parts of engineering. In large sectors of British industry until the 1980s management sought trade union cooperation, working with trade union officers and, at shop floor level, with shop stewards (their number possibly quadrupling in the 1970s), supporting closed shop agreements and arranging for union dues to be deducted directly from pay (check-off systems covering over 72 per cent of trade unionists by 1978) (Fox 1985: 397). British trade unionism reached its peak in 1979, with 12,639,000 members and a density of 53.4 per cent.

However, by the 1980s and 1990s the British system of industrial relations characterized by voluntarist principles and widening collective bargaining was no longer prevalent in much of the private sector of the British economy in the face of increased competition in the international economy and governments hostile to its presumptions. While the contrast with the 1960s and 1970s was great, there were, as Blyton and Turnbull (1998: 188–200) have emphasized, some underlying continuities. Collective bargaining remained stronger in the public sector, and even the drop here was due in large part to the introduction of review bodies for teachers and nurses (which did not mark the collapse of the unions). The 1980s and 1990s also saw a continuing trend towards decentralized bargaining. In much of the private sector bargaining moved to company or plant level. Industry-wide bargaining ended in such sectors as iron and steel, engineering, water, electricity, cement, banks, multiple retailing, road passenger transport, and for journalists in newspapers (Brown 1993: 189–200; Kessler and Bayliss 1995: 107–14).

This late twentieth-century fall in collective bargaining appeared to be more than an acute part of the pattern of expansion during upswings in the economy and in strike activity with decline during downturns. According to the Workplace Industrial Relations Survey for 1984–90 overall collective bargaining fell from 71 to 54 per cent, with the fall in the private sector being from 52 to 41 per cent (Milner 1995: 69–91; Kelly 1998: 95–6). Other research (the Labour Force Surveys) has suggested that by 1996 overall collective bargaining may have declined to cover only 37 per cent of the workforce (Blyton and Turnbull 1998: 190). Unlike earlier in the century, the late twentieth century revealed no signs of a major recovery in the coverage of collective bargaining. McIlroy (1995: 387–8) has summed the situation up: 'Collective bargaining was becoming a minority phenomenon, increasingly decentralised and more restricted in scope.'

The decline in coverage of collective bargaining and the fall in trade union membership were partly due to an anti-trade union political climate. The Thatcher and Major governments positively encouraged employers to ignore or oppose trade unions and to reject collective bargaining. For instance, the 1993 Trade Union Reform and Employment Rights Act protected employers from legal action for paying trade union members lower wages than non-trade unionists. It also took away from the Advisory, Conciliation, and Arbitration Service (ACAS) the duty of encouraging the extension of collective bargaining. In such a climate there were fewer attractions for employers to act together. The Workplace Industrial Relations Surveys also reported a withering of employers' associations, with establishments which were members of them falling from 25 to 13 per cent between 1980 and 1990. By the late twentieth century they were most prevalent in construction, engineering, and textiles (Kessler and Bayliss 1995: 195–6).

Yet these declines were very much part of more competitive labour market conditions which were experienced by other industrialized countries. Trade

Table 9.2. Trade union densities, 1950–2000

Year	Britain	France	Germany	Sweden	USA
1950	43.8	23.9	33.1	67.7	28.0
1970	48.5	21.4	33.0	80.4	27.4
1990	38.1	10.8	32.9	81.5	15.5
2000	28.8	9.7	25.0	80.0	12.8

Source: Bain and Price (1980: 40, 89, 134, 143). The 1970–2000 union densities are drawn from the OECD's *Labour Market Statistics* (2005).

unionism and collective bargaining were weakening beyond Britain (see Table 9.2 for a selection of trade union densities, with Sweden being exceptional).

With collective bargaining weakened and the 1980–93 legislation mostly still in place during Tony Blair's premiership (from 1997), the voluntarist system aired before the 1894 Royal Commission on Industrial Relations and embodied in the 1968 Donovan Report appears less central and inevitable in some recent reassessments of British industrial relations. Howell (2005: 2) has argued that, 'contrary to most scholarship, the state has played a central role in the construction of industrial relations institutions in Britain in the last hundred years or so'. Others, such as Hanson (1991) and Bassett (1986), have emphasized the remedying in Britain of what are seen as peculiarly, or acutely, British industrial relations ills. More generally, some of these authors and such studies as 'The Japanization of British Industry?' have placed changes in an international economy ('global') context, highlighting the changes introduced to survive in the face of Japanese and other competition (Ackroyd et al. 1988; Oliver and Wilkinson 1992; Grant 1996: 203–33).

In revisiting the role of the state in British industrial relations Howell argued for 'three distinct industrial relations systems, running from 1890–1959', in which 'the Collective Laissez-Faire System' was constructed, the late 1950s to 1979, marked by the decentralization of industrial relations, and 1979–97, the decollectivization of industrial relations. In defining phases, linked to international economic pressures, he was following several earlier writers (though different writers selected different dates).

In considering the role of the state in the formation of modern British industrial relations many historians have selected either the mid-1870s or the early 1890s. The mid-1870s marked the beginning of a new legal era for the trade unions, the legislation of 1871 and 1875 providing the framework in which they could function effectively. This period also marked the start of a major downturn in the international economy and Britain facing severer competition, notably from Germany and the USA. As a result, Richard Price and others have argued, firms adapted work practices to meet the new, adverse conditions and as a result relations between employers and employees seriously deteriorated.[8]

The early 1890s shared these problems but in addition were marked by serious industrial conflict, ranging from the end of the New Union disputes to trials of strength in cotton, coal, and engineering. In these years Gladstone's last government felt the need to intervene in the 1893 coal dispute, Board of Trade officials mediated in disputes, and, in 1896, the legal basis for government intervention in disputes, the Conciliation (Trades Disputes) Act, reached the statute book. Like so much Victorian social legislation the 1896 Conciliation Act was permissive: the state became involved only if both sides agreed that it should, and then any recommendations were not legally binding (Davidson 1985).[9] The 1896 Act remained the basis for much of government intervention in industrial relations until the Industrial Relations Act 1971.

In a Whig-style account state intervention should have evolved steadily from the early to mid-1890s onwards. What is very clear is that it did not, though it could be argued that the state did reshape the framework of British industrial relations in 1906 after the Taff Vale judgment, 1902, and some earlier legal decisions which had undercut what was widely understood to have been the legal position after the 1871 and 1875 legislation.

State intervention in industrial relations occurred when industrial disputes caused major social misery, as in the case of Lord Penrhyn's slate quarrymen in North Wales in 1896–97 and 1899–1903 or threatened to disrupt substantial parts of the economy, as in the case of a threatened railway strike in 1907. In the case of the quarrymen, Lord Penrhyn did not wish for conciliation and rebuffed C. T. Ritchie, the Conservative President of the Board of Trade. In the case of the 1907 rail dispute, David Lloyd George displayed considerable skills in securing a settlement. Before the First World War much depended on political will and ability. Lloyd George and Winston Churchill as Presidents of the Board of Trade (1905–08 and 1908–10) intervened with some degree of success, whereas the efforts of various Cabinet ministers (including an unfocused Lloyd George) during the 1912 Port of London dispute were a dismal failure (Clegg et al. 1964: 212–14, 424–6; Wrigley 1976: 13–15, 55–8, 74–6).

While it can be said that the state set the major parameters of industrial relations in Britain until the 1970s with the Trades Disputes Act 1906, this was far from a carefully considered move. Most of the Liberal ministers intended to return trade union law to where they believed the framers of the 1871 and 1875 legislation had intended it to be. However, Sir Henry Campbell-Bannerman, the Prime Minister, agreed to more extensive immunities for the trade unions than his legal colleagues wished.

[8] On the 1871 and 1875 legislation see Curthoys (2004) and Price (1980).
[9] See also the essays by Brown, Davidson, Wrigley, and others in Wrigley (1982).

After the extensive First World War changes in industrial relations, there was a somewhat similar desire in this, as in many other matters, to go 'back to 1914'. Austen Chamberlain, the Chancellor of the Exchequer, expressed business concerns about state intervention in industry as well as in industrial disputes. In August 1919 he observed of state control of wool, 'The moment you began control you were inevitably driven to complete control which, if prolonged, led to nationalisation . . . Control eliminated all the usual motives which induced economic production.' Of government involvement in strikes, he commented in early 1919 that 'in recent years there has been an increasing reliance placed on the government as the ultimate arbiter in labour disputes, with the result that strikes were prolonged by the fact that neither side would say the last word as to what they were prepared to concede, as they expected the government to be called in'. While a minority of employers, such as Dudley Docker, a prominent member of the Federation of British Industries, for a while favoured government participation in restructuring British industry, most did not.[10] This was especially so after the post-war boom of 1919–20 ended and the accompanying threat of serious industrial and social unrest had greatly lessened. With the severe 1921–22 recession and the 34.8 per cent drop in British trade union membership between 1920 and 1923, labour was notably weaker in the labour market and there was less impetus for either collective bargaining or state intervention.

There is a reasonable case for seeing the direct role of the state in industrial relations rolled partly back after 1920, rather than to follow Keith Middlemas in believing that from the First World War British governments exhibited 'corporate bias', with unelected trade unions and employers' organizations involved in decision making and so becoming 'governing institutions'. While the trade unions and employers' associations were consulted by government, their influence over policy was not that great. Rather, as Rodney Lowe has commented, government policy was for 'the decentralisation, not the centralisation, of responsibility. Each industry was to be responsible for its own affairs whilst government itself stood above the fray.' However, the state did affect levels of wages and bargaining through increased social welfare provision after 1908 (Middlemas 1979; Lowe 1987: 185–210, 211).

In broader terms, the framework of the British industrial relations system was only modified a little between the wars. While many of the 1915–20 innovations were repealed or withered away after several years (as was the fate of the Whitley committees in several industries), the Industrial Courts Act 1919 remained and was a notable addition to governments' powers (to the continuing Conciliation Act 1896). Under the Act a standing court was set up and this enabled ad hoc courts of inquiry to be appointed regarding specific

[10] War Cabinet minutes, 28 Jan. and 5 Aug. 1919; National Archives CAB 23/9/30 and 15/160, as well as Wrigley (1990: 94, 312). On Docker, see Davenport-Hines (1984).

disputes, as was done in regard to port labour and also engineering in the period after the First World War. As arbitration under the Act was voluntary, employers were less keen to use the legislation after 1926, when the trade unions were weaker (Sharp 1950: 347–60).

The other notable change was the Trades Disputes Act 1927. The General Strike in 1926 provided Stanley Baldwin's government with the occasion to bring in trade union legislation which much of the party had desired since the 1906 Trades Disputes Act. As well as banning general strikes, the Act made picketing more difficult, banned civil servants and local government workers from joining unions affiliated to the TUC, and made the trade unions' political levy a matter of contracting in not contracting out. These measures survived until May 1946, then being repealed after the election of a majority Labour government in 1945.

After the Second World War there was less political will for the state to disengage from industrial relations than after the First World War and no economic shock of the dimension of the 1921–22 recession. Whereas in 1919–21 the government had pressed ahead with decontrolling industry, in 1945–51 a majority Labour government nationalized sectors of the economy and thereby greatly increased the numbers of employees whose wages and conditions of work were directly or indirectly determined by the state. Such responsibilities were mostly discharged through national collective bargaining. The major pressures for change were concern at rising inflation in conditions of near full employment, the linked issue of the erosion of the competitive strength of British exports (and eventually of British manufactured goods in the home market), the considerable number of unofficial strikes, especially in car manufacturing and printing, and the undercutting of the 1906 legal framework by several judicial judgments (notably *Rookes* v. *Barnard*, 1964, and *Stratford* v. *Lindley*, 1965). The inflationary pressures led to a series of incomes policies, voluntary and statutory, in 1948–49 and then from 1957 to 1979, and to the involvement of the trade unions and employers' associations in discussing national economic planning in the National Economic Development Council (NEDC). Set up in 1961, the NEDC had substance in its earlier years, but was increasingly marginalized in the 1980s and abolished at the beginning of 1993.

The 1906 legal framework was temporarily replaced by the Industrial Relations Act 1971 and (as yet) more generally by a series of legislative measures between 1980 and 1993.[11] One major impact of this legislation was on the ability of the trade unions to engage in industrial disputes. Before strikes were called, the support of union members had to be sought and secured by secret ballot (under the Trade Union Act 1984 and the Employment Act 1988). The Trade Union and Employment Rights Act 1993 went much further, requiring that trade unions

[11] For shrewd assessments of this legislation Auerbach (1990), as well as Davies and Freedland (1993).

should not only give seven days' notice but also provide employers with lists of the employees who would be involved. Under the Employment Act 1982 strikes were only legally protected if they concerned 'wholly or mainly' employment issues affecting those involved and their own employer. Other legislation made it illegal to apply pressure to secure a closed shop.

Another aspect of the legislation regulated trade union government. The provisions of the 1988 Employment Act included giving trade union members the right to demand a ballot before industrial action and, when a majority favoured it, the right not to be disciplined by their union if they refused to take part. It also established a Commissioner for the Rights of Trade Union Members who could provide legal advice and financial assistance to any trade union member who wished to take legal action against their own union.

The 1980–93 legislation also ended various aids to union recognition and to extending collective bargaining. For instance, the 1993 legislation protected employers from legal action if they gave trade union members lower wages than non-trade unionists. Alongside such measures, the legislation also removed many employee rights, thereby favouring employers.

With this legislation, especially the 1988 and 1993 measures, the pendulum had swung a long way from the favourable 1906 legislation. The trade union organizations were presumed to be not only obstacles to economic growth but also the exploiters of many of their own members. They were no longer valued participants in facilitating economic growth but were best shunned. While the Blair government (from 1997) restored the right to be a trade union member, it also was committed to the provision of a flexible labour force in the face of globalization and did not go in for the wholesale reversal of the 1980–93 legislation that the trade union leadership had hoped for.

The Thatcher–Major legal framework for the conduct of industrial relations was intended, among other things, to remedy one of the alleged 'British diseases', strike proneness. This was a very long-running concern. The reader of a paper at the Royal Statistical Society in January 1880 complained, 'Striking has become a disease, and a very grave disease, in the body social' (Bevan 1880: 35–54 quoted in Cronin 1982: 74).

The strike waves of the late nineteenth and early twentieth centuries— 1871–73, 1889–90, 1911–13, and 1919–20—all occurred during upturns in the trade cycle, when the labour market was favourable to strike action. James Cronin has pointed to the greater number of workers involved on average in the 1910–13 disputes (780) than those of 1889–92 (350) and their considerable degree of success (44 per cent of strikers winning, 42 per cent securing compromises, and only 14 per cent being defeated). Cronin has also commented on those involved in strikes in 1911–13, marking 'a further shift from skilled craftsmen towards the newer, more "proletarian" workers in industry and transport, with mines, dockers, railwaymen, and textile workers especially prominent' (Cronin 1982: 74–98; 1979).

This pre-1914 unrest aroused much anxiety among the propertied classes. Jenkins (1967: 260) wrote of the hot August 1911, 'This torrid weather brought violence closer to the surface and gave an added menace in the eyes of the official classes, to any threat which emerged from the foetid and overcrowded quarters of the industrial towns.'[12] King George V's secretary made Asquith aware of the king's concerns, writing,

He desires me . . . to urge most strongly on the Government the importance (and it is also their duty . . . to devise a scheme which although not entirely preventing strikes (perhaps that is not possible) would to a large extent prevent a threatened strike from coming to a head, and might be the means of preventing 'sympathetic' strikes from taking place. Under any circumstances he hopes that what is called 'peaceful picketing', which most people now condemn, will be put an end to by legislation. (Quoted in Jenkins 1967: 261)

Thus the king wished to return trade union law not just to before the 1906 legislation but before that of 1871 and 1875. Asquith, however, was diplomatically inactive on this request.

The British industrial unrest of 1910–14 was far from being unique. While there are major statistical differences in the ways countries have collected strike data making precise comparisons hazardous, nevertheless broad patterns of change are discernible for most European countries. In the period 1910–14, as so often later, British levels of strikes were in the middle of the range. According to Crouch's figures for days lost per thousand trade union members in 1910–14, at least France (8,883), Italy (6,452), and Norway (5,607) were

Table 9.3. Average number of working days lost in disputes per annum in the UK, 1901–45 (000s)

Years	All industries and services	Coal mining	% of coal mining
1901–9	3,596	1,315	36.6
1910–14	16,119	8,808	54.6
1915–18	4,230	1,072	25.3
1919–21	49,136	32,519	66.2
1922–5	11,724	1,861	15.9
1926	162,233	146,434	90.3
1927–39	3,126	869	27.8
1940–5	1,984	949	47.8

Source: Calculated from Board of Trade and Ministry of Labour Annual Reports on Strikes and Lock-outs. Department of Employment, *British Labour Statistics: Historical Abstract 1886–1968* (London: HMSO, 1971), 396.

---

[12] In such purple prose he was following the memorable earlier account by Dangerfield (1935).

markedly worse than the UK (3,886) by this measure, with at least Germany (3,577), Austria (2,570), the Netherlands (1,861), Sweden (1,813), and Denmark (1,509) better (Crouch 1993: 123). However, with the severe post-First World War industrial unrest, a common fear in Britain was that Britain would follow much of Eastern and Central Europe into red revolution, not that British unrest was exceptional.[13]

After the 1921 recession, with the exception of the General Strike, 1926, strikes were not seen as a major problem in inter-war Britain, nor as a peculiarly British issue. Using Colin Crouch's measurement of days lost per thousand trade union members in 1921–5, the levels are lower than for 1910–14 and 1919–21, but with the UK fourth highest (5,183), behind Norway (12,109), Ireland (5,467), and Sweden (5,366) but ahead of France (5,001), Germany (4,2301), Denmark (3,852), the Netherlands (2,679), Austria (1,827), and Finland (1,348). The British position reflects the strong trade union opposition to cuts in wages and increases in working time, notably in 1921–23. In the later 1930s (1934–38) the UK was among the lowest (320), ranking below Ireland (2,620), Denmark (1,478), Finland (1,031), Norway (986), Belgium (928), and Sweden (780) but above the Netherlands (160) and Switzerland (120) (Crouch 1993: 152, 173). What is clear is that a lower level of strikes in the mid-1930s compared to the early 1920s was common in free economies across Europe.

Major concern about strikes was expressed again with a strike wave in 1957–62 (see Table 9.4) marked by unofficial strikes, including in the car industry which was then an important export industry. The Donovan Report

Table 9.4. Average number of working days lost in disputes per annum in the UK, 1946–2000 (000s)

Years	All industries and services	Coal mining	% of coal mining
1946–56	2,157	588	27.3
1957–62	4,835	478	9.9
1963–67	2,428	253	10.4
1968–80	11,708	496	4.2
1981–83	4,444	401	9.0
1984	27,135	22,484	82.9
1985–90	3,600	812	22.6
1991–2000	519	7	1.3

Note: From 1983 the statistics include also coke, mineral oil, and natural gas, and from 1994 also electricity.

Sources: Ministry of Labour *Gazette; Employment and Productivity Gazette;* Department of Employment *Gazette; Labour Market Trends.*

---

[13] On the post-1917 fears, see Maier (1975) and Wrigley (1993).

concluded, 'By far the most important part in remedying the problem of unofficial strikes and other forms of unofficial action will . . . be played by reforming the institutions of whose defects they are a symptom' (Royal Commission 1968: 266–7, para. 1052). However, both leading Labour and Conservative politicians felt a political imperative was to go further than strengthen voluntarist collective bargaining institutions. The Labour government's legal proposals, *In Place of Strife* (1969), and the succeeding Conservative government's legislation, the Industrial Relations Act 1971, politicized strikes, with sixteen substantial strikes of political protest losing some 6 million working days in 1969–72 (Durcan et al. 1983: 170, 438).

The main causes of the upsurge in industrial unrest in the late 1960s and 1970s were claims for increases in wages and other wage issues. Between 1945 and 1968 such matters were the principal cause of around 44–8 per cent of strikes but from 1969 to 1979 wage issues were deemed the key cause in 57 per cent of strikes, falling back to 38 per cent in 1981 to 1995 (Durcan et al. 1983: 143, 181–3; Wrigley 2003a: 45).

A major feature of strikes in twentieth-century Britain was that they were not spread evenly across the country, across industries, or even within large industrial, workplaces. At various times coal, docks, engineering, and car manufacturing have experienced relatively high levels of strikes. Even when allowance has been made for the presence of such industries, some regions have been more strike prone than others. Knowles (1952: 185–209), in his classic study of strikes, found that for 1911–45 South Wales, the West Riding of Yorkshire, Lancashire and Cheshire, Northern Ireland, and Scotland had notably more strikes than other areas. Later writers have followed Knowles in emphasizing geographic dimensions of strikes. Gilbert (1996: 128–61) has pointed to the development of new industries, commenting that this, 'away from older heartlands of union organization, militancy and established industrial communities, has led to relatively low levels of strike activity'. Yet he has also noted 'that the history of strikes also exhibits some degree of . . . "regional resilience" '. A good illustration of such points was the differing strike experiences of different car manufacturing plants, with the Ford plant at Halewood on Merseyside having the area's traditional higher level of strikes.

Another feature of British strikes in the twentieth century was that many were concentrated in strike-prone parts of strike-prone industries. A Department of Employment analysis of strikes in 1971–73 found that in this notably turbulent period strikes were most likely in larger industrial units, but that overall 'only five per cent of plants experienced stoppages and of those over two-thirds had only one stoppage'. Within this 5 per cent, 5 per cent 'accounted for a quarter of stoppages and two-thirds of days lost in manufacturing' (Smith et al. 1978).

Nevertheless, for a country whose international competitiveness in industrial goods was declining any substantial number of strikes in export industries naturally led to concern. Whether Britain was in some way exceptional in its level of strikes was another matter. The Royal Commission under Lord Donovan drew on International Labour organization statistics to assess this, and suggested that Britain was in an intermediate group of countries with more strikes than a group including France, Germany, and Japan but with fewer than another group including Italy, Canada, Australia, Ireland, and the United States. This sparked off a substantial debate about the problems of comparability of international strike statistics (Wrigley 2003*a*: 49–50).

While it is wise to be cautious in making international comparisons, even allowing for different definitions and efficiency in the collection of strike statistics, there are patterns which remain over decades and which undermine notions of strikes in the 1960s and 1970s being a peculiarly British phenomenon. Table 9.5 presents working days lost per thousand workers for 1961–89, thus going two decades beyond the period of the Donovan Report.

From the table and similar assessments it appears that Britain's relative position remained broadly the same, at least until the 1990s. An upsurge in strikes in 1968–80 was experienced by other countries, though Britain's position deteriorated within the intermediate group of countries (ones at neither the higher or lower ends of a rank order of proneness to strikes) in the late 1960s and 1970s. As Kessler and Bayliss (1995: 214) have remarked of the British strike record under Margaret Thatcher, 'the reductions in the UK's incidence were not larger than those of its main competitors, nor did they bring it anywhere near the extremely low incidence in Germany and the Netherlands'.

Table 9.5. Working days lost per thousand workers in ten countries, 1961–89

	Annual averages		All industries	
	1861–9	1970–9	1980–9	1980–9
Australia	424 (5)	1,298 (3)	770 (2)	350 (4)
Canada	1,026 (3)	1,840 (1)	960 (1)	470 (2)
France	321 (6)	312 (7)	150 (8)	80 (8)
Germany (West)	24 (9)	92 (9)	50 (9)	50 (9)
Ireland	1,114 (2)	1,163 (5)	530 (4)	380 (3)
Italy	1,438 (1)	1,778 (2)	290 (7)	620 (1)
Japan	239 (8)	215 (8)	20 (1)	10 (10)
Sweden	18 (10)	42 (10)	330 (5)	180 (6)
United Kingdom	274 (7)	1,088 (6)	740 (3)	330 (5)
United States	1,001 (4)	1,211 (4)	330 (5)	120 (7)

Notes: The first three columns are for mining, manufacturing, construction, and transport and communication; the fourth column gives all industries and services for the final decade. The figures in brackets give the rank order.

From the mid-1980s the coverage of the French figures changed markedly. Also the French series omits 1968.

Source: *Employment Gazette*, Dec. 1971, Oct. 1971, Oct. 1973, Jan. 1981, and Dec. 1991.

In very broad terms the British level of strikes has risen and fallen along with the movement of strikes in other major developed economies. Just as there are residual patterns which last over long periods of times for certain regions or areas of the UK, so there are residual patterns among competing developed countries. Trade union strength in a period of full employment can affect a country's relative position in a league of the strike prone, especially if industrial relations becomes politicized (as happened in Britain in 1968–74); and determined state hostility to trade unionism and collective bargaining, as in Britain and the USA in the 1980s and early 1990s, can also alter the position.

Yet, what is clear is that the effect of state action (including new laws) needs to be seen in a comparative context and within the major trends in the international economy. As Kelly (1998: 106) has commented, 'there is more than enough evidence to demonstrate long-term fluctuations in patterns of worker mobilization and state and employer counter-mobilization', even if there are variations in timing in different countries. In recent years there have been greater efforts to understand industrial relations in wider contexts than one country.[14]

Whether or not trade union membership rises and the coverage of collective bargaining extends again if international economic conditions change remains to be seen. Table 9.6 reports the situation at the end of the century. The decline of the old staple industries, which were heavily unionized in the mid-twentieth century, did not doom British trade unionism. A major feature of British trade unionism over 250 years has been the rise and fall of prominent unionized occupations. For instance, much of the growth of trade unionism in its peak period, 1964–79, came from the unionization of white-collar workers. Whereas in 1911 some 11.6 per cent of white-collar workers were in trade unions and under 13 per cent of all trade unionists were white-collar workers,

Table 9.6. UK employment and collective bargaining, autumn 2001 (in millions)

	Covered by collective agreements	Not covered	Total
Union members	5.5 (22%)	1.7 (7%)	7.2 (29%)
Non-union members	3.4 (14%)	14.1 (57%)	17.5 (71%)
Total	8.9 (36%)	15.8 (64%)	24.7 (100%)

Source: Metcalf (2003: 184) originally drawn from Brook (2001).

[14] Throughout the twentieth century there were comparative studies. For examples, see De Montgomery (1922), Marquand (1939), and Bamber and Lansbury (1993). For a study of the impact of the international economy on labour generally, see Wrigley (2000a: 201–15), For a highly sophisticated comparative analysis see Crouch (1993).

by 1979 about 44 per cent of all white-collar workers were trade union members and of all trade unionists 40 per cent were white-collar workers. At the end of the twentieth century trade unionism and collective bargaining had shrunk but possibilities for growth appeared to be present.[15]

References

Ackers, P., and Wilkinson, A. (eds.) (2003). *Understanding Work and Employment: Industrial Relations in Transition*. Oxford: Oxford University Press.

Ackroyd, S., Burrell, G., Hughes. M., and Whitaker, A. (1988). 'The Japanization of British Industry?' *Industrial Relations Journal*, 19/1: 11–23.

Auerbach, S. (1990). *Legislating for Conflict*. Oxford: Oxford University Press.

Bain, G., and Price, R. (1980). *Profiles of Union Growth: Comparative Statistical Portrait of Eight Countries*. Oxford: Blackwell.

Bamber, G. J., and Lansbury, R. D. (eds.) (1993). *International and Comparative Industrial Relations: A Study of Industrialised Market Economies*, 2nd edn. London: Routledge.

Bassett, P. (1986). *Strike Free: New Industrial Relations in Britain*. London: Macmillan.

Beloff, M. (1979). 'On the Problems of Writing Contemporary History'. Paper for the Institute of Historical Research, July.

Bevan, G. P. (1880).'The Strikes of the Past Ten Years'. *Journal of the Royal Statistical Society*, 93.

Blyton, P., and Turnbull, P. (1998). *The Dynamics of Employee Relations*, 2nd edn. London: Palgrave.

Board of Trade (1910). *Report on Collective Agreements between Employers and Workpeople in the United Kingdom*. Cd. 5366. London: His Majesty's Stationery Office.

Brook, K. (2001). 'Trade Union Membership: An Analysis of Data from the Autumn 2001 LFS'. *Labour Market Trends*, July: 343–54.

Brown, W. (1993). 'The Contraction of Collective Bargaining in Britain'. *British Journal of Industrial Relations*, 31/2: 189–200.

Bullock, A. (1967). *The Life and Times of Ernest Bevin*, ii: *Minister of Labour 1940–1945*. London: Hutchinson.

Butterfield, H. (1931). *The Whig Interpretation of History*. New York: W. W. Norton.

Charles, R. (1973). *The Development of Industrial Relations in Britain 1911–1939*. London: Hutchinson.

Clegg, H. A. (1985). *A History of British Trade Unions since 1889*, ii: *1911–1933*. Oxford: Clarendon Press.

—— (1994). *A History of British Trade Unions since 1889*, iii: *1934–1951*. Oxford: Clarendon Press.

—— Fox, A., and Thompson, A. F. (1964). *A History of British Trade Unions since 1889*, i: *1889–1910*. Oxford: Clarendon Press.

Collini, S. (1991). 'The Whig Interpretation of English Literature: Literary History and National Identity', in his *Public Moralists, Political Thought and Intellectual Life in Britain 1850–1930*. Oxford: Clarendon Press.

---

[15] For a major assessment see Metcalf (2003: 170–87).

Conservative Political Centre (1966). *Trade Unions for Tomorrow: The Memorandum of Evidence Presented to the Royal Commission on Trade Unions and Employers' Associations by the Inns of Conservative and Unionist Society*. London.

Cronin, J. E. (1979). *Industrial Conflict in Modern Britain*. London: Croom Helm.

—— (1982). 'Strikes 1870–1914', in C. Wrigley (ed.), *A History of British Industrial Relations 1875–1914*. Brighton: Harvester Press.

Crouch, C. (1993). *Industrial Relations and European State Traditions*. Oxford: Clarendon Press.

Curthoys, M. (2004). *Governments, Labour and the Law in Mid Victorian Britain: The Trade Union Legislation of the 1870s*. Oxford: Clarendon Press.

Dangerfield, G. (1935). *The Strange Death of Liberal England*. London: Constable.

Davenport-Hines, R. (1984). *Dudley Docker*. Cambridge: Cambridge University Press.

Davidson, R. (1985). *Whitehall and the Labour Problem in Late Victorian and Edwardian Britain*. London: Croom Helm.

Davies, P., and Freedland, M. (1993). *Labour Legislation and Public Policy: A Contemporary History*. Oxford: Clarendon Press.

De Montgomery, B. G. (1922). *British and Continental Labour Policy*. London: Kegan Paul, Trench and Trubner and Co.

Dickens, R., Gregg, P., and Wadsworth, J. (eds.) (2003). *The Labour Market under New Labour: The State of Working Britain*. London: Palgrave.

Durcan, J. W., McCarthy, W. E. J., and Redman, G. P. (1983). *Strikes in Post-War Britain: A Study of Stoppages of Work Due to Industrial Disputes 1946–73*. London: Allen and Unwin.

Edwards, P. (ed.) (1995). *Industrial Relations: Theory and Practice in Britain*. Oxford: Blackwell.

Flanders, A. (1954). 'Collective Bargaining', in A. Flanders and H. A. Clegg (eds.), *The System of Industrial Relations in Great Britain: Its History, Law and Institutions*. Oxford: Basil Blackwell.

—— and Clegg, H. A. (eds.) (1954). *The System of Industrial Relations in Great Britain: Its History, Law and Institutions*. Oxford: Basil Blackwell.

Fox, A. (1985). *History and Heritage: The Social Origins of the British Industrial Relations System*. London: Allen and Unwin.

Geary, D. (1981). *European Labour Protest 1848–1939*. London: Methuen.

Gilbert, D. (1996). 'Strikes in Post-War Britain', in Chris Wrigley (ed.), *A History of British Industrial Relations 1939–1979*. Cheltenham: Edward Elgar.

Gospel, H. (1996). 'Employers and Managers: Organisation and Strategy 1914–1939', in C. Wrigley (ed.), *A History of British Industrial Relations*, vol. ii. Cheltenham: Edward Elgar.

Grant, D. (1996). 'Japanization and New Industrial Relations', in Ian J. Beardwell (ed.), *Contemporary Industrial Relations: A Critical Analysis*. Oxford: Oxford University Press.

Hanson, C. G. (1991). *Taming the Trade Unions: A Guide to the Thatcher Government's Employment Reforms, 1980–1990*. London: Macmillan.

Howell, C. (2005). *Trade Unions and the State. The Construction of Industrial Relations Institutions in Britain, 1890–2000*. Princeton: Princeton University Press.

Jaffe, J. A. (2000). *Striking a Bargain: Work and Industrial Relations in Britain 1815–1865*. Manchester: Manchester University Press.

Jenkins, R. (1967). *Asquith*. London: Fontana.

Kelly, J. (1998). *Rethinking Industrial Relations: Mobilization, Collectivism and Long Waves.* London: Routledge.

Kessler, S., and Bayliss, F. (1995). *Contemporary British Industrial Relations*, 2nd edn. London: Macmillan.

Knowles, K. G. J. C. (1952). *Strikes: A Study in Industrial Conflict.* Oxford: Blackwell.

Lorwin, V. R. (1954). *The French Labor Movement.* Cambridge, Mass.: Harvard University Press.

Lowe, R. (1987). 'The Government and Industrial Relations 1919–1939', in Chris Wrigley (ed.), *A History of British Industrial Relations 1914–1939.* Brighton: Harvester Press.

Lyddon, D. (2003). 'History and Industrial Relations', in P. Ackers and A. Wilkinson (eds.), *Understanding Work and Employment: Industrial Relations in Transition.* Oxford: Oxford University Press.

McIlroy, J. (1995). *Trade Unions in Britain Today*, 2nd edn. Manchester: Manchester University Press.

Magraw, R. (1982). *A History of the French Working Class*, vol. ii. Oxford: Blackwell.

Maier, C. S. (1975). *Recasting Bourgeois Europe.* Princeton: Princeton University Press.

Marquand, H. A. (ed.) (1939). *Organized Labour in Four Continents.* London: Longmans, Green and Co.

Metcalf, D. (2003). 'Trade Unions', in R. Dickens, P. Gregg, and J. Wadsworth (eds.), *The Labour Market under New Labour: The State of Working Britain.* London: Palgrave.

Middlemas, K. (1979). *Politics in Industrial Society.* London: Deutsch.

Milner, S. (1995). 'The Coverage of Collective Pay-Setting Institutions in Britain 1895–1990'. *British Journal of Industrial Relations*, 33/1: 71–91.

Ministry of Labour (1961). *Industrial Relations Handbook.* London: Her Majesty's Stationery Office.

Mokyr, J. (ed.) (2003). *The Oxford Encyclopedia of Economic History*, vol. v. Oxford: Oxford University Press.

Oliver, N., and Wilkinson, B. (1992). *The Japanization of British Industry.* Oxford: Blackwell.

Pollard, S. (1965). 'Trade Unions and the Labour Market 1870–1914'. *Yorkshire Bulletin of Economic and Social Research*, 17: 98–112.

Price, R. M. (1980). *Unions and Men: Work Control in Building and the Rise of Labour, 1830–1914.* Cambridge: Cambridge University Press.

Royal Commission on Trade Unions and Employers' Associations (1965). *Written Evidence of the Ministry of Labour.* London: Her Majesty's Stationery Office.

—— (1968). *Report.* Cmnd. 3623. London: Her Majesty's Stationery Office.

Sharp, I. G. (1950). *Industrial Conciliation and Arbitration in Great Britain.* London: Allen and Unwin.

Smith, C. T. B., Clifton, R., Makeham, P., Creagh, S. W., and Burns, R. V. (1978). *Strikes in Britain.* London: Her Majesty's Stationery Office.

Swain, G. (1983). *Russian Social Democracy and the Legal Labour Movement.* London: Macmillan.

Terry, M. (1995). 'Trade Unions: Shop Stewards and the Workplace', in P. Edwards (ed.), *Industrial Relations: Theory and Practice in Britain.* Oxford: Blackwell.

Visser, J. (1989). *European Trade Unions in Figures.* Deventer: Klower.

Whiteside, N. (1987). 'Social Welfare and Industrial Relations 1914–1939', in C. Wrigley (ed.), *A History of British Industrial Relations 1914–1939.* Brighton: Harvester Press.

Wrigley, C. (1976). *David Lloyd George and the British Labour Movement*. Hassocks: Harvester Press.

—— (ed.) (1982). *A History of British Industrial Relations 1875–1914*. Hassocks: Harvester Press.

—— (1987). 'The First World War and State Intervention in Industrial Relations, 1914–1918', in C. Wrigley, *Cosy Co-operation under Strain: Industrial Relations in the Yorkshire Woollen Industry 1919–1930*. York: Borthwick Institute.

—— (1990). *Lloyd George and the Challenge of Labour*. Hemel Hempstead: Harvester-Wheatsheaf.

—— (ed.) (1993). *Challenges of Labour: Central and Western Europe 1917–1920*. London: Routledge.

—— (1996). 'The Second World War and State Intervention in Industrial Relations, 1939–1945', in C. Wrigley (ed.), *A History of British Industrial Relations, 1939–1979*. Cheltenham: Edward Elgar.

—— (2000*a*). 'Organized Labour and the International Economy', in C. Wrigley (ed.), *The First World War and the International Economy*. Cheltenham: Edward Elgar.

—— (ed.) (2000*b*). *The First World War and the International Economy*. Cheltenham: Edward Elgar.

—— (2003*a*). *British Trade Unions since 1933*. Cambridge: Cambridge University Press.

—— (2003*b*). 'Unions', in J. Mokyr (ed.), *The Oxford Encyclopedia of Economic History*, vol. v. Oxford: Oxford University Press.

10

Unemployment

Ian Gazeley and Andrew Newell

10.1 Introduction

In 1909 William Beveridge published the book *Unemployment: A Problem of Industry*. His title implies to us that he thought movements in British unemployment were related to the cycle in world trade and changes in the relative prosperity of different industries. In many respects Beveridge viewed unemployment as a structural problem. A hundred years later, looking at the twentieth century in retrospect, our conclusion is quite similar for all but the last decade of the twentieth century. We have to add another cause that at the time he might have considered unlikely: British monetary policy.

Our first port of call will be the historical data. Although, as we will see, there are genuine difficulties with comparing unemployment rates across time, Feinstein (1972) shows that in the first fourteen years of the century unemployment cycled between 2 per cent and 8 per cent of the workforce. By contrast, in the inter-war years, marked by two major depressions, the unemployment rate never fell below 7 per cent and peaked at just over 15 per cent (about 3 million workers). After the Second World War unemployment remained abnormally low for over two decades: it did not pass 2 per cent until 1963 and reached 5 per cent of the workforce in 1976, peaking in 1983 at 12.5 per cent according to the Office of National Statistics (ONS) data.[1] We aim to review the reasons why unemployment was so high in the 1920s and 1930s, so low in the 1950s and 1960s, why it rose to much higher levels in the 1980s and why it seemed to fall after the mid-1990s.

In section 10.2 we discuss the measurement of unemployment and examine movements in the unemployment rate, in historical and international perspective. We describe unemployment by industry, region, duration, age, sex, and occupation. In section 10.3 we sketch a theoretical framework capable of

---

[1] ONS data give a different peak from registration or claimant count measures, which peak in 1986.

elucidating the mechanisms via which international and domestic economic events impact upon unemployment, and place that model in its intellectual context. Section 10.4 discusses and analyses the changes in unemployment from 1918 to 2000. In the conclusion we briefly revisit broad explanations for the passage of unemployment during the century.

10.2 The facts

The International Labour Office (ILO) defines the unemployed as those people not in work, actively seeking a job, and willing to start work within a reasonable time horizon. By the 1980s, in most developed market economies, unemployment rates were estimated from labour force surveys. Prior to that, data were provided from the operation of unemployment insurance and unemployment assistance schemes. In the United Kingdom, the operation of state unemployment insurance has provided data since 1911. Before this date there exist some data from trade union unemployment schemes covering mainly skilled workers in export goods-producing industries.

Using trade union data the Board of Trade produced an index of unemployment, which averages 4.5 per cent for the period 1870–1913. The extent to which this index provides a reliable measure of unemployment is questionable (Boyer and Hatton 2002). The main concerns relate to the coverage and labour force weights used in the construction of the index. These are derived from membership figures of some craft unions and are heavily biased towards shipbuilding and metals prior to 1890. The unskilled are not represented in the index and short-time working is ignored.[2] The latter is a problem for coal mining and textiles, where short-time working was used in preference to lay-offs. Boyer and Hatton (2002) have produced revised estimates of industrial unemployment for this period that they claim are more representative. Their revised series is also largely based on union data, weighted using employment shares from decennial population censuses, but also includes allowances for short-time working and a proxy for unemployment among unskilled workers (males receiving poor relief in workhouses). Neither the Board of Trade nor Boyer and Hatton include a measure of unemployment in agriculture. Between 1870 and 1913 their revised index suggests a mean industrial unemployment rate of 6.6 per cent, with essentially the same peaks and troughs but significantly less volatility than the Board of Trade index.

In 1911 the National Insurance Act Part II introduced a compulsory unemployment insurance scheme for all grades of worker in shipbuilding,

---

[2] The boundary between a worker on short time and an unemployed worker is problematic. For instance, a worker with a commitment from an employer to start work in the near future would not be considered unemployed by the ILO definition.

engineering, and building and construction (see Thane 1996). This was extended in 1916 to cover munitions work and various other trades.[3] In 1920, the Unemployment Insurance Act extended compulsory contributory unemployment insurance to all manual and non-manual workers earning up to £250 per annum, except domestic servants, agricultural workers, and certain trades where the risk of unemployment was considered low (Garside 1990: 37).[4] The number of workers covered by the scheme rose from 2.3 million in 1911 to 11.75 million in 1920. From the administration of this scheme, the Ministry of Labour published monthly totals of the number of insured workers who were 'wholly unemployed' and those that were 'temporarily stopped'.

The official data published by the Ministry of Labour also underestimate total unemployment during the inter-war period. Because compulsory insurance covered the export industries first of all, and these industries were generally experiencing greater vicissitudes in output, the official data overstate the percentage rate of unemployment in the economy as a whole. At the same time they understate the total numbers who were unemployed (because some workers in industries not covered by the scheme would have been unemployed). There is also a specific problem of under-recording female unemployment. Between 1921 and 1930 unemployment benefit was subject to a 'genuinely seeking work test'. Deacon (1981) reckons that some 3 million claims were disqualified under the provisions of this clause, the majority of whom were women. From 1925 an individual means test was introduced, which led to 2.5 times as many disqualifications among women as men until it was abolished in 1928. The 'genuinely seeking work test' was finally repealed in March 1930, but from October 1931 the 'Anomalies Regulations' made it harder for married women to register as unemployed (they were debarred if they were deemed to have 'abandoned insurable employment' or could not 'expect to obtain insurable employment' in the district in which they were resident (Deacon 1976). Feinstein's (1972) widely-cited unemployment series attempts to adjust the inter-war data for all these deficiencies using unemployment data recorded in the 1931 Population Census.[5] The official data indicate a mean of 14.2 per cent 1921–38, whereas the average in Feinstein's series is 10.9 per cent.

Following the 1942 Beveridge Report, the reform of social security after the Second World War extended unemployment insurance to virtually the entire male labour force. The 1946 National Insurance Act required individuals who were without work and who were seeking employment to register for work and it

[3] Including machine woodwork, repair of metal goods, manufacture of munitions, chemicals, rubber, leather, bricks, wooden cases, artifical stone, and other artificial building materials (Garside 1990: 34).

[4] For example, public servants and railwaymen. Agriculture workers were included in the scheme in 1936.

[5] The census was carried out after the abolition of the genuinely seeking work clause and before the introduction of the Anomalies Regulations.

is from these data that the official statistics on unemployment are derived. Almost all unemployed men registered for work. This is not the case for married women and, as a consequence, it is reckoned that the post-Second World War unemployment figures underestimate total unemployment by about one-fifth (Metcalf et al. 1982). This was because the post-war insurance system was based upon the conception of a male breadwinner, with married women treated as dependants. The assumption of a neat division between the male sphere of work and the female sphere of home became increasingly inappropriate with the rise in participation of married women in the labour market during the post-war period.

For the period after the Second World War, when unemployment insurance became universal until about 1980, the data on unemployment are more consistent. Thereafter, repeated and important changes to the rules governing entitlement to unemployment benefit occurred. Nearly all of these changes acted so as to reduce the official unemployment count (Unemployment Unit Briefing 1990). The key change was in October 1982 when the official unemployment count ceased to be based on registration and instead became based upon those receiving unemployment benefit. During the 1980s, serious squabbles arose over what measured unemployment might have been on an unchanged definition. The Department of Employment published historical data on the basis of the current unemployment definition (but not a current count on a pre-1980 definition). For example, in 1986, the official average count was 13.5 per cent. By 1989 this had been revised downwards to 11.8 per cent (Glynn 1991) and the 2005 estimate for that year is 11.25 per cent.

It has been suggested that to make the inter-war data comparable with the post-Second World War unemployment figures to 1982, it is necessary to multiply the official inter-war data by 0.8 and the post-war totals by 1.3 (Metcalf et al. 1982).[6] On the basis of multiplying the inter-war data by 8/13 the inter-war average becomes 8.7 per cent, which makes the rise in unemployment in the 1980s seem significantly more severe (Glynn and Booth 1987). The introduction of the Labour Force Survey, providing a questionnaire-based estimate of unemployment, facilitates easier comparison based on the ILO definition. In the late 1980s the official claimant count and estimates using the ILO definition from the Labour Force Survey diverged considerably. In the 1990s these two measures were much closer, probably due to reforms of the rules for claiming unemployment benefit that have moved the definition of a claimant closer to the ILO definition.

Figure 10.1 gives Feinstein's (1972) and current Office of National Statistics estimates of the unemployment rate. The main story told by this graph is not in dispute, despite the major changes in measuring unemployment previously discussed. Note first the fairly regular and quite large unemployment cycles in the

---

[6] These correction figures are averages over the trade cycle, as registration is a contracyclical.

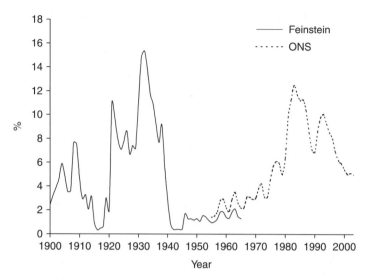

Figure 10.1 The British unemployment rate in the twentieth century

Notes: The series 'Feinstein' is from Feinstein (1972); see text for discussion. The series 'ONS' is from the Office of National Statistics, and is their attempt to make a long Second World War series consistent with the Labour Force Survey estimates used since the late 1980s.

trade union data up to 1910. The 1914–18 and 1939–45 wars show up as periods of very low unemployment. The inter-war period, 1919–39, is a period of unequalled turbulence containing two depressions. The period from 1945 looks quite different again. Initially, unemployment stayed very low, but then cycles around a trend that grew gradually at first, through the 1960s and early 1970s, and then exploded in two great bursts. The first surge was in the mid-1970s; the second was in the early 1980s. The unemployment rate then fell fast through the late 1980s. The early 1990s recession and recovery are also clearly visible.

10.2.1 *International comparison*

If comparison over time of UK unemployment is problematic, comparisons between countries prior to the mid-1950s are also fraught with similar difficulties. From 1955 the OECD started to produce international estimates of unemployment using a standard definition. Table 10.1 gives estimates of average annual rates of unemployment for the United Kingdom and ten other countries for the 1920s and 1930s. Those calculated by Galenson and Zellner (1957) are average industrial unemployment rates derived from a variety of sources depending on country, including trade union returns, insurance data, and census reports. For comparison, Table 10.1 also reports Maddison's (1964) estimates of economy-wide unemployment. These provide significantly lower

Table 10.1. Average international unemployment rates, 1921–38

	Galenson and Zellner 1921–29	Galenson and Zellner 1930–38	Maddison 1921–29	Maddison 1930–38
Australia	8.1	17.8		
Belgium	2.4	14.0	1.5	8.7
Canada	5.5	18.5	3.5	13.3
Denmark	18.7	21.9	4.5	6.6
France	3.8	10.2		
Germany	9.2	21.8	4.0	8.8
The Netherlands	8.3	24.3	2.4	8.7
Norway	16.8	26.6		
Sweden	14.2	16.8	3.4	5.6
UK	12.0	15.4	6.8	9.8
USA	7.7	26.1	4.9	18.2

Source: Eichengreen and Hatton (1988: table 1.2, p. 9).

estimates of unemployment for Europe, making the experience of the United States appear comparatively severe, although Maddison's estimates for the 1930s are thought to be too low (Eichengreen and Hatton 1988). As far as the experience of the United Kingdom is concerned, Galenson and Zellner's data suggest that the UK fared relatively poorly in the 1920s, with unemployment rates that exceeded all other countries outside Scandinavia. In contrast, during the 1930s, unemployment in the United Kingdom was lower than most other countries. Of the countries listed in Table 10.1, only France and Belgium had lower unemployment than the UK, 1930–38.

Figure 10.2 plots unemployment rates for the European Union (without Britain), the United Kingdom, and the United States for 1955 to 2003. These rates have been standardized for international comparison by the OECD. All these unemployment rates are higher after 1975 than before, especially those of Europe and the United Kingdom. By contrast, the United States appears to have had a more constant unemployment history. The international nature of many of the peaks and troughs is also evident. Some of these have more or less agreed origins. The OPEC oil crises of 1973 and 1979 caused serious inflationary recessions. Reaction to the second of these shocks had particularly severe unemployment consequences, as governments of all the major Western economies adopted firm deflationary policies in the early 1980s. The worldwide recession of the early 1990s is also clearly visible.

10.2.2 Unemployment by industry and region

At the end of the twentieth century when multiple job holding was not unusual and where moving between industries was typical within an individual's

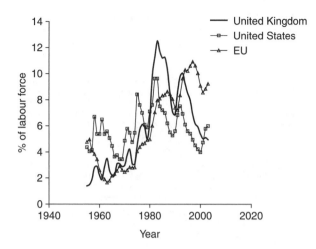

Figure 10.2 OECD standardized unemployment rates, 1955–2003

employment life cycle, the idea of 'industrial unemployment' rates may have seemed quite odd. This was not the case, however, at the beginning of the century, when the majority of workers would have entered an industry with the expectation of remaining in that industry for life. Indeed, in cultural terms, industrial occupation was of crucial importance in defining individual identity, especially for men.

The individual industries have quite distinct incidences of unemployment during the twentieth century. Prior to the First World War, export industries were subject to cyclical unemployment, with a trade cycle of about 7–11 years. During the inter-war period, the great rise in unemployment affected the old staple trades disproportionately. Table 10.2 shows that, even at the top of the trade cycle in 1924, 1929, and 1937, unemployment in old staples was generally considerably worse than unemployment in new industries. During the worst of the depression, unemployment in new industries increased significantly, but unemployment in the staples was chronic. In 1932, nearly two-thirds of all shipbuilders, nearly half of all iron and steelworkers, about a third of all coal miners and cotton textile workers, and about a fifth of all wool textile workers were registered as unemployed.

Because the spatial location of industry reflected the pattern established during the initial stages of industrialization, staple industries remained concentrated in the north of England, Wales, and Scotland. New industries, which were not as dependent upon water, coal, and mineral deposits, tended to be located in southern Britain near to metropolitan areas with good road and rail communication. As a consequence, the industrial structure largely explains the regional pattern of unemployment for much of the twentieth century.

Table 10.2. Industrial unemployment rates

	1924	1929	1932	1937
Old staples				
Coalmining	5.8	19.0	34.5	16.1
Shipbuilding	30.3	25.3	62.0	24.4
Cotton	15.9	12.9	30.6	10.9
Wool textiles	8.4	15.5	22.4	8.8
Iron and steel	22.0	20.1	47.9	11.4
New industries				
Chemicals	9.9	6.5	17.3	6.8
Cars and aircraft	8.9	7.1	22.4	5.0
Gas, water, electricity	6.3	6.1	10.9	8.3
Electrical engineering	5.5	4.6	16.8	3.1

Note: Data refer to the average of the numbers of insured workers unemployed in the UK at January and July each year.

Source: Adapted from Garside (1990: table 5, p. 13).

Table 10.3 shows how regional unemployment rates varied in the United Kingdom from before the First World War. The war appears as a distinct break in the historic pattern of unemployment. Before 1914, industrial areas of northern Britain, Wales, and Scotland were very much more prosperous, with fairly low average unemployment with peaks and troughs following a distinct cyclical pattern. After the First World War, a trade cycle is still apparent, but the average level of unemployment is significantly higher in these regions.

The uneven spatial impact of unemployment was also highlighted by the Ministry of Labour in its annual reports,[7] which described the United Kingdom in terms of 'two nations'. Roughly speaking, a line drawn between the Bristol Channel and the Wash would demarcate 'inner' (southern) and 'outer' (northern) Britain (Glynn and Booth 1987). The Midlands did not fit quite so comfortably into this picture. These were bell-weather regions where unemployment rates tended to be more strongly cyclical than other regions.

In the twenty years following the end of the Second World War, this pattern in the geography of unemployment was still apparent: unemployment rates in the north were still twice those of the south, while those evident in Wales and Scotland were roughly three times as large. But because unemployment was low in every region (except in Northern Ireland), geographical differences in the rate seemed much less important. The increase in unemployment during the mid-1970s and early 1980s more or less followed the geographical pattern established after the First World War, and once again, the spatial incidence of unemployment was viewed in terms of a north–south divide. The two-nations

---

[7] For example 1938, quoted in Constantine (1980).

Table 10.3. Regional unemployment rates UK, 1912–95

	1912–13	1932	1937	1949	1958	1963	1976	1986	1995	2000
England										
London	8.7	13.1	8.2							7.0
South-east	4.7	13.1	6.1	1.1	1.4	1.0	4.4	8.7	8.0	3.3
East Anglia				1.1	1.4	1.0	5.0	8.9	6.4	3.6
South-west	4.6	16.4	7.1	1.4	2.2	1.5	6.6	9.9	7.1	4.1
West Midlands	3.1	21.6	6.0	0.6	1.6	0.9	6.5	14.0	8.4	6.0
East Midlands	2.5	21.6	6.0	0.7	1.8	1.1	5.3	11.3	7.6	4.8
North-east	2.5	30.6	9.2	0.7	1.8	1.1	6.1	13.8	8.9	5.9
North-west	2.7	26.3	12.9	1.7	2.7	2.1	7.6	14.5	8.8	5.4
North	2.9		19.1	2.6	2.4	3.3	8.5	16.9	10.5	8.4
Wales	3.1	38.1	24.3	4.0	3.8	2.6	7.8	14.2	8.4	6.3
Scotland	1.8	29.0	15.2	3.0	3.8	3.6	7.6	14.3	8.4	6.5
Northern Ireland				6.5	9.3	6.6	11.5	19.1	12.2	6.1

Notes: The regions are not identical in this table. For 1912–13, 1932, 1937 the data refer to insured workers in July and are derived from Beveridge (1944: table 12, p. 73; 1936). The data for 1949, 1958, and 1963: annual average data from *British Labour Statistics: Historical Abstract*; 1976, 1986, and 1995: July data from, respectively Department of Employment *Gazette* (Nov. 1976), *Employment Gazette* (Dec. 1986), and *Labour Market Trends* (Dec. 1995). Data for 2000 are from the *Labour Force Survey*. Figures for East Anglia are not given separately, but are aggregated. North-eastern is Yorkshire and Humberside from 1949.

pattern of unemployment rates broke down in the 1990s, when unemployment rates differed little between regions, and only in Northern Ireland was unemployment significantly greater than it was in the south-east.

In the 1930s, long-duration unemployment was also predominantly concentrated in 'outer Britain', as Table 10.4 shows. The proportion of those unemployed for a year or more in London and the south-east was very low, at around 4–6 per cent. According to Crafts (1987), the proportion of long-term male unemployment in the UK rose from 10.7 per cent in September 1929 to 27.1 per cent in September 1937 (from 16.1 per cent to 34.0 per cent over the same dates if casual and temporary stopped are omitted (Crafts 1987: 420). This increase in long-term unemployment in the early 1930s is what Beveridge referred to as the 'legacy of the Great Depression' (Beveridge 1944: 66). However, compare this with the next severe depression in 1986. At this date 41 per cent of the unemployed had been unemployed for more than one year.[8] That proportion was lower in the south than it was in the north, Wales, or Scotland. Similar changes happened in France, Germany, and Italy. Between 1979 and 1990 the share of the unemployed out of work for more than a year

---

[8] Between the end of the Second World War and the mid-1970s, the proportion of long-term unemployed among unemployed women was little more than half that of men. Between the 1970s and 1980s, the incidence of long-term unemployment increased especially for women, with near equality by 1995.

Table 10.4. Share of unemployed with current spell over one year, by region, UK, 1932–95

	1932 Men	1938 Men	1986			1995		
			Men	Women	All	Men	Women	All
London	0.044	0.058						
South-east	0.038	0.066	0.41	0.29	0.37	0.42	0.29	0.39
East Anglia	ditto	ditto	0.39	0.28	0.35	0.35	0.25	0.29
South-west	0.088	0.086	0.38	0.28	0.34	0.35	0.24	0.33
West Midlands	0.146	0.159	0.52	0.37	0.47	0.43	0.30	0.40
East Midlands	ditto	ditto	0.46	0.30	0.41	0.39	0.26	0.36
Yorkshire and Humberside	0.196	0.250	0.46	0.32	0.42	0.39	0.27	0.36
North-west	ditto	ditto	0.43	0.35	0.40	0.39	0.26	0.36
North	ditto	ditto	0.50	0.36	0.46	0.41	0.27	0.38
Wales	0.210	0.307	0.47	0.31	0.42	0.36	0.24	0.33
Scotland	0.276	0.297	0.45	0.31	0.41	0.36	0.24	0.33
Northern Ireland			0.56	0.33	0.49	0.60	0.39	0.55
United Kingdom			0.46	0.31	0.41	0.40	0.27	0.37

Source: Crafts (1987: table 3, p. 422) and *Employment Gazette* (Dec. 1986), *Labour Market Trends* (Dec. 1995).

rose from 30 to 40 per cent in France, from 20 to 50 per cent in Germany, and from 37 to 70 per cent in Italy. Notably, this did not happen in the United States, where the share hovered below 5 per cent throughout. Through the 1990s long-term unemployment fell more heavily in Britain than in the other large European economies.

10.2.3 *Unemployment by age and gender*

During the inter-war period insurance data suggest that unemployment rates were greater for men than for women, as Tables 10.5 and 10.6 show. If we consider the rates of registered unemployment, the proportion of women employed is about half that of men in April 1927, November 1932, and November 1935. In February 1931 the proportion of women unemployed is much closer to the proportion of men unemployed and this reflects changes in the rules governing the administration of unemployment benefit (that is, after the repeal of the 'genuinely seeking work' clause and before the introduction of the Anomalies Regulations discussed previously). Similarly, according to the 1931 census, average unemployment was 12.7 per cent for men and 8.6 per cent for women (Hurstfield 1986). Of course, women's labour force participation was also much lower than men's (see Chapter 7), so women accounted for a small proportion of the registered unemployed—about 14 per cent in 1933 according to Thomas (1988). On average, women also had unemployment spells of shorter duration than men. The tendency for women to withdraw from the labour force at marriage (either voluntarily or through the operation

Table 10.5. Male unemployment rates by age, 1927–38

Age	April 1927	February 1931	November 1932	November 1935	February 1938
16–17	2.1		4.6	4.6	4.1
18–20	8.8	15.8	16.3	8.2	8.2
21–4	8.8	23.3	23.5	17.8	12.5
25–9	11.0	21.3	22.7	15.3	11.1
30–4	9.3	22.0	21.9	15.3	11.4
35–9	9.2	22.3	21.4	17.1	13.0
40–4	9.5	22.3	22.4	17.1	13.5
45–9	10.8	24.4	23.1	19.6	15.1
50–4	11.3	27.1	26.5	19.6	17.6
55–9	13.0	28.5	26.9	25.2	19.9
60–4	15.1	34.5	32.0	28.2	23.6
18–64	10.2	23.1	22.9	17.3	13.6

Source: Thomas (1988: table 3.6, p. 117).

Table 10.6. Female unemployment rates by age, 1927–38

Age	April 1927	February 1931	November 1932	November 1935	February 1938
16–17	2.2		3.1	4.7	5.5
18–20	5.1	13.3	7.9	7.3	8.3
21–4	5.1	18.4	9.1	8.5	10.6
25–9	4.3	20.5	9.3	8.0	10.7
30–4	4.1	24.1	11.8	8.0	11.7
35–9	4.5	27.2	10.9	11.5	12.8
40–4	4.3	26.5	9.4	11.5	13.8
45–9	4.6	27.8	17.3	15.5	15.1
50–4	5.2	30.4	18.3	15.5	17.3
55–9	4.8	32.9	20.6	22.2	19.8
60–4	5.5	30.6	16.4	23.8	24.5
18–64	4.8	20.3	10.4	9.3	11.6

Source: Thomas (1988: table 3.6, p. 117).

of marriage bars) helps explain both lower labour force participation and shorter duration unemployment as recorded in the official data. However, the official unemployment count is based on a particular construction of unemployment that distorts and underestimates the extent of female unemployment, especially among married women workers.

Tables 10.5 and 10.6 also show how unemployment varied by age during the inter-war period. In general terms, young workers under 21 had the lowest unemployment rates. This is true for both boys and girls. Amongst men and women, a higher proportion of workers over 55 years old were unemployed. According to Beveridge, the risk of becoming unemployed was much the same for all adults over 35 years old, although the probability of re-employment declined with age. Thus, older workers experienced longer spells of unemployment, which largely accounts for the higher proportion of older workers who were without work.[9] According to Eichengreen's (1987: 20–1) analysis of the individual data collected for the *New Survey of London Life and Labour*, unemployment by age was lowest amongst prime age workers and highest for young adults and older workers. Low unemployment rate among juveniles is likely to be due to the pay structure, in which young workers' wages were relatively low until age 21, but were then subject to a discrete increase.

Table 10.7 shows how unemployment varied with age after the Second World War. During the golden age of the 1940s, 1950s, and 1960s, young workers made up a tiny fraction of the unemployed and the incidence of long-term unemployment among young workers was especially low. Notice in Table 10.7 how the proportion of youth unemployment increased from the late 1960s. In the 1970s and 1980s, about a third of all male unemployed were young workers aged less than 24 years. For women, the young made up an even greater fraction of the unemployed: in 1976 nearly two out of every three women who were

Table 10.7. The distribution of unemployment by age, mid-year 1947–95

	Age groups (% share in total)				Total
	Under 20	20 to 39	40 to 54	55 and over	
Men 1947	5.4	37.6	31.4	25.5	189,897
Men 1958	7.5	41.5	27.4	23.6	260,103
Men 1963	11.0	38.5	25.2	25.3	322,320
		18 to 24	25 to 49	50 and over	Total
Men 1965		18.8	38.9	42.2	136,510
Men 1971		27.3	41.0	31.8	628,263
Men 1976		36.1	39.3	24.6	1,030,712
Men 1986		32.1	54.6	13.3	2,231,500
Men 1995		25.3	58.8	15.3	1,758,600
	Under 20	20 to 39	40 to 54	55 and over	Total
Women 1947	12.8	55.4	27.5	4.3	65,849
Women 1958	13.4	48.9	27.2	10.5	103,516
Women 1963	22.7	43.6	23.7	10.0	107,872
		18 to 24	25 to 49	50 and over	Total
Women 1965		41.9	37.6	20.5	63,473
Women 1971		52.5	29.5	18.0	112,568
Women 1976		65.4	25.0	9.6	371,758
Women 1986		44.1	48.7	7.3	1,048,100
Women 1995		36.6	48.7	14.7	569,700

Sources: July data, various issues of Ministry of Labour *Gazette*, Department of Employment *Gazette*, *Employment Gazette*, and *Labour Market Trends*.

[9] Thomas suggests that older workers were also more vulnerable to unemployment than younger workers during the early 1930s (1988: 120).

unemployed were aged between 18 and 24 years.[10] Despite this huge increase in the proportion of young workers in the unemployment total, they still made up a relatively small proportion of the long-term unemployed. Older men and women were a smaller fraction of the unemployed in the 1970s, 1980s, and 1990s than they were during the golden age. Older workers, however, formed a disproportionately large share of the long-term unemployed: in the 1980s and 1990s, roughly half the long-term unemployed were aged over 50 years.

10.2.4 *Unemployment by occupation*

During the inter-war period, unemployment varied inversely with social class, so that the 'risk of unemployment fell as social class rose' (Thomas 1988: 123). This is illustrated in Table 10.8 which contains data derived from the 1931

Table 10.8. Unemployment rate (%) by occupation, England and Wales, 1931

	Men	Women
Professional	3.7	2.7
Semi-professional	14.5	17.2
Employers and managers	1.4	0.9
Clerical	5.6	4.3
Foremen, supervisors	5.1	4.4
Skilled manual	12.1	12.9
Semi-skilled manual	11.9	9.7
Unskilled manual	21.5	11.1

Source: Thomas (1988: table 3.9).

Table 10.9. Unemployment rate (%) by occupation, Great Britain, 1975–95

	1975	1985	1989	1993	1995	2000
Professional	1	1	2	4	2	1.3
Employers and managers	2	4	2	6	4	2.1
Intermediate and junior non-manual	3	7	4	7	6	2.0
Skilled manual and own account non-professional	3	11	7	12	11	4
Semi-skilled manual and personal service	5	15	9	15	13	4.5
Unskilled manual	7	17	16	18	14	7.7
Total	4	9	6	10	8	4.8

Source: *General Household Survey*, 1995, and authors' calculations from Office of National Statistics data.

[10] These are July figures. In the 1970s school leavers and students were entitled to claim unemployment benefit.

Population Census. Male manual workers had the highest risk of unemployment and female managers the lowest. A similar relationship is evident in the post-Second World War data. Table 10.9 shows that between 1975 and 1995 unemployment rates for the unskilled and semi-skilled were consistently higher than for skilled and professional workers, and roughly proportionally so.

10.3 The natural rate of unemployment and the NAIRU

The history of unemployment and unemployment policy over the last hundred years is interwoven with the history of economic thought. Keynes's *General Theory* (1936), which virtually single-handedly started the sub-discipline of macroeconomics, was written as a response to the high unemployment of the inter-war years. In 1940 the macroeconomics of Keynes had barely begun to be absorbed by professional and academic economists, yet within a decade it had become orthodoxy (see Tomlinson 1987) in a Britain that was, perhaps coincidentally, enjoying negligible unemployment for the first time in recorded history. In the 1970s, the re-emergence of large-scale unemployment alongside high inflation was the single most influential event in the destruction of the international Keynesian hegemony in macroeconomic thought. Later, in the 1980s, new developments in macroeconomics were again inspired by the mass unemployment of the period.

This section sets out in a straightforward way the economic theory of unemployment. The rest of the chapter can be read without this section, but we think understanding will be enhanced if this section is absorbed. The main aims are twofold. First, we establish the factors that affect the level of unemployment. Secondly, we develop the idea that some factors are likely only to affect the amount of unemployed people temporarily, while other factors are likely to have more permanent effects.

10.3.1 *A basic model of equilibrium unemployment*

(a) THE DEMAND FOR LABOUR

In the short run of the microeconomics textbook, the demand for labour is determined by the profit-maximizing decisions of firms. The factors that will determine labour demand include: the size of the existing stock of capital, the state of technical and managerial knowledge, the levels of real wages, and real prices of other variable inputs, such as raw materials. A Keynesian macroeconomist would, in contrast, link the demand for labour much more directly to the aggregate demand for goods and services. A compromise between these two positions is to allow Keynesian aggregate demand effects in the short run but assume a return to the profit-maximizing position in the medium run. The

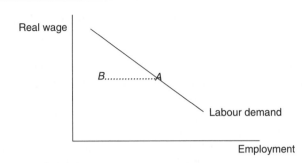

Figure 10.3 Labour demand

downward sloping line in Figure 10.3 is the medium-term labour demand schedule. Along this line, as the real wage[11] rises, firms find it profit maximizing to lower the level of employment.

At point A, or any other point on the labour demand curve, firms are in their medium-run position, having absorbed previous changes to aggregate demand for goods. Point B represents the position of employment and real wages immediately after a contraction in the demand for goods and services, if we assume that the initial response to a contraction in demand for goods is to lay off workers, rather than to cut wages and/or prices. In the medium term, when the contraction in demand has been absorbed by price and wage changes, the economy will return to a point on the labour demand curve. The behaviour of labour supply and the process of wage determination will determine the eventual resting point on the curve.

(b) THE SUPPLY OF LABOUR

In twentieth-century Britain, despite great long-run changes in the supply of labour, there was not much cyclical variation in labour market participation. This fact allows us the convenient simplification of developing a model with a fixed number of participants. Aside from participation, the other relevant aspect of labour supply is search intensity. In urban labour markets especially, most potential employers and employees are unknown to each other, so must seek each other out. In early twentieth-century Britain social observers began to recognize the imperfections in this process and began campaigning for government intervention. Board of Trade labour exchanges were introduced in 1908, in an attempt to improve these information flows.

Holding everything else constant, variations in the intensity of search will affect the level of unemployment. To understand why, suppose all unemployed workers increase their search intensity. Remember the inflow of

---

[11] The ratio of average wages to the average price of output.

job vacancies to the market and the inflow of workers into unemployment are both constant. This increase in search intensity would increase the number of matches struck per period and so reduce the average duration of a spell of unemployment.[12] So, the same number of people are made unemployed per week, but they remain unemployed for less time. It follows that there are fewer of them at any point in time[13] and unemployment is lower.

All economic theories of job search predict that a fall in the ratio of unemployment benefit to wages[14] increases search intensity. Thus, models of search intensity will generally predict that higher wages, by raising search intensity, reduce unemployment *ceteris paribus* and vice versa. This is summarized in Figure 10.4. The vertical line to the right of the diagram represents the labour force. The reaction of search intensity to wages generates the *effective labour supply* curve, EL^S, linking high wages to low unemployment. The horizontal distance from the EL^S curve to the labour force is the measure of unemployment. Equilibrium wages, employment, and unemployment are given by the intersection of labour demand and EL^S.

This is a complete model of the equilibrium rate of unemployment or, in Friedman's (1968) terminology, the natural rate of unemployment. What changes equilibrium unemployment? First, in the long run, capital accumulation and technical innovation tend to shift the demand for labour to the right, raising wages and employment. This may seem odd at first, as capital accumulation and technical innovation are often undertaken to reduce labour input. But there is a second, ultimately dominant effect: the optimal level of output

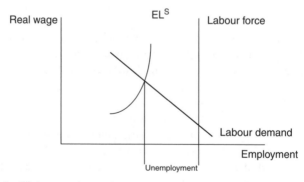

Figure 10.4 Equilibrium employment

---

[12] And reduce the average duration of a vacancy.

[13] Some may find this confusing. It is possible that everybody else searching harder has a negative impact on an individual's chance of getting a job. This would weaken the connection between search intensity and the level of unemployment.

[14] The replacement rate.

increases, so much so as to effect a net increase in labour demand. This is the process that raises living standards in the long run. What happens to unemployment? If unemployment benefits are raised in line with wages, then the EL^S curve shifts up as well and equilibrium employment and unemployment is unchanged. Over a shorter time horizon, however, technical change can have negative effects on employment. Rapid industrial change, for instance, could result in a higher level of *structural* unemployment, i.e. mismatches between the available vacancies and the skills of the unemployed. This can be represented in the diagram by a leftward shift of the EL^S curve.

Secondly, fiscal policy (taxation and expenditure policy) can also affect the natural rate of unemployment. Income taxes, indirect taxes, and employment taxes all create a wedge between the real wage paid by firms and the real wage received by workers. Thus, in principle, tax increases raise real labour costs and lower employment and increase unemployment. Similarly, rises in real raw material prices also raise equilibrium unemployment, by reducing labour demand and lowering equilibrium employment and wages. This assumes, plausibly, that over the medium term firms react to higher material prices by cutting output and employment rather than substituting workers for materials.

What about monetary policy? In Britain after the mid-1990s monetary policy consisted of manipulating interest rates with the target of keeping medium-term price inflation at a steady, low level. Most economists take the view that interest rates, through their effects on consumer and investment spending, will influence demand for goods and services and hence employment and unemployment, but only in the Keynesian short run, so that the equilibrium level of unemployment in unaffected.

Thirdly, labour market policy will affect the natural rate of unemployment. Any increase in costs associated with hiring or firing labour, such as a rise in statutory redundancy pay, will raise equilibrium unemployment.[15] Training schemes should increase the effectiveness of the unemployed as job seekers, and hence lower the natural rate. On the other hand, the generosity of the unemployment benefit system will also affect the natural rate of unemployment. In terms of Figure 10.4, an increase in unemployment benefits, or a lengthening of the period of benefit entitlement, will shift the EL^S curve to the left, raising unemployment.

10.3.2 *Extensions and alternatives*

The most influential work on post-1950 unemployment in the UK was undertaken by Layard and Nickell in a series of papers (hereafter LN, 1985, 1986, and 1987) and culminating in the book Layard et al. (1991). Their theoretical

---

[15] Such costs, though not incurred unless a worker is made redundant, increase the adverse risks associated with job creation and so reduce employment.

framework emphasized price and wage setting. They derived a curve similar to the labour demand curve from modelling the price-setting behaviour of firms. They also derived a curve similar to the EL^S curve, but from their analysis of wage-setting behaviour. The resulting model of equilibrium unemployment is very similar in predictions to the model of section 10.3.1. The differences of derivation are important, though.

The emphasis LN put on wage and price setting, rather than labour demand and supply, derives in part from a tradition of linking unemployment to the processes determining the rate of inflation. For them, at the intersection of the two curves, inflation is unchanging, reflecting a steady point in the wage–price spiral. The equilibrium unemployment rate is renamed the NAIRU (non-accelerating inflation rate of unemployment).

The emphasis on wage and price setting suggests a role for wage-setting institutions, such industrial confederations, trade unions, and incomes policy makers.[16] Some have argued, for instance, that the national structure of wage bargaining can influence unemployment. Bruno and Sachs (1985) borrowed the term corporatism from political scientists to describe centralized wage-bargaining systems. In the presence of powerful industrial unions, a centralized wage-bargaining system (or an incomes policy fully backed by all sides) might deliver greater sensitivity of wages to unemployment, and thus a lower equilibrium unemployment rate. In terms of Figure 10.4, the idea is that centralized bargaining, or corporatism, might move the EL^S curve to the right and make it steeper. Blanchard and Wolfers (2000) interpret the diversity of unemployment experience across industrialized countries in the last twenty years as being due to common shocks impacting differently upon economies with different institutions. We discuss the history of such British institutions in section 10.4 below.

So far, the analysis has employed the distinction between the medium run and the short run as a heuristic device. The idea that some forces have strong, but ultimately transient effects on unemployment, while others have permanent effects, is powerful. It can, however, become a tyranny. One of the most valuable contributions of Layard and Nickell (1985, 1986) was to suggest a plausible mechanism whereby a temporary macroeconomic recession might create a long-lasting rise in unemployment.

We can illustrate this as follows. Amend the model of Figure 10.4, by dividing the unemployed into two groups: the short-term unemployed, those who have been unemployed for less than a year, and the long-term unemployed, whose duration is greater than a year. Assume that after a year out of work, the unemployed become discouraged enough to cease searching for work forever.

---

[16] The term 'incomes policy' barely exists any more, but it was a major part of anti-inflation policy in Britain and many other countries in the 1960s and 1970s. It is discussed in section 10.4.

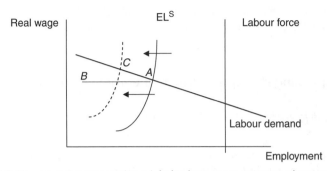

Figure 10.5 How a temporary recession might lead to permanent umemployment

This is an unnecessarily severe assumption, but it allows us to tell a simple story. An increase in the proportion of long-term unemployed in the labour force will shift the EL^S curve to the left. In other words, as before if, on average, workers search less hard for work, then there will be more unemployment.

Now consider a sharp decline in aggregate demand. In Figure 10.5, employment drops from A to B. How is this reduction engineered? Since they face costs of adjustment, such as redundancy payments, initially firms will not replace workers who leave. Vacancies will fall. Beyond this, some firms will lay workers off. The existing unemployed and newly laid-off workers will experience delays in finding work and more people will enter long-term unemployment, or in other words, will become discouraged searchers, though nominally still participating in the labour market. The impact of this is illustrated by the dotted lines representing the new, leftward-shifted labour force and EL^S curves.

Now imagine the medium term, where the economy is restored, by real wage adjustment, to somewhere on the labour demand curve. The new equilibrium will be C, where employment is lower than it was at A, unless the discouraged become newly encouraged. If they do not regain enthusiasm for search, unemployment will have risen permanently in response to a temporary shock. The deep message is that a recession might cause, for instance, an increased culture of dependency on unemployment benefits that lasts beyond the duration of the recession. This model would also predict a rise in long-term unemployment after a recession.

Let us summarize this section. Changes in aggregate demand for goods and services are the primary influences on unemployment in the short term, though supply-side shocks like the oil price hikes also influence unemployment in the short run. Some would argue that the effects could be long lasting, as in the preceding discussion. In the medium term, supply-side influences, such as the tax wedge, labour market policy, the wage-bargaining structure, the pace of industrial change, the pace of capital accumulation, and technical progress can all play a part in determining the equilibrium unemployment rate.

10.4 Explaining changes in British unemployment, 1918–2000

10.4.1 *The post-First World War depression*

In the years immediately following the Great War the British economy experienced two violent swings in economic activity, as economic boom gave way to severe recession. The boom started in April 1919 and lasted for about a year. It was the result of a high level of effective demand for both consumer and capital goods, as wartime controls and restrictions were rapidly abandoned, fuelled by low interest rates and plentiful credit. In addition, the war had been financed primarily through borrowing and the government was running a large budget deficit. By the beginning of 1920, the economy was at near full employment, industrial production was almost at its pre-war level, and both prices and wages were rising strongly (Howson 1975).

During the subsequent recession that began in April 1920, the official unemployment rate increased from 1.4 per cent to 16.7 per cent in the space of a year. Gross Domestic Product fell by 16 per cent in nominal terms and by 8 per cent in real terms between 1920 and 1921, making this the more severe of the two inter-war depressions. Why did this depression occur, why was it so severe, and why was it so persistent?

The depression coincided with a marked change in monetary policy. The rate of interest was raised to 6 per cent in November 1919 and again to 7 per cent in April 1920. This policy of 'dear' money lasted nearly a year and was motivated by a fear of inflation. Wholesale prices in 1918 were roughly double their 1913 level, but by 1919 they were treble pre-war levels (Cairncross and Eichengreen 1983). Because of the lags involved, it is likely that the tightening of monetary policy in the autumn of 1919 was of more importance in precipitating the depression than was the raising of interest rates to 7 per cent in April 1920. Although, according to Howson (1975: 24), this 'came just at the right time to ensure that the (over-)optimistic expectations of businessmen (who had apparently believed the prosperity generated by the restocking boom would last for ever) . . . were replaced in the shortest possible time by deep pessimism, which was later reflected in a drastic downturn in investment'.

In 1919 the government had grappled with a fundamental policy conflict between expenditure dictated by its pledge to social reform and reconstruction and the objective of returning to the gold standard at the pre-war parity. Initially, fear of unemployment and industrial unrest dominated over the restoration of parity (a policy that was supported by the Treasury and Bank of England), but in the first quarter of 1920 there was a change in the government's fiscal stance as the budget moved from deficit to surplus. Thus deflationary fiscal policy was implemented at the same time as monetary policy was tightened.

In August 1918 the Cuncliffe Committee recommended a return to the gold standard at the pre-war parity at the earliest opportunity, through the imposition of high interest rates. The value of sterling had been pegged against the United States dollar at about $4.76 in January 1916. After the armistice, considerable intervention was required to maintain sterling at this value and Britain left the gold standard in March 1919, whereupon the value of sterling fell. It reached a low of $3.63 in July 1921 after which sterling appreciated to $4.70 in March 1923. It is not clear whether the appreciation of sterling was simply the result of the change in domestic interest rates or whether there was an additional effect from the decision to return to gold (Miller and Sutherland 1994).

In April 1925 Britain returned to the gold standard at the pre-war parity. Keynes argued that the costs of this 10 per cent overvaluation would fall primarily on the export industries.[17] The extent to which his prognosis was correct has been hotly debated ever since. The contrast between the fortunes of the staples and 'new' industries is revealing in this context. Between 1920 and 1924, employment growth in the new industries was about 2 per cent per year and in 1924 unemployment was below 9 per cent, while in cotton, shipbuilding, and iron and steel unemployment remained 15 per cent.[18] Although most agree that monetary and exchange rate policy worsened the depression experienced by the staple trades during the 1920s, calculations of purchasing power parity (assuming that in 1913 exchange rates and price were at equilibrium) are extremely sensitive to the price index chosen as a comparator and do not universally support Keynes's claim of overvaluation (Cairncross and Eichengreen 1983). However, Redmond's (1984) calculation of real effective exchange rates suggests that between 1913 and 1925, British prices did indeed rise relative to its principal trading partners, by between 5 and 10 per cent, as a consequence of the restoration of the pre-war parity.

By 1924 export volumes were still significantly below their 1913 levels, while imports had regained their pre-war levels. For the remainder of the 1920s, staple trades experienced deep-rooted structural problems, which were aggravated by government monetary policy.[19] During the second half of the 1920s interest rates were high relative to earlier periods. This was despite contemporary concern over the negative impact high interest rates would have on

[17] Based on a comparison of British and US prices. Keynes (1931) argued that prices in the UK had risen by 10 per cent relative to those in the USA between 1913 and 1925.

[18] New industries are chemicals, electricity and electrical engineering, hosiery, silk and rayon, and vehicles. See Cairncross and Eichengreen (1983).

[19] Although Bank rate was reduced to 4% after the return to gold, it was increased to 5.5% in December 1925, where it remained until April 1927, after which it was reduced to 4.5% until February 1929 (Howson 1975).

domestic industry and employment.[20] High rates were necessary to maintain the value of sterling because of the need to attract short-term capital inflows to balance long-term foreign lending (Cairncross and Eichengreen 1983). Redmond calculates that by 1929, British domestic wholesale prices had declined sufficiently to eliminate the 5–10 per cent difference in British prices compared with its trading partners as a consequence of the overvaluation of sterling (Redmond 1984). This suggests that the Bank of England's Bank rate policy was effective in deflating the domestic price level and partly responsible for a reduction in output (relative to trend) and increased unemployment.

In addition, staple industries faced a number of serious structural difficulties. During the First World War, there was an increase in world capacity, markets had been lost to foreign competitors, and industries such as cotton faced new competition from man-made fabrics. To help combat these changes, British exports required a decline in their relative price.[21]

In view of the level of demand for British exports, it might be expected that there would have been downward wage adjustment. During 1919 the length of the working week was reduced from about 54 to 48 hours across a swath of British manufacturing, without offsetting reductions in wages. According to Dowie (1975), on average the reduction in the working week was 13 per cent (ibid.). It is unlikely that this increase in hourly pay was fully compensated by corresponding increases in labour productivity (Broadberry 1990). Prior to the First World War wages varied significantly by region. Flat-rate bonuses were paid to workers in key industries during the First World War. The implementation of these national bonuses represents an important step towards national wage bargaining. Money wages also increased regularly as a consequence of increases in the cost of living or selling price of output through the operation of sliding scale agreements (Gazeley 2003: ch. 3). These increases continued through the post-war boom (usually with about a three-month lag on price changes), before beginning to fall sharply at the end of 1920, as national bonuses were withdrawn and prices fell. After the end of 1922, however, money wages in most industries remained sticky before gradually increasing from the mid-1930s onwards.

For all of the changes in earnings there were very few changes in wage rates. In many manufacturing industries, wage rates during the 1920s were still based on rates agreed in the period before the First World War.[22] During the war and post-war boom wages benefited from national bonuses and increases resulting

[20] For a discussion of the different views held by the Treasury and Bank of England on this matter see Cairncross and Eichengreen (1983).

[21] Though the extent to which demand was price elastic is also a matter of debate.

[22] Though in 1919 several new wage rate agreements were negotiated following the reduction in length of the working week.

from sliding scale adjustments. During the subsequent depression, national bonuses were withdrawn and price falls triggered reductions in the sliding scales component of wages. Downward pressure on wages was resisted by trade unions, whose membership had roughly doubled from 25 per cent to 48 per cent of the workforce between 1914 and 1920, before gradually falling away in the early 1920s.

10.4.2 The natural rate of unemployment between the wars

Many scholars, prominently Hatton (2003),[23] have argued that the high unemployment that persisted in Britain throughout the inter-war years was partly due to a high underlying or natural rate of unemployment, as well as due to the transient effects of the demand shocks that generated the two major recessions.[24] There are three main theories of an increase in the natural rate. The first of these is that there were changes in wage-setting institutions that made wages more rigid. We have already seen that money wage adjustments were required in the early 1920s as prices fell in response to the deflationary pressure derived from the policy decision to return sterling to the gold standard at the pre-war parity (see Dimsdale 1984; Eichengreen and Hatton 1988; Dimsdale et al. 1989).

As Thomas (1994) points out, comprehensive industry-level bargaining expanded rapidly through the British economy during and after the First World War and particularly after the Whitley Reports of 1917–18. Over a similar period there was the establishment of trades boards, i.e. public bodies setting minimum wage rates in low-paying industries. The first of these boards were set up in 1908, but they expanded rapidly to cover 3 million workers by 1921. According to Sells (1939), in the mid-1930s, the Ministry of Labour estimated that 2.7 million workers were in trades covered by statutory wage-fixing machinery. Allowing for double counting, Sells reckons that in total approximately 11 million industrial and agricultural workers, from a total of about 15 million, were covered by national wage fixing in one form or another in the mid-1930s.[25] Thomas claims (1994) that many collective bargaining agreements embodied a wage floor, below which indexation was suspended. These wage floors, or bargained minima, survived in many pay scales throughout the period.

---

[23] See also Hatton and Boyer (2002).

[24] Inevitably it is hard to test this hypothesis directly given the brevity of the period and the domination of the unemployment rate series by two great events.

[25] Sells (1939: 48–9). The 2.7m workers covered by statutory wage fixing were estimated as 1.136m trade board workers (*Gazette* (1935), 127), 0.742m agricultural workers, 0.2m road haulage, 0.615m underground coal miners (*Gazette* (Oct. 1923), 383). A full list of trade boards industries is given in Sells (1939: 188).

Hatton (2003) argues that the change in wage setting to industry-level bargaining was vital. He applies a model due to Calmfors and Driffill (1988), in which changes in the degree of centralization of bargaining affect the equilibrium rate of unemployment. Two forces are at work in this model. On the one hand, as the bargaining unit increases in size its product market power increases, allowing higher wages. On the other hand as the bargaining unit increases its share of the labour market, it also increases its share of the negative employment consequences of raising wages and this mediates its wage. The feature of the Calmfors and Driffill model that Hatton highlights is that unemployment and wages are highest at intermediate levels of centralization.

Does this model explain high inter-war unemployment? We believe that Hatton is looking in the wrong place. First, we have seen from Table 10.3 that unemployment was particularly concentrated in the staple industries whose products were heavily oriented to export markets. The Calmfors–Driffill model was explicitly a closed economy model, which remains one of its great weaknesses. It is a common observation that British staple industries were hit by an exogenous shock in the immediate post-First World War years, in the form of increased world capacity coupled with a reduction in the volume of world trade. It is likely that this led to a change in their market power (something that is not addressed in the Calmfors–Driffill model), which would weaken the position of bargaining units to pass on wage increases. Secondly, the Calmfors–Driffill model does not include a parameter for the relative bargaining strength of workers and employers within the bargaining unit. If unions became weaker at the same time as bargaining became more centralized, their neat conclusion would not necessarily hold. We believe that after 1920, as unemployment increased, and particularly after the failure of the 1926 General Strike, the position of unions weakened. Add the likely increase in the demand elasticity of British exports to the post-1926 weakening of trade unions and you have strong forces working against the Hatton hypothesis.

The second theory is that increased scope and generosity of unemployment insurance raised the natural rate. The National Insurance scheme was extended in 1920 to cover about two-thirds of the workforce. At the same time there was a gradual drift towards a two-tier benefit system. Workers who were covered by the National Insurance scheme and who met the qualifications for benefit were entitled to receive Unemployment Benefit as a right. Benefits were extended to the dependants of claimants in November 1921 and the money value of the benefit paid to a family of two adults and three children increased from 11s. in December 1919 to 23s. in November 1921 to 32s. in March 1930 (Gazeley 2003).

Those who were either in industries outside the insurance scheme, or who were in industries covered by the scheme, but had not made sufficient contributions or who had exhausted their entitlement to unemployment benefit, often received the benefits 'as if' they were entitled. These benefits had a variety of names during the 1920s ('out of work donation', 'uncovennated benefit', 'extended benefit', 'transitional payments', and in the 1930s 'public assistance'). Although these were generally subject to a means test and tougher job search rules, they were of unlimited duration from 1924 onwards.

Benjamin and Kochin (1979) provocatively claimed that the unemployed were an 'army of willing volunteers' created by this expansion of the unemployment insurance system. Their claim, supported by some suggestive but fragile statistical evidence, invoked a controversy because it seemed to attack the view that inter-war unemployment was largely involuntary.[26] A decade or so later, after the publication of more reliable studies of the impact of the unemployment benefit system on the search behaviour of individual unemployed workers,[27] a consensus emerged that the best guess was that the benefit system played a significant but minor role in raising core unemployment in the period.

The third major theory of a raised natural rate is structural change, the subject of Chapter 1. The staple industries remained a very large depressed sector with high unemployment that were particular vulnerable to world shocks, while new industries experienced much lower levels of unemployment. As Newell shows in Chapter 2 there were historically very high levels of structural turbulence during the recessions of 1920/21 and 1930/31. Additionally, there was no growth of employment in the staples, even after the big shake-outs of 1920/21 and 1930/31, until the impact of rearmament from 1935/36 onwards. Since these staple industries were heavily concentrated in particular localities, and often based on bespoke skills that by nature were not easily transferable, the long decline in the staples almost certainly led to higher mismatch unemployment throughout the period. The problem with establishing the extent or importance of mismatch unemployment is that it is difficult to separate from the aggregate business cycle. To try to get around this problem, Brainard (1992) developed an index of the cross-industrial variation of stock market returns, which 'accounts for one-quarter of the total unemployment over the inter-war years', and though his index may not only reflect industrial change, the result is suggestive (Brainard 1992: 29).

10.4.3 *The Slump, 1930–32*

The centre of the initial shock was probably the United States. The New York stock market crash of 1929 seemed to impart a further downward push to an

---

[26] The distinction between voluntary and involuntary unemployment, with its strong moral overtone, bedevilled serious discussion of unemployment among economists for more than a generation.   [27] See, *inter alia*, Narendranathen et al. (1985); Eichengreen (1987).

economy that was already slowing down. In early 1930 there seemed to be a brief lull before the setting in of the 'slide into the abyss' (Kindleberger 1973: 128). The Great Depression hit the UK during 1930 and 1931. It arrived principally as a collapse of exports. By 1931 exports were only 69 per cent of their 1929 level. This fall in exports was greater than the total fall in GDP. The only other component of GDP to fall significantly in that period was inventory accumulation, which collapsed in 1931; clearly a reaction to the export crunch. Unemployment increased from 7.3 per cent in 1929 to 15.1 per cent in 1931 and peaked in 1932 at 15.6 per cent. The export collapse was not initially accompanied by a decline in imports, though this did follow, modestly, in subsequent years. Thus a large trade deficit emerged, from a small trade surplus in 1929, with exports at only 70 per cent of imports in 1931. Britain had experienced exchange rate crises of increasing severity in 1927 and 1929, before finally being forced off the gold standard in September 1931 (Cairncross and Eichengreen 1983). One of the immediate consequences of the abandonment of the gold standard was the rapid depreciation of sterling ($3.24 by December 1931), before rising sharply in 1933–34. The depreciation of sterling probably aided domestic industry by making exports relatively cheaper (Cairncross and Eichengreen 1983), but it is likely that the most important macroeconomic consequence of the abandonment of the gold standard was that it allowed domestic interests rates to fall.

The explanation for the fast recovery from the slump commands no unanimity in the literature. However, the Bank of England's decision to reduce Bank rate to 2 per cent in 1932, where it stayed for the rest of the 1930s, was of crucial importance. Cheap money allowed for the return on the 5 per cent War Loan to fall to 3.5 per cent, which reduced the debt payments as a percentage of National Income from 8.3 per cent in 1932 to 4.6 per cent in 1935 (Cairncross and Eichengreen 1983). It is also led to a reduction in the mortgage rate from 6 to 4.5 per cent, which provided a stimulus to house building. The increase in house building accounted for 17 per cent of the increase in GDP between 1932 and 1934 (Worswick 1984). Cheap money also provided a stimulus to manufacturing investment, which began to increase in 1933–34. Thus, the main engine of GDP growth between 1932 and 1936 was investment expenditure, which increased by over 40 per cent.

From 1935 onwards, government expenditures on rearmament provided an increase demand for engineering, shipbuilding, iron and steel, aircraft, and motor vehicle construction. Government expenditure on defence rose from 2.7 per cent of GDP in 1935–36 to 7.7 per cent in 1938–39 (Middleton 1985). According to Thomas (1983), British rearmament created 0.45 million jobs in 1935 and 1.5 million in 1938. This represents an important change in fiscal policy that sustained economic recovery through the late 1930s. By 1941 unemployment had fallen to 1.2 per cent of the labour force, and for the rest of the war remained less than 0.6 per cent.

10.4.4 *Why was unemployment so low after the Second World War?*

We identify three generic types of explanation: those that emphasize aggregate demand factors, whether autonomous or related to the Keynesian revolution in policy making; those that emphasize corporatist wage setting; and natural rate models. There are a number of variants of each of these explanations and they are by no means always independent. For example, those that stress the role of autonomous demand-side factors may also acknowledge the role of Keynesian demand management. Also, corporatist institutional explanations tend to see government commitment to full employment as a prerequisite. We should note here that econometric studies have not yet provided an answer to the question of low unemployment. Hatton and Boyer (2002) admit that they cannot explain the low unemployment in Britain in the 1950s.

Despite disagreements over precise definition and origin, most would accept that the Keynesian revolution was a relatively gradual one, spanning the decade of the 1940s, and having its genesis in the 1930s (see Tomlinson 1987). Several other things need to be emphasized in this context. First, Keynesian hegemony was not restricted to UK policy making, but evolved somewhat later in Western Europe and, most importantly, the United States, where Samuelson's influence on policy making played a key role (Blaug 1990). Secondly, Morgan (1990) has emphasized the degree of heterogeneity among early Keynesians and it is not clear that Keynes would have necessarily approved of the analysis and policy prescription of all those claiming brotherhood after his death. Thirdly, the origins of the Keynesian era of economic policy making were rooted in controlling inflation, not unemployment. Keynes's role as an adviser to the Churchill wartime coalition government was primarily to devise policy that would tackle wartime inflation. As Tomlinson (1987) points out, the Keynesian revolution coincided with traditional Treasury objectives and the policy Keynes recommended, of heavy taxation, and deferred consumption via compulsory saving and rationing, fitted well with Treasury concerns over wartime borrowing. Fourthly, after the Second World War, the transition from war to peace was clearly managed better than had been the case after the First World War. Extensive controls adopted during the war (over prices, investment, imports and raw materials, and rationing of important items of consumption) were very gradually abandoned in favour of demand management and state control of the commanding heights of the economy (Cairncross 1985, 1994).

Stewart (1986, 1991) provides the most celebrated defence of the impact of the Keynesian revolution in policy making on employment. His argument, succinctly put, is that unemployment was low because governments successfully undertook counter-cyclical demand management. Stewart accepts the argument of Matthews (1968) that post-war governments were for the most part grappling with inflationary, rather than deflationary gaps, but nevertheless maintains that at crucial periods, governments stimulated demand (through a mix of fiscal and monetary policy), when 'the growth in demand fell below the growth of the economy's productive potential' (1986: 145). The occasions of these Keynesian acts of demand management were, according to Stewart, the early 1950s, the late 1950s, the early 1960s, and the beginning of the 1970s. It is clear, however, that government policy was not always stabilizing (Dow 1964; Brittain 1969), due to errors in forecasting and mistiming of interventions.

Central to Stewart's analysis is the full employment pledge enshrined in the 1944 Employment White Paper that committed the government to 'the maintenance of a high and stable level of employment after the war', as one of its policy aims. This is not the same as committing governments to full employment, but very rapidly after the war governments did commit themselves to full employment as their primary policy goal. At the time of publication of Keynes's General Theory, he defined full employment as 6 per cent of the labour force, while for Beveridge it was 8.5 per cent in 1942 (as a precondition for the welfare state), but fell rapidly to 3 per cent by the time of the publication of *Full Employment in a Free Society* (Beveridge 1944: 21).

Matthews (1968), in a seminal article, argued that post-war full employment was not due to Keynesian demand management per se, but increased levels of private investment compared with those prevailing before the war. Similar views are expressed in Matthews et al. (1982); although here the authors also stress the role of exports.

The institutional explanation for low post-war unemployment focuses on wage bargaining and particularly tripartite, corporatist wage-setting institutions. The existence of corporatism provides a powerful explanation of both low unemployment in the 'golden age' and the subsequent rise in unemployment during the early 1970s. Although Middlemas (1979) and Hannah (1983) trace the origins of 'corporate bias' to the 1920s, it is during the Second World War that the position and influence of labour was transformed (after the fall of France with the formation of the increasingly Labour-dominated wartime coalition government led by Churchill). There are two strands to this argument. The first is the familiar 'people's war' thesis that the sacrifices made by people during the war would have a utopian post-war reward in the form of a 'new Jerusalem', which, although subject to some revision lately (Smith 1986; Calder 1991), remains an important explanation of the desire for social planning, reconstruction, and a more egalitarian post-war society.

Secondly, the requirements of total war also transformed the political position of labour. Bevin, former general secretary of Britain's largest union, the Transport and General Workers' Union, assumed almost dictatorial control over the process of production and direction of labour and transformed the Ministry of Labour 'into one of the commanding heights of the home front' (Addison 1991). The war also vastly strengthened the shop stewards movement. When Labour won the 1945 general election with a landslide majority, it legislated for a comprehensive welfare state. Full employment formed an integral part of post-war desires, partly as a response to the experience of the mass unemployment of the early 1930s.

Most writers see the twenty-five years after the end of the Second World War as a period of social democratic consensus based on the ideas of Beveridge and Keynes, although Morgan (1990) has suggested that the extent of the congruence between Labour and Conservative governments' industrial and social policy during the 1950s has been overdone in many accounts. Kavanagh argues that post-war economic planning was based on a 'social contract' in which governments would take responsibility for ensuring full employment and trade union leaders would urge wage moderation and responsible industrial relations on their members (1990). The maintenance of full employment was to be achieved through the use of Keynesian techniques of demand management. Social planning had a universal welfare state based on Beveridge's recommendations as its centrepiece.

Corporate decision making required the establishment of apparatus for the tripartite management of the economy. It is important to note that social and economic planning were intimately connected in the minds of their proponents. Beveridge saw full employment as one of the preconditions for the successful implementation of his blueprint for the post-war welfare state, and the construction of his vision was important for post-war economic management because it raised significantly the share of government expenditure in GDP (Tomlinson 1987), thus making, in theory at least, demand management that much easier. According to Middlemas (1979), the post-war settlement raised employers and trade union representatives to the status of 'governing institutions'. This tripartite system started during the war with planning in the form of the Reconstruction Advisory Council and culminated in the 1960s with the National Economic Development Council.

This form of corporatism could result in lower unemployment at any given wage level, as we saw in section 10.3. Initially in the post-war period, trade union leaders were able to deliver wage restraint, for example during 1948–50, but gradually industrial relations became increasingly disharmonious as unofficial or 'wildcat' strikes became more frequent and powerful unions exercised less restraint and governments resorted, usually with key trade union leaders' acquiescence, to compulsory incomes policies (Jones 1987). Moreover, the strengthened shop stewards rigorously defended restrictive practices and overmanning which further weakened competitiveness. The rise in the power of industrial labour was not matched by employers' organizations, which remained relatively weak (Phelps Brown 1987). The institutionalization of the 'annual pay round', a phenomenon absent in the inter-war period, provided the conditions for wage 'leapfrogging' in the labour market as employers found that they were able to pass on increased costs while maintaining profitability.

During the 1960s, government responded to rising wage inflation by using incomes policies and by attempting to reform the trade union law. Although incomes policies were successful in the short term, the same cannot be said for Labour's 1969 attempt to reform trade unions. At the end of the 1960s the post-war settlement was under immense strain as wages exploded and militancy increased. This phenomenon took place throughout the Western countries (Nordhaus 1972). It may be that an internal contradiction of corporatism had finally worked itself out. Once unemployment really did appear to have been eradicated, a generation of workers who had no direct experience of the depression, and were not participants in the post-war settlement, had no reason to stick with the deal agreed by their union leaders.

Low unemployment in the golden age may, of course have had little to do with demand management or the great institutional agreements designed to deliver wage restraint. It may be that Britain was experiencing a low equilibrium or natural rate of unemployment. Why was the equilibrium rate low? Newell and Symons (1990) argue that British workers had a low equilibrium rate of unemployment because they had a low taste for it, as they had strong preferences for 'home and hearth'. Evidence for this is higher marriage rates, lower divorce rates, larger family sizes, and increased fertility in all age groups from the end of the Second World War until the mid-1960s.

10.4.5 *The great rise in unemployment, 1975–85*

The most influential studies of the rise in unemployment were made by Layard and Nickell (1985, 1986, and 1987). Their statistical work found the key factors influencing unemployment were: measures of the level of world trade, export price competitiveness and fiscal stance, tax and import price wedges, unemployment benefit generosity,[28] union power,[29] a proxy for incomes policy, and a measure of the extent of mismatch.

Layard and Nickell divide the period 1956 to 1983 into four eras: the low unemployment period from 1956 to 1966, when the male unemployment rate averaged just under 2 per cent; the eight years surrounding 1970 when the unemployment rate of men averaged just under 4 per cent; the late 1970s, from 1975 to 1979, with an average male unemployment rate 7 per cent; and the early 1980s, when unemployment of men averaged just under 14 per cent. The estimated impacts of the various factors on unemployment are summarized in Table 10.10.

As we have already seen, the rise in the unemployment rate from the 1956–66 period to the 1967–74 period (about 2 percentage points) was due to, in order of importance: a rise in union power, an increase in unemployment

[28] Measured by the replacement rate, the ratio of unemployment benefits to average earnings.　　　　[29] Measured by the mark-up of union over non-union wages.

Table 10.10. Changes in the male unemployment rate, 1956–83 (percentage point changes)

Periods	1956–66 to 1967–74	1967–74 to 1975–79	1975–79 to 1980–83
Employer's labour taxes	0.42	0.67	0.78
Benefit replacement rate	0.54	−0.09	−0.10
Union power	0.84	0.86	0.57
Real import prices	−0.36	1.01	−0.67
Mismatch	0.14	0.18	0.44
Aggregate demand factors	0.47	0.82	5.14
Incomes policy	0.00	−0.31	0.43
Total	2.05	3.14	6.59
Actual change	1.82	3.01	7.00

Source: Layard and Nickell (1985, table 6, p. 77).

benefit generosity, and adverse aggregate demand changes. The rise from 1967–74 to 1975–79 (about 3 percentage points) is estimated to be due to, again in order of importance: increases in the tax and import price wedge, a further rise in union power, and further adverse aggregate demand effects.

The rise in the unemployment rate from 1975–79 to the early 1980s (about 7 percentage points) is due in the main to adverse aggregate demand changes, with small extra effects coming from union power and the degree of mismatch.

In summary, in the Layard and Nickell account, the slow rise in unemployment in the decade up to the late 1960s and early 1970s was due most importantly to a rise in union power. Most of the available indices seem to reflect greater militancy in the UK, as in many other countries, over this period; see Flanagan et al. (1983), for instance. In the model of section 10.3, this translates into a leftward shift of the EL^S curve and higher wages and unemployment. During the 1970s, the most important cause of increasing unemployment was the OPEC oil embargo of 1973/74. According to Layard and Nickell's data, this raised real import prices by over 35 per cent between 1972 and 1974. Recall that in our model a rise in real import prices shifts both the labour demand and the EL^S curves to the left. Lastly, the great rise in unemployment from the late 1970s to the early 1980s is almost completely a fall in aggregate demand, caused mainly by combination of tight fiscal and monetary policy, but also slightly later by a contraction in world trade. The tightening of monetary and fiscal policy was very much recognized at the time. The first Thatcher government was committed to lowering inflation using monetary policy without resorting to incomes policy. A fiscal tightening was seen as a necessary bulwark to support the new monetary stance. At the same time the second oil price hike raised unemployment and inflation.

Let us remind ourselves of the dogs that did not bark. First, Layard and Nickell estimate almost no effect on unemployment from technological change and capital shortage. This must be partly due to the assumption, used to construct their model, that the unemployment rate is unaffected by capital and technology in the long run. Bean (1994) summarizes other investigations into this possibility. No robust effects have been found.

Secondly, the impact of mismatch is similarly negligible (see Table 10.10, last column). This is one of their most controversial findings. Many observers find it difficult to believe that the dislocations associated with, for instance, the great contraction of manufacturing in the early 1980s and the rationalization and eventual privatization of much of the public sector did not create significant mismatch unemployment. Rosen's discussion of Jackman et al. (1991) is a strong attack on these lines.

Thirdly, Layard and Nickell find little impact of incomes policy on unemployment. Recall that moderation of wage claims by unions should have the effect of shifting the EL^S curve to the right, and perhaps making it steeper, so that incomes policy should reduce wage pressure and lower unemployment. Layard and Nickell find this effect to be tiny, lowering unemployment by one-third of one percentage point in the late 1970s. This is mildly surprising, since there was fairly universal acceptance that incomes policy played a part in lowering inflation in the late 1970s (Jones 1987).

10.4.6 Mid-1980s to mid-1990s

The unemployment generated by the recession of the early 1980s was massive and prolonged, peaking at over 3 million workers. It is perhaps useful to repeat Layard and Nickell's theory of this persistence. They found that the long-term unemployed exerted little downward pressure on wages, in contrast to the significant effect found with respect to the short-term unemployed. The consequence is that long-term unemployment could persist.

Governments during the 1980s and 1990s made considerable efforts to cajole the unemployed into more assiduous job search. This took two forms. First, the expansion of active labour market policies, that is, policies designed to help job seekers. Secondly, there were reforms of benefit entitlements. Among active policies, the Restart programme, introduced in 1986, entailed re-interviewing the long-term unemployed and training them in job search techniques. Restart is credited (see, for instance, OECD 1996) with much of the fall in long-term unemployment from 1986 to 1990. In 1990 the government introduced individual assessments for the long-term unemployed, and sent some on courses, called Jobclubs, to improve their job-finding ability. By 1996 there were eight different schemes, with about 1.5 million places, in operation to help the long-term unemployed with job search skills and vocational training.

Unemployment benefit reforms included the provision in the 1989 Social Security Act that introduced an 'actively seeking work' clause into the conditions for unemployment benefit entitlement. Later, in 1996, the government also reduced entitlement to non-means-tested unemployment benefit from twelve to six months with the introduction of job seekers' allowance.

After 1997, the Labour government's New Deal combined benefit reform and active labour market policy. This was initially aimed at those less than 25 years of age. After six months' unemployment a young person would be offered: employment (with employers subsidized to hire a young person for a period of six months), full-time education, or environmental or voluntary sector work. Those unwilling to take one of these four options lost 40 per cent of their benefit.

Between 1986 and 1989 the UK experienced a macroeconomic boom fuelled by, among other things, the interplay between financial market liberalization, asset price inflation, and the emergence of high levels of private sector debt. This together with the labour market policy measures described above helped to reduce the unemployment rate from its 1986 peak of 13 per cent to about 7 per cent by 1989.

The end of the boom was initially very gradual, but became a severe recession that lasted until 1992. It is generally ascribed to a tightening of monetary policy following an outbreak of inflation in the late 1980s. Unemployment peaked in 1993 at around 10 per cent of the workforce, somewhat below the 1980s peak, and fell continuously to the end of the century. Interestingly, neither the post-1993 fall in unemployment, nor the depreciation of sterling following the British withdrawal from the Exchange Rate Mechanism of the European Monetary System in 1992, seemed to cause upward pressure on wages, unlike previous similar episodes.

Many observers (see, for instance, OECD 1996) explained this lack of wage pressure by arguing that a reduction in the equilibrium unemployment rate occurred through the 1990s. This reduction is seen as a manifestation of a major increase in the flexibility of the British labour market. The main causes of this change are seen as: the deregulation of the 1980s, the changes in the treatment of the unemployed noted above, and the weakening of the trade union movement,[30] through restrictive legislation and the defeat of key unions in major industrial disputes (Brown and Wadhwani 1990).

The fall in union influence is reflected in the proportion of union members among employees, which stood at 33 per cent in the mid-1990s compared to just over 50 per cent in 1980. The OECD cites a number of other indicators of

---

[30] The Employment Acts of 1980, 1982, 1988, and 1990 restricted the activities of trade unions: employers were not required to negotiate or recognize trade unions, secondary picketing was strictly controlled, trade union civil immunity for the consequences of unlawful industrial action was removed, and closed shop practices were effectively ended.

increased flexibility (1996: 89–90): the increasing diversity of hours worked, decentralization of wage bargaining; an increase in temporary work; and an extension of performance-related pay. In terms of Figure 10.3, we can think of most of these changes, for instance the weakening of unions in collective bargaining, as shifting the EL^S curve to the right. Some reforms, such as a move to more short-contract labour and a greater willingness on behalf of workers to embrace new technologies, will shift the labour demand curve to the right.

Not only did Britain's unemployment improve in comparison with the recent past, but also in comparison with the experience of OECD countries in general, and similar EU countries in particular. In a major study of late twentieth-century unemployment in the OECD countries, Nickell and van Ours (2000) ask why British unemployment fell faster that that of other countries in the 1990s. Their conclusion was that the major cause was the collapse of unionization, which according to their calculations accounts for 2.8 of the 4 percentage point reduction in the British natural rate of unemployment between the late 1980s and late 1990s.

10.5 Conclusions

What should the reader take away from our account? We have discussed various macroeconomic shocks leading to short-run slumps, but the harder aspects to explain are the long period differences in average unemployment. Begin with the high unemployment of the 1920s and 1930s. The literature points to three explanations: changing wage-setting institutions, expanded unemployment insurance, and structural change. There is no consensus as to their relative importance, though the best guess is that benefits probably played a minor role. As for the other two explanations, the fact that the unemployment rates in 'outer Britain' were so much higher than in the rest of the country is suggestive of a structural problem. The old staple industries, which relied on exports, were heavily concentrated in the north of England, Scotland, and Wales. As a consequence of their heavy reliance on trade, these industries were more vulnerable to external shocks. It is difficult to believe this would have been different under any other set of wage-setting institutions.

Next we come to the low unemployment of 1945–65. The first key point is that the government adopted a very gradual approach to dismantling the war economy. This, plus the absence of monetary policy blunders, seems the most likely reason why the brief but devastating boom–bust of 1919–21 was not repeated in the late 1940s. Why did unemployment stay low? On demand side we have the investment boom, partly a worldwide phenomenon. This was possibly encouraged by the stable environment pledged by the adoption of Keynesian policy making, as well as by the wholesale application of technologies devised during the Second World War. This may have been accommodated on the supply side by institutional arrangements designed to deliver wage moderation.

What of the rise in unemployment from the 1960s to the 1980s? Let us knowingly oversimplify the economists' view and say that the initial rise in unemployment was due to growing union militancy, with help from OPEC, and the later rise was due mainly to the fiscal squeeze of the early 1980s. The (oversimplified) historian's view is that the post-war settlement delivered low unemployment in the twenty years after 1945, but its breakdown and subsequent abandonment by the first Thatcher government led to higher unemployment in the 1980s and 1990s. How different are these two explanations?

The rise of union militancy could be interpreted (indeed we have suggested it) as the first sign of breakdown in the post-war settlement. Also the fiscal squeeze of the early 1980s could be interpreted as the act of a government proving itself liberated from the settlement. Interestingly, historians are most concerned with the role of institutions, but have an implicit economic model that is usually highly Keynesian. The economists' story acknowledges the power of institutions, but refrains from asking why this power rises and falls or why it is exercised at some times and not at others.

In an authoritative study of unemployment in the industrialized countries Nickell (1997) summarizes the labour market features associated with high unemployment. These are: generous and indefinite unemployment benefit regimes in combination with few or no active labour policies; high levels of unionization undisciplined by centralized coordination; high payroll taxes and high minimum wages for young people; poor educational standards. From the early 1980s to the late 1990s, the British government curtailed the generosity of the benefit regime as well as developing a substantial range of active labour market policies. Also, as we have seen, the level of unionization fell heavily. These are the key reasons why there was a fall in British equilibrium unemployment during the period.

How do we reconcile our discussion of the golden age of 1945–65 with Nickell's findings? In that period unemployment benefits were no less generous than in the early 1980s, and, indeed, universal for the first time in British history. The basic benefit was more or less indefinite. Britain was quite unionized, though the growth of white-collar unionization had not yet taken place. Crucially, however, at the beginning of the period, moderation in wage bargaining was delivered by trade union leaders as part of the post-war settlement. It should not be forgotten, though, that there was no major global macroeconomic disruption over the period. If unemployment started low in 1945 because of careful demilitarization, then, in terms of the Layard and Nickell model, there were no shocks to drive the economy into high unemployment.

As for the fall in unemployment after 1993, the main explanations seem to be the deregulation of the labour market that occurred most prominently under Thatcher and the overhaul of unemployment policy away from benefits payments to active assistance with job search and retraining. Is unemployment still a problem of industry, as Beveridge would have had us believe nearly a hundred years ago? We've seen that Nickell and van Ours consider that the collapse of unionization was responsible for the fall in unemployment in the 1990s. But one of the reasons for that collapse in unionization must be the final elimination of the old, regionally concentrated industries of Britain's industrial past. The answer to our question is, 'No, not any more'.

References

Addison, P. (1991). *The Road to 1945*, 2nd edn. London: Pimlico.

Bean, C. R. (1994). 'European Unemployment: A Survey'. *Journal of Economic Literature*, 23: 573–619.

Benjamin, D., and Kochin, L. (1979). 'Searching for an Explanation of Unemployment in Interwar Britain'. *Journal of Political Economy* 87: 441–70.

Beveridge, W. (1909). *Unemployment: A Problem of Industry*. London: Longman.

—— (1936). 'An Analysis of Unemployment'. *Economica*, NS, 3: 12.

—— (1942). *Report on Committee on Social Insurance and Allied Service*. Cmd. 6404. London: His Majesty's Stationery Office.

—— (1944). *Full Employment in a Free Society*. London: Allen and Unwin.

Blanchard, O. J., and Wolfers, J. (2000). 'The Role of Shocks and Institutions in the Rise of European Unemployment'. *Economic Journal*, 110: 1–33.

Blaug, M. (1990). *John Maynard Keynes*. London: Macmillan.

Booth, A. (1983). 'The Keynesian Revolution in Policy Making'. *Economic History Review*, 36: 103–23.

—— (1984). 'Defining a Keynesian Revolution'. *Economic History Review*, 37: 263–7.

Boyer, G., and Hatton, T. J. (2002). 'New Estimates of British Unemployment, 1870–1913'. *Journal of Economic History*, 62: 643–75.

Brainard, S. L. (1992). 'Sectoral Shifts and Unemployment in Inter-War Britain'. NBER Working Paper Series, No. 3980.

Brittain, S. (1969). *Steering the Economy: The Role of the Treasury*. London: Secker and Warburg.

Broadberry, S. (1990). 'The Emergence of Mass Unemployment: Explaining Macroeconomic Trends in Britain during the Trans-World War 1 Period'. *Economic History Review*, NS, 43/2: 271–82.

Brown, W., and Wadhwani, S. (1990). 'The Economic Effects of Industrial Relations Legislation since 1979'. *National Institute Economic Review*, 131: 57–70.

Bruno, M., and Sachs, J. D. (1985). *Economics of Worldwide Stagflation*. Oxford: Blackwell.

Cairncross, A. (1985). *Years of Recovery: British Economic Policy 1945–51*. London: Methuen.

—— (1994). 'Economic Policy and Performance, 1945–1964', in R. Floud and D. McCloskey (eds.), *The Economic History of Britain since 1700*, iii: *1939–92*. Cambridge: Cambridge University Press.

—— and Eichengreen B. (1983). *Sterling in Decline: The Devaluations of 1931, 1949 and 1967*. Oxford: Blackwell.

Calder, A. L. (1991). *The Myth of the Blitz*. London: Jonathan Cape.

Calmfors, L., and Driffill, J. (1988). 'Centralisation of Wage Bargaining and Macroeconomic Performance'. *Economic Policy*, 6: 13–61.

Constantine, S. (1980). *Unemployment in Britain between the Wars*. London: Longman.

Crafts, N. F. R. (1987). 'Long Term Unemployment in Britain'. *Economic History Review*, 40: 418–32.

Deacon, A. (1976). *In Search of the Scrounger: The Administration of Unemployment Insurance in Britain, 1920–1931*. Occasional Papers on Social Administration. London: Bell (for the Social Administration Research Trust).

—— (1981). 'Unemployment and Policy in Britain since 1945', in B. Showler and A. Sinfield (eds.), *The Workless State*. Oxford: Robertson.

Dimsdale, N. H. (1984). 'Real Wages and Employment in the Inter-war Period'. *National Institute Economic Review*, November.

—— Nickell, S. J., and Horsewood, N. (1989). 'Real Wages and Unemployment in Britain during the 1930s'. *Economic Journal*, 99/396: 271–92.

Dow, J. C. R. (1964). *The Management of the British Economy, 1945–60*. Cambridge: Cambridge University Press.

Dowie (1975). '1919 to 1920 is in Need of Attention'. *Economic History Review*, NS 28/3: 429–50.

Eichengreen, B. (1987). 'Unemployment in Inter-War Britain: Dole or Doldrums?' *Oxford Economic Papers*, 39: 597–623.

—— and Hatton, T. J. (1988). 'Inter-War Unemployment in International Perspective: An Overview', in B. Eichengreen and T. J. Hatton (eds.), *Inter-War Unemployment in International Perspective*. NATO ASI Series, Series D. Behavioural and Social Sciences 43. Dordrecht: Kluwer Academic Publishers.

Feinstein, C. H. (1972). *National Income, Expenditure and Output of the United Kingdom 1855–1965*. Cambridge: Cambridge University Press.

—— (ed.) (1983). *The Managed Economy*. Oxford: Oxford University Press.

Flanagan, R. J., Soskice, D. W., and Ulman, L. (1983). *Unionism, Economic Stabilisation and Incomes Policy: European Experience*. Washington: The Brookings Institution.

Friedman, M. (1968). 'The Conduct of Monetary Policy'. *American Economic Review*, 58: 1–17.

Galenson, W., and Zellner, A. (1957). 'International Comparison of Unemployment Rates', in *The Measurement and Behaviour of Unemployment*. NBER, Princeton: Princeton University Press.

Garside, W. R. (1990). *British Unemployment 1919–39: A Study in Public Policy*. Cambridge: Cambridge University Press.

Gazeley, I. (2003). *Poverty in Britain 1900–1965*. Basingstoke: Palgrave Macmillan.

Glynn, S. (1991). *No Alternative? Unemployment in Britain*. London: Faber.

—— and Booth, A. (1987). *The Road to Full Employment*. London: Allen and Unwin.

Greene, W. (1994). *Econometric Analysis*, 2nd edn. New York: HarperCollins.

Hammermesh, D., and Rees, A. (1993). *The Economics of Work and Pay*, 5th edn. New York: HarperCollins.

Hannah, L. (1983). *The Rise of the Corporate Economy*, 2nd edn. London: Methuen.

Harris, J. (1983). 'Did British Workers Want the Welfare State?', in J. Winter (ed.), *The Working Class in Modern British History*. Cambridge: Cambridge University Press.

Hatton, T. (2003). 'Unemployment and the Labour Market, 1870–1939', in R. C. Floud and P. A. Johnson (eds.), *The Cambridge Economic History of Modern Britain*. Cambridge: Cambridge University Press.

—— and Boyer, G. (2002). 'New Estimates of British Unemployment, 1870–1913'. *Journal of Economic History*, 62: 643–75.

Hatton, T., and Boyer, G. (2003). 'Unemployment and the UK Labour Market before, during and after the Golden Age, 1946–1973'. Mimeo, ANU.

Hennessy, P. (1993). *Never Again: Britain 1945–51*. London: Vintage.

Howson, S. (1975). *Domestic Monetary Management in Britain 1919–38*. Cambridge: Cambridge University Press.

Hurstfield, J. (1986). 'Women's Unemployment in the 1930s: Some Comparisons with the 1980s'. *Explorations in Sociology*, 21.

Jackman, R., Layard, R., and Savouri, S. (1991). 'Mismatch: A Framework for Thought', in F. Padoa Schioppa (ed.), *Mismatch and Labour Mobility*. CEPR (Centre for Economic Policy Research). Cambridge: Cambridge University Press.

Jefferys, K. (1987). 'British Politics and Social Policy during the Second World War'. *Historical Journal*, 30: 123–44.

—— (1991). *The Churchill Coalition and Wartime Politics 1940–45*. Manchester: Manchester University Press.

Jones, R. (1987). *Wages and Employment Policy 1936–1985*. Oxford: Blackwell.

Kavanagh, D. (1987, 1990). *Thatcherism and British Politics: The End of Consensus*. Oxford: Oxford University Press.

—— (1992). 'The Postwar Consensus'. *Twentieth Century British History*, 3: 175–90.

Keynes, J. M. (1931). 'The Economic Consequences of Mr Churchill', in *Essays in Persuasion*. London: Macmillan, 1st pub. *Evening Standard*, 22, 23, 24 July 1925.

—— (1936). *The General Theory of Employment, Interest and Money*. London: Macmillan.

Kindleberger, C. (1973). *The World in Depression, 1929–39*. Berkeley and Los Angeles: University of California Press.

Layard, R., and Nickell, S. J. (1985). 'The Causes of British Unemployment'. *National Institute Economic Review*, 111: 62–85.

—— —— (1986). 'Unemployment in Britain'. *Economica*, 53: S121–S169.

—— —— (1987). 'The Labour Market', in R. Dornbusch and R. Layard (eds.), *The Performance of the British Economy*. Oxford: Oxford University Press.

—— —— and Jackman, R. (1991). *Unemployment: Macroeconomic Performance and the Labour Market*. Oxford: Oxford University Press.

Maddison, A. (1964). *Economic Growth in the West*. London: Allen and Unwin.

Matthews, R. C. O. (1968). 'Why Has Britain Had Full Employment since the War?' *Economic Journal*, 82: 195–204.

—— Feinstein, C. H., and Odling-Smee, J. C. (1982). *British Economic Growth 1856–1973*. Oxford: Clarendon Press.

Metcalf, D., Nickell, S. J., and Floros, N. (1982). 'Still Searching for an Explanation of Unemployment in Inter-War Britain'. *Journal of Political Economy*, 90/2: 386–99.

Middlemas, K. (1979). *Politics and Industrial Society: The Experience of the British System since 1911*. London: André Deutsch.

Middleton, R. C. (1985). *Towards the Managed Economy: Keynes, the Treasury and the Fiscal Policy Debate of the 1930s*. London: Methuen.

Miller, M., and Sutherland, A. (1994). 'Speculative Anticipations of Sterling's Return to Gold: Was Keynes Wrong?' *Economic Journal*, 104/425: 804–12.

Minford, P. (1985). *Unemployment Cause and Cure*. Oxford: Basil Blackwell.

Morgan, K. (1990). *Britain since 1945: The People's Peace*. Oxford: Oxford University Press.

Narendranathen, W., Nickell, S., and Stern, J. (1985).'Unemployment Benefits Revisited'. *Economic Journal*, 95: 307–29.

Newell, A., and Symons, J. (1990). 'The Passing of the Golden Age', in R. Brunetta and C. Dell'Aringa (eds.), *Labour Relations and Economic Performance*. London: Macmillan.

Nickell, S. J. (1997). 'Unemployment and Labor Market Rigidities: Europe versus North America'. *Journal of Economic Perspectives*, 11: 55–74.

—— and Van Ours, J. (2000). 'The Netherlands and the United Kingdom: A European Unemployment Miracle?' *Economic Policy*, 30: 135–80.

Nordhaus, W. (1972). 'The Worldwide Wage Explosion'. *Brookings Papers in Economic Policy*, 72: 432–65.

OECD (Organization for Economic Cooperation and Development) (1996). *OECD United Kingdom Country Report 1996*. Paris: OECD.

Phelps Brown, H. (1983). *The Origins of Trade Union Power*. Oxford: Clarendon Press.

Redmond, J. (1984). 'The Sterling Overvaluation in 1935: A Multilateral Approach'. *Economic History Review*, 37: 520–32.

Sells, D. (1939). *British Wages Boards*. Washington: The Brookings Institution.

Smith, H. (ed.) (1986). *War and Social Change*. Manchester: Manchester University Press.

Stewart, M. (1986, 1991). *Keynes and After*. Harmondsworth: Penguin.

Thane, P. (1996). *Foundations of the Welfare State*. London: Longman.

Thomas, M. (1983). 'Rearmament and Economic Recovery in the Late 1930s'. *Economic History Review*, 36: 552–79.

—— (1988). 'Labour Market Structure and the Nature of Unemployment Insurance in Inter-War Britain', in B. Eichengreen and T. J. Hatton (eds.), *Inter-War Unemployment in International Perspective*. NATO ASI Series, Series D. Behavioural and Social Sciences 43. Dordrecht: Kluwer Academic Publishers.

—— (1994). 'Wages in Interwar Britian: A Sceptical Inquiry', in G. Grantham and M. McKinnon (eds.), *Labour Market Evolution*. London: Routledge.

Titmuss, R. (1950). *Problems of Social Policy*. London: His Majesty's Stationery Office.

Tomlinson, J. (1987). *Employment Policy: The Crucial Years 1939–55*. Oxford: Clarendon Press.

Winch, D. (1972). *Economics and Policy*. London: Fontana.

Worswick, G. D. N. (1984). 'The Sources of Recovery in the United Kingdom in the 1930s'. *National Institute Economic Review*, 110/November.

11

Education and the Labour Market

Michael Sanderson

One of the many functions of education is to provide the labour force for an industrializing society. As such it has both responded to and helped to shape the changing occupational structure of British society. For the twentieth century this has been as shown in Table 11.1. Unsurprisingly the professional and managerial class has increased especially since the Second World War, and in the last twenty years, clerical workers have increased up to 1980 and stabilized since and this has been matched by a sharp reduction in the proportion of manual workers. In broad terms, this is consistent with universal literacy and the gradual extension of secondary education for all. More controversially there has been the more recent concern to change higher education from being a privilege for less than 10 per cent of the population to the normal expectation for a half. Let us consider first the relation of education and jobs at the start of the century, 1900–14.

I

By the 1900s virtually all children were literate (Vincent 1989). Between 1870 and 1902 over 2,000 school boards had complemented Anglican and other religious societies in building and running schools. Elementary education became compulsory from 1880 and then free from 1891 and was taken over by the new local education authorities from 1902. Accordingly enrolment rates at the elementary level rose from 119.8 per 1,000 in 1871 to 343.2 by 1901 and 373.1 by 1911 (Broadberry 2003: 59) and this drove up literacy rates to 98–100 per cent by 1914. All classes attended elementary schools but the vast majority, 60 per cent, were skilled and semi-skilled manual workers (Rose 1993: 118). An Edwardian elementary education was not designed to enable children to 'rise' and so these children made up the vast bulk of the 1900s working class—the agricultural labourers, domestic servants, factory hands, and dockers—that 80

Table 11.1. The occupational structure in Britain, 1911–98 (%)

	1911	1921	1931	1951	1961	1971	1979		1984	1990	1998
Professional	4.05	4.53	4.60	6.63	9.0	11.07	17.1	Managerial/ professional/ technical	29.1	31.8	36.6
Employers and managers	10.14	10.46	10.36	10.50	10.10	12.43	12.9	Clerical/ secretarial	16.0	17.0	15.0
Clerical	4.84	6.72	6.97	10.68	12.70	13.90	16.0	Craft and related	17.7	16.0	12.2
Foremen and manual workers	80.97	78.29	78.07	72.19	68.10	62.60	54.0	Sales and personal services	14.3	15.0	18.8
								Manual operatives	11.6	10.6	9.4
								Other	11.2	9.6	8.0

Sources: Routh (1980: 5, 45); Halsey (1972: 113) and Wolf (2002: 49) for 1984–98.

per cent of the occupational structure in 1911 who were manual workers. Children were already being inured to work while at school, making boots, artificial flowers, bookkeeping at home with mother, out of (and even in) school hours (Davin 1996: 168–9). Yet it may be argued that the chief value of an elementary school education to the labour force was not what it taught but the social values it instilled—order, discipline, cleanliness, deference to authority, and the tolerance of boredom at work (Baines 1981: 173).

The century began with a radical change in the creation of a post-elementary area of education, a kind of nebulous no man's land between elementary and secondary schools. Some of this was controversial and even of doubtful legality but it had important implications for occupational structure and the labour market. Elementary schools were divided into seven standards and most children left before completing all of them. But many able and possibly ambitious children had passed through all seven before wishing to leave school since there was no mandatory leaving age. Various devices catered for these post-elementary children in Victorian times, culminating in the higher grade school. These were substantial separate buildings often of conspicuous quality operating as pseudo-secondary schools though formally still elementary. They fulfilled a valuable purpose in shaping the Edwardian aristocracy of labour as we shall see. But some influential educational administrators detested them, notably Sir Robert Morant the future Permanent Secretary of the Board of Education. The grounds for opposition were chiefly twofold. First it could be claimed that they were illegal since they were manifestly post-elementary schools financed by rates intended to be confined to the elementary. Second, Morant saw them as a cul-de-sac, taking able working-class children and keeping them within the working class. He wanted a system giving full opportunities to such children by enabling them to enter grammar schools and universities to facilitate social mobility and the circulation of elites. The higher grade schools, in his view, were a dead end impeding this vision.

Disputes over the system culminated in the Cockerton judgment of 1899 which declared the higher grade schools illegal. The consequent 1902 Education Act and its aftermath then reshaped the system. The Act brought into being the new local education authorities one of whose duties was to create new municipal rate-supported grammar schools. Following the Act, Regulations in 1904 required grammar schools to teach classics (to enable Oxbridge entry) and 1907 Regulations provided for scholarships to grammar schools, 25 per cent of whose places were to be reserved for such award winners from elementary schools. Morant also valued the provision of vocational education. Accordingly he encouraged or sanctioned central schools and junior technical schools for those whose bent was practical, commercial, and technical rather than academic. Let us now consider the implications for the formation of the labour force of these different types of schools.

Higher grade schools had gradually emerged since 1876. The ablest children in elementary schools who had passed beyond the seven standards of such schools were given a kind of post-elementary education with subjects such as French, chemistry, and physics. While the proportions of lower middle-class pupils were roughly the same as in secondary grammar schools, the higher grade schools had far fewer middle-class and far more working-class pupils than the latter. They undoubtedly made a valuable contribution to the economy at the turn of the century (Vlaeminke, 2000: 61, 109, 155, 176). At Fairfield Road HGS in Bristol boys in the period 1898–1906 went into engineering, the building trades, plumbing, carpentry, while girls studied cookery and domestic science and aimed to teach such subjects. At St George's, Bristol, 1902–06, of 140 girls, 38 per cent became teachers, 18 per cent secretaries, 15 per cent went into business posts, and 14 per cent into various jobs—shop assistants, librarians, telephonists. An analysis of four other schools in Bristol and Birmingham 1902–07 shows the spread of occupations as in Table 11.2.

Table 11.2. Occupations of ex-pupils of four higher grade schools in Bristol and Birmingham, 1902–07

Occupation	Number	%
Clerks, typists	217	32.8
Teachers	180	27.2
Unspecified skilled trades	121	18.3
Accountants, bank clerks, civil servants, librarians	56	8.5
Engineers	50	7.5
Chemists, laboratory assistants	23	3.5
Designers and draughtsmen	11	1.7
Unskilled	4	0.6

Source: Vlaeminke (2000).

Meriel Vlaeminke (2000: 155) presents a powerful case for the HGS as channelling children whose education might have been restricted to elementary schools and jobs into admirably worthwhile occupations. She is clear that the vast majority of such children 'entered occupations which required training or further education, carried some status and offered above average security'. About three-quarters of the intake in HGSs were lower middle-class and skilled artisans, but whereas 7 per cent of the intake was unskilled working class yet fewer than 1 per cent of ex-pupils became such (Reader 1987: 144).

The junior technical schools had been sanctioned in 1906 by Sir Robert Morant. They were created as English versions of the German trade continuation schools and French *écoles primaires supérieures* providing education combined with trade training for 13+ teenagers as a preparation for technical college and apprenticeship (Sanderson 1994; McCulloch 1989). They tapped the abilities of youngsters whose inclinations were mechanical and craft rather than academic. There were about thirty-seven of them by 1914 and that they did successfully supply this area of the labour market is suggested by the future occupations of boys from a technical school in Leeds 1905–12 (see Table 11.3; Welpton 1913: 243–4).

The JTSs were in many ways complemented by central schools. Sheffield in 1878 was possibly the first followed by other major cities. Their particular emphasis was on commercial, rather than technical education. They provided for the future clerks for business and professional offices, bookkeepers, shop assistants, and others in the retail and distributive trades.

The middle classes ensured that their offspring gained a secondary education through, at least, a fee-paying grammar school. These were old existing ones, joined by the newly created LEA grammar schools from1902. We can see what area of the labour market they supplied by reference to Hull and Bristol grammar schools. At Hull 'the great majority left to enter banks, shipping and insurance offices, some to take up civil service clerkships, a few to be articled to

Table 11.3. Occupations of ex-pupils of Holbeck and Woodhouse Technical Schools in Leeds ,1905–12

Occupation	%
Mechanical engineering	49.6
Electrical engineering	8.5
Draughtsmen	8.5
Building trades	5.2
Other skilled occupations	11.1
Commercial occupations	10.4
Unskilled	6.7

Source: Welpton (1913).

Table 11.4. Occupations of ex-pupils of various public schools, 1906–11

Percentage entering	Clifton 1907	Marlborough 1906	Merchant Taylors 1911	Mill Hill 1907	Winchester 1900–09
University	39	32	13	25	69.8
Professions	22	23	22	26	33.1
Business	25	23	25	32	32.2
Armed forces	18	14	11	1	14.9
Other occupations	16	14	20	11	9.3
Unknown	35	32	28	31	—
Civil service					6.2

Sources: Reader (1966: appendix 2); Bishop and Wilkinson (1967: 68).

solicitors, accountants, dentists' (Lawson 1963: 265).[1] At Ipswich of 136 boys (1894–1906) 'a very large number of boys entered the business houses of Ipswich and provided the nucleus round which many of these concerns have developed' (Gray and Potter 1950: 141). In fact 41.2 per cent went into business, 36 per cent into the professions (ecclesiastical, medical, legal, engineering, scholastic), and 10.3 per cent into the armed services. It is unsurprising, the grammar school boys usually going directly into local businesses (perhaps often their fathers') to become future managers and rather fewer into professions.

The upper middle class preferred to send their sons away to public boarding schools with higher expectations. The contribution to the labour force of a sample of public schools is as shown in Table 11.4. The similarities are notable, with about a quarter to a third of boys going into both business and the professions. But more would be going to university than would grammar school boys. W. D. Rubinstein (1993: 116–18) has importantly refined this picture by showing that for Eton, Harrow, Rugby, Winchester, St Paul's, Cheltenham, and Mill Hill at the start of the twentieth century (1895–1900) a consistently higher proportion of boys went into professions than fathers and conversely a smaller proportion went into business that had been the case with paternal occupations in the same schools. In all of Rubinstein's seven schools more boys were entering professions than business. It was part of that rise of professional society on which Harold Perkin (1989: 119–21) laid emphasis and which is evident in Table 11.1.

The older English universities before 1914 made only a limited contribution to the labour force (see Table 11.5). The broad similarity of the Oxford and Cambridge figures is evident. Both had moved away from being predominantly educators of clergymen as they had been in Victorian times. Cambridge more than Oxford provided for the secular professions of law, medicine, and the military but Oxford predominated as a supplier to business and industry.

[1] The dates seem to cover the period 1898–1910.

Table 11.5. Occupations of graduates of Oxford and Cambridge, 1850–1913

	Cambridge 1850–99	Cambridge 1902–07	Oxford 1900–13
Holy orders	38	25	17.9
Law	14	16	10.2
Medicine	7	9	5.6
Business, engineering	7	24	28.8
Armed forces	—	6	3
Teaching	12	5	6.5
Government service	6	4	5.8
Farmers and planters	7	3	4.2
Others	9	8	18

Sources: Cambridge 1850–99: Jenkins and Caradog-Jones (1950); Cambridge 1902–07: Roach (1959: 288); Oxford: D. I. Greenstein in Harrison (1994: 56) reclassified to relate to the Cambridge figures. Greenstein.

This was in spite of the fact that Cambridge was far superior to Oxford in the sciences, engineering, and even business economics. It suggests that business preferred to recruit from Oxford for social reasons.[2] Otherwise Oxford and Cambridge were adjusting to the more secular professional and business labour market of the 1900s.

Whatever the limitations of Oxbridge they probably did not matter so much since another major educational change of the 1900s was the creation of six civic universities as independent chartered institutions. Most had begun in the 1870s and 1880s as technical schools to support local industry. They accepted women students from the start (and Manchester from 1873) and usually merged with a pre-existant medical school to become full universities. As a result the output of students was commonly a third into industry, a third to medicine, and a third (most women) to teaching. This was evident at Birmingham, the first of the civic universities (Ives et al. 2002: 65). In a rare piece of evidence students in 1893–4 were asked their intended future careers. Almost all men indicated engineering, especially electrical, assaying, analytical chemistry, whilst most women were intending to be teachers. This three-way split—industry, teaching, medicine— was quite typical of the new civics (Sanderson 1972: 100–1). In the Welsh colleges teaching and the Church completely predominated.[3] In Scotland, by contrast, the range of graduate careers was much wider before 1914, but with a well-known heavy emphasis on medicine (see Table 11.6).[4]

Technical education for the labour force in Edwardian England was good, as it had not been in the 1870s and 1880s. It has been a fallacy to regard the whole

[2] See Sanderson (1999: 52–4) for a consideration of this paradox.

[3] Sanderson (1972: 136–7). At Aberystwyth and Bangor teachers and clergy were over 70% of the output.

[4] Robertson (1990) has full data on all the Scottish universities. See also Anderson (1992).

Table 11.6. Occupations followed by Scottish graduates, 1860–1914 %

	Glasgow	Aberdeen	Edinburgh
Medicine	36.5	39.2	53.3
Clergy	14.6	14.3	9.4
Law	6.0	4.6	4.8
Engineering/science	6.5	1.2	2.8
Teacher, lecturer	23.4	29.8	18.5
Others	13.1	11.0	11.1

Source: Robertson (1990).

Table 11.7. Indicators of the growth of scientific and technical education, 1900–14

	(a) University students	(b) Students graduating in science or technology in civic universities	(c) Cumulative stock of (b)	(d) City and Guilds examination passes	(e) Students in technical college evening classes	(f) Day students in engineering in four colleges	(g) RSA papers sat
1900	17,839	378	4,984	8,114	475,000	376	9,808
1910	26,432	1,231	14,300	14,105	708,000 (1911)	613	30,000 (1911)
1914	26,711			14,570			

Sources: (a) Lowe 1982; (b) and (c) Roderick and Stephens (1974); (d) Millis (1925); (e) Pollard (1989: 179); (f) Guagnini (1993); (g) Hudson and Luckhurst (1954).

period 1870–1914 as a unity with the defects of the earlier period still attributed to the later. Institutionally the situation was transformed. The City and Guilds of London was created in 1879 and founded two large colleges in London, and more importantly ran a national system of technical examinations. In 1882 Quintin Hogg began his polytechnic movement in Regent Street, expanding to eleven 'polys' by 1898. Most importantly the Technical Instruction Act of 1889 enabled towns to raise rates to build and run local technical colleges and some 160 were created by 1898. There were the new civic universities chartered between 1900 and 1909 and the new junior technical schools as we have seen. Also many firms ran educational classes for their own workers (Fitzgerald 1993). Something of this rapid growth and its extent may be seen in Table 11.7.

Moreover English apprenticeship still thrived in spite of the complaints of 'decline' and the advent of skill-substituting machine tools. Apprenticeship was the distinctive English way and in this contrasted with the Continental emphasis on publicly financed colleges. Apprenticeship rationally spread the balance of cost and benefits between employers, employees, and consumers rather than the taxpayer (Nicholas 1985). It also delivered the required skilled labour for the labour force (Floud 1982). What was remarkable was not the decay of apprenticeship but its survival compared with the USA (Elbaum 1991). Indeed Broadberry (2003: 64–5) finds apprentices as a percentage of persons engaged in industry as satisfactory, much in line with Germany and superior to the USA (GB 2.48 per cent (1906), Germany 2.99 per cent (1907), USA 0.28 per cent (1900)), and he rejects criticism of the inadequacy of technical training before 1914.

Broadly the connection of education and the labour market in the 1900s was good. There was universal literacy, finely graded differences between types of post-elementary working-class education and between them and the grammar and public schools—all leading to different strata of labour aristocracy and middle-class employment. Technical education was ample and the two different types of university education, Oxbridge and the civics, catered for different social classes and career outcomes.

II

A major feature of the inter-war years was the restructuring of the relation of elementary to secondary education, and this too was to have implications for the labour market. The Victorian assumption was that the working classes received only an elementary education and that the secondary stage was appropriate only for the middle class. In the 1900s the beginnings of a ladder of opportunity was created with scholarships to the grammar school ring-fenced for ex-elementary school pupils. Yet still, except for the exceptionally able, education related to social class and hence to subsequent jobs. The new call in the 1920s was for 'secondary education for all' (Tawney 1922).[5] As mass literacy had been achieved between 1880 and 1914 so universal experience of secondary education was the next goal.

The school leaving age was raised to 14 by the Fisher Act in 1918 thus extending school life well beyond Victorian assumptions of an elementary schooling. The Hadow Committee of 1926 recommended that children from elementary schools should sit the 11+ examination and on its results be decanted into grammar schools, modern schools, and, a few, into junior technical schools (Hadow 1926). In practice it was recognized that LEAs were unlikely to build new schools, especially in the depression that shortly followed the publication of the Report. Accordingly since many post-11 children would stay behind in their former—now all-age—elementary schools these were reorganized as primary schools (up to 11) but with senior classes beyond. Children in these senior classes rose from 163,106 pupils in 1927 to 818,827 by 1938. The whole structure below the grammar school was not always clear-cut.

---

[5] Simon (1974) and Sutherland (1990) are also valuable surveys of this period.

The 'modern' sector envisaged by Hadow comprised a wide variety of nomen-clature and types. There were children in senior schools, senior classes in elementary schools, non-selective central schools barely distinguishable from the former, selective central schools veering towards the grammar school—the true secondary schools. In the public mind 'senior' was easily confused with 'secondary' and it was in various governments' interest to encourage this belief that all children were receiving a secondary education in the sense of post-primary. By 1935 83.2 per cent of children left elementary schools (including seniors) straight for employment, 11.4 per cent left for secondary grammar schools, and the residual 5.4 per cent for other full-time education, presumably selective central and JTSs (Carr-Saunders and Caradog-Jones 1937: 119–23). So how did this relate to the labour market?

The leading educational psychologist of the day, Dr (later Sir) Cyril Burt, had a clear view of how intelligence related to schools and hence to jobs (see Table 11.8).[6] This was a root of the 80/20 view of the labour market: that society needed about 20 per cent of the population in some kind of knowledge-able authority and the rest to carry out their instructions.

Turning to realities, how did elementary school pupils fit into the labour mar-ket? Detailed evidence from Norwich in the 1930s is shown in Table 11.9. The contribution to the labour market is what one would expect, a high proportion going into a few jobs—factories and distributive trades—with some of the ablest reaching up to clerical, retail, skilled engineering, and tailoring work.

Between the elementary school and the grammar school the middle ground served more specific purposes. Central schools still retained a commercial bias. The junior technical schools remained closely linked to a few occupations as intended (Table 11.10). This strong emphasis on the production of skilled

Table 11.8. Dr Cyril Burt's view of the relation of intelligence, schooling, and labour, 1926 and 1938

	Intelligence	Schooling	Future occupations
Top	10%	Secondary school scholarship children	Professional, administrative, and executive
	10%	Central and other post-elementary schools	Clerical and technical
	68.5%	Ordinary children who stayed at elementary school until 14	Skilled labour
	10%	Dull and backward	Unskilled labour
Bottom	1.5%	Feeble-minded	Institutionalized or casual labour

Source: PRO ED 10/147.

[6] PRO ED 10/147, Evidence of Dr Cyril Burt to the Hadow Committee. He sent the same evidence to both the Hadow (1926) and Spens (1938) Committees saying that his views remained unchanged.

youth was appropriate for the time. C. G. Renold (1928) of the noted engineering firm found that he had less need for unskilled and semi-skilled men but an increasing demand for skilled craftsmen who made up the largest category of his labour force. The grammar school contribution to the labour force can be seen from various schools. At 'Hightown Grammar' 1917–20 the most common future destinies were as shown in Table 11.11.

It may be noted at this stage that these grammar school outcomes are rather disappointing. Very few were using the grammar school as a bridge to further or higher education as was intended. Most went into, presumably local, clerical and technical jobs. It may also be regrettable that the less intelligent fee payers took up technical occupations more than the more able scholarship holders who preferred clerical work. It confirmed the prejudice that technical work was inferior to white-collar office work. Conversely it was wasteful but explicable that the less intelligent but wealthier fee payers proceeded to further education more than their abler, less affluent, scholarship boy counterparts.

Table 11.9. Occupations of ex-elementary pupils in Norwich in the 1930s (%)

Boys		Girls	
Distributive trades	28.0	Boot and shoe factories	33.2
Boot and shoe factories	25.6	Confectionery factories	14.2
Engineering	9.4	Shop assistants	10.4
Sheet metal workers	8.1	Tailoring	10.1
Clerks	5.9	Box making	4.6
And small proportions in building, joinery and furniture manufacture, porters, messengers, gardeners.		And small proportions in domestic service, packers, laundry work, hairdressing, clerks.	

Sources: Rackham (1940: 28); Zmroczek (2004). The boys' figures are from Rackham, girls from Zmroczek.

Table 11.10. Occupations of ex-JTS pupils in England and Wales, 1930

Boys	%	Girls	%
Construction	46.7	Commercial	56.5
Engineering	29.9	Dressmaking	17.8
Commercial	12.3	Tailoring	7.1
Building	5.6	Domestic service	4.5
Nautical	1.2	Millinery	3.2
		Upholstery	2.5
		Cookery	1.7
Smaller proportions to cookery, book production, photography, music trades, tailoring, hairdressing, silversmith, painting and decorating, boot and shoe.		Smaller proportions to hairdressing, photography, laundry, construction trades.	

Source: 1930–1 XII *Board of Education Annual Report 1930*.

Table 11.11. Occupations of ex-pupils of 'Hightown Grammar', 1917–20 (%)

Scholarship boys (i.e. the most intelligent ex-elementary boys)		Fee payers (i.e. not able enough to pass the 11+ examination)	
Clerical	35.5	Higher technical	23
Higher clerical and banks	10.7	Clerical	17
Further education	10.7	Further education	12
Technical	10.0	Technical	11
Higher technical	8.9	Skilled apprenticeship	11
(46.2% clerical 18.9% technical jobs)		(45% technical 17% clerical jobs)	

Source: Lacey (1970: 16). The scholarship boys' figures are presented with decimal places, the fee payers are not.

We shall return to consider this in the context of the range of schooling shortly. There is similar evidence for Norwich which has full data for the LEA grammar schools for 1931–9: 32.9 per cent of boys (about a third) became clerks, 12.3 per cent went into engineering and industry, 10.3 per cent into local government, and 7.3 per cent became shop assistants. Of girl grammar school pupils 45.9 per cent became clerks, and 13 per cent shop assistants. Only 3.4 per cent of boys and 7.6 per cent of girls went on to university or training college (Rackham 1940: 28). Finally, the same was found around Balham, where from four grammar schools in 1937 57 per cent of boys had become clerks, 16 per cent were in technical jobs, and only 8 per cent had gone into professional careers to which they might have expected a grammar school to lead.[7]

This gap may have been made up by the independent public schools where there was a shift in the output of boys from industrial and commercial careers to the 'safe' professions not so affected by the depression of trade. Of boys leaving Winchester 1918–27 32 per cent went into business and industry and 38 per cent into professions (clergy, medicine, teaching, civil service, military) (Bishop and Wilkinson 1967: 69). By 1938–40 (boys born 1920–2) the figures had widened to 7 per cent and 84 per cent respectively and the same trends are evident at Bradfield, Epsom, Durham, Gresham's Holt, and Aldenham (Sanderson 1997).

That much of what we have seen of schooling in the inter-war years is what we would expect, with important exceptions, suggests a fair match between educational levels and the labour market. But some aspects prompt comment. First some of the jobs taken by elementary school children seem to overlap with the grammar school. This was so with clerks and shop assistants. This

---

[7] ED 12/472 Enquiry into conditions of employment of ex-secondary schoolboys by Balham Rotary Club, 26 Aug. 1937.

suggests that in elementary schools there was a good deal of trapped talent of intelligent children who could not proceed further due to social factors such as the hidden costs of uniforms, books, and stationery in secondary schools, the narrow career horizons of much of the working class, the imperative of early school leaving and working to support family budgets. In 1935 73 per cent of children of high intelligence who should have been in grammar schools were still in elementary schools and destined to leave at the minimum school leaving age of 14 (Gray and Moshinsky 1935). Places left unfilled by the intelligent working-class pupils were filled by fee payers, half of whom were not of the ability to benefit from the academic education of the grammar school. This accounts for the disparity of outcomes of scholarship and fee payers at 'Hightown' (see Table 11.11). Secondly, the LEA grammar schools were not really acting as elite schools as much as Morant would have hoped. Relatively few pupils progressed to professions or higher education. More often they provided the solid clerical/technical expertise needed in their local towns and one expects that many borough treasurers and engineers, bank and department store managers, emerged from them.

Thirdly, several pupils at both elementary and grammar schools would have been better served by attending the under-provided junior technical schools—the engineers and tailors from Norwich elementary schools, the 'technical' boys (45 per cent of fee payers) at 'Hightown' grammar. The JTSs increased from 78 in 1919 to 248 by 1938 yet provided for only 1.4 per cent of all schoolchildren in the 1930s (Bailey 1990: 100–1). There were various factors behind this lack of development. JTSs were more expensive to build and run than grammar schools. It seemed unjustifiable to spend more on the education of children who had failed the 11+ than on those who had passed. Moreover they entailed administrative trouble for the LEA since the entry age was 13, which meant that JTS pupils had to be temporarily accommodated in some other kind of school before transference. The Hadow Report of 1926 had taken a cool view of the JTSs and was suspicious of them as channelling working-class pupils into working-class jobs. Finally, although nearly a half of JTS output went into the building trades yet only 2 per cent of building firms employed such entrants (Sanderson 1987: chs. 3 and 4). This links with the often noted indifference of employers to school performance as the fourth element distorting links between the school system and the labour market as expressed in Cyril Burt's neat table.[8]

Technical education in the inter-war years has received much criticism. It was provided in technical colleges with 353,675 students and evening institutes with 740,790 students in 1936. This was reckoned to be one in fifteen of employed persons (Richardson 1939: 23). However sizeable this seems there

---

[8] Keeble (1992: 65 and ch. 4). See also the Hadow Report: 'most employers attach comparatively little significance to any form of school record'.

were reservations. Most of this education took place in the evening after work when students were tired. Technical education ('T' in Board of Education terminology) was what happened 'after tea'. Lord Eustace Percy deplored that whereas in Germany and USA most technical education was day education to meet the needs of industry yet 'in this country between 80 and 90 per cent of our classes are evening classes attended by students in their own time and according to their own predilections . . . happy go lucky'.[9] Also the large numbers in institutes were mostly studying commercial subjects, secretarial, clerical, and bookkeeping skills, which were valuable but not at the hard edge of manufacturing industry. There were wide variations in the enthusiasm for technical education across different industries (Richardson 1939: 367–8). Day release was much more accepted in newer and more successful industries like chemical (58/10,000 employees), engineering (43), food and catering (40), than in older, failing ones like mining (6) and textiles (4). The Balfour Committee likewise found a spectrum of appreciation of technical education from mechanical engineering and shipbuilding at one end to cotton and woollens at the other (Balfour 1927: 191–216). Some thought that technical education was becoming too academic. Percy took this view and attributed it to the lack of clear indications from employers of what they wanted. The Chief Inspector of Technical Education also thought this form of education was drifting away from its purposes, that 'engineering instruction is far better suited to the needs of the student who is ambitious to rise to a position of considerable responsibility in the industry than to those of the student who has the equally laudable ambition of being an excellent craftsman' (Abbot 1933: 69). Finally there was not much take-up of technical qualifications. The Ordinary and National Diplomas had been started in 1920 but by 1938 there were only 3,317 successes at ONC and 1,668 at HNC (Albu 1980).

Keith Burgess (1994) thinks it unfair to blame the government for defects in this area because of the divergent or negative messages it was receiving from employers. Very few valued full-time technical education whereas about a half (49.1 per cent) preferred it concurrent with work. Most actually valued personal qualities of initiative and character rather than technical knowledge: 'it was the experience of British employers themselves that made them neglectful of skills formation relevant to the productive economy.'

Compared with other levels of the educational system the universities were marginal in terms of scale: the 40,000 British students of the 1920s and 50,000 of the 1930s represented respectively 1.5 per cent of the potential university age group in 1924–25 and 1.7 per cent in 1938–39. Their output to the labour market was correspondingly limited. This limitation was also partly a consequence of changes in the subject balance of students over the inter-war years

---

[9] ED 24/1875, Letter, Lord Eustace Percy (Board of Education) to Sir Philip Cunliffe Lister (Board of Trade), 5 Oct. 1927.

Table 11.12. The changing balance of subject specialisms in British universities, 1920–39

	Arts	Pure science	Technologies
1920/21–1924/25	39.8	17.0	13.5
1935/36–1938/39	46.5	16.3	9.7

Sources: Reports of the University Grants Committee, 1925, 1930, 1936; Annual Returns 1920–39.

(Table 11.12). In spite of the industrial commitment of the civic universities, teaching was the largest career outlet for arts and pure science graduates. At Birmingham 80 per cent of arts graduates became teachers in the 1920s and 1930s and less predictably 80–90 per cent of women pure scientists did so also. Men scientists entering teaching varied over the 1930s from 37.5 to 64.9 per cent, tracking depression and recovery (Ives et al. 2002: 258–61). This was typical of the civics, where arts faculties were 'a kind of preparatory school to the Department of Education'.[10] There was a certain dysfunction in the universities' excessive output of teachers and their own specific labour market. Many graduates best suited to secondary education taught in elementary schools: 39 per cent of Birmingham, 60 per cent of Manchester, and 80 per cent of Exeter graduate teachers did so in the 1930s. As individuals they were avoiding graduate unemployment but from the viewpoint of the educational system these graduates must have enriched the senior elementary and central schools and brought a 'secondary' element to the merely 'senior' sector.

Otherwise industry was a significant employer especially of civic university applied scientists (Table 11.13). Although there was a widening of the labour market for the graduate in industry—aircraft, food canning, the film industry, dyestuffs, and department stores—there was a marked imbalance in their production. Between 1926 and 1939 4,000 chemists graduated but only 300 chemical engineers, only 15 metallurgists a year graduated from the late 1920s through the 1930s, and there were shortages of geology graduates for the oil industry. There was clearly an avoidance of economic risk. A graduate chemist could fall back on the security of teaching; a chemical engineer, metallurgist, or geologist less evidently so. Relative incomes did not even out these disparities. A non-residential public schoolmaster would earn around £300–£420 in the mid-1930s, only a little less than managers at around £440. The slight income differences were more than offset by the preference for security.

At Oxford and Cambridge the output was more diversified, with teaching not so dominant and graduates taking up a wider range of professions. The

[10] Ives et al. (2002) citing Truscott (1951: 260).

Table 11.13. Percentages of graduates in civic universities entering careers in industry and business in the 1920s and 1930s

	1920s	1930s
Liverpool	52	
Leeds		17–21.8
Newcastle	50–60	27.9–41.3
Exeter		6–17.2
Birmingham	32.3	

Source: Sanderson (1972: 279).

Table 11.14. Occupations of Cambridge male graduates, 1937–38

	%
Banking and business	31
Teaching	16
Miscellaneous	14
Medicine	12
Law	11
Administration	10
Church	6

Source: Spens (1946).

1937–38 Cambridge survey of 2,295 male graduates is shown in Table 11.14, which may suggest the higher social backgrounds and wider career horizons of Cambridge graduates. As with the public schools there was a swing to the professions and away from business, reflecting the economic climate of the time. Of 651 sons of businessmen leaving Cambridge 1937/38 only 22.7 per cent went into business, the rest entered professions (Spens 1946).

Oxford too showed a wider contribution to the labour market than the civic universities though in some ways not so much as Cambridge (Table 11.15). The predominance of teaching as a career is still there, not so much as in civic universities but more than Cambridge. Conversely Oxford made a lesser contribution to business than Cambridge and considerably less than some of the more industrial civic universities. Oxford's strength was in providing recruits for the civil service and professions as well as that of teaching. Daniel Greenstein (1994: 67, 70–1) attributes this to men from modest backgrounds seeking advance through examination success and meritocratic middle-class professions. Most arts men who entered business and industry, by contrast, did so through family connections.

Table 11.15. Occupations entered by Oxford graduates, 1920s and 1930s

	Arts graduates		Science graduates	
	1920s	1930s	1920s	1930s
Male				
Business	22.05	17.74	16.68	19.10
Civil service	16.07	19.62	10.66	10.01
Teachers	37.32	34.33	34.0	32.73
Clergy	10.35	16.98	2.0	3.64
Medicine	—	0.76	33.33	29.09
Law	10.08	7.93	—	0.91
Military and police	0.55	1.13	1.33	3.64
Female				
Business	8.62	10.3	1.35	5.55
Civil service	2.65	9.69	6.75	4.44
Teachers	63.57	55.15	63.51	70.0
Medicine	1.99	0.61	20.27	10.0
Law	7.29	5.46	—	—

Sources: Greenstein in Harrison (1994: 68–9, 74–5).

III

The 1944 Education Act is, exaggeratedly, considered a watershed in the creation of the post-war education system. It raised the school leaving age to 15 and abolished fee-paying grammar schools. Thus by making the 11+ examination the sole entry requirement the Act excluded academically inadequate middle-class fee payers who had compromised the academic intent of the grammar school in the inter-war years. The Act did not specify what types of schools LEAs should run but the existing tripartite system of Morant and Hadow was perpetuated. The grammar school was now selective, and the JTS was upgraded to a secondary technical school with an entry age of 11. Secondary modern schools (using the Hadow term) were the heirs of the old central, senior elementary, higher elementary, higher grade schools stretching back to the turn of the century. It was hardly a true tripartite system but was in the curious ratio of pupils (in 1952/53) of 4 per cent STS:28 per cent grammar school:68 per cent secondary modern. How did these three forms of state school relate to the labour market?

The secondary modern school provided about two-thirds of school leavers and since only about 0.3 per cent went on to further full-time education the bulk went straight into employment, about a half with no training (Taylor 1963: 56, 62). They provided labour as shown in Table 11.16. There were clearly gender differences as the majority of boys became apprentices and clerks whereas girls took up secretarial and shop work. In the East End, of 177 leavers of a secondary modern school 4.5 per cent went into 'intermediate'

Table 11.16. Occupations of ex-secondary modern school pupils, 1956 %

	Clerical	Apprentices	Forces and police	Nursing	Distribution	Unskilled	Misc.	Unknown
Boys	6.3	55.2	8.1	—	6.3	13.1	0.9	9.9
Girls	2.6	6.2	—	1.0	32.3	21.3	1.6	11.4

Source: Reworked from Veness (1962: 66).

Table 11.17. Occupations of ex-grammar school pupils 1956 %

	Professional	Clerical	Apprentices	Forces or police	Nursing	Distributive	Misc.	Unknown
Boys	35.8	22.6	24.5	15.1	—	1.9	—	—
Girls	25.9	57.6	—	5.9	1.2	—	9.4	—

Source: Veness (1962: 66).

jobs (insurance broker, trainee manager, commercial artist), 49.7 per cent into skilled jobs (butcher, compositor, motor mechanic), and 24.8 per cent into semi- and unskilled work (building labourer, fish porter, store keeper, van boy) (Willmott 1966: 102) . Finally in Sheffield, of the leading jobs taken by secondary modern boys 40 per cent went into steel and engineering firms, 9 per cent into painting and decorating, 6 per cent into woodwork, and 4 per cent each became butchers, van boys, cutlers, shop assistants (Carter 1962: 102). The secondary modern schools clearly supplied the bulk of the working-class labour market. Yet without sixth forms they could offer no bridge to the universities or professions. One cannot know how many secondary pupils might have proceeded further, but the Crowther Report (1959: 72) finding that 22 per cent of Army and 29 per cent of RAF National Servicemen had been allocated to schools lower than their abilities warranted suggests that it was considerable.

This contrasts with the role of the grammar school which was intended to prepare pupils for the professions and higher education—goals beyond the secondary modern. At Manchester Grammar School of 798 boys 70 per cent went to universities and 20 per cent to other colleges. A third of the sample went into industry mostly as scientists, (Graham and Phythian 1965). In another, lower-status, grammar school the output was more widely spread (Table 11.17). The grammar school was largely pre-empting its pupils into the middle-class though in the latter case with some overlap at the skilled apprentice and clerical level. Penny Summerfield (1988) likewise finds for Lancashire 1911–51 the sharp decline of girls' jobs in textiles, clothing, and domestic service and the corresponding rise in careers in commercial, secretarial, and administrative work.

The contrast of the predominantly higher-education professionals of the grammar schools and the untrained manual workers of the secondary moderns and especially the increasing doubts about the validity of the chasmal selection at 11 led to demands to eradicate the division by the creation of the comprehensive school in the 1960s. The comprehensives had academic, technical, and commercial streams culminating in sixth forms. Late developers, those misallocated at 11, and especially those whose narrow horizons and poverty of ambition had been grounded in family attitudes and confirmed by the secondary modern found a new lease of life. At Creighton School (Davies 1976: appendix 3), a merger of a grammar school and a secondary modern, about a fifth (19.6 per cent) of its pupils in 1975 went to higher education. Some of these must have been pupils who, had they stayed in secondary modern schools, would not have had these opportunities.[11]

The third part of the tripartite system was the old JTS, now secondary technical school. This continued with its traditional role producing apprentices for the engineering and construction trades. The output of one school for 1956 was as shown in Table 11.18 and in another engineering, banking, insurance, printing, engraving, journalism, surveying, metal refining, paint technology, tent making (Kingsland 1965). But now that they were secondary schools they too sent pupils to universities and CATs, almost all for science and applied science degrees (Kingsland 1965). Yet their manifest value to the labour market did not commend them. They were quite the smallest sector of the tripartite system and were destined for extinction. They had peaked at 324 in 1946 and declined to 184 by 1964. Most LEAs decided to invest in grammar schools

Table 11.18. Occupations of ex-secondary technical school pupils, 1956 (%)

	Boys	Girls
Apprentices	55.4	14.8
Clerical	30.3	78.7
Professional	8.9	—
Forces and police	5.4	—
Nursing	—	1.6
Distribution	—	4.9

Source: Veness (1962: 66).

[11] My father was the headmaster of a secondary modern school in Preston in the 1950s. The ceiling of ambition and achievement was gaining apprenticeships with Dick Kerr's electrical engineering works. In the 1960s he became head of a large purpose-built comprehensive (not the result of a merger) in the same town. This had a sixth form (the French master became an HMI) and pupils went to universities.

which were cheaper and preferred by parents, psychologists did not believe that technical aptitudes were detectable for selection at 11 and the new secondary moderns took over some of the workshop training. Most important Sir David Eccles, the Minister of Education, saw no specific purpose in the schools and decided in 1955 to approve no more. The STSs became absorbed into bilateral grammar schools and then into comprehensives. Pupils fell from 101,913 (3.7 per cent of pupils) in 1960 down to 2,502 (0.06 per cent of pupils) by 1985. The decline of this small but significant sector had crucial knock-on effects for the labour market higher up the scale, as we shall see.

Outside the state sector the relationship of the public schools to the labour market changed significantly in the post-war years. That ex-public school men made up a high proportion of elite occupations is well known. Over the whole period 1939–84 it was 73 per cent but declining from 83 per cent in 1939 to 60 per cent by 1984.[12] A later survey by *The Economist* taking 100 leaders of British life still found 66 per cent were ex-public school.[13] This gradual decline in public school men in traditional elite (largely public service) occupations suggests some spreading of public school men into a wider range of occupations, notably business and industry. In 1956/7 already nearly a half of public school leavers took up careers in industry and commerce, of whom just over a third were doing so through university (Snow 1959: 97).

John Wakeford found for the public school which was the subject of his research in 1963 that 2,644 old boys had entered the labour market in the ways shown in Table 11.19. The largest specific occupations in the table were medical practitioners (8.8 per cent), managers in engineering and allied trades (7.4 per cent), managers in mining and production (6.1 per cent), accountants,

Table 11.19. Careers entered by boys from a public school, 1963 (%)

1	Employers, managers in central and local government, industry, commerce, larger establishments.	33
2	Ditto smaller establishments	1
3	Professional workers, self-employed	11
4	Professional workers, employees	25
5	Intermediate non-manual workers	5
6	Junior non-manual workers	3
7	Skilled manual	1
8	Farm employers and managers	6
9	Armed forces	3
10	Indefinite, other, retired	4
11	Students	8

Source: Wakeford (1969, appendix 3, pp. 228–31).

[12] Reid et al. (1991). The 'elite' were ambassadors, high court and appeal judges, directors of clearing banks, undersecretaries and above, major generals, air vice marshals, rear admirals and above, Anglican assistant bishops and above.   [13] *The Economist*, 19 Dec. 1992: 22.

company secretaries (5.7 per cent), lawyers (4.1 per cent), and technologists (4.0 per cent).

This change may be attributed to various factors. First, there was already a swing to business and industry before 1914 which was halted in the inter-war years. The revival of economic growth post-war restored confidence that careers in industry and commerce were worth pursuing. Second, in 1955 an Industrial Fund for the Advancement of Scientific Education was established for public and direct grant schools (Weinberg 1967: 71–3). By 1957 141 leading firms had contributed £3 million for building science laboratories. This gave recipient schools an advantage over maintained grammar schools which gained no such matching support from the state. Third, as public schools became more expensive so increasingly pupils came from business back-grounds.[14] Boys from such backgrounds were more likely imbued with monetary rather than public service ideals in career choice and their parents would see a public school education as an investment yielding a high-income career for the child—business and industry—and no longer the Church or academe. Fourth the public school prejudice against science as the counterpart of the reverence for classics was fast evaporating. John Rae of Westminster found that in 1965 almost all his Queens Scholars were classicists but by 1975 most were scientists and half his leavers were studying science at university with engineering as the most popular profession (Rae 1981: 160–1).

The area where the post-war education system and the labour market have been most disengaged has been that of vocational education, sometimes referred to as VET (vocational education and training). We have seen that the STS was effectively removed from the system after 1955. This staunched the flow of intelligent, technically minded youngsters up to apprenticeship and forms of technological higher education. A consequence has been the perpetual complaint of a shortage of manually skilled craftsmen in the labour supply. The Carr Report deplored 'the serious shortage of skilled workers in the 1950s . . . the present intake into craft apprenticeship, is inadequate' (1958: 2, 11). It persisted. Companies with skills shortages rose from 2 per cent in the 1970s to 20 per cent by 1990 (Wooldridge 1990: 5) by which year Sir John Cassells noted that two-thirds of firms reported difficulties in recruiting carpenters and bricklayers and the supply of mechanical fitters, electricians, and building craftsmen was only a half to two-thirds that of Germany (Cassells 1990: 5, 8). In 2004 the Construction Industry Council estimated that 500,000 skilled jobs disappeared between 1990 and 1995, about a quarter of the total workforce,[15] and Patricia Hewitt (Secretary of State for Trade and Industry) has deplored that 130,000 jobs were left unfilled in 2003 for lack of skilled applicants.[16]

---

[14] Weinberg (1967: 161–3): 'businessmen comprised the largest group of parents.'

[15] *Financial Times*, 'In the Pipeline', 20 Nov. 2004.

[16] Patricia Hewitt, *Six O'Clock News*, BBC Radio 4, 26 Oct. 2004.

This long-term perceived defect was met with a whole gamut of devices of varying degrees of effectiveness. Industrial training boards were created from 1964 following the Industrial Training Act of that year. It was intended to mark a shift from a system in which employers bore (and failed to bear) the chief responsibility for training to one in which the state was to take a more positive role. This was further reinforced by the Employment Training Act of 1973. But neither created a national training system or succeeded in widening employers' time horizons about training their labour (Sheldrake and Vickerstaff 1987: ch. 6). The industrial training boards were mostly abolished in the 1980s. Schemes and acronyms followed each other with dizzying rapidity—Training Opportunities Scheme (TOPS) in 1972, Youth Opportunities Programme (YOP) in 1978, Youth Training Scheme (YTS) in 1983, Technical and Vocational Education Initiative (TVEI) also in 1983, the Certificate of Pre Vocational Education (CPVE) in 1985, the National Certificate of Vocational Qualifications (NCVQ) in 1986, Employment Training (ET) in 1988, Training and Enterprise Councils (TECs) in the 1980s, Youth Training (YT) in 1990, the General National Vocational Qualification (GNVQ) in 1993, Modern Apprenticeship in 1995. Almost all these developments met severe criticism as reducing unemployment figures rather than providing training, being too costly, uncoordinated, or irrelevant to manufacturing industry's needs (Aldcroft 1992; Wolf 1997, 2002; Finegold and Soskice 1988).

This proliferation of schemes and initiatives which smacks of desperation was underlain by the collapse of apprenticeship, from 389,000 in 1964 to 87,000 by 1990, as more able youngsters were swept up in university expansion (Gospel 1993). All the while there was a running commentary by analysts adversely comparing British performance in the VET of teenagers with that of foreign competitors, notably Germany.[17] Optimists put faith in city technology colleges initiated in 1987 which were to emphasize IT and practical skills (even pop music) and to be financed by private firms. Private capital was not forthcoming and only fifteen were created, no substitute for the 324 STSs of 1946 (Walford and Miller 1991).

Underlying all this was dissension between the Department of Education and Science, the Manpower Services Commission, and the Treasury. The former saw itself as concerned with educational aims but was seen by Margaret Thatcher as insufficiently energetic in addressing the relation of education to the world of work. The MSC, with stronger powers and more concerned with 'Manpower', moved into the educational sphere with many of these schemes, creating a tension between itself and the DES. Yet the MSC was also motivated by the concern not only to increase industrial efficiency but to assuage the unemployment-driven social unrest exemplified by the urban riots of 1981.

[17] E.g. Prais and Wagner (1983) and several other NIESR papers by S. J. Prais, Hilary Steadman, Andy Green, and others.

The Treasury meanwhile took the view that paying for training was the employers' duty not its own.[18] Indeed, Sheldrake and Vickerstaff (1987:54) suggest that the defects of Britain's VET have been underlain by a deep ambivalence of whether the training of the labour force is a private matter in which individual employers and employees calculate their personal benefits, or whether it is a collectivist matter of concern for the state about the enrichment of society and the economy as a whole. They see this more than anything differentiating Britain from the more free market solutions of USA and Japan, the state intervention of France, and the corporatist joint public and private approach of Germany.

Yet there is a piquant paradox that would have surprised critics of this dismal period of British VET. In spite of our comparative admiration of Germany and Japan yet British GDP growth 1990–98 was higher than that of Japan, Germany, and France, has been consistently higher in Britain than Germany and France since 2000, and higher than Japan in three of those five years. It gives the educationalist pause that his field of enquiry is not the only one, and far from the most important, affecting these matters (Maddison 2001: 43, 47, 55, 59, 67; OECD 2004: 184–206). However, the skills gap still remains. A recent survey of the proportion of employees not proficient at their jobs in various industries shows a spectrum. It varies from 9–10 per cent in the fast-expanding hospitality and leisure, food and drink sectors to 5–6 per cent in photography, media, and construction.[19] The national average is 7.5 per cent of the labour force as not proficient. Hope for the future is being placed in city technology colleges and the replacing of failing comprehensive schools by skills academies. Two hundred of these are expected by 2010, partly financed by businessmen and strongly oriented in curriculum towards the world of work—rivals M & S and Arcadia cooperating to create a Skills Academy for fashion is an indicative exemplar.

At the level of higher education the established universities continued to serve the labour market predictably. At Birmingham, the output figures for 1964 were as shown in Table 11.20, with a high proportion going into industry and commerce not only for technologists and scientists but also for arts men. Otherwise teaching was the main outlet especially for women.

Cambridge and Oxford, as in the inter-war years, were more diversified, possibly reflecting the greater prestige of Oxbridge in the eyes of employers and the higher social class and wider career horizons of students. At Cambridge in 1952/53 the output was as in Table 11.21. The output to teaching is very similar to that of Birmingham, and that to industry and commerce somewhat

---

[18] Valerie Bayliss, 'Policy Thinking in the 1980s and 1990s: All Change or No Change?' ESRC Seminar, Institute of Education, University of London, 13 Dec. 2002.

[19] *Financial Times*, 21 Mar. 2005. These were calculations of 23 skills councils for the sectors to which they relate.

Table 11.20. First employment of Birmingham University graduates, 1964

	Arts		Science		Technology (male)
	Male	Female	Male	Female	
Teaching	28	55	25	45	1
Industry and commerce	just over 20	just under 10	29	12	70
Public service	about 5	10	5	15	10
Training courses	10	15	—	5	—
Research	over 20	under 10	40	24	20

Source: Ives et al. (2002: 263–4). The figures are close approximations based on graphs.

Table 11.21. The employment of Cambridge graduates of 1952 and 1953

	Male	Female
Agriculture	3	—
Industry	24	6
Commerce	8	—
Law	5.8	—
Medicine	8	11
Other professions	6.3	2
Church	6	—
Research	4	—
Schoolteaching	15	24
University teaching	9	20
Local or central government	5	10
Military	2	—
Journalism, arts, entertainment	2	—

Source: Craig (1963: 18, 71). The data for men are fuller than for women. The survey was for graduates of 1952 and 1953.

higher but with a greater diversification into the professions. The Oxford data give the fullest evidence of the changing relation of the graduate to the labour market Table 11.22. Certain important social trends are evident. For men there was a move away from traditional professions—the Church, education, and even medicine. Law increased its attractions and even induced scientists to switch direction. Scientists also increasingly joined the civil service. But the chief change was the sharp increase of male scientists going into business and finance. Yet Greenstein points out that this was not so much into manufacturing but into banking and accountancy. Paradoxically, high academic achievers were (naively) drawn to university teaching and the civil service, lower achievers (more worldly wise) to finance and business. For women, by contrast, education, taking over half women graduates, enhanced its attractions, largely

Table 11.22. Careers of Oxford graduates, 1946–47

	Arts			Science		
	1946–52	1953–59	1960–67	1946–52	1953–59	1960–67
Male						
Business and finance	30.49	36.24	31.46	27.86	32.82	41.76
Civil service	14.39	7.74	13.34	7.17	7.61	9.26
Education	35.08	38.41	33.13	29.71	36.23	26.34
Clergy	6.75	5.07	3.33	2.12	1.05	0.82
Medicine	0.87	0.73	0.42	27.32	18.64	17.08
Law	8.50	7.01	12.92	0	0.26	1.24
Social work	0.44	1.93	1.46	0.27	0.53	0.82
Armed forces and police	1.96	1.45	1.67	0.53	0	0.62
Female						
Business and finance	17.12	15.88	15.56	13.46	17.65	14.29
Civil service	13.37	9.41	12.43	6.42	4.41	5.72
Education	43.32	58.82	51.82	49.35	56.62	57.71
Medicine	0.54	0	0.52	19.87	17.65	14.29
Law	2.14	0.59	5.18	0	0	0
Social work	3.21	4.71	5.18	1.28	2.94	2.86

Sources: Greenstein in Harrison (1994, ch. 3: 67–77).

accounted for by the expansion of university teaching in the 1960s. And whereas there was little change in the proportions of women entering business or the civil service, women were increasingly attracted to law and the relatively new profession of social work. Greenstein suggests that Oxford women graduates were more socially homogeneous than men and accordingly preferred careers where academic accreditation was more important than an advantageous family background.

Perhaps the development that has had the most contentious implications for the labour market in the post-war years has been the expansion of new higher education. Students had risen from 68,452 in 1946–47 to 107,699 by 1960–61. Independent universities had been created and expanded at Nottingham, Southampton, Hull, Exeter, Leicester, and Keele. Yet only about 4 per cent of school leavers gained university places by 1960 and this was unusually low in international terms, socially inequitable, and leading to complaints from industry of a shortage of expertise and an intense demand for graduates (Sanderson 1972: 352–3). In this context the 'new' universities of the 1960s were created—Sussex, East Anglia in Norwich, Warwick, Lancaster, Kent, Essex, and Stirling. Although the Robbins Report (1963), had not stressed economic motives in advocating the expansion yet it was an expectation. In some ways this was to be disappointed. The new universities, with the possible exception of Warwick, did not generally relate themselves closely to future occupations. They were located near old non-industrial cities, in greenfield parkland sites, and their curricula tended to stress the liberal arts and social studies rather than subjects which prepared more directly for the world of work (Beloff 1968: 39). Various factors pushed them in this direction. The so-called 'Dainton swing' was the shift of sixth formers' preferences at A level away from science and technology to the arts and social studies and accordingly the newer universities had to respond in what their own curricula could offer. Second, costs per student were lower and staff/student ratios higher in the softer social studies than any other subject.[20] Both individual universities and the government as their paymaster were concerned to expand as quickly and cheaply as possible, at the risk of distancing themselves from the labour market. Third, there were strong steers from outside. The future University of East Anglia, seeking to devise a useful 'relevant' curriculum in its planning stage, was told firmly by the relevant professional bodies that there was no need for any more provision for law, medicine, or architecture, and even more so by the UGC that it must keep clear of agricultural or engineering studies (Sanderson 2002: 57–8, 65–6). Other new universities of the 1960s must have been receiving similar advice. An enforced neglect of vocational studies and an overemphasis on the liberal arts and initially high levels of graduate unemployment in the early days were a consequence. Both were suggestive of a mismatch between the 1960s expansion and the labour market.

It could be argued that this did not matter because there was to be a parallel expansion of higher technological education. In 1956 eleven leading technical colleges were designated as CATs, colleges of advanced technology, to do degree standard work validated by the Council for National Academic Awards. In 1965 these became universities and in 1966 a further group of technical colleges, initially twenty-seven and ultimately thirty, were designated as polytechnics to teach at degree level, likewise under the CNAA. It was hoped that this creation of a sector of higher education awarding or teaching for technological degrees would match the arts and social studies orientation of the 'new' universities. Some may have hoped that they would take on a prestigious hard vocational role such as that filled by the French *grandes écoles* or the German *Technische Hochschulen*, but it was not to be so.

Yet here too things went wrong as this new sector drifted away from its intended relation to the labour market. If traditional universities could not attract enough quality students in science and technology then the ex-CATS and polytechnics could not do so either. Moreover there was a sentiment that 'proper' universities, unlike technical colleges, offered a wide range of cultural studies. Accordingly 'policy drift' set in as the new technological sector cleaved

---

[20] Morris (1977: 83). Costs per student in 1969: £1,976 in social studies; £2,339 in arts; £3,350 in science; £4,240 in engineering.

to the liberal academic model. For example in 1963 the CATs told Robbins that they intended to have 80 per cent of their students in science and technology (two-thirds in technology) and only 20 per cent in arts and social sciences. By 1974 only two-thirds of their students were in science and technology (less than a half in technology) and a third in arts and social sciences (Venables 1978: 295). The polytechnics did likewise. They moved from 57.9 per cent of their students in engineering, technology, and science and only 2.2 in the arts in 1965–66 to 33.9 and 20 respectively by 1978–79 (Pratt and Burgess 1974: 77; Matterson 1981: 67).

The most important debate at the beginning of the century is over the proposal to raise the proportion of school leavers going to university from 43 to 50 per cent with students being paid for up front but paying back their fees when they begin earning.[21] The justification is partly economic, that higher education generates £34 billion for the economy, one in five businesses tap into university skills, and 80 per cent of new jobs created by 2010 will require degree-level qualifications. This will be facilitated by upgrading to university status further colleges not doing research or awarding post-graduate degrees.[22]

This further expansionism has met criticism that it will lead to a glutting of the labour market and that already the post-1960s expansion has led to 'too many graduates chasing too few jobs'. In consequence 40 per cent of graduates were not using university-acquired skills in their work since each year 400,000 new graduates are competing for 416,000 'knowledge worker posts' with the 7.8 million graduates already at work in the British economy. Accordingly graduate starting salaries fell from £13,422 in 2002 to £12,659 in 2003 (Brown and Hesketh 2004). The prospect of expansion, some think, is simply huge numbers of graduates with large debts on low incomes. Moreover proliferating inferior universities merely give further advantages in the job market to middle-class students with personal social qualities from the 'best' universities (Brown and Scase 1994).

Yet there are counter-arguments. That 'studies may not lead to the jobs and careers associated with a university degree in the past' (Brown and Hesketh 2004: 25) is beside the point since they never have done. Universities at least since the 1850s have always sent graduates out into ever widening spheres of labour. The clergy and schoolmasters of the 1840s were joined by the civil servants of the 1850s, marine engineers of the 1890s, business economists of the 1920s, through to the surfers (Plymouth) and millionaire comedian entertainment entrepreneurs (Cambridge) of the present day. Each succeeding generation has explored new areas of labour that would have astonished predecessors. What is a 'graduate job'? In my own department there were no graduate secretaries ten years ago but now four out of the seven are. It reflects

---

[21] Clarke (2003). Charles Clarke (MP for Norwich), address at UEA, 31 Jan. 2003.
[22] *Financial Times*, 17 July 2004.

the fact that the job has changed from the shorthand typist to executive administrator with discretionary powers. The same is so in the steel industry and in banking where it is not felt that their graduates, employed in formerly non-graduate areas, are underutilized (O'Mahony 2003: 130–1). Secondly, it is often overlooked that Charles Clarke intends the expansion to be 'mainly through two year work-focused foundation degrees' to meet the skills gap of higher technical work—'we are not choosing between more plumbers and more graduates: we need both'.

As Clarke's last statement suggests, the skills shortage has been highlighted in the public imagination by his emphasis on plumbers. For example Pimlico Plumbers, founded in the 1970s, now takes ex-graduate professionals who see better career prospects than in banking or public relations.[23] Lambeth Technical College—sixty applicants per place—is the stepping stone to careers with plumbing firms paying salaries of £50,000–£90,000 a year. Plumbing is also being urged as a career for women who will be necessary to meet the estimated need for 29,000 new plumbers by 2007.[24] The same point is true for farrier blacksmiths, whose shortage has likewise driven salaries up to £40,000–£70,000.[25] All kinds of 'Ragged Trousered Philanthropist' Victorian working-class jobs are becoming highly paid areas of middle-class self-employment and entrepreneurship. If Charles Clarke's expansion of two-year work-focused degrees meets these areas all will be well. In any case we can be more optimistic than Brown, Hesketh, and Scase. Over the last twenty years or more the demand has sharply increased for all kinds of managerial and professional workers reflected in their relative wages. To be specific the expanding output of UEA, a 1960s new university, has been comfortably absorbed in the last forty years (Sanderson 2002: 413). Leaving aside graduates in the sciences, computing, and law, virtually all of whom are employed in professional work, even the arts graduates are not far behind. English, history, languages, art, music, social sciences all had more than 90 per cent of their graduates working in graduate professions. Yet unlike the scientists who more usually were in careers closely related to their degrees, arts graduates were more likely to be following one not so closely related to their original discipline—but of professional degree status nonetheless. This would not have been predictable in 1960 by those sceptical of the value of expansion. It gives pause to those sceptical that universities will fail to adjust to the labour market of the next forty years.

[23] *Posh Plumbers*, BBC 2 TV, 7 June 2004. Note also *Today*, Radio 4, 28 Sept. 2004, discussion with a man who left a degree in economics at UCL for plumbing.

[24] *Daily Telegraph*, 6 May 2004, on plumber Pauline Brown featuring an Equal Opportunities Commission advertising campaign to encourage women into plumbing. Ms Brown is an ex-psychology graduate.

[25] *The Archers*, BBC Radio 4, 29 Sept. 2004. The agricultural story editor clearly wished to emphasize this point as being likely to surprise urban audiences. Similarly *Women's Hour*, 16 Nov. 2004, featured a woman lawyer turned thatcher.

There are already signs that many universities are reshaping parts of their curricula. This is to meet national problems of skills shortage and to attract students now faced with high fees and debts and taking a more calculating view of their studies and employability. Post-1992 universities especially are dropping academic subjects and mounting more work-related courses like computer game design and risk management. London Metropolitan has culled English literature and replaced it with music and media management for budding 'pop' entrepreneurs. Older universities have likewise made judicious changes, Essex making its mathematics more applied, UEA dropping physics but introducing pharmacy. It is a welcome reversal of the trend of the 1960s and 1970s when technological universities tried to mould to an inappropriate academic model. Many have rediscovered the Victorian truth that being vocationally useful is both a response to the market and an honourable aim.[26]

IV

How could one tell whether education has related well to the labour market over the twentieth century and whether it has appropriately matched economic needs? Historians have taken various approaches to this question.

First is the calculation of rates of return. Here the costs of education and earnings forgone in the period of education are related to the extra earnings accruing from this training. The latter are seen as a yield on education as the original investment over a working lifetime expressed as an annualized rate of return. Various estimates of this are optimistic. Ziderman (1973) found that the rate of return for graduates was 15 per cent in 1961 before the expansion of the new universities, though falling to a still respectable 7 per cent by 1973. R. A. Wilson likewise studying the 1960s and 1970s found good rates of return for all subjects, 16.5 per cent in 1966/67 and 15.5 per cent in 1970/71, which were virtually identical with those for engineering and technology (Wilson 1981: 57). A BP/LSE Survey made in the late 1980s found that the returns for boys doing A level were 6.04 per cent and for girls 9.80 per cent and the returns on higher education were 7.08 per cent for males and 5.84 per cent for females. Generally the lower the social origins of the pupils the higher the rates of return above these averages (Bennett et al. 1992). Sir Ron Dearing's Committee in 1997 estimated that the return on doing a degree was of the order of 11–13 per cent. Finally Charles Clarke's major policy statement of 2003 stresses that honours graduates earn on average 64 per cent more than those who have no degree and that the rate of return (he does not specify) from higher education in the UK is higher than in any other OECD country (2003: 11). This suggests that for the post-war years, when these studies originate, there has been a

---

[26] *Financial Times*, 1 Nov. 2004, Report of *FT*'s own survey of seventy universities.

rough match of education and the labour market since employers have proved willing to reward it.

Secondly, historians have tried to relate productivity levels to educational development and to estimate formally the contribution of education to growth. Stephen Broadberry (2003) finds that there were several features about the relation of education to productivity that were creditable in the UK. First, in spite of the exaggerated admiration for German education shared by Edwardians and subsequent historians, between 1911 and 1950 German labour productivity remained consistently around only 70–75 per cent of that of the UK. Secondly, he argues that before 1950 there was no clear shortfall of vocational skills in Britain. German superiority in intermediate skills was offset by a British advantage in higher-level skills especially in services. Conversely the USA's advantage in higher-level skills was offset by Britain's in intermediate-level skills. The surprising outcome is that relative vocational skill levels were remarkably similar across the three competitor countries over the first half of the twentieth century. Relative vocational skill levels, where UK = 100 were as shown in Table 11.23. Thirdly, a major factor in the US superiority may also relate to educational factors in that one marked area of US advance was the spread of secondary education from the First World War which can be related to the sharper increase in productivity in services—rather than industry. In short, Broadberry does see connections between education and economic performance and that Britain was not badly served in its formation of a labour market.

Mary O'Mahony (2003), following on from Broadberry, takes a less optimistic view of the post-1950s situation. Although primary, secondary, and higher enrolments increased, so they did in all competitor countries. Yet apprentice and articled trainees as a proportion of employees was lower than that of Germany. But whereas German proportions increased from 4.6 to 6.3 per cent, between 1960 and 1980, those for Britain declined from 3.6 to 2.6 per cent over the same time. Stocks of qualified persons as a percentage of employees were as shown in Table 11.24, which indicates Britain's lag behind USA in higher education and behind Germany in intermediate skills. She notes, 'Britain's skill deficiency is apparent in all sectors of the economy' and

Table 11.23. Relative vocational skill levels, 1910–50 (UK = 100)

	USA/UK	Germany/UK
1910	96.9	99.8
1930	100.9	99.2
1950	100.4	99.2

Source: Broadberry (2003: 72).

this related to the lower labour productivity (see Table 11.25). UK productivity was lower than that of major competitors, the gap somewhat less in 1999 than twenty years earlier but still there. Both Broadberry and O'Mahony find a clear link between education and productivity, optimistically so before 1950, less so from the late 1960s to the 1980s. And this is in accord with our own account here.

Likewise Matthews et al. (1982: 111) find the growth of labour quality resulting from improvements in education: annual percentage growth rates rose to 0.5 per cent in the period 1873–1913 and remained at 0.5 or 0.6 per cent thereafter until 1973. They also see education as the most important source of the improvement of labour quality.

Thirdly, we are particularly impressed that education has been a powerful force enabling upward social mobility as the neglect of it has had the reverse effect. Andrew Miles (1999: 30, 144, 185) found that by the early twentieth century increasing literacy was associated with greater social fluidity than experienced by the Victorians, as sons of Class V fathers mostly moved higher. He notes that the generation marrying 1899–1914 gained from bureaucratization and the spread of basic education and 'the battle to seek out any advantage switched from the labour market to education'. To take two indicators over the sweep of the twentieth century: 58 per cent of people moving from working to middle class had taken school examinations and 12.8 per cent had gone to university. Yet only 15.1 per cent of those falling from middle to working class had taken school examinations and a tiny 0.5 per cent had been to university. A. H. Halsey's (1986: 125) figures state this clearly (Table 11.26).

Table 11.24. Stocks of qualified persons as a percentage of employees by skill level in the UK, USA, and Germany

	Higher level			Intermediate level		
	UK	USA	Germany	UK	USA	Germany
1978/79	6.8	15.8	7.0	21.8	11.4	58.5
1998	15.8	27.7	15.0	33.9	18.6	65.0

Source: O'Mahony (2003: 125, 129).

Table 11.25. Comparative labour productivity in various countries, 1979, 1999

	UK	USA	France	Germany
1979	100	154	131	130
1999	100	130	129	117

Source: O'Mahony (2003).

Table 11.26. The educational experience of the middle class and the upwardly mobile, 1972 (%)

	Private primary schooling	Selective secondary schooling	School exams	Some FE qualification	University degree
Stable middle class	32	88.4	82.0	33.1	29.8
Lower middle to middle	11.7	67.9	62.1	34.1	13.5
Working to middle	1.6	63.1	58.5	32.3	12.8

Source: Halsey (1986: 125).

Table 11.27. The educational experience of the working class and the downwardly mobile, 1972 (%)

Middle to working	3.8	33.5	15.1	7.0	0.5
Lower middle to working	3.0	21.9	8.1	1.8	0.1
Stable working class	0.6	14.7	4.6	0.4	0.1

Source: Halsey (1986: 125).

This may be contrasted with figures for the downwardly mobile to the working class and with the stable working class itself (Table 11.27). These various approaches through rates of return, productivity and growth, social mobility, all suggest that there is a connection between education and the economy.

The previous section suggests that from various points of view the connection of education and the labour market was broadly well matched. Indeed it would be surprising if it were not so in an advanced Western industrial country like Britain. Virtually universal literacy was achieved, types of post-elementary education had been stratified on German lines in the 1900s, higher education expanded with a strong scientific and technical element. The curriculum of schools and universities diversified from the old liberal education based on classics and pure mathematics to a wide range of subjects of intended utility. All this was underlain by a widening access, from elementary schools to grammar schools, 'secondary education for all', the abolition of fee paying by the 1944 Act, and the changing concept of universities from elite to mass institutions. This was all appropriate for the kind of changing social structure we saw in Table 11.1—the rise of a professional and managerial class—a similar increase in the need for secretarial work, sales, and personal services, the corresponding decline of manual, especially unskilled, work.

Yet there are cross-currents and discordances in this relationship of education and the supply of labour. First the efficient flow of ability through the education system into the most appropriate jobs was vitiated by social-class differences. Although places were set aside in grammar schools—initially 25 per cent rising to 40 per cent—for children from elementary schools, yet the poverty of working-class families in the 1920s and 1930s led to failure to take up these places. Even after 1944 social factors prevented the 11+ examination from adequately selecting 'intelligence'. Parental poverty restricted the horizons of such children in pre-1944 elementary schools and post-1944 secondary moderns and limited the level in the labour market to which they could aspire. The same factors to a lesser extent informed the different career outcomes of grammar and public schoolboys in this time and the contemporary concern to widen the social-class intake into the 'best' universities. The trapping of talent in jobs lower than ability might merit has been a recurrent feature of the system.

Secondly, the overlapping of outcomes between supposedly different levels of the system also suggests a lack of clear match. We have noted the disappointing output of grammar schools in the inter-war years. In a context in which less than 2 per cent of 18-year-olds went to university, many grammar school pupils entered clerical and technical jobs barely distinguishable from those taken by ex-elementary school pupils. The system was further confused by the misty borderland of former HGSs, central schools selective and non-selective, senior schools, rural area schools, between the elementary and secondary grammar schools. Third, at least the JTS and STS had much more targeted purpose and output than the above schools but their neglect, one would argue, was an important gap in the provision the education system should have provided in labour formation. The high proportion of boys who started to become technicians after an academic grammar school education suggests this, as does the plethora of 'initiatives' by the MSC and others since 1970 to replicate the virtues of the STS, lost after 1955.

Finally, we have seen various points where the education system did not seem to be responsive to what was needed in the labour force. The swing of university students away from science and technology in the inter-war years and 1960s, and the lack of chemical engineers, metallurgists, and oil geologists in the same period, were indicative. So was the discouragement of the 1960s universities from professional studies, even engineering and computing. In our own time there have been constant complaints about a skills gap. University physics and chemistry departments close despite GEC's complaints about the shortage of physicists before its demise and GSK's concern about the shortage of good chemistry graduates despite starting salaries of £34,000.[27] Universities have to mediate two markets, that of sixth formers and their subject preferences on the one hand and the demand of employers for their students on the other. Ultimately higher education has to be more responsive to the former than the latter and dysfunctions arise when students are insufficiently aware of the rewards or limitations of their degree choice and the careers to which they may

---

[27] *Financial Times*, 18 Mar. 2005, on Glaxo.

lead. Above all an even better match of education and the labour market will be gained for the future by a narrowing of the skills gap. More vocational studies in schools are intended to counteract the resentment of non-academic teenagers at long, compulsory, too-academic schooling and their craving for the world of work. The replacing of some comprehensives by CTCs and skills academies (ghostly resurrections of the old JTS and STS) is a move in this direction. The old Victorian reverence for liberal education which has been arguably an impediment to the acceptance of vocationalism and specialized technical skill training is being eroded along with many of its snobberies. It is not self-evident that the classicist, historian, philosopher, or literary critic is 'superior' to the fashion designer, website manager, recording studio sound engineer, or chef. The labour market has need of them all as Britain becomes a wealthier economy more demanding of sophisticated services and consumer goods.

References

Abbott, A. (1933). *Education for Industry and Commerce in England*. Oxford: Oxford University Press.

Albu, A.(1980) 'British Attitudes to Engineering Education: A Historical Perspective', in K. Pavitt (ed.), *Technical Innovation and British Economic Performance*. London: Macmillan.

Aldcroft, D. H. (1992). *Education, Training and Economic Performance 1944 to 1990*. Manchester: Manchester University Press.

Anderson, R. D. (1992). *Universities and Elites in Britain since 1800*. London: Macmillan.

Bailey, B. (1990), 'Technical Education and Secondary Schooling 1905–1945', in P. Summerfield and E. Evans (eds.), *Technical Education and the State since 1850*. Manchester: Manchester University Press.

Baines, D. E. (1981). 'The Labour Supply and the Labour Market 1860–1914', in R. Floud and D. McCloskey (eds.), *The Economic History of Britain since 1700*. Cambridge: Cambridge University Press.

Balfour, A. (1927). *Factors in Industrial and Commercial Efficiency* (Committee on Industry and Trade). London: His Majesty's Stationery Office.

Beloff, M. (1968). *The Plateglass Universities*. London: Secker and Warburg.

Bennett, R., Glennerster, H., and Newton, D. (1992). *Learning Should Pay*. Poole: BP Educational Service.

Bishop, T. H. J. H., and Wilkinson, R. (1967). *Winchester and the Public School Elite*. London: Faber and Faber.

Broadberry, S. (2003). 'Human Capital and Skills', in R. Floud and P. Johnson (eds.), *The Cambridge Economic History of Modern Britain*, vol. iii. Cambridge: Cambridge University Press.

Brown, P., and Hesketh, A. (2004). *The Mismanagement of Talent*. Oxford: Oxford University Press.

—— and Scase, R. (1994). *Higher Education and Corporate Realities*. London: UCL Press.

Burgess, K. (1994). 'British Employers and Education Policy, 1935–1945: A Decade of Missed Opportunities'. *Business History*, 36/3: 29–45.

Carr, R. (1958). *Training for Skill: The Recruitment and Training of Young Workers in Industry.* London: Her Majesty's Stationery Office.

Carr-Saunders, A. M., and Caradog-Jones, D. (1937). *A Survey of the Social Structure of England and Wales.* Oxford: Oxford University Press.

Carter, M. P. (1962). *Home, School and Work.* London: Pergamon Press.

Cassells, Sir J. (1990). *Britain's Real Skill Shortage and What to do About it.* London: Policy Studies Institute.

Clarke, C. (2003). *The Future of Higher Education.* Cm. 5735. London: Her Majesty's Stationery Office.

Craig, C. (1963). *The Employment of Cambridge Graduates.* Cambridge: Cambridge University Press.

Crowther, Sir G. (1959). *Fifteen to Eighteen.* London: Her Majesty's Stationery Office.

Davin, A. (1996). *Growing up Poor: Home, School, Street in London 1870–1914.* London: Rivers Oran Press.

Davies, H. (1976). *The Creighton Report: A Year in the Life of a Comprehensive School.* London: Hamilton.

Dearing, Sir R. (1997). *National Committee of Inquiry into Higher Education: Higher Education in a Learning Society.* London: Her Majesty's Stationery Office.

Elbaum, B. (1991). 'The Persistence of Apprenticeship in Britain and its Decline in the United States', in Howard Gospel (ed.) *Industrial Training and Technological Innovation.* London: Routledge.

Finegold, D., and Soskice, D. (1988). 'The Failure of Training in Britain: Analysis and Prescription'. *Oxford Review of Economic Policy*, 4/3: 21–53.

Fitzgerald, R. (1993). 'Industrial Training and Management in Britain', in N. Kawabe and E. Daito (eds.), *Education and Training in the Development of the Modern Corporation.* Tokyo: University of Tokyo Press.

Floud, R. (1982). 'Technical Education and Economic Performance in Britain 1850–1914'. *Albion*, 14: 153.

Gospel, H. (1993). 'Whatever Happened to Apprenticeship Training in Britain?' *Studies in Economics* (University of Kent), 93/14.

Graham, J. A., and Phythian, B. A. (1965). *The Manchester Grammar School 1515–1965.* Manchester: Manchester University Press.

Gray, I. E., and Potter, W. E. (1950). *Ipswich School 1400–1950.* Ipswich: Harrison.

Gray, J. L., and Moshinsky, P. (1935). 'Ability and Opportunity in English Education'. *Sociological Review*, 27/2.

Greenstein, D. (1994). 'The Junior Members,1900–1990: A Statistical Profile', in B. H. Harrison (ed.), *The History of the University of Oxford Vol. VIII The Twentieth Century.* Oxford: Oxford University Press.

Guagnini, A. (1993). 'Worlds Apart, Academic Instruction and Professional Qualifications in the Training of Mechanical Engineers in England 1850–1914', in R. Fox and A. Guagnini (eds.), *Education, Technology and Industrial Performance in Europe 1850–1939.* Cambridge: Cambridge University Press.

Hadow, Sir H. (1926). *Board of Education Report of the Consultative Committee on the Education of the Adolescent.* London: His Majesty's Stationery Office.

Halsey, A. H. (1972). *Trends in British Society since 1900.* London: Macmillan.

—— (1986). *Change in British Society.* Oxford: Oxford University Press.

Harrison, B. H. (1994). *The History of the University of Oxford*, viii: *The Twentieth Century*. Oxford: Oxford University Press.

Hudson, D., and Luckhurst, K. W. (1954). *The Royal Society of Arts*. London: John Murray.

Ives, E., Drummond, D., and Schwarz, L. (2002). *The First Civic University: Birmingham 1880–1980*. Birmingham: University of Birmingham Press.

Jenkins, H., and Caradog-Jones, D. (1950). 'The Social Class of Cambridge University Alumni of the 18th and 19th Centuries'. *British Journal of Sociology*, 1: 93–116.

Keeble, S. P. (1992). *The Ability to Manage: A Study of British Management 1890–1990*. Manchester: Manchester University Press.

Kingsland, J. C. (1965). 'Cray Valley Technical High School for Boys', in R. E. Gross (ed.), *British Secondary Education*. Oxford: Oxford University Press.

Lacey, C. (1970). *Hightown Grammar*. Manchester: Manchester University Press.

Lawson, J. (1963). *A Town Grammar School through Six Centuries*. Oxford: Oxford University Press.

Lowe, R. (1982). 'The Extension of Higher Education in England', in K. H. Jarausch (ed.), *The Transformation of Higher Learning 1860–1930*. Chicago: University of Chicago Press.

Lindley, R. M. (ed.) (1981). *Higher Education and the Labour Market*. Guildford: Society for Research into Higher Education.

McCulloch, G. (1989). *The Secondary Technical School: A Usable Past?* Lewes: Falmer.

Maddison, A. (2001), *The World Economy: A Millennial Perspective*. Paris: OECD.

Matterson, A. (1981). *Polytechnics and Colleges*. London: Longman.

Matthews, R. C . O., Feinstein, C. H., and Odling-Smee, J. C. (1982). *British Economic Growth 1856–1973*. Oxford: Clarendon Press.

Miles, A. (1999). *Social Mobility in Nineteenth and Early Twentieth Century England*. Manchester: Manchester University Press.

Millis, C. T. (1925). *Technical Education: Its Development and Aims*. London: Edward Arnold.

Morris, V. (1977). 'Investment in Higher Education', in C. Baxter, P. J. O'Leary, and A. Westoby (eds.), *Economics and Education Policy: A Reader*. London: Longman.

Nicholas, S. (1985). 'Technical Education and the Decline of Britain 1870–1914', in I. Inkster (ed.), *The Steam Intellect Societies*. Nottingham: University of Nottingham Press.

OECD (2004). *Economic Outlook*, vol i. Paris: OECD.

O'Mahony, M. (2003). 'Employment, Education and Human Capital', in R. Floud and P. Johnson (eds.), *The Cambridge Economic History of Modern Britain*, vol. iii. Cambridge: Cambridge University Press.

Perkin, H. (1989). *The Rise of Professional Society*. London: Routledge.

Pollard, S. (1989). *Britain's Prime and Britain's Decline*. London: Edward Arnold.

Prais, S. J., and Wagner, K. (1983). *Schooling Standards in Britain and Germany: Some Summary Comparisons Bearing on Economic Efficiency*. NIESR Discussion Paper 60, Industry Series 14.

Pratt, J., and Burgess, T. (1974). *Polytechnics: A Report*. London: Pitman.

Rackham, C. (1940). *Education in Norwich 1920–1940*. Norwich: WEA.

Rae, J. (1981). *The Public School Revolution: Britain's Independent Schools 1964–1979*. London: Faber.

Reader, D. (1987). 'The Reconstruction of Secondary Education in England 1869–1920', in D. Muller, F. Ringer, and B. Simon (eds.), *The Rise of the Modern Educational System 1870–1920*. Cambridge: Cambridge University Press.

Reader, W. J. (1966). *Professional Men*. London: Weidenfeld and Nicolson.

Reid, I., Williams, R., and Rayner, M. (1991). 'The Education of the Elite', in G. Walford (ed.), *Private Schooling*. London: Paul Chapman.

Renold, G. C. (1928). 'The Nature and Present Position of Skill in Industry'. *Economic Journal*, 38, December: 593–604.

Richardson, W. A. (1939). *The Technical College*. Oxford: Oxford University Press.

Roach, J. P. C. (1959). 'The University of Cambridge', in *The Victoria County History of Cambridgeshire*, iii: *The City and University of Cambridge*. Oxford: Oxford University Press.

Robertson, P. L. (1990). 'The Development of an Urban University: Glasgow, 1860–1914'. *History of Education Quarterly*, 30/1, Spring: 47–78.

Roderick, G. W., and Stephens, M. (1974). 'Scientific Studies and Scientific Manpower in the English Civic Universities 1870–1914'. *Science Studies*, 4/1: 41–63.

Rose, J. (1993). 'Willingly to School: The Working Class Response to Elementary Education in Britain 1875–1918'. *Journal of British Studies*, 32, April: 114–38.

Routh, G. (1980). *Occupation and Pay in Great Britain 1906–79*. London: Macmillan.

Rubinstein, W. D. (1993). 'Education, the "Gentleman" and British Entrepreneurship', in *Capitalism, Culture and Decline in Britain 1750–1990*. London: Routledge.

Sanderson, M. (1972). *The Universities and British Industry 1850–1970*. London: Routledge and Kegan Paul.

—— (1987). *Educational Opportunity and Social Change in England, 1900–1980s*. London: Faber.

—— (1994). *The Missing Stratum: Technical School Education in England 1900–1990s*. London: Athlone Press.

—— (1997). 'The English Public Schools and the Economic Depression of the 1930s', in P. Lanthier and H. Watelat (eds.), *Private Enterprise during Economic Crises*. New York: Legas.

—— (1999). *Education and Economic Decline 1870–1990s*. Cambridge: Cambridge University Press.

—— (2002). *The History of the University of East Anglia 1918–2000*. London: Hambledon.

Sheldrake, J., and Vickerstaff, S. (1987). *The History of Industrial Training in Britain*. Aldershot: Avebury.

Simon, B. (1974). *The Politics of Educational Reform 1920–1940*. London: Lawrence and Wishart.

Snow, G. (1959). *The Public School in the New Age*. London: G. Bles.

Spens, W. (1946). *University Education and Business: A Report by a Committee Appointed by the Cambridge University Appointments Board 1937–8*. Cambridge: Cambridge University Press.

Summerfield, P. (1988). 'Family, School and Work. Girls' Education and Employment in Lancashire 1900–1950', in M. Dick (ed.), *Education and Employment: Initiatives and Experiences*. History of Education Society Conference Papers.

Sutherland, G. (1990). 'Education' in F. M. L. Thompson (ed.), *The Cambridge Social History of Britain 1750–1950*, vol. iii. Cambridge: Cambridge University Press.

Tawney, R. H. (1922). *Secondary Education for All*. London: George Allen and Unwin.

Taylor, W. (1963). *The Secondary Modern School*. London: Faber and Faber.

Truscott, B. (1951). *Red Brick University*, 2nd edn. Harmondsworth: Penguin.

Venables, Sir P. (1978). *Higher Education Developments: The Technological Universities*. London: Faber and Faber.

Veness, T. (1962). *School Leavers*. London: Methuen.

Vincent, D. (1989). *Literacy and Popular Culture in England 1750–1914*. Cambridge: Cambridge University Press.

Vlaeminke, M. (2000). *The English Higher Grade Schools: A Lost Opportunity*. London: Woburn Press.

Wakeford, J. (1969). *The Cloistered Elite*. London: Macmillan.

Walford, G., and Miller, H. (1991). *City Technology College*. Milton Keynes: Open University Press.

Weinberg, I. (1967). *The English Public Schools*. New York: Atherton Press.

Welpton, W. P. (1913). *Primary Artisan Education*. London: n.p.

Willmott, P. (1966). *Adolescent Boys of East London*. London: Routledge and Kegan Paul.

Wolf, A. (1997). *GNVQs 1993–97: A National Survey*. London: FEDA.

—— (2002). *Does Education Matter?* London: Penguin.

Wooldridge, A. (1990). *Education and the Labour Market: An English Disaster*. London: Social Market Foundation.

Ziderman, A. (1973). 'Does It Pay to Take a Degree?' *Oxford Economic Papers*, NS 25: 262–74.

Zmroczek, J. (2004). 'The Education and Employment of Girls in Norwich 1870–1939'. Ph.D. thesis, University of East Anglia.

12

Britain's Twentieth-Century Productivity Performance in International Perspective

Stephen Broadberry and Mary O'Mahony

12.1 Introduction

This chapter provides an overview of Britain's labour productivity performance during the twentieth century, incorporating the catching-up and convergence perspective. By taking account of levels of labour productivity, as well as growth rates, we will see that it is possible to arrive at a more sanguine evaluation of Britain's twentieth-century performance than is common in much of the literature. Until recently, the literature was dominated by a 'declinist' perspective, emphasizing the slower rate of productivity growth in Britain compared with other countries (Kirby 1981; Wiener 1981; Dintenfass 1982; Pollard 1984; Barnett 1986; Elbaum and Lazonick 1986; Alford 1988). However, following important papers by Abramovitz (1986) and Baumol (1986) on the convergence of productivity and living standards, a more balanced view has become possible.

The central idea in the convergence literature is that there is a negative correlation between the productivity growth rate and the initial level of productivity. This can be explained most intuitively by the fact that it is easier for a lagging economy to imitate via adoption of technology or organization from abroad than to innovate at the frontier. However, it also follows in a simple neoclassical growth model, since in a world of diminishing returns to capital, a country with a low level of capital per worker and hence a low level of labour productivity will have high returns to capital and hence attract investment. Since Britain had a relatively high level of productivity in the late nineteenth century, the finding of slower productivity growth in Britain is only to be expected within this framework. Furthermore, it should not be overlooked that per capita income in 2000 was around four and a half times higher than it had been in 1900, representing a considerable increase in living standards over the century.

However, there is a danger of taking the revisionism of the convergence framework too far and taking too optimistic a view of Britain's twentieth-century productivity performance (Rubinstein 1993; Booth 2001). Crafts and Toniolo (1996) continue to see British performance as disappointing, even allowing for differences in catch up potential, since Britain was not just caught up by many countries, but also fell behind. Furthermore, Britain has been slow to close the productivity gap that has opened up with North America and much of Western Europe (Broadberry and O'Mahony 2004).

One way of guarding against an excessively optimistic interpretation of Britain's productivity performance is to delve beneath the aggregates to look at sectoral variations in comparative productivity performance. We present results for the US/UK and Germany/UK comparisons, so as to provide coverage of both North America and Western Europe. In addition to highlighting areas of weakness as well as strengths, this helps to shed light on the long-term development of the British economy. We show that the high levels of overall labour productivity achieved in late nineteenth-century Britain were under-pinned by high levels of labour productivity in agriculture and services rather than in industry, together with a highly favourable structure. In particular, Britain's high level of development at this time shows up in a relatively small share of the labour force in agriculture, a sector with relatively low value added. One strand of the literature has drawn attention to the substantially higher levels of labour productivity in American industry compared with British industry during the nineteenth century as a result of land abundance and labour scarcity (Habakkuk 1962). Nevertheless, if there has been a long-standing British labour productivity gap in industry, it has not trended upwards (Broadberry 1997*a*, 1997*b*). This means that over the long run, the overall deterioration in Britain's comparative labour productivity performance must be concentrated in agriculture and services, together with the effects of structural change. Structural change matters because of the later movement of labour out of agriculture, a relatively low value-added sector, in other countries. However, the long-run stationarity of comparative labour productivity in industry is quite consistent with shorter periods of disappointing perform-ance, which were later reversed. This pattern occurred during the period 1950–79, for example, with Britain much slower than Germany to close the large productivity gap that had opened up with the United States across the Second World War, so that Germany overtook Britain. However, Britain then closed the gap with Germany during the 1980s (Broadberry and Crafts 2003).

The chapter also offers a quantitative overview of explanations of Britain's productivity performance. Before the Second World War, Britain, in common with the rest of Europe, had a productivity gap with the United States, particu-larly in industry. Since the 1970s, there has also been a productivity gap with Europe. This section draws on growth accounting and levels accounting to quantify the factors behind Britain's productivity performance during the twentieth century, focusing on the roles of physical capital, human capital, and innovation.

12.2 Britain's aggregate productivity performance

The rate of labour productivity growth in Britain has tended to be slower than in most other major economies which have been perceived as Britain's main competitors, throughout most sub-periods since 1870. This is shown in panel (*a*) of Table 12.1, with Britain having the slowest labour productivity growth during the periods 1870–1913, 1913–29, 1929–38, and 1973–90. Furthermore, although the United States grew more slowly during 1950–73, this was the period when the growth rate gap between Britain and most continental European economies and Japan was at its peak. A similar pattern of a lagging British growth rate appears in data on GDP per capita and GDP per employee. This pattern of relatively slow growth in Britain has tended to generate a rather pessimistic and critical tone to much of the literature on British economic history during the twentieth century.

This view has been tempered in more recent years by a consideration of comparative levels of labour productivity, shown here in panel (*b*) of Table 12.1. Consideration of these data tends to lead to a more optimistic view, showing Britain starting out in 1870 with the highest level of labour productivity. The faster growth of other countries can thus be explained as part of the process of

Table 12.1. Rates of growth and comparative levels of GDP per hour worked

(*a*) Growth rates (% per annum)

	1870–1913	1913–29	1929–38	1938–50	1950–73	1973–90	1990–98
UK	1.2	1.5	0.9	2.3	3.1	1.7	3.1
USA	1.9	2.4	1.5	3.2	2.7	1.4	1.7
Germany[a]	1.8	1.4	1.1	−0.8	6.0	2.4	2.4
France	1.7	2.4	2.9	0.5	5.1	2.9	1.7
Japan	1.9	3.5	2.3	−0.6	7.7	3.0	2.1

(*b*) Comparative levels (UK = 100)

	1870	1913	1929	1938	1950	1973	1990	1998
UK	100	100	100	100	100	100	100	100
USA	87	116	136	144	161	148	141	126
Germany[a]	61	80	79	81	56	105	116	111
France	52	65	75	89	72	113	138	123
Japan	18	23	32	37	26	72	89	82

[a] Former West Germany for the period after 1950.

Sources: Maddison (1995: table J-5; 2001: table E-7).

catching up. However, whilst this can be seen as applying to Japan throughout the twentieth century, and to France and Germany into the early post-Second World War period, it cannot be used to explain the forging ahead of the United States between 1913 and 1950, nor the continued growth of the French and German productivity lead until 1990. Why were other countries able to forge ahead, and why was the British economy so slow to catch up once it had fallen behind?

12.3 Sectoral productivity performance

12.3.1 Overview

The data in Table 12.1 refer to GDP per hour worked. To provide a sectoral breakdown of Britain's comparative labour productivity performance,

Table 12.2. Comparative labour productivity levels by sector, 1869/71 to 1990: GDP per person engaged (UK = 100)
(a) US/UK

	Agriculture	Industry	Services	Aggregate economy
1869/71	86.9	153.6	85.9	89.8
1889/91	102.1	164.1	84.2	94.1
1909/11	103.2	193.2	107.4	117.7
1919/20	128.0	198.0	118.9	133.3
1929	109.7	222.7	121.2	139.4
1937	103.3	190.6	120.0	132.6
1950	126.0	243.5	140.8	166.9
1973	131.2	214.8	137.4	152.3
1990	151.1	163.0	129.6	133.0

(b) Germany[a]/UK

	Agriculture	Industry	Services	Aggregate economy
1871	55.7	91.7	62.8	59.5
1891	53.7	99.3	64.4	60.5
1911	67.3	127.3	73.4	75.5
1925	53.8	92.3	76.5	69.0
1929	56.9	97.1	82.3	74.1
1935	57.2	99.1	85.7	75.7
1950	41.2	91.8	83.2	74.4
1973	50.8	121.1	120.1	114.0
1990	75.4	111.0	134.9	125.4

[a] Former West Germany for the period after 1950.
Sources: Derived from Broadberry (1997b, 1997c).

however, requires working in terms of output per person engaged. The figures in Table 12.2 for the US/UK and Germany/UK comparisons show levels and trends that are very similar to Maddison's (1995, 2001) well-known comparative data on GDP per hour worked until about 1973, when hours worked per person engaged began to diverge between Europe and America.

Around 1870, aggregate GDP per person engaged in the United States was about 90 per cent of the British level, but US overtaking occurred in the 1890s. The United States then forged ahead, reaching a peak labour productivity lead around 1950, after which Britain slowly narrowed the gap. In 1871, aggregate GDP per person engaged in Germany was less than 60 per cent of the British level. Although this had risen above 75 per cent before 1914, the First World War provided a significant setback to Germany. By the late 1930s, German labour productivity had reached about 80 per cent of the British level, but the Second World War provided another setback. Thereafter, Germany returned to the catching-up path and overtook Britain during the 1960s. Germany continued to forge ahead until 1979, and during the 1980s comparative aggregate labour productivity fluctuated without trend until German reunification.

The natural starting point for the sectoral analysis of Britain's comparative productivity performance is the widely acknowledged fact that comparative productivity trends in manufacturing have differed from trends in the aggregate economy (Broadberry 1993). The US/UK and Germany/UK comparative labour productivity trends in manufacturing are shown here in Figure 12.1. In contrast to the situation at the aggregate level, in manufacturing there is no long-run trend in comparative labour productivity. In 1870, US labour productivity in manufacturing was roughly twice the UK level, and this was also the case in the late twentieth century. Although there have been periods of sustained deviation from this two-to-one US labour productivity advantage,

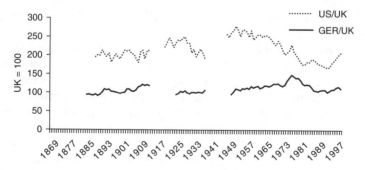

Figure 12.1 Comparative labour productivity in manufacturing
Source: Broadberry (2004*a*).

particularly following major wars, in the long run there has always been a return to this ratio. The sharp increase in the US/UK comparative labour productivity ratio in manufacturing between 1938 and 1950, and the subsequent downward trend between 1950 and 1979, should be interpreted in this light. Similarly, there has been no long-run change in the Germany/UK comparative labour productivity ratio, with Germany roughly on a par with Britain in both 1870 and 1990.

This large US labour productivity advantage in manufacturing since at least the mid-nineteenth century has attracted a great deal of attention since it was linked by Habakkuk (1962) to the abundance of land and natural resources in the United States. Habakkuk's argument was that resource abundance led to labour scarcity and hence (1) substitution of capital for labour in manufacturing and (2) labour-saving technical progress. The first result, of resource abundance leading to greater capital intensity in manufacturing, goes through so long as there is a complementarity between capital and resources (Ames and Rosenberg 1968). The second result, of resource abundance leading to labour-saving technical progress has been demonstrated by David (1975), drawing on a model of endogenous localized technical change from Atkinson and Stiglitz (1969).

Broadberry (1997a) extends the argument into the twentieth century with the incorporation of human capital. The resource-using machinery was substituted for skilled labour in the United States, making good use of US natural resource abundance and skilled labour scarcity. However, US mass production methods were not well suited to European conditions of natural resource scarcity and skilled labour abundance. The large, homogeneous US market reinforced these technological differences, since mass production technology produced standardized products. US mass production technology can be seen as coexisting with European flexible production technology, with a process of innovation on one side of the Atlantic mirrored by imitation on the other side of the Atlantic, and with technical progress adapted to local circumstances on both continents.

To make these ideas more concrete, it is helpful to focus on a particular industry, motor vehicles. Already by the end of the nineteenth century, substantial differences had emerged between the European and American industries, with US firms building long runs of standard cars, assembled by semi-skilled labour from bought-in components, while European firms tended to use skilled craft workers to produce parts in-house, and to assemble them on a more customized basis (Lewchuk 1987). Production census data for the period 1907–09 capture these differences very well, with output per worker substantially higher in the United States than in Britain or Germany (Broadberry 1997a). The process of standardization and the substitution away from skilled labour received a further boost with developments at Ford during the First World War, with the introduction of a moving assembly line, high wages in return for hard driving of the labour force, and the extreme pursuit of volume by the removal of all variation in the product (any colour you want so long as it's black!).

Although there was clearly technological cross-fertilization between the European and American car industries, with Ford and General Motors producing in Europe as well as America, differences in demand patterns (more varied in Europe), and relative factor prices (cheaper skilled labour and more expensive energy in Europe), meant that in Europe there was much greater model variety than in America, the labour force relied more heavily on skilled craft workers, and machinery remained more general purpose and less specialized (Bardou et al. 1982; Foreman-Peck 1982; Lewchuk 1987). Whilst American car producers remained technological leaders for much of the twentieth century, with European producers having to adapt American technology to European conditions, the tables were turned from the 1970s, with the revival of flexible production on the basis of numerically controlled machine tools and computer-aided design (Milgrom and Roberts 1990; Juergens et al. 1993; Broadberry 1994). Having a skilled labour force with experience of building to custom became once again an asset (Edquist and Jacobsson 1988). Again, however, given differences in factor proportions and demand patterns between countries, differences in production strategies and productivity outcomes have persisted (McKinsey Global Institute 1993).

Since manufacturing was the biggest industrial sector, and since agriculture had shrunk in importance to around 2 or 3 per cent of the labour force in all three countries by the late 1980s, reconciling the trends and levels of comparative productivity performance in manufacturing and the whole economy seemed to require a loss of British productivity leadership in services. This was first established by Broadberry (1997b, 1997c, 1998) using a nine-sector breakdown. However, to bring out the crucial importance of services for understanding Britain's comparative productivity performance since 1870, it is sufficient to consider the results on the basis of a three-sector breakdown, covering agriculture, industry, and services.

Britain's loss of productivity leadership in services coincided with the 'industrialization' of market services in the United States, which involved the transition from a customized, low-volume, high-margin approach to business organized on the basis of networks to a more standardized, high-volume, low-margin business with hierarchical management. As with the related introduction of mass production in manufacturing, the industrialization of services led to sustained growth of labour productivity. However, the gains from the introduction of the technology and organization of industrialized services provision varied by sector over time (Broadberry and Ghosal 2002).

Again, to make the idea of the industrialization of services more concrete, it is helpful to focus on a particular example. Here, we consider shipping. As Boyce (1995) notes, shipping ventures in the nineteenth century were usually conducted by networks. A group of agents would each make an initial invest-ment, which would allow the purchase of a ship and other necessary items. The aim of the venture might be to take a cargo between two cities (say London and Buenos Aires), find a cargo for the return voyage, and then sell the ship or undertake another venture. Agents would bring different skills and commer-cial contacts as well as initial capital. However, there was much scope for opportunistic behaviour, since it was difficult to monitor the actions of agents over long distances. Suppose, for example, that there were difficulties in finding a return cargo in Buenos Aires, which reduced the profitability of the venture. How could the other partners in the venture find out whether or not this was the fault of the agent in Buenos Aires? In these circumstances, group reputation and the associated persistence of group membership could be used to provide a solution to the incentive problem and deter opportunistic beha-viour. You only trade with people you can trust, and that trust can take a long time to build up. The economic mechanisms underpinning these networks of trust have been analysed formally by Greif (1989, 2000).

During the late nineteenth century, however, a number of developments per-mitted the evolution of a more anonymous, high-volume 'industrial' approach to shipping. First, the scale of business increased as world population, incomes, and trade grew. Second, communications improved with the spread of the tele-graph and then the telephone. And third, the transition from sail to steamships improved the predictability of sailing times. These developments all made it more feasible to establish a regular scheduled service between two ports, requir-ing investment in a fleet of ships, the establishment of a bureaucracy to run the regular service, and a marketing organization to secure sufficient demand to fill the capacity. This led to the establishment of shipping lines, which required Chandler's (1977) three-pronged investment in production, management, and marketing. This led to a dramatic increase of concentration in shipping, with the eight-firm concentration ratio in the British fleet reaching 42.5 per cent by 1918/19, and 100 per cent in the liner section (Boyce 1995: 128–9).

Further steps in the industrialization of shipping came after the First World War with the replacement of steam ships by motorships, and the associated development of large oil tankers to replace the declining oil trade (Sturmey 1962). These developments led to a further squeeze on tramp shipping. After the Second World War, the growth of the oil tanker business accelerated, and the dry cargo business moved towards containerization, with dramatic changes in oper-ating methods, leading to much higher labour productivity (Channon 1978).

12.3.2 *Sectoral analysis of the US/UK case, 1870–1990*

The importance of services to the changing US/UK comparative labour productivity level in the aggregate economy over the period 1870–1990 can be seen in the sectoral breakdown of comparative productivity levels in panel (*a*) of Table 12.2. To get the full picture, however, requires adding to this the sectoral breakdown of employment in the two countries, shown in Table 12.3. Panel (a) of Table 12.2 illustrates the point raised in the previous section that the long-run trends in comparative labour productivity for the aggregate economy owe rather less to trends in industry than is usually assumed in accounts of comparative productivity performance. Hence, for example, between circa 1890 and 1990, the US labour productivity lead in industry declined slightly,

Table 12.3. Sectoral shares of employment in the United States, the United Kingdom and Germany, 1870–1990 (%)

(a) United States

	Agriculture	Industry	Services
1870	50.0	24.8	25.2
1910	32.0	31.8	36.2
1920	26.2	33.2	40.6
1930	20.9	30.2	48.9
1940	17.9	31.6	50.5
1950	11.0	32.9	56.1
1973	3.7	28.9	67.4
1990	2.5	21.8	75.7

(b) United Kingdom

	Agriculture	Industry	Services
1871	22.2	42.4	35.4
1911	11.8	44.1	44.1
1924	8.6	46.5	44.9
1930	7.6	43.7	48.7
1937	6.2	44.5	49.3
1950	5.1	46.5	48.4
1973	2.9	41.8	55.3
1990	2.0	28.5	69.5

(c) Germany[a]

	Agriculture	Industry	Services
1871	49.5	29.1	21.4
1913	34.5	37.9	27.6
1925	31.5	40.1	28.4
1930	30.5	37.4	32.1
1935	29.9	38.2	31.9
1950	24.3	42.1	33.6
1973	7.2	47.3	45.5
1990	3.4	39.7	56.9

[a] Former West Germany for the period after 1950.

Sources: Derived from Broadberry (1997b, 1997c, 1998).

while the United States went from a position of lower labour productivity to a 33 per cent lead in the aggregate economy. That is not to say that industry did not matter, particularly in shorter-run fluctuations of comparative labour productivity. Indeed, Broadberry (1997a) notes that the US labour productivity lead in manufacturing increased significantly across the First World War and again across the Second World War, but in each case, the increase was not sustained.

Note, secondly, that although the trend of comparative labour productivity in agriculture moved in the same direction as in the aggregate economy, with the United States overtaking Britain, this was not the really significant contribution of agriculture to changing comparative productivity performance at the aggregate level. The greater significance of agriculture was in its declining share of the labour force, which can be seen for both countries in Table 12.3. The decline in agriculture's share of employment had a significant impact on aggregate labour productivity because agriculture is a relatively low value-added activity. Hence countries which have retained a large share of the labour force in agriculture have also remained poor.[1] Shifting labour from agriculture into higher value-added industrial and service sectors hence acted to boost aggregate labour productivity. Note, however, that this shift out of agriculture occurred rather later in the United States than in Britain, thus contributing to the US catching up. Whereas in about 1870, agriculture accounted for just 22.2 per cent of employment in Britain, it still accounted for a full half of the US labour force. By 1990, however, agriculture accounted for less than 3 per cent of employment in both countries.

An important point to note in panel (a) of Table 12.2 is that comparative labour productivity trends in services broadly mirror comparative labour productivity trends for the economy as a whole. The USA overtook Britain in services during the 1890s, and forged ahead to the 1950s. Furthermore, since services grew in importance throughout the period in both countries, it is this loss of British productivity leadership in services that largely explains Britain's loss of overall productivity leadership (Broadberry and Ghosal 2002). Services also played an important role in shorter-run fluctuations, frequently mirroring the patterns in the aggregate economy.

12.3.3 *Sectoral analysis of the Germany/UK case, 1870–1990*

The importance of services to the changing Germany/UK comparative labour productivity level in the aggregate economy over the period 1870–1990 can be seen in the sectoral breakdown of comparative productivity levels in panel (b) of Table 12.2, together with the sectoral employment data in Table 12.3. Again, the

---

[1] Note that rich New World countries such as Australia and Canada conform to this pattern, with labour force shares of agriculture well under 5% by the end of the twentieth century.

first point to note is that the long-run trends in comparative productivity levels for the aggregate economy are less affected by trends in industry than is commonly thought. Thus, for example, between 1911 and 1990, the German labour productivity lead in industry declined while for the aggregate economy Germany went from three-quarters of the British level to a lead of more than 25 per cent. However, over shorter periods, there have been substantial movements in comparative Germany/UK levels in industry. Broadberry (1997a) emphasizes the German forging ahead in manufacturing during the 1970s, with Germany attaining close to a 50 per cent labour productivity lead by the end of the decade. This was not sustained, however, and by the end of the 1980s, most of the German lead had been eliminated (Broadberry and Crafts 2003).

Secondly, although Germany's comparative productivity position in agriculture has improved since the late nineteenth century, agricultural labour productivity remained much lower in Germany than in Britain in 1990. Again the declining importance of agriculture as a share of the labour force requires emphasis. Since the shift of labour out of low value-added agriculture occurred much later in Germany than in Britain, and even substantially later than in the United States, this had important implications for the lateness of German catching up at the aggregate economy level. With such a large share of the German labour force tied up in low-productivity agriculture before the Second World War, the overall labour productivity level was bound to be much lower in Germany than in Britain. On the other hand, once Germany shifted decisively out of agriculture after the Second World War, overall catching up was rapid.

For the Germany/UK case in panel (b) of Table 12.2, comparative labour productivity trends in services broadly mirror comparative labour productivity trends for the economy as a whole, as for the US/UK case in panel (a). Again, the key to understanding Germany's overtaking of Britain at the aggregate level was the loss of British productivity leadership in services (Broadberry 2004b). Services also played an important role in the shorter-run fluctuations, frequently mirroring the patterns in the aggregate economy.

12.3.4 *Developments since 1990*

The period from the mid-1990s is seen as a watershed in comparative productivity analysis since it represents the first time in decades that US productivity levels gained ground on major EU countries for a sustained period of time. It is also a period when Britain narrowed the gap with large European countries. Table 12.4 shows comparative levels of output per hour worked for the sector division shown in previous tables, but also shows figures for the market economy and market services. This confirms that aggregate trends are not being driven by trends in non-market services (health, education, and public administration), where outputs are frequently measured by inputs.

Table 12.4. Comparative labour productivity levels by sector: output per hour worked (UK = 100)

	1990	1995	2001
United States			
Total economy	138.4	124.4	123.9
Agriculture	162.3	137.8	187.4
Industry	151.9	133.2	130.3
Services	133.1	121.4	120.6
Market services[a]	149.9	136.3	139.0
Market economy[b]	148.8	134.0	136.9
Germany[c]			
Total economy	123.5	118.7	117.0
Agriculture	37.4	39.6	46.9
Industry	126.1	105.0	103.8
Services	126.9	127.7	122.7
Market services[a]	145.5	141.1	131.1
Market economy[b]	134.8	124.8	121.2
France			
Total economy	139.1	128.0	122.3
Agriculture	61.0	71.5	78.0
Industry	133.9	120.1	119.9
Services	152.2	137.7	127.2
Market services[a]	169.8	145.8	126.2
Market economy[b]	142.6	129.3	120.7

[a] Transport, communications, distribution, hotels and catering, financial and business services, and personal services.
[b] Total economy excluding health, education, public administration, and real estate.
[c] Unified Germany.
Source: Updated estimates from O'Mahony and de Boer (2002).

Table 12.4 confirms the previous findings that Britain has a significant productivity shortfall relative to the United States, Germany, and France, in all sectors other than agriculture. However it also shows that whereas Britain has lost some ground relative to the United States since 1995 in the market economy, Britain has gained on France and Germany, in particular in market service sectors. Again as in the previous sections, developments in service sectors dominate the trends, with the United States forging ahead in market services, in particular relative to France and Germany. The dramatic turnaround in the fortunes of US service industries has been increasingly noted in the literature and is now acknowledged to be highly influenced by the adoption and diffusion of information technology (O'Mahony and van Ark 2003; Triplett and Bosworth 2003). The information technology age appears also to have coincided with a turnaround in British productivity performance relative to large EU countries. However, despite the faster growth rate of labour productivity, Britain has not yet caught up with the other large EU countries in terms of labour productivity levels. This reflects the fact that Britain had fallen substantially behind during the 1970s and 1980s.

12.4 Explaining Britain's productivity performance

Before the Second World War, Britain, in common with the rest of Europe, had a productivity gap with the United States, particularly in industry. Since the 1970s, there has also been a productivity gap with Europe. This section draws on growth accounting and levels accounting studies of productivity performance to identify the proximate causes, with particular emphasis on physical capital and human capital.

12.4.1 Physical capital to 1990

Much of the literature on international comparisons suggests that labour productivity growth rates differ at least in part because of differences in capital stock growth (Denison 1967; Maddison 1987). Hence it is of some interest to

Table 12.5. Comparative total factor productivity levels by sector, 1869/71 to 1990 (UK = 100)

(a) US/UK

	Agriculture	Industry	Services	Aggregate economy
1869/71	99.5	154.2	86.5	95.2
1889/91	123.0	139.6	64.3	83.3
1909/11	118.7	150.9	71.6	90.5
1919/20	133.1	158.3	92.1	108.2
1929	118.0	187.8	92.0	112.7
1937	119.2	161.2	89.1	105.9
1950	132.6	217.6	110.2	138.1
1973	125.9	202.2	120.6	137.4
1990	138.8	157.3	119.8	125.3

(b) Germany[a]/UK

	Agriculture	Industry	Services	Aggregate economy
1871	58.4	90.5	67.2	61.6
1891	59.8	91.6	65.5	63.2
1911	71.6	106.1	76.4	75.4
1925	57.0	92.9	83.6	74.3
1929	59.3	96.0	90.0	78.5
1935	59.6	97.1	88.8	78.2
1950	44.7	89.4	89.3	76.2
1973	48.1	105.7	127.6	108.6
1990	65.4	98.5	139.0	116.5

[a] Former West Germany for the period after 1950.

Sources: Derived from Broadberry (1997b, 1997c, 1998).

consider the role of capital in explaining international differences in labour productivity levels. For the US/UK case at the aggregate level, trends in comparative total factor productivity (TFP) in panel (a) of Table 12.5 and labour productivity in panel (a) of Table 12.2 are similar, but with TFP differences generally smaller than labour productivity differences. This means that capital has a role to play in explaining labour productivity differences, but not enough to eliminate TFP differences altogether. One point worth noting here is that whereas the United States overtook Britain before the First World War in terms of labour productivity, it was only between the wars that the United States gained a TFP advantage. This would be consistent with the emphasis of Abramovitz and David (1973, 1996) on the importance of capital rather than TFP in American economic growth during the nineteenth century. It is also consistent with McCloskey's (1970) claim that Victorian Britain did not fail, at least in the sense that the United States was still catching up in terms of aggregate TFP levels. In services, too, note that US overtaking of Britain also occurred later in terms of TFP than in terms of labour productivity.

For the Germany/UK case, comparing panel (b) of Tables 12.5 and 12.2 we see that trends are very similar for comparative TFP and labour productivity at the aggregate level, with differences in TFP generally smaller than differences in labour productivity. Again, as in the US/UK case, this means that capital has a role to play in explaining labour productivity differences, but not enough to eliminate TFP differences altogether. Note that in industry, Germany had caught up with Britain in terms of TFP as well as labour productivity before the First World War. In services, higher capital intensity in Britain throughout the period means that until 1950 the British TFP lead was smaller than the British labour productivity lead, but that from 1973 the German TFP lead was greater than the German labour productivity lead.

When considering the more recent periods, the increasing importance of information and communications technology (ICT) equipment in the past two decades has led to significant changes in the method employed to measure capital input, with capital services increasingly replacing capital stocks as the main measure being employed in national accounts. Essentially the difference between the two measures relates to methods employed to aggregate across asset types, which in turn requires detailed investment series not available in the historical data. Hence comparisons across countries based on this new measure are confined to the period from 1990 and discussed in the section on growth accounting below.

12.4.2 Formal education and human capital

The most basic indicator of human capital is the level of education of the labour force. Table 12.6 provides data on formal schooling in Britain, the United States, and Germany. The data are presented in the form of enrolment

Table 12.6. Educational enrolment rates per 1,000 population under age 20, 1870–1990

(*a*) Britain

	Primary	Secondary	Higher
1871	118.6		
1881	238.4		
1891	285.8		
1901	344.7		1.6
1911	374.1	11.1	
1921	371.8	24.1	3.8
1931	380.6	31.7	
1938	357.1	37.1	4.8
1951	323.1	164.4	8.7
1961	299.8	233.2	13.9
1971	337.4	258.0	26.0
1981	327.4	327.4	30.5
1991	333.1	279.1	46.8

(*b*) United States

	Primary	Secondary	Higher
1870	390.6	4.2	
1880	404.5	4.6	
1890	492.5	10.3	
1900	478.9	18.7	
1910	475.6	26.8	
1920	472.9	56.1	15.8
1930	479.2	99.6	23.1
1938	472.2	147.1	29.8
1950	409.6	125.2	52.0
1960	436.6	138.6	62.5
1970	443.0	187.4	111.5
1980	389.0	248.7	167.0
1990	434.1	213.3	191.1

(*c*) Germany[a]

	Primary	Secondary	Higher
1871	364.7	9.5	0.8
1880	362.4	9.6	1.0
1890	365.5	10.1	1.3
1900	372.1	10.6	1.8
1911	372.4	10.9	2.3
1925	291.2	35.4	4.0
1933	383.2	38.3	6.4
1939	345.6	34.5	2.6
1950	410.6	52.3	6.9
1960	332.9	73.9	12.5
1970	368.2	123.1	19.7
1980	332.0	226.9	60.7
1990	286.6	191.4	99.8

[a] Former West Germany for the period after 1950.

Sources: Broadberry (2003, 2004*a*).

rates per 1,000 population under the age of 20, to facilitate international comparisons (Mitchell 1975; Flora 1983; Mitch 1992; Goldin 1998; Lindert 2001).

First, it is clear that Britain lagged behind both Germany and the United States in the provision of mass primary education until about 1900, as has been widely noted in the history of education literature and demonstrated quantitatively by Easterlin (1981). However, it is widely accepted that the official data on primary enrolments in England and Wales overstate the British shortfall due to under-recording. Lindert (2001) provides a corrected series using data on the number of child scholars from the 1871 Census of Occupations, which shows primary enrolments per 1,000 population in England and Wales having already reached 137.5 by 1871. This suggests that the British lag in primary education may not have been as great as suggested by the official data in Table 12.7, but it does not eliminate the lag.

Secondly, both Britain and Germany lagged behind the United States in the development of mass secondary education between the two world wars. This has been noted by historians of education such as Ringer (1979: 252–3), and has also been emphasized recently in the work of Goldin (1998). Thirdly, both Britain and Germany lagged behind the United States in the provision of mass higher education after the Second World War. By 1990, tertiary enrolment ratios in Britain and Germany were still a long way behind US levels.

Two points should be borne in mind when interpreting these trends. First, the transfer from primary to secondary education has generally occurred at a later age in the United States and Germany than in Britain, affecting the breakdown between primary and secondary education. Secondly, however, it is not possible to give enrolment ratios for narrower age bands, as the difference between primary and secondary education was a matter of class as well as age before the Second World War.

Previous attempts to provide a link between education and productivity have focused on industry, where the link between the tasks that most workers actually perform on the shop floor and the skills learned in school seems rather tenuous. In services, by contrast, the link between education and the tasks performed by most office workers seems rather closer. Although Goldin and Katz (1996) claim that the early development of mass secondary schooling in the United States was important in the development of batch and continuous process methods in the early twentieth century, the argument goes against the grain of an earlier view which sees the development of mass production in the United States as substituting away from skilled labour (Habakkuk 1962; Braverman 1974). Furthermore, Goldin's (1998) own evidence on the cross-state variation in the level of schooling shows a negative relationship between high school graduation and the share of the labour force in manufacturing. As David and Wright (1999) note, a long period of time undoubtedly elapsed before industrial employers learned to make effective use of the supply of high school graduates. The move to mass secondary schooling surely makes more sense when seen in the context of the organizational and technological changes occurring in the rapidly expanding service sector during the first half of the twentieth century. High levels of formal education can thus be seen as one factor behind the early industrialization of services in the United States.

12.4.3 Vocational training and human capital

Not all human capital is accumulated in schools, so it is important to supplement the data on formal education with data on vocational training. It is also important to draw a distinction between higher-level and intermediate-level vocational training. Higher-level training is taken to cover vocational qualifications at the standard of a university degree, including membership of professional institutions, while intermediate-level training is taken to cover craft and technician qualifications above secondary level but below degree level, including non-examined time-served apprenticeships (Prais 1995: 17). We begin with intermediate-level skills, paying particular attention to developments in the service sector since the Second World War.

Table 12.7 provides apprentice-to-employment ratios in Britain, Germany, and the United States. As well as economy-wide ratios, estimates are also provided on a sectoral basis where available. Data are taken from official sources including occupational censuses for all three countries and various inquiries into apprenticeship training. Traditionally, apprenticeships have been concentrated in the industrial sector, and this is reflected in Table 12.7. The most striking finding is the much lower proportion of apprentices in US industry compared with both Britain and Germany throughout the period. The most important factor here is the different approaches to training in manufacturing on the two sides of the Atlantic, with US manufacturing oriented towards mass production with unskilled or semi-skilled labour and European manufacturing more oriented towards flexible production with skilled craft workers (Broadberry 1997a).

In services, although apprentice-to-employment ratios were also substantially lower in the United States than in Britain and Germany throughout the period, the transatlantic gap was smaller than in industry before the Second World War. This reflected the fact that the absolute numbers involved in service sector apprenticeship were small, even in Germany. After the Second World War, however, the German lead in the provision of intermediate-level vocational training in services became substantial, with the spread of apprenticeship into services. Given the importance of developments within services for the German overtaking of Britain in terms of aggregate labour productivity during the post-Second World War period, this German lead in the provision of intermediate-level vocational skills in services is of major significance.

Turning to higher-level vocational training, an important aspect of human capital accumulation was the early development in Britain of professional

Table 12.7. Apprentices as a percentage of persons engaged in Great Britain, Germany, and the United States, 1895–1991

(a) Great Britain

	Agriculture	Industry	Services	Whole economy
1906		4.19	0.65	2.48
1925		5.02	0.50	2.54
1951	0.17	3.22	0.59	1.87
1961	1.41	4.61	2.69	3.56
1966	1.34	5.08	3.18	4.01
1971	1.11	4.05	2.74	3.28
1981	0.56	3.67	1.98	2.58

(b) Germany[a]

	Agriculture	Industry	Services	Whole economy
1895		7.67	1.60	2.99
1907		6.38	1.60	2.87
1925		7.64	0.40	3.18
1933		6.48	0.48	2.28
1950	0.50	7.87	3.89	4.75
1957	0.73	6.95	6.33	5.70
1962	0.77	4.78	5.65	4.62
1969	1.60	4.99	5.50	4.89
1980	3.47	7.94	5.29	6.34
1988	3.89	7.39	5.31	6.08

(c) United States

	Agriculture	Industry	Services	Whole economy
1880		0.95	0.07	0.25
1900		0.87	0.06	0.28
1920		0.91	0.06	0.34
1930		0.56	0.03	0.19
1940		0.47	0.02	0.16
1952		0.74	0.03	0.26
1960		0.72		0.24
1970		0.98		0.31
1975		1.00		0.29
1991		0.84		0.20

[a] Former West Germany for the period after 1950.
Source: Broadberry (2003: 112).

bodies, an important function of which was to oversee professional training (Carr-Saunders and Wilson 1933; Reader 1966). The majority of these qualified professionals worked in the service sector, where Britain had a labour productivity lead over Germany and the United States in the late nineteenth century.

Table 12.8. Professionals in Britain, the United States, and Germany, 1880–1991
(a) Higher professionals in Great Britain, 1881–1991 (000s)

	1881	1911	1931	1951	1971	1991
Church	38	44	48	49	41	34
Medicine	21	35	46	62	80	115
Law	20	26	23	27	39	82
Engineering	24	24	51	138	343	542
Writing	7	15	21	26	51	79
Armed forces	8	14	16	46	40	34
Accounting	13	11	16	37	127	171
Science	1	7	20	49	95	114
Total	132	176	240	434	816	1,173

(b) Higher and lower professions as a % of total employment in Great Britain, the United States, and Germany, circa 1880 to 1950 (%)

	1880	1890	1900	1910	1920	1930	1950
Great Britain	3.6	3.7	4.0	4.1	4.3	4.4	6.1
United States	3.1	3.7	4.0	4.4	5.0	6.1	7.5
Germany			2.6	2.8	2.6	3.0	3.5

Source: Broadberry (2003: 116).

Table 12.8 presents data on the employment of professionals in the three countries since 1881. The British data allow a distinction between higher and lower professions, and data on the higher professions are shown in panel (a). The definition is taken from Routh (1965), and corresponds broadly with the concept of higher-level skills employed here, requiring a qualification at the standard of a university degree (Prais 1995). Although the key higher professions in the nineteenth century were in the Church, medicine, and law, the twentieth century has seen the growing importance of engineering, science, and accounting. Increasingly, these professions have come to be restricted to graduate entry, so that in recent times information on professional associations does not substantially alter the picture of human capital levels gleaned from data on higher education.

To measure the growth of the professions on a comparative basis, it is necessary to include the lower professions as well as the higher professions, in panel (b) of Table 12.8. Britain started the period with a higher share of the occupied population in the professions, but the United States had pulled ahead by the end of the nineteenth century. Although much of the existing literature on the professions concentrates on social aspects and eschews quantification, the idea of a leading role for Britain in the professionalization of society during the nineteenth century and a leading role for the United States during the first half of the twentieth century does seem to be widely accepted (Perkin 1996; Gilb

1966). In Germany, the effects of the large agricultural sector with low value added, and the resulting low per capita incomes, can be seen in the restricted growth of the professions, in line with the stunted growth of the service sector. Figures for the inter-war period suggest a substantially smaller professional sector in Germany through to 1950 (McClelland 1991).

For some professional groups, it is possible to chart the growth of qualifications on a comparative basis. Broadberry (2003: 118) shows that the share of professional accountants in the British labour force has been unusually high compared with the United States, and especially compared with Germany, throughout the twentieth century. Although the high degree of reliance on professional accountants in Britain has been widely noted in the contemporary business literature, the long-standing nature of this reliance has been less widely commented upon (Handy et al. 1988; Matthews et al. 1997). Matthews et al. (1997) explain it at least in part by the nature of the British capital market, with its emphasis on market transactions rather than German-style long-term internalized relationships, which generated an early and growing need for independent auditors.

Although British services almost certainly had a human capital advantage over the United States during the late nineteenth century in terms of the proportion of workers with higher-level professional qualifications, this was increasingly offset by the rapid growth of higher education in the United States, particularly after the Second World War.

In the period since 1979, increased data availability from labour force surveys means that it is possible to present comparisons of the stocks of skilled workers, combining qualifications attained through both formal education and vocational training. Table 12.9 presents the percentage of the workforce

Table 12.9. Skill proportions of the workforce, aggregate economy, 1979–2000 (%)

	US	UK	France	Germany
1979				
Higher	18.7	8.3	5.6	4.2
Intermediate	17.4	28.2	54.9	61.2
Low	63.9	63.5	39.5	34.6
1989				
Higher	23.7	10.8	8.2	6.0
Intermediate	21.4	35.3	61.1	67.0
Low	54.9	53.9	30.7	27.0
2000				
Higher	27.6	18.6	11.7	8.2
Intermediate	25.3	37.0	67.3	71.7
Low	47.1	44.4	21.0	20.1

Source: O'Mahony et al. (2004).

with qualifications at three levels, namely Higher (degree or equivalent), Intermediate (secondary school qualification at age 18 and certified vocational qualifications deemed above the level achieved by pupils leaving school at age 16), and Low skills (no certified qualifications). This illustrates the well-known finding that Britain has a skills gap relative to the United States at the higher level but performs better than the European countries in this respect. However, Britain has a large gap in intermediate skills relative to the European countries.

Compared with Germany and France, Britain has shown a greater narrowing of the higher skills gap with the US, in particular during the 1990s. This has resulted from a more rapid expansion of higher education in Britain than in Germany or France, so that by the beginning of the twenty-first century, Britain was sending roughly the same share of its young people to university as the United States. To the extent that degree and equivalent qualifications are those most in demand in adopting and using information technology, it could be argued that Britain has upgraded its skill base more successfully than the other European economies. However, the intermediate skills gap remains very large, with Britain still in a position where a large section of the working population have no more than basic skills. Note that the categorization by skill group for the United States does not include high school graduates in the intermediate group since this is an attainment rather than a qualification measure—all pupils in the US who finish high school graduate—and so it is difficult to compare with the European economies. If high school graduates were included, then the US intermediate proportions would be about 57 per cent in both 1979 and 2000, comparable to proportions in France and Germany.

12.4.4 Growth accounting

Growth accounting estimates, showing the contributions of labour quality, physical capital, and TFP to UK labour productivity growth, are shown in Table 12.10. These estimates are derived by weighting inputs by their shares of value added, assuming constant returns to scale and perfect markets. Traditionally, growth accounting is used to break down the growth of output into the parts attributable to the growth of factor inputs and residual TFP growth:

$$g_Y = \alpha g_K + \beta g_H + \gamma g_L + g_{TFP} \tag{1}$$

where g_Y, g_K, g_H, and g_L are the growth rates of output, physical capital, human capital, and raw labour, respectively, and α, β, and γ are the shares of each factor in national income. Here we are interested in accounting for labour productivity growth, so subtracting the growth of raw labour from both sides

Table 12.10. Growth of output and labour productivity in Britain and the contributions of labour quality, capital deepening, and TFP, 1873–1973 (percentage points per annum)

	1873–1913	1913–24	1924–37	1937–51	1951–73	1973–89	1989–2000
Output	1.8	−0.1	2.2	1.8	2.8	1.8	2.8
Hours worked	0.9	−2.3	1.5	0.1	−0.5	0.1	−0.5
Output per hour	0.9	2.2	0.7	1.7	3.3	1.7	3.3
Contributions of:							
Labour quality	0.5	1.2	0.4	0.7	0.5	0.7	0.5
Capital per hour	0.4	1.2	0.1	0.3	1.0	0.3	1.0
TFP	0.0	−0.2	0.2	0.7	1.8	0.7	1.8

Sources and notes: 1873–1973: derived from Matthews et al. (1982: 208, 501); 1973–2000: derived from the data in O'Mahony and van Ark (2003), backdated to 1973 using data in O'Mahony (1999).

under the assumption of constant returns to scale ($\alpha + \beta + \gamma = 1$) yields the accounting identity used in Table 12.10:

$$g_Y - g_L = \alpha(g_K - g_L) + \beta(g_H - g_L) + g_{TFP} \qquad (2)$$

The left-hand side is now the growth of output per hour worked, and this can be accounted for by capital deepening, an improvement in the quality of the labour force, and residual TFP growth.

For the period 1873–1973, the data in Table 12.10 are taken from the study by Matthews et al. (1982). The growth of output per hour worked shows a U-shaped pattern, with relatively slow growth during the peak-to-peak inter-war period 1924–37. However, note that the high labour productivity growth across the First World War was largely the result of the sharp reduction in the length of the working week from 54 to 47 hours in 1919–20 (Dowie 1975; Broadberry 1990). Note also that the number of hours worked ceased to grow substantially after the end of the 1930s as population growth slowed down and annual hours worked per person continued to decline. Before the Second World War, labour productivity growth was largely explained by capital deepening and improvements in the quality of the labour force. However, after the Second World War, TFP growth became more important.

For the period since 1973, data are taken from O'Mahony (1999) and O'Mahony and van Ark (2003).[2] These estimates suggest a decline in output growth and labour productivity growth in the period after 1973, which fits in

---

[2] Physical capital input is based on a finer division of asset types. In particular ICT assets are distinguished from other equipment and given a relatively high weight due mainly to their rapid depreciation and hence high marginal productivities. The labour quality adjustment is also based on a finer division by type of labour, so care must be taken in making comparisons with the pre-1973 period.

with the widely accepted view of slower growth in the western world at this time (Matthews 1982). These figures also suggest that the period since 1989 has seen a return to the labour productivity growth of the golden age of the 1950s and 1960s. Again, as during the golden age, this rapid labour productivity growth is only partly explained by the rapid growth of physical capital and skills, leaving an important role for TFP growth.

12.4.5 *Accounting for comparative productivity levels*

A more complete picture can be obtained by breaking down Britain's productivity gap with the United States, Germany, and France. To do this requires adapting the growth accounting identity (2), which compares labour productivity in a single country at different points in time and assesses the contributions of changing factor inputs and TFP. We now need to compare labour productivity between different countries at a single point in time, and assess the contributions of differences in labour quality, capital intensity, and TFP:

$$ln\ Y/L^{US} - ln\ Y/L^{UK} = (ln\ A^{US} - ln\ A^{UK}) + \alpha\ (ln\ K/L^{US} - ln\ K/L^{UK})$$
$$+ \beta\ (ln\ H/L^{US} - ln\ H/L^{UK}) \tag{3}$$

The term on the left-hand side of (3) is the proportional labour productivity difference between two countries, superscripted by USA and UK. This is explained by differences in TFP, differences in capital intensity, and differences in the quality of the labour force.

For the period to 1973, data in Table 12.11 are taken from Broadberry (2003), and work in terms of accounting for the differences in output per person engaged. For the US/UK comparison, labour quality made little contribution to explaining the total labour productivity gap, which rose from 17.7 percentage points in 1910 to 66.9 percentage points by 1950, before narrowing to 52.3 percentage points in 1973. Capital intensity made the biggest contribution to explaining the US/UK labour productivity gap before 1950, after which TFP became more important. This echoes the growing importance of TFP in explaining the growth of British labour productivity after the Second World War, noted in the earlier discussion of Table 12.10. For the Germany/UK case, by contrast, TFP was the most important factor behind the labour productivity gap until 1950. However, it must be stressed that this was a negative labour productivity gap, with Britain achieving higher levels of labour productivity as a result of higher TFP levels. By 1973, however, we see the growing importance of labour force quality in explaining the emergence of a German labour productivity advantage over Britain, with capital intensity playing a secondary role, and any remaining British TFP advantage being of minor importance.

Table 12.12 brings the story up to the beginning of the twenty-first century, but working in terms of differences in output per hour worked. The key finding

323

is that in 2000, as in 1973, TFP plays a much bigger role in explaining Britain's labour productivity gap with the United States than it does in explaining Britain's labour productivity gap with continental Europe. In 2000, whereas TFP explains around half of Britain's labour productivity gap with the United States, it explains only a very small part of Britain's labour productivity gap with Germany. Furthermore, in the comparison with France, TFP is higher in Britain despite labour productivity being higher in France. Tables 12.11 and 12.12 taken together are thus consistent with the view that accumulation of

Table 12.11. Contributions of labour quality, capital intensity, and TFP to Britain's labour productivity gap, 1910–73 (percentage points)

(*a*) US/UK

	Labour quality	Capital intensity	TFP	Total labour productivity gap
1910	−1.9	30.1	10.5	17.7
1929	0.6	23.6	15.2	39.4
1950	0.3	20.9	45.7	66.9
1973	1.9	10.8	39.6	52.3

(*b*) Germany/UK

	Labour quality	Capital intensity	TFP	Total labour productivity gap
1910	−0.1	0.2	−24.6	−24.5
1929	−0.6	−5.6	−19.7	−25.9
1950	−0.6	−2.6	−22.6	−25.6
1973	9.5	5.4	−0.9	14.0

Source: Broadberry (2003: 125–6).

Table 12.12. Decomposition of comparative labour productivity levels, 2000

	US/UK	Germany/UK	France/UK
Total economy:			
Total labour productivity gap	24.3	16.8	20.7
Percentage contribution to comparative labour productivity:			
Labour quality	0.4	3.7	3.6
Physical capital	12.6	11.7	17.1
TFP	11.3	1.4	−0.2

Source: Own calculations employing data underlying O'Mahony and de Boer (2002) and O'Mahony and van Ark (2003).

physical and human capital largely explains the overtaking of Britain by continental European economies such as Germany and France in the post-war period. Accumulation appears also to have played an important role in US forging ahead in the first half of the twentieth century. However, during the post-war period, US labour productivity leadership has rested largely on innovation leading to higher levels of TFP.

12.5 Concluding comments

The catching-up and convergence perspective recognizes a negative relationship between the starting level of productivity and subsequent productivity growth, which helps to avoid too pessimistic an evaluation of Britain's productivity performance during the twentieth century. For Britain in 1900 had a relatively high level of productivity, and subsequently grew more slowly than other countries which were catching up. However, this framework cannot provide a complete explanation, since Britain had already been overtaken by the United States in 1900, and continued to fall further behind until the 1950s. Furthermore, Britain was not only caught up by most West European countries by the end of the 1960s, but also continued to fall behind during the 1970s. Although the relative decline was stemmed during the 1980s, it was not decisively reversed, and by the end of the twentieth century Britain continued to have a substantial labour productivity gap with both the United States and continental Europe.

The sectoral breakdown of Britain's comparative productivity performance sheds light on the factors behind British relative decline. We see that Britain's position in the late nineteenth century was quite fragile because overall productivity leadership rested on a precocious release of labour from low value-added agriculture, combined with a large, labour-intensive industrial sector that did not achieve particularly high levels of labour productivity. As other countries industrialized, Britain's overall productivity leadership was threatened, and a loss of labour productivity leadership in services exacerbated the problem. The low point of Britain's comparative productivity performance was reached during the post- Second World War period, with the widespread adoption of Fordist mass production methods in industry and an acceleration in the 'industrialization' of services. Difficulties of adjustment to these new forms of technology and organization led to substantial relative economic decline in Britain during this period. However, with a return to more flexible forms of production based on ICT from the 1980s, in both industry and services, Britain's relative economic decline has been stemmed, and has recently shown signs of being reversed.

Physical capital and human capital have both played an important part in Britain's productivity performance, accounting for large portions of British labour productivity growth and Britain's labour productivity gaps with the United States and continental Europe. However, the importance of technology and organization also shows up in the contribution of TFP.

References

Abramovitz, M. (1986). 'Catching Up, Forging Ahead and Falling Behind'. *Journal of Economic History*, 46: 385–406.

—— and David, P. A. (1973). 'Reinterpreting Economic Growth: Parables and Realities'. *American Economic Review*, 63: 428–39.

—— —— (1996). 'Convergence and Deferred Catch-up', in R. Landau, T. Taylor, and G. Wright (eds.), *The Mosaic of Economic Growth*. Stanford, CA: Stanford University Press, 21–62.

Alford, B. W. E. (1988). *British Economic Performance, 1945–1975*. London: Macmillan.

Ames, E., and Rosenberg, N. (1968). 'The Enfield Arsenal in Theory and History'. *Economic Journal*, 78: 827–42.

Atkinson, A. B., and Stiglitz, J. E. (1969). 'A New View of Technological Change'. *Economic Journal*, 79: 573–8.

Bardou, J. P., Chanaron, J. J., Fridenson, P., and Laux, J. M. (1982). *The Automobile Revolution: The Impact of an Industry*. Chapel Hill, NC: University of North Carolina Press.

Barnett, C. (1986). *The Audit of War: The Illusion and Reality of Britain as a Great Nation*. London: Macmillan.

Baumol, W. J. (1986). 'Productivity Growth, Convergence and Welfare: What the Long-Run Data Show'. *American Economic Review*, 76: 1072–85.

Booth, A. (2001). *The British Economy in the Twentieth Century*. Basingstoke: Palgrave.

Boyce, G. H. (1995). *Information, Mediation and Institutional Development: The Rise of Large-Scale Enterprise in British Shipping, 1870–1919*. Manchester: Manchester University Press.

Braverman, H. (1974). *Labor and Monopoly Capital: The Degradation of Work in the Twentieth Century*. New York: Monthly Review Press.

Broadberry, S. N. (1990). 'The Emergence of Mass Unemployment: Explaining Macroeconomic Trends in Britain during the Trans-World War I Period'. *Economic History Review*, 43: 271–82.

—— (1993). 'Manufacturing and the Convergence Hypothesis: What the Long-Run Data Show'. *Journal of Economic History*, 53: 772–95.

—— (1994). 'Technological Leadership and Productivity Leadership in Manufacturing since the Industrial Revolution: Implications for the Convergence Debate'. *Economic Journal*, 104: 291–302.

—— (1997a). *The Productivity Race: British Manufacturing in International Perspective, 1850–1990*. Cambridge: Cambridge University Press.

—— (1997b). 'Forging Ahead, Falling Behind and Catching-Up: A Sectoral Analysis of Anglo-American Productivity Differences, 1870–1990'. *Research in Economic History*, 17: 1–37.

—— (1997c). 'Anglo-German Productivity Differences 1870–1990: A Sectoral Analysis'. *European Review of Economic History*, 1: 247–67.

Broadberry, S. N. (1998). 'How did the United States and Germany Overtake Britain? A Sectoral Analysis of Comparative Productivity Levels, 1870–1990'. *Journal of Economic History*, 58: 37–407.

—— (2003). 'Human Capital and Productivity Performance: Britain, the United States and Germany, 1870–1990', in P. A. David and M. Thomas (eds.), *The Economic Future in Historical Perspective*. Oxford: The British Academy and Oxford University Press.

—— (2004*a*). 'The Performance of Manufacturing', in R. Floud and P. Johnson (eds.), *The Cambridge Economic History of Modern Britain*, iii: *Structural Change, 1939–1999*. Cambridge: Cambridge University Press.

—— (2004*b*). 'Explaining Anglo-German Productivity Differences in Services since 1870'. *European Review of Economic History*, 8: 229–62.

—— and Crafts, N. F. R. (2003). 'UK Productivity Performance from 1950 to 1979: A Restatement of the Broadberry–Crafts View'. *Economic History Review*, 56: 718–35.

—— and Ghosal, S. (2002). 'From the Counting House to the Modern Office: Explaining Anglo-American Productivity Differences in Services, 1870–1990'. *Journal of Economic History*, 62: 967–98.

—— and O'Mahony, M. (2004). 'Britain's Productivity Gap with the United States and Europe: A Historical Perspective'. *National Institute Economic Review*, 189: 72–85.

Carr-Saunders, A. M., and Wilson, P. A. (1933). *The Professions*. Oxford: Oxford University Press.

Chandler, A. D., Jr. (1977). *The Visible Hand: The Managerial Revolution in American Business*. Cambridge, Mass.: Harvard University Press.

Channon, D. F. (1978). *The Service Industries: Strategy, Structure and Financial Performance*. London: Macmillan.

Crafts, N. F. R., and Toniolo, G. (1996). 'Postwar Growth: An Overview', in N. F. R. Crafts and G. Toniolo (eds.), *Economic Growth in Europe since 1945*. Cambridge: Cambridge University Press.

David, P. A. (1975). *Technical Choice, Innovation and Economic Growth*. Cambridge: Cambridge University Press.

—— and Wright, G. (1999). 'Early Twentieth Century Productivity Growth Dynamics: An Inquiry into the Economic History of "Our Ignorance" '. Unpublished, All Souls College, Oxford.

Denison, E. F. (1967). *Why Growth Rates Differ: Post-War Experience in Nine Western Countries*. Washington: The Brookings Institution.

Dintenfass, M. (1982). *The Decline of Industrial Britain, 1870–1990*. London: Routledge.

Dowie, J. A. (1975). '1919–20 is in Need of Attention'. *Economic History Review*, 28: 429–50.

Easterlin, R. A. (1981). 'Why isn't the Whole World Developed?' *Journal of Economic History*, 41: 1–19.

Edquist, C., and Jacobsson, S. (1988). *Flexible Automation: The Global Diffusion of Technology in the Engineering Industry*. Oxford: Blackwell.

Elbaum, B., and Lazonick, W. (eds.) (1986). *The Decline of the British Economy*. Oxford: Clarendon.

Flora, P. (1983). *State, Economy and Society in Western Europe, 1815–1975: A Data Handbook in Two Volumes*. Frankfurt: Campus Verlag.

Foreman-Peck, J. (1982). 'The American Challenge of the Twenties: Multinationals and the European Motor Industry'. *Journal of Economic History*, 43: 405–31.

Gilb, C. L. (1966). *Hidden Hierarchies: The Professions and Government*. New York: Harper & Row.

Goldin, C. (1998). 'America's Graduation from High School: The Evolution and Spread of Secondary Schooling in the Twentieth Century'. *Journal of Economic History*, 58: 345–74.

—— and Katz, L. (1996). 'Technology, Skill, and the Wage Structure: Insights from the Past'. *American Economic Review, Papers and Proceedings*, 86: 252–7.

Greif, A. (1989). 'Reputation and Coalitions in Medieval Trade: Maghribi Traders'. *Journal of Economic History*, 49: 857–82.

—— (2000). 'The Fundamental Problem of Exchange: A Research Agenda in Historical Institutional Analysis'. *European Review of Economic History*, 4: 251–84.

Habakkuk, H. J. (1962). *American and British Technology in the Nineteenth Century*. Cambridge: Cambridge University Press.

Handy, C., Gordon, C., Gow, I., and Randlesome, C. (1988). *Making Managers*. London: Pitman.

Juergens, U., Malsch, T., and Dohse, K. (1993). *Breaking from Taylorism: Changing Forms of Work in the Automobile Industry*. Cambridge: Cambridge University Press.

Kirby, M. W. (1981). *The Decline of British Economic Power since 1870*. London: Allen and Unwin.

Lewchuk, W. (1987). *American Technology and the British Vehicle Industry*. Cambridge: Cambridge University Press.

Lindert, P. H. (2001). 'Democracy, Decentralization, and Mass Schooling before 1914: Appendices'. Working Paper No. 105, Agricultural History Center, University of California, Davis.

McClelland, C. E. (1991). *The German Experience of Professionalization: Modern Learned Professions and their Organizations from the Early Nineteenth Century to the Hitler Era*. Cambridge: Cambridge University Press.

McCloskey, D. N. (1970). 'Did Victorian Britain Fail?' *Economic History Review*, 23: 446–59.

McKinsey Global Institute (1993). *Manufacturing Productivity*. Washington: McKinsey.

Maddison, A. (1987). 'Growth and Slowdown in Advanced Capitalist Economies: Techniques of Quantitative Assessment'. *Journal of Economic Literature*, 25: 649–98.

—— (1995). *Monitoring the World Economy, 1820–1992*. Paris: OECD.

—— (2001). *The World Economy: A Millennial Perspective*. Paris: OECD.

Matthews, D., Anderson, M., and Edwards, J. R. (1997). 'The Rise of the Professional Accountant in British Management'. *Economic History Review*, 50: 407–29.

Matthews, R. C. O. (ed.) (1982). *Slower Growth in the Western World*. London: Heinemann.

—— Feinstein, C. H., and Odling-Smee, J. C. (1982). *British Economic Growth, 1856–1973*. Oxford: Oxford University Press.

Milgrom, P. and Roberts, J. (1990). 'The Economics of Modern Manufacturing: Technology, Strategy and Organisation'. *American Economic Review*, 80: 511–28.

Mitch, D. F. (1992). *The Rise of Literacy in Victorian England: The Influence of Private Choice and Public Policy*. Philadelphia: University of Pennsylvania Press.

Mitchell, B. R. (1975). *European Historical Statistics, 1750–1970*. London: Macmillan.

O'Mahony, M. (1999). *Britain's Productivity Performance, 1950–1996: An International Perspective*. London: National Institute of Economic and Social Research.

O'Mahony, M. and de Boer, W. (2002). 'Britain's Relative Productivity Performance: Has Anything Changed?' *National Institute Economic Review*, January: 38–43.

—— and van Ark, B. (2003). *EU Productivity and Competitiveness: An Industry Perspective. Can Europe Resume the Catching-up Process?* Brussels: European Commission, Enterprise publications.

—— Robinson, C., and Vecchi, M. (2004). 'Skill Biased Technological Change'. Unpublished, National Institute of Economic and Social Research, London.

Perkin, H. (1996). *The Third Revolution: Professional Elites in the Modern World*. London: Routledge.

Pollard, S. (1984). *The Wasting of the British Economy: British Economic Policy, 1945 to the Present*, 2nd ed. London: Croom Helm.

Prais, S. J. (1995). *Productivity, Education and Training: An International Perspective*. Cambridge: Cambridge University Press.

Reader, W. J. (1966). *Professional Men: The Rise of the Professional Classes in Nineteenth-Century England*. London: Weidenfeld & Nicolson.

Ringer, F. K. (1979). *Education and Society in Modern Europe*. Bloomington: Indiana University Press.

Routh, G. (1965). *Occupation and Pay in Great Britain, 1906–1960*. Cambridge: Cambridge University Press.

Rubinstein, W. D. (1993). *Capitalism, Culture and Decline in Britain, 1750–1990*. London: Routledge.

Sturmey, S. G. (1962). *British Shipping and World Competition*. London: Athlone.

Triplett, J. E., and Bosworth, B. P. (2003). 'Productivity Measurement in Service Industries: "Baumol's Disease" has been Cured'. *Federal Reserve Bank of New York Economic Policy Review*, 9/3: 23–33.

Wiener, M. J. (1981). *English Culture and the Decline of the Industrial Spirit, 1850–1980*. Cambridge: Cambridge University Press.

13

Immigration and the Labour Market

Dudley Baines

This chapter discusses the main features of British immigration and emigration in the twentieth century and their effect on the labour market. We will see that, for a long time, there were strict rules governing who could enter the country and work, but this policy was never related to the needs of the labour market, as the government saw it. A recent survey concluded that the UK was probably the only European country where immigration policy was not, specifically, related to the labour market (Hansen 2000). For long periods there were no restrictions on the entry of certain groups but this was part of a blanket policy, which had little directly to do with the labour market. Selective policies were introduced on occasion, but they were usually a short-term (and possibly unconsidered) political reaction to an immediate political problem. A major consideration is that for the majority of the twentieth century, Britain has had a net outward migration balance. This was related to immigration policy in several ways. Returning British emigrants were an important component of immigration. And, in some years, immigration policy was constrained because it was related to the concept of the British Empire (later, Commonwealth).

One consequence of the relative lack of official interest in the characteristics of individual immigrants is that data concerning immigration are limited. Before the Second World War, annual inward sailings—obviously an unsatisfactory measure—often have to be used as a proxy for immigration. A stricter definition of immigrant was used after the Second World War, but that must have underestimated the true flow since there was a major break of trend in 1964 when the UN definition of immigrant was adopted. One important group (the Irish) have virtually never been counted, except from the stock of Irish-born residents.[1] Finally, the main sources concerning the characteristics of the migrant stock have only recently been available, for example in the (partly

[1] Before 1991, it was not acceptable to ask questions about ethnic origin in the census. Respondents were normally asked to give their place of birth, but not, in every census, that of their parents, so that British-born children of immigrant parents could not be identified. It was

panel) *Labour Force Survey* (LFS), which was started in 1979. Before 1992 the sample was small, however.[2]

It is important to note that the majority of immigrants to Britain were not from an ethnic minority. Although ethnicity has dominated the literature, only 30 per cent of the immigrants since the Second World War came from the New Commonwealth (and Pakistan).[3] (Even if was assumed that all immigrants from the Old Commonwealth, Western Europe, and the USA were white and all the rest were from an ethnic minority, a gross over-assumption, the majority of immigrants, in virtually every year, would have been white.)

13.1 British immigration

Tables 13.1 and 13.2 show the most important features of British immigration since the Second World War. The years may be divided into four periods. In the first period (1946–63), the IPS data show that there was heavy emigration to the New Commonwealth (76,000 p.a.), but do not record the countervailing net immigration of more than a million from continental Europe and Ireland. New Commonwealth immigration in this period was very low (32,000 p.a., 8,000 net), many of whom were returning expatriates. In the second period, (1964–73) emigration (still mainly to the Old Commonwealth) exceeded immigration by about 50,000 p.a. (Table 13.3) Irish immigration fell, but movement to and from the USA and Western Europe increased. The main feature was an increase in ethnic minority immigration of 83,000 p.a. (31,000 net) despite increasing restriction.[4] The next period (1973–82) saw the effect of the restrictions on New Commonwealth immigration, which fell by 25 per cent. There was also a fall in (mainly Old Commonwealth) emigration of about 30,000 p.a. In the last period (1983–99), immigration resumed its upward trend from 153,000 in 1981 to 332,000 (80,000 net) in 1998 and 480,000 (171,000 net) in 2001.[5] But, over the whole period, the rate is still small—not much more than 1/000 of the population (ONS 2000: 370). New Commonwealth immigration

thought that if people were asked to answer sensitive questions, the census as a whole might be compromised.

[2] From 1992, the LFS was taken every quarter. Sixty-four thousand households (about 167,000 individuals) are tracked for five consecutive quarters. Previously, characteristics could only be examined by pooling, at the cost of losing longitudinal data.

[3] i.e. Pakistani, Bangladeshi, Chinese, Indian, African, and West Indian immigrants. Pakistan left the Commonwealth in 1972, but is included for statistical purposes. Hence, the acronym NCWP. The Old Commonwealth includes Canada, Australia, and New Zealand. South Africa also left the Commonwealth and was subsequently readmitted. South African migration is excluded from both New and Old Commonwealth totals.

[4] Estimates of net Irish migration are +15,000 p.a. in 1961–71 and +15,000 in 1971–81, partly because of increasing returns to Ireland.

[5] Immigration fell significantly in the four years 1986, 1987, 1992, 1993, as we would expect from the trade cycle.

Table 13.1. Immigration and emigration, by origin and destination (000s p.a.), 1946–63 (extra-European only)

	Old C	New C	USA	EC/EU	Other	All
In p.a.	+21	+32	+9	n./a.[a]	+11	+72
Out p.a.	−76	−26	−20	n./a.[a]	−13	−135
% of in	29.0	44.6	11.8	n./a.[a]	14.5	100
1964–72 (All destinations)						
In p.a.	+45	+83	+21	+40	+30	+218
Out p.a.	−134	−52	−27	−40	−29	−280
% of in	20.1	38.0	9.4	18.2	13.8	100
1973–82 (All destinations)						
In p.a.	+35	+60	+17	+30	+42	+184
Out p.a.	−76	−47	−24	−39	−43	−227
% of in	18.8	32.9	9.0	16.5	23.0	100
1983–2001 (All destinations)						
In: p.a.	+42	+70	+26	+79	+87	+305
Out p.a.	−54	−30	−31	−74	−53	−241
% of in	+13.8	+22.8	+8.5	+26.0	+28.6	100

Notes: Old C = 'Old Commonwealth' (mainly Canada, Australia, New Zealand)

New C = 'New Commonwealth' (mainly India, Pakistan, Bangladesh, West Indies, Hong Kong, Singapore). South Africa is excluded from both.

[a] About 250,000 Continental Europeans and 800,000 Irish are thought to have entered (net of returns) in this period.

Source: OPCS (later, ONS), *Population Trends*.

Table 13.2. Recorded net migration p.a., 1946–2001 (000s p.a.)

	In	Out	Net
1946–63	+72	−136	−63
1964–72	+218	−286	−68
1973–82	+184	−227	−44
1983–2001	+305	−241	+64

Source: OPCS (later, ONS), *Population Trends*, various issues.

was little higher than in the previous period (70,000 p.a.) but returns fell—as we would expect with continued restrictions. Irish immigration also fell. The main change in the period was large gross (relatively small net) flows between Britain and other developed countries, particularly the EU and the USA. But, by the late 1990s, net flows from poorer countries began to increase, leading to media interest.

This chapter will concentrate on the most important migration streams. We start with a discussion of the implications of Empire (later Commonwealth) migration. For the greater part of the century this largely comprised British emigration to the white Dominions, but in the later 1950s, the flows

Table 13.3. Immigrants of working age, United Kingdom, 1979 and 2000, by birthplace

	1979	2000
Old Commonwealth	0.7	0.4
West Indies		
Africa	0.3	0.6
India	1.2	1.2
Pakistan	0.4	0.7
Bangladesh	0.1	0.3
Chinese	0.2	0.2
Other non-white	0.6	1.2
Irish	1.4	0.8
EU	1.0	1.4
New Commonwealth	0.4	0.8
Other Europe (non EU)	0.4	0.4
Other white	0.9	1.3
White UK-born	92.2	88.3
Non-white UK-born	0.5	2.4

Notes: Working age = 16–60 for women and 16–65 for men.
'Old Commonwealth' = Australia, New Zealand, Canada.
Source: Dustmann et al. (2003: 21).

increasingly comprised ethnic minority immigrants into the UK. The tensions related to this movement mirrored the transition from a 'British' Empire to a multi-ethnic 'Commonwealth'. We will also consider what used to be termed 'alien' (i.e. non-British or Empire) immigration. Unlike Empire migration, alien immigration was controlled for most of the twentieth century. Ironically, soon after New Commonwealth immigration began to be restricted Britain entered the European Community (later Union), which gave EU citizens free access to the British labour market. Hence, the entry of some 500 million people which (in theory) had been free became severely restricted, and the entry of some 300 million which had been restricted became free.

13.2 Empire/Commonwealth migration

The data are not easy to interpret, but if we take the net outward movement of British passengers as a proxy, between 1900 and the First World War, some 3.5 million people must have left the country for extra-European destinations and some 1.5 million returned—net emigration of 2 million or a mean net emigration rate of over 3.5/000 p.a. (Table 13.4). (In other words, the very high return rate was already well established in the early twentieth century.) Over a half of the emigrants went to Empire destinations, and a further 30 per cent to the USA. Substantial British emigration to overseas destinations continued after the First World War (more than 2.1/000 p.a. net in 1919–29). Canada,

Table 13.4 Emigration (outward passenger movement) to extra-European destinations, 1900–38 (millions)

	Outward	Inward	Net
1900–14	−3778.8	+1578.4	−2201.4
1919–29	−1789.8	+675.8	−1114.0
1930–38	−319.2	+482.6	+163.4
1919–38	−2109.0	+1158.4	—950.6

Note: Gross outward passenger movement was 3,779.8 million, and gross inward 1,578.4 million (net 2,201.4 million). The estimate of 2 million assumes some double entry.
Source: Carrier and Jeffrey (1953: 91–3).

Emigration (outward passenger movement) to extra-European destinations by country, 1900–1938 (% of all emigrants)

	USA	Canada	Australia NZ	Other
1900–14	30.8	37.2	13.4	17.7
1919–38	16.4	28.9	15.4	39.3

Source: Carrier and Jeffrey (1953: 96–7).

Australia, and New Zealand remained important destinations (44 per cent of all emigrants). Fewer emigrants went to the USA. Thirty-six per cent of Empire emigrants were assisted and, for the first time, some of the assistance came from the UK government through the Empire Settlement Act (1922) (Constantine 1990: 16). Assistance prioritized agricultural labourers, children, and domestic servants. (The latter were seen as helping the post-war 'surplus women' problem.) But there was little government concern about population losses to the economy, either from a quantitative or qualitative perspective. British emigrants were not seen as a loss of labour, but as 'the British overseas'—an ideological construct which, for example, meant that they would fight for Britain in time of war (Constantine 1990: 8). Emigration fell massively in the 1930s. Inward movement exceeded outward by some 150,000, reflecting the serious depression in the traditional British destinations.

British emigration after the Second World War initially followed the pre-war pattern. Recorded emigration from Britain to overseas destinations fluctuated around 150,000 p.a. until the late 1950s and then fell to around 100,000 p.a.[6]

[6] After the Second World War, 'emigration' and 'immigration' were defined more strictly than hitherto. Short-stay migrants who stayed less than a year and those who had lived abroad less than a year were excluded. Before 1964, UK data include only movement by sea, and exclude movement to and from the UK from other parts of Europe. Since 1964, the International Passenger Survey has sampled arrivals and departures although movement to and from the Republic of Ireland is excluded. Data from the two periods cannot be spliced.

But the true level must have been higher since recorded emigration jumped from 107,000 to 273,000 in 1964 when data collection was improved; see Figures 13.1 and 13.2. Before 1970, over a half of this emigration continued to be to the 'Old Commonwealth' countries (Canada, Australia, New Zealand). Australia, in particular, had very generous subsidies for British immigrants. But changed economic circumstances made it more difficult, even for British immigrants, who were prioritized, to enter these countries. Moreover, large numbers of British emigrants returned in the 1960s.[7] Hence, after 1970, emigration shifted to a much wider set of destinations, including much higher flows to Western Europe and the United States.

Irish immigration had been important since the first half of the nineteenth century. However, since they were British nationals, even after Southern Irish

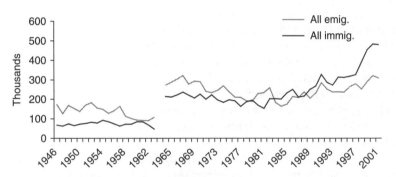

Figure 13.1 Immigration and emigration, 1946–2001

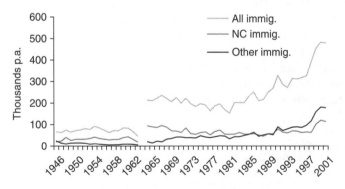

Figure 13.2 'Ethnic minority' immigration into the UK, 1946–2001

---

[7] In fact, many of the so-called 'ten pound' emigrants (£10 was the fare) returned to the UK—23% by 1966 (Jupp 1998: 95).

independence in 1922, Irish immigration was unrecorded. Net migration may be estimated from the stock of Irish-born enumerated in the census. Net inward movement fluctuated between 10,000 and 30,000 p.a. in the 1920s and was probably nearer to the higher level in the 1930s (Walshaw 1941: 72). The Irish were the only significant civilian immigrants during the Second World War when between 100,000 and 150,000 are thought to have entered, plus another 50,000 who served in the British armed forces (Delaney 2000*a*: 130).

After the war, the British economy experienced serious labour shortages, caused by reconstruction, war deaths of prime aged males, and (to some extent) emigration, leading to substantial Irish immigration. Stock data imply net immigration of some 800,000 in the 1950s, equivalent to 16 per cent of the home population and comparable with contemporary flows from southern to northern Europe (Delaney 2000*b*).[8] It also largely countervailed the heavy emigration of the period (Table 13.4). Irish immigration placed the British authorities in some difficulty. Work permits for Irish immigrants had been considered as early as 1928, but were rejected on the grounds that the Free State was a Dominion (i.e. comparable to Canada). Despite the clear importance of Irish immigration to the recovery from the war, and the numbers of Irish-born workers in the new National Health Service, both Labour and Conservative governments considered regulation. (Ireland had ceased to be a Dominion in 1948.[9]) This would have created the equivalent of 'gastarbeiter'. But political sensitivities prevailed. No Irish government would have contemplated a recruitment agreement with the UK, since official policy was to eliminate emigration (Delaney 2000*b*: 342–3). In addition, since the Republic/Ulster border was open, restrictions on Irish immigration would imply immigration controls between two parts of the UK, which was politically impossible. Irish migration fell to 150,000 (net) in both the 1960s and 1970s, partly driven by increasing returns. By the later twentieth century, changes in the Irish economy made Britain less-attractive to highly educated emigrants, although less-skilled immigration continued (Hale 2000: 95).[10] By the 1990s, the 444,000 remaining Irish-born in Britain were older than the native population and relatively unskilled (Woolford 1994).[11] Of course, some Irish immigration had always been temporary—i.e. comprised of 'target earners'—emphasizing the close connection between the British and Irish labour markets.

---

[8] The birthplace of Irish-born included people who stated that they had been born in 'Ireland'. Hence, the Irish-born population includes some people who had been born in Ulster. The majority would have been born in the Republic, however.

[9] Under wartime emergency powers Irish wartime immigration was controlled in both countries.

[10] In the 1990s, 16% of construction workers were Irish-born compared with 7% of British-born.

[11] A half of the Irish-born were over 50. Age-specific participation was relatively high, however.

The first significant ethnic minority immigrants came from the West Indies. Active recruitment (by London Transport among other employers) coincided with the (1952) McCarran–Walter Act, which restricted West Indian immigration into the USA, the traditional destination. By 1964, there were 300,000 West Indians in the UK, most of whom were recent arrivals. The 1960s also saw new flows from Pakistan, Hong Kong, and Singapore (PRO 2000: 13).

As British citizens, these immigrants had the right to live and work in the UK, which had recently confirmed by the Nationality Act of 1948.[12] Of course, in 1948, it was difficult for poor people to exercise this right. The problem for British politicians in the immediate post-war period was that they were anxious to create a multiracial Commonwealth (including an independent India). Hence, official restrictions on New Commonwealth immigration would be problematic. The Foreign Office was encouraging West Indian immigration at the time, for example (Hansen 2000: 26). British politicians did not have to face this issue in 1948 since most New Commonwealth entrants in the 1940s were elite immigrants, such as students and businessmen, who did not impinge on the bulk of the population. But the New Commonwealth immigrants of the late 1950s and early 1960s were different. There were already 'visible' immigrant communities in some British cities, leading to anxieties about jobs and housing that could be exploited by one or two openly racist politicians (Anwar 1995: 17–18). In fact, working-class immigrants, of whatever ethnic origin, had never universally been welcomed in Britain. In the nineteenth century hostility had been directed at the Irish and in the early twentieth century at the Jews, for example.

Political pressure reached a peak in the early 1960s. The Conservative government had already requested some New Commonwealth governments to restrict emigration (Spencer 1994: 38). But in 1962, they passed the Commonwealth Immigrants Act. This introduced a controlled voucher system, based on the 'needs' of the British economy. But these were not economically well-thought-out 'needs'. Vouchers were issued fairly freely, at first, but immigration remained an important issue in the 1964 election, and the incoming Labour government, not to be outdone on the immigration issue, severely restricted the issue of vouchers.[13] By 1965, the UK had the most severe immigration controls in Western Europe with the exception of Switzerland.

The Commonwealth Immigrants Act changed the nature of immigration. All Commonwealth citizens still had equal access to the UK, but, in practice, few vouchers were given to unskilled workers, which had the desired effect, which was seriously to reduce the number of ethnic minority immigrants. In

---

[12] British subjects did not have the same right to enter other Commonwealth countries.
[13] Three types of vouchers were introduced in 1962. Category A was for those with a job offer and B for those with scarce skills. Any immigrant could apply for a Category C voucher, but the numbers were limited by ballot. It was the C vouchers that were abolished in 1965.

the short run, however, the immigration rate increased, as people attempted to 'beat the ban'. New Commonwealth immigration, which had averaged only 33,000 a year in 1954–59, rose to 136,000 in 1961 and 95,000 in the first six months of 1962, including large numbers from the Indian subcontinent. Hence, inflammatory predictions regarding the future size of the ethnic population seemed to have been confirmed.

Unsurprisingly, the 1962 Act did not satisfy the demand for restriction. The voucher scheme was ended in 1971 and replaced with the concept of 'patriality'. Only British citizens with a British-born parent, or EU nationals, could enter without a work permit requested by an employer, although there were exceptions.[14] In practice, work permits were only given to highly skilled immigrants, mainly from developed countries. Further restrictions included removing the right of entry from the inhabitants of the few remaining British colonies (by then called Dependent Territories) in 1981.[15] But at the same time, the Race Relations Act of 1968 prohibited racial discrimination. This was a gesture to the immigrant communities, but it also made a political point. Discrimination would only be minimized if ethnic minority immigration was restricted.

Restriction changed the character, as well as the skill balance, of New Commonwealth immigration. Before 1962, most ethnic minority immigrants were single workers, many of whom may not have intended to stay.[16] But changes in immigration rules made temporary immigration virtually impossible. Moreover, since work permits were difficult to obtain, immigrants sought to enter via other categories, which, for ethnic minorities, exceeded work permit applications. For example, between 1962 and 1978 dependants of ethnic minority immigrants, despite attempts to control them, outnumbered those entering as workers by nearly three to one. (Holmes 1988: 275–7; Coleman 1996: 196).[17] By 1991, more ethnic minority immigrants had entered since the most restrictive legislation was passed in 1971, than had before (Armitage 1994).

The shift away from 'economic' entry mirrored developments in continental Europe. The end of 'catch-up' growth in Western Europe led to severe reductions in the number of temporary 'gastarbeiter'. Western European governments expected that these immigrants would return to their native countries, but most declined, forcing European governments to choose between a policy

---

[14] The main exceptions, where immigrants could work without a permit, were for short 'working holidays', 'au pairs', and seasonal agricultural workers (mainly from Eastern Europe). See Rees (1993: 91).

[15] The purpose was to make it even more difficult for Hong Kong natives to enter Britain following the expected takeover by China. (Natives of the Dependent Territories only regained their right of entry in May 2002.)

[16] Males usually predominated, except for the West Indians, where, in some years, women were in the majority.

[17] Between 1962 and 1968, 140,000 entered as workers and 510,000 as depandants. (Anwar 1995: 275).

of compulsory repatriation or accepting a permanent immigrant labour force. Hence, the 'gastarbeiter' became permanent workers and were soon joined by their dependants (Baines 1998).

13.3 Other immigrants

The foreign-born population of Britain in 1901 was only some 186,000 (0.6 per cent of the population), many of whom were not immigrants. The first substantial immigrant flow was of Eastern European Jews: 120,000 entered Britain, between the 1880s and the First World War (Gartner 1960). Opposition to Jewish immigration led to the first attempt to control immigration into the UK, the Aliens Act of 1905. This was passed in a period of anti-Jewish tension, but was limited to controlling the entry of 'destitute and undesirable aliens', i.e. those who were thought likely to become a public charge (Rees 1993: 91). There was no discussion of the effects of unrestricted immigration on the labour market. In fact, the Act was not strictly enforced, partly because of a change in government. In fact, fewer than 5 per cent of Jewish immigrants were rejected (Garrard 1971: 107). The 1905 Act was extended in 1921 when the Aliens (Restriction) Act introduced permits for alien settlement. The Act was passed at a time when unemployment was politically important and was much more restrictive. In effect, alien immigrants required a permit that was only granted on a case-by-case basis.[18] There was no serious attempt to match immigrants with labour demand, however, and many of the entry decisions must have been arbitrary. A by-product of the 1921 Act, however, was that immigration from Europe could be measured. At the outbreak of the Second World War about 231,000 aliens (i.e. those who had not taken British nationality) were registered with the police, of which 206,000 had entered since 1921 (Carrier and Jeffery 1953: 75). The largest single group was some 50,000–9,000 Jewish refugees.

It is thought that 460,000 foreigners (i.e. non-British citizens) entered the UK in the five years following the Second World War (Anwar 1995). Since aliens had no right of entry, in effect, they could only enter if they had been recruited. The two main groups were, the 'Polish Resettlement Corps' and 'European Volunteer Workers'. One hundred and sixty thousand members of the Polish armed forces decided to remain in the UK, joined by 40,000 dependants.[19] One hundred and one thousand 'European Volunteer Workers',

---

[18] An indication of the increase in the degree of control is that the 1921 legislation affected all incoming passengers, including those travelling first class (the 1905 legislation applied only to steerage passengers) and even those returning from short visits abroad.

[19] Out of 249,000 members of the Polish armed forces under overall British control (many returned to Poland).

mainly from Eastern Europe and including a large number of women, were recruited from displaced person camps (Kay and Miles 1992: 19; PRO 2000: 30–1). The Poles were treated generously compared with the EVWs. The latter were directed to areas of labour shortage—i.e. agriculture, coal mining, and textiles—incidentally, deflecting any trade union opposition.[20] Most settled permanently. And in the early 1950s, about 50,000 (mainly southern) Italians entered, many of whom were directly recruited. They were also directed into particular occupations, but as with the EVWs, restrictions were lifted for those who stayed.

Immigration from outside the Commonwealth increased in the later 1960s and from the Continent after Britain's entry into the EU in 1973. This led to complete mobility between EU countries. By the 1980s and early 1990s, immigration from the EU averaged 76,000 p.a. but only 5,000 net. Immigration from and to the USA was also large (27,000 p.a.) but net migration was effectively zero.[21] Much of this movement was so-called 'elite' migration of highly skilled workers between similar labour markets who either did not need a work permit or had no difficulty in acquiring one. ('Elite' immigrants included British returnees. In the exceptional years of the mid-1980s, returning British emigrants were nearly as numerous as British emigrants.) Finally, in the late 1990s the immigration rate increased sharply.

13.4 Refugee immigration

In effect, the British government had no policy towards refugees in the twentieth century. Decisions seem to have been made in an ad hoc way. For example, whether the refugees would be economically beneficial was rarely considered. The largest refugee group in the twentieth century was some 250,000 refugees from Belgium during the First World War. But they were expected to return, as all did. Hence, the Belgian refugees tell us little about British refugee policy. In fact, Britain has not been generous to refugees. Less than 60,000 Jewish refugees were accepted in the 1930s—not a very generous number in the circumstances.[22] Similarly, at the time of the Hungarian Uprising in 1956, the Home Secretary stated that Britain was not an immigration country, and could

---

[20] A survey of 340,000 displaced persons in German and Austrian camps found that 34% of males were from skilled and 13% from managerial and professional occupations. The proportion for women was 19% and 13%, respectively. There were examples of doctors from the Baltic states directed to cleaning jobs in British hospitals (Kay and Miles 1992: 98).

[21] Note that under IPS definitions, a 'migrant' has to intend to 'settle' for at least a year. In fact, the average stay of a returning immigrant (defined in this way) in the later twentieth century was four years.

[22] 23% (46,000) of aliens registered in 1939 were from 'the German group' (presumably including Austria) but this excludes children. Some of them probably left the country.

not be expected to take many refugees. Only 16,000 were accepted (Patterson 1969: 2). Moreover, the motives for granting entry could be mixed. Apparently, the government tried to 'cherry pick' the most desirable Jewish immigrants in the 1930s, for example (Holmes 1988). Similarly mixed motives were probably in play when the 'Polish Resettlement Corps' and 'European Volunteer Workers, who technically were refugees, entered after the second war. They were directed to areas and occupations with the greatest labour shortage.

The episodes of the Kenyan and Ugandan Asians are instructive. Following Kenyan independence, residents of Asian origin faced severe discrimination. They believed that they had been offered British passports and, hence, entry into the UK as insurance against such an eventuality. But this was in 1968, at the height of an immigration crisis, which was dominating politics. The government was on the horns of a dilemma and, desperate to find a way out, decreed that, because of recent legislation, the particular British passports held by the Kenyan Asians did not give entry.[23] However, when the Kenyan government expelled the Asians, the government's hand was forced: 84,000 entered. The case of the Ugandan Asians in 1972 was different. By then it was clear that their entry guarantee was no longer valid. But since they were also in the process of physical expulsion they too were given entry (28,000 entered) (Hansen 2000: 28–32, 158–60).

There was at no time any argument concerning the benefits to the UK economy of the Asian immigrants. Government policy was entirely determined by political opposition to *all* ethnic minority immigration. In fact, the East African Asians were, on average, older than typical immigrants, a high proportion had owned businesses in East Africa, and 40 per cent of the adults had A levels (18+) or higher qualifications. Many continued as successful entrepreneurs in the UK—characteristics that suggest that they were a net gain to the economy and a net loss to the economies of the East African countries (Robinson 1995: 333, 336).

As is well known, the number of refugees ('asylum seekers' in British parlance) increased substantially in the 1990s. The criteria for accepting refugees were very tightly drawn, allowing the UK government, until recently, to restrict refugee immigration to a trickle. The majority of applicants were rejected, usually on the grounds that they were economic migrants, and did not have a 'well-founded fear of persecution'—a rather subjective criterion. In the early 1990s, there were over 500,000 applicants for political asylum annually to EU countries, of which about 50,000 were to the UK. About 10 per cent were successful.

---

[23] At one point it was argued that British passports issued by the High Commission in Nairobi before independence were less valid for this purpose than passports issued by the British embassy in Nairobi after independence, because the latter had been issued in the UK, but the former had not.

British geography means that direct clandestine entry is difficult. Since direct entry as a refugee is also difficult, a common means has been to enter in one relatively open category—i.e. as tourists or students—and then to claim asylum.[24] In the 1990s, so-called 'switchers' made up two-thirds of refugees in the UK and presented many problems (including the measurement of immigration).[25]

13.5 The effect of immigration on the labour market

The quantitative effects of immigration on the labour market in the UK have been relatively small. Measured by place of birth, 4.8 million people (8 per cent of the population) were immigrants in 2000. About 47 per cent were UK citizens (Spencer 1997: 49). This was about 9 per cent of the working age population, a rise of two percentage points since 1979 (Table 13.4). On the other hand, by the early twenty-first century, immigration was (directly) responsible for more than a third of UK population growth, although population growth was very slow, of course.[26] The ethnic minority population, as self-defined in the *Labour Force Survey*, was about 4 million, or something over 7 per cent of the population.[27]

Since, up to the early twenty-first century, the number of immigrants into the UK has been relatively small, the main effect on the labour market is likely to have been because the characteristics of the immigrants were different from those of the native population—or, possibly, because the characteristics of immigrant children who were born in the UK were different. Hence, the effect of immigration on the labour market depends *inter alia* on age structure, participation rates, and the relative skill level of immigrants and natives. (The latter includes the formal qualifications and whether they were undervalued compared with native qualifications.)

13.6 Participation

Most systematic evidence concerning the characteristics of the immigrant population is taken from the *Labour Force Survey*. As we have seen, the LFS only

[24] The political situation in the 1990s meant that the origins of the refugees were diverse, including Afghanistan, the Balkans, and parts of Africa.

[25] A Home Office survey estimated that the IPS under-counted immigration in the 1980s and early 1990s by 20,000 p.a. (200,000 in all) and that this rate is rising (Coleman 1996). Following the 2001 census, the IPS data for 1991–2001 were increased (Table 13.1).

[26] Taking the EU as a whole, where, typically, natural population growth was lower and the immigration rate was higher than in the UK, immigration was responsible for about 85% of all population growth.

[27] The corresponding figures for 1971, 1981, and 1991 were, respectively, 1.4 million, 2.2 million, and 3.1 million.

began in 1979 and it was 1992 before a sufficiently large sample, was taken. Hence, it has only been possible to rigorously analyse immigrant groups in the last few years. (One of many advantages of the post-1992 LFS is that it allows the characteristics of Irish-born immigrants to be analysed in more detail than hitherto.) Moreover, recent research allows the characteristics of ethnic minority immigrants and ethnic minority natives to be distinguished. This fills a gap, since most of the existing literature concerning immigrant performance fundamentally concerned ethnicity. (The attention given to ethnic minorities is unsurprising, given the political issues which we discussed above.)

Table 13.3 shows the number of immigrants of working age in 2000—i.e. the potential contribution of immigrants to the UK labour force. Since immigrants are younger than the native population (90 per cent of late twentieth-century immigrants were under 30 on arrival, for example) the share of immigrants in the labour force (9 per cent) has been proportionally greater than in the population as a whole (8 per cent) and it grew faster than the native population. Table 13.3 also shows the changes since 1979. The main growth was in immigrants from Europe (EU and non-EU) and 'other'. ('Other' comprises everywhere else except the Commonwealth and the United States.) The share of West Indian and Irish-born fell substantially. Nor did New Commonwealth immigrants significantly increase their share of the working age population. (The main growth in ethnic minority immigrants was from African and Asian countries which were outside the Commonwealth.) Overall, the share of ethnic minority immigrants in the working age population rose from 3.5 per cent to 4.6 per cent, while the share of white immigrants rose from 4.1 per cent to 4.7 per cent.

However, immigration has increased the size of the paid labour force rather less than we might expect. Normalizing for age, participation rates for immigrants were very varied. Studies show that participation depends on how long the immigrant had been in the country, his or her education levels, whether their qualifications were recognized, and the ability to speak good English. Cohort effects have also been important—immigrants who arrived in some years were more likely to be in employment than those who arrived in other years (Dustmann et al. 2003).

Overall, and normalizing for age and gender, we find that only 64 per cent of immigrants were in employment in 2000, compared with 75 per cent of the native population. There are important differences between immigrant groups, however. White immigrants and white natives have identical participation rates. Ethnic minority participation rates are low, and, in fact, lower than in 1979. The explanation is partly cultural; for example, married women from Pakistan and Bangladesh have very low participation rates in the paid labour force. But the main reason is that they had high unemployment rates. (This also applied to minority natives, although to a lesser extent.) In the late 1990s, males and females from ethnic minorities were two and a half times more likely to be unemployed than whites. (The most affected were Pakistan- and Bangladesh-born immigrants.) High immigrant unemployment rates may be interpreted in several ways. Ethnic minority immigrants were disproportionately in the 15–24 age group—the most likely to be unemployed. (Minority immigrants were more likely to be unemployed, holding age constant, however.) Another possible explanation is that immigrants were disadvantaged by the development of internal labour markets, which pushed the immigrants as recent arrivals into the secondary labour market where their chances of being laid off were higher. In turn, this was probably related to the ability of the immigrants to speak good English. In 2000, the ability to speak English increased immigrant participation *ceteris paribus* by about 20 per cent. Several surveys have confirmed, as we would expect, that immigrants who arrived at a young age had much better facility in English than older immigrants (LFS 1996–98; Shields and Wheatley-Price 2002; Dustmann et al. 2003).[28]

Some ethnic minority immigrants were more likely to be self-employed than natives and white immigrants. This was particularly true of South Asian immigrants. Twenty-five per cent of employed immigrants of South Asian origin were self-employed compared with only 13.8 per cent of all immigrants and 10.7 per cent of (all) UK-born people. But these groups—i.e. Pakistan- and Bangladesh-born—had the highest unemployment rates. Hence, it is not the case that ethnic minority immigrants had been able to compensate for their low participation in the formal labour market by self-employment. Moreover, as we will see, the ethnic groups with the lowest participation rates also had relatively the lowest earnings.

13.7 Skills

It would be fair to say that, with the exception of the immediate post-war period, the UK economy has rarely been labour short, but it has been skills short. Hence, immigrants who improved the skills balance would have been beneficial. Immigration policy (even when unintended) sometimes had this effect. For example, restrictions on ethnic minority immigrants in the early 1960s, in effect, not only increased the mean skill levels of the fewer minority immigrants who entered, but also the average skill level of immigrants who came increasingly from more developed countries.

There were exceptions, however. Many EU immigrants, who did not require work permits, were relatively unskilled. But the more skilled non-EU

---

[28] It may be significant that Irish unemployment rates (normalized for age and qualifications were lower than, for example, ethnic Pakistani or Bangladeshi rates. (In 1993, 38% of Irish workers had no qualifications at all compared with 26% for the UK.) This may have been because Irish longevity of stay had eliminated prejudice.

immigrants more than compensated. By the mid-1990s, immigrants (and returned UK emigrants) were more likely to be 'professionals, employers or managers' than the native population, so that the skill balance was inward (Salt 1995: 18). Finally, the large increase in immigration at the very end of the century may have led to a marginal decline in the average skill levels of entrants, as it apparently did in the USA (Borjas 2000: 4).

There was very high variance in the qualifications held by immigrants. In 2000, immigrants were more likely to have a university degree than UK-born population (19 per cent compared with 15 per cent). (Black African, Indian, and Chinese-born immigrants are more likely to have university degrees.) But immigrants were more likely to have had no qualifications at all. And 32 per cent of immigrants had qualifications that were unrecognized—i.e. were not useful for employment purposes—compared with only 12 per cent of the UK-born population.

Of course, skill gains to the labour market have to be offset against skill losses through emigration. Historically, DominioNn immigration controls always favoured skilled workers. Hence, it is likely that, in the early post-war years, the economy was losing human capital. But from 1970s, the migration balance with these countries (and the USA) became zero, which implies that the human capital losses were no longer occurring. There is evidence from the IPS which measured skilled migration between 1968 and 1993. In that period, the UK lost 1,628,000 'managerial or professional' workers and gained 1,455,000. But all the net loss occurred before 1983. The years 1983–93 showed a net gain. The main losses according to the IPS occurred in the 'manual or clerical' category—477,000, or about 18,000 p.a. Further (partial) evidence concerns the 'brain drain' of scientists and engineers, which was another topic of media interest. Two separate surveys of university departments and research centres, covering the years 1975–92, showed, however, that the number of qualified scientists and engineers who had left was no greater than those who arrived and that their quality was similar (Royal Society 1993) The main difference was that the inward-bound scientists were younger.

13.8 Earnings

Earnings are normally explained by reference to human capital theory. Wages are related to the qualifications brought to the labour market by the worker and the effect of on-the-job learning ('learning by doing'). In the case of immigrants, wage levels may be affected by prejudice and also because their qualifications may not adequately be recognized. In 2000, white immigrant earnings (conditioned for age and skills) were, on average, 20 per cent above UK-born white workers (£403 per week compared with £338). The differential rises with length of stay. On the other hand, earnings of ethnic minority immigrants were about

10 per cent below UK-born white earnings (UK-born minority earnings were closer to white UK-born) (Kempton 2002: 14–5). This pattern confirmed earlier work, which showed that there was no white immigrant/white native earnings gap, but a 25 per cent white/non-white immigrant earnings gap (Chiswick 1980; Bell 1997).

Two factors should be born in mind, however. Immigrants, on average, have taken up employment in the most prosperous parts of the country, and particularly in London. This may explain why white immigrant earnings exceeded native, because UK-born workers are less responsive to income differentials than immigrants (see below). It is also possible that there are cohort effects— i.e. the labour market was particularly prosperous in the late twentieth century when the immigration rate increased. Cohort effects may also have affected minority earnings, since many entered the labour market when conditions were less buoyant. The effect of adaptation may only be measured from 1992, however.

There were major differences in earnings between different ethnic groups. In 2000, average earnings of Pakistan- and Bangladesh-born immigrants were 48 per cent and 25 per cent below native white earnings. Even if we condition for age and skills, the differences only fall to 40 per cent and 20 per cent, respectively. In other words, the reason why Pakistan- and Bangladesh-born immigrants have fared poorly in the labour market is that, on average, they have relatively low skills—reflecting their relatively poor educational attainment. But, most important, they are poorly rewarded for the skills that they do have. Hence, minority workers were less likely to be in non-manual occupations (43 per cent cf. 47 per cent). But again, it was largely he Pakistani and Bangladeshi immigrants who dominated. Other minority immigrants were not relatively unskilled, nor were white immigrants (Sly 1995: 258; Dustmann et al. 2003: 44).

It is clear that some ethnic minority workers received relatively low earnings, holding skills constant. Skills are not only qualifications, of course, but include experience. The ILS makes it possible to distinguish returns to education and returns to experience, but only from 1992. Holding occupation and other characteristics constant, a study in 1992–94 showed that returns to education were exceptional for white immigrants (about double the returns to education for natives). But returns to education for ethnic minority workers were lower than returns to white native workers. An additional year of education increased earnings by about 5 per cent for white natives and 10 per cent for white immigrants but only by 4–4.5 per cent for ethnic minority workers. The lowest returns to education were to those of West Indian origin (Bell 1997: 342).

This result is surprising, since educational participation was higher among many ethnic minorities than among the white population (Blackaby et al. 1994: 183, 192, 196; Woolford 1994; Berthoud 1999: 70–9). On the other hand, returns to experience (i.e. post-formal education) were not much lower for ethnic minority workers than for white natives. Hence, the conclusion of (the rather few) studies is that ethnic minority qualifications were undervalued (Jones 1993: 31–2, 43; Hatton and Wheatley Price 1998: 36–7). Similar results have been obtained in the USA.[29]

13.9 Location

A large proportion of the immigrants and minority natives live in London and the proportion rose through the late twentieth century. Moreover, the share increased through the period. By 2000, 40 per cent of the immigrants lived in London compared with only 9 per cent of the white native population. And 45 per cent of the minority UK-born population lived in London. One reason is that London has a relatively high proportion of occupations with high earnings (e.g. in internationally traded services). It has been the main destination for elite migrants (including corporate transferees) and is the main reason for the relatively high earnings of white, and some ethnic minority, immigrants (holding other characteristics constant).

But London has a distinctive labour market in another sense. In common with the other 'world cities' (New York and Los Angeles) it has a relatively high proportion of low-productivity service occupations. This explains its attraction for less-skilled immigrants, some but not all of whom are from ethnic minorities. Some of the south-east towns have the same distinctive employment pattern (except that the high earners are mainly commuters), for example, Bedford, St Albans, and Milton Keynes. London also attracted many young immigrants whose earnings have often been below the level that would attract significant numbers of migrants from the more distant UK regions. (This group includes health professionals and teachers; Salt and Kitching 1992: 153–5). There are two probable explanations. Housing costs increase the opportunity cost of inter-regional migration within the UK. The south-east region has been, in part, a self-contained housing market (Hamnet 1992: 57). Secondly, many of the immigrants have made an investment in career development, either directly (nurses learning new skills) or indirectly (learning English), which countervails the high housing cost in the south-east.

Outside London, immigrants (particularly ethnic minority immigrants) have been concentrated in a relatively small number of cities. The one-time cotton towns of north Lancashire, the one-time woollen towns of the West Riding of Yorkshire, and Leicester are well-known examples. Their history is well known. The textile industries were in decline because of Far Eastern competition. The employers looked for cheaper immigrant labour, thus providing the entrée for the minority immigrants. The industries were not saved. Some of

---

[29] 7% less than for whites for the same educational attainment, including experience, controlling for period, location, and age (Betts and Loftson 2000: 77).

the immigrants moved to more prosperous parts of the country, others did not. But for every multiracial city in the UK, there are far more where the ethnic minority population is small. In other words, the UK is not a multiracial society, but several of the important cities are very multiracial.

13.10 Conclusion

By 2000, the number of immigrants (i.e. foreign-born) had reached 4.8 million, or 8 per cent of the population. Net immigration since 1990 has, on average, been less than 100,000 per year, or less than 2/000. The current rate which is considered to be exceptionally high is about 3.5/000 or 4/000 of the labour force. Hence, any effect on the labour market is likely to have been qualitative; the immigrants could have been particularly skilled or particularly unskilled. We have seen that over the last fifty years, or so, the net balance of skills has been different at different times, but on average the effect of the skills mix has been neutral. Hence, immigration has not worsened the well-known skills shortages in the UK labour market.

In the standard textbook formulation, the effect of immigration on an economy depends on the degree to which the economy (and the labour market) is open. In a closed economy with no technical change, immigration increases real income but reduces real income per capita. The effect on real income therefore depends on whether the immigrants brought complementary skills which allowed the existing workers to be more productive and also whether there was a large externally traded sector, which would increase returns to the additional workers. There could be an effect on the distribution of income, even if income rose overall. This would depend on the openness of the labour market—e.g. how upwardly mobile were any workers who were displaced by immigrants. A tentative conclusion is that recent immigration into the UK has been beneficial. Most immigrants have entered places with the highest labour demand and lowest unemployment, suggesting that their skills were complementary. This would mean that immigration has increased the average wage level in the UK, which was a tentative conclusion of recent research (Dustmann et al. 2003). This contrasts with US studies that have shown the opposite, primarily because of a negative effect on unskilled earnings.

The effect of immigration policy in the UK on the labour market is fairly clear. The UK government has never had a consistent immigration policy, either in general or connected to the needs of the labour market. The Home Office, which is responsible for immigration, has only just begun to take an interest in its economic effects. Hence, the literature is sparse. (There is relatively little concerning the effects of non-minority immigration, for example.) Even in the post-Second War period, when there was a labour shortage, only very limited recruitment was undertaken. The labour shortages could largely be met by (uncontrolled) Irish immigration. Moreover, policies have been subordinated to larger political considerations, as in the case of Empire emigration which was taken for granted. Or, as in the case of ethnic minority immigration, the policy was an ad hoc reaction to a political crisis. The relative rise in the skills base of immigrants after the 1960s was an unintended consequence of the legislation. With only a few exceptions, the policy concerning refugees was to take as few as possible. The key consideration was to avoid any social problems that their political opponents could blame on immigration. This implied restrictions, of course, which before the 1960s were strongly applied to 'aliens' and from the 1960s, for the first time, to ethnic minority immigrants who up to that time had been considered to be 'British'. Ethnic minority immigration since the 1960s has probably been greater than was intended at the time, however.

References

Anwar, M. (1995). 'New Commonwealth Immigration to the UK', in R. Cohen (ed.), *The Cambridge Survey of World Migration*. Cambridge: Cambridge University Press, 274–8.

Armitage, R. (1994). 'Retrospective Revisions to Population Estimates for 1981–90'. *Population Trends*, 77: 33–6.

Baines, D. E. (1998). 'European Immigration since 1945', in M. S. Schulze (ed.), *Western Europe: Economic and Social Change since 1945*. London: Longmans, 177–90.

Bell, B. D. (1997). 'The Performance of Immigrants in the UK: Evidence from the General Household Survey'. *Economic Journal*, March: 333–44.

Berthoud, R. (1999). *Young Caribbean Men and the Labour Market: A Comparison with Other Ethnic Groups*. London: Joseph Rowntree Trust.

—— Lakey, J., Modood, T., Nazroo, J., Smith, P., Virdee, S., and Beishon, S. (1997). *Ethnic Minorities in Britain: Diversity and Disadvantage*. London: Policy Studies Institute.

Betts, J. R., and Loftson, M. (2000). 'Educational Attainments of Immigrants', in G. Borjas (ed.), 'Introduction', in *Issues in the Economics of Immigration*. Chicago: University of Chicago, NBER (National Bureau of Economic Research).

Bielenberg, A. (ed.) (2000). *The Irish Diaspora*. Harlow: Longman.

Blackaby, D. H. (1986). 'An Analysis of the Male Racial Earnings Differential in the UK Using the General Household Survey'. *Applied Economics*, 18: 1233–42.

—— Drinkwater, S., Leslie, D. G., and Murphy, P. D. (1994). 'A Picture of Male and Female Unemployment among Britain's Ethnic Minorities'. *Scottish Journal of Political Economy*, 44/2: 182–97.

—— Clark, K., Leslie, D. G., and Murphy, P. D. (1997). 'Black–White Male Earnings and Employment Prospects in the 1960s and 1970s'. *Economics Letters*, 46: 273–9.

Borjas, G. (ed.) (2000). 'Introduction', in *Issues in the Economics of Immigration*. Chicago: University of Chicago, NBER (National Bureau of Economic Research).

Brooks, D. (1975). *Race and Labour in London Transport*. Oxford: Oxford University Press.

Brown, C, (1984). *Black and White Britain*. London: Heinemann/Policy Studies Institute.

Busulu, L. (1986). 'Recent Patterns of Migration from and to the United Kingdom.' *Population Trends*, 39: 35–41.

—— (1991). 'A Review of Migration Data Sources'. *Population Trends*, 66: 45–7.

Carrier, N. H., and Jeffery, J. R. (1953). *External Migration: A Study of the Available Statistics, 1815–1950*. London: Her Majesty's Stationery Office.

Champion, T. (1996). 'Population Review: (3) Migration to, from and within the United Kingdom'. *Population Trends*, 83: 5–16.

Chiswick, B. R. (1980). 'The Earnings of White and Coloured Male Immigrants in Britain'. *Economica*, 47: 81–7.

Coleman, D. A. (1996). 'U.K. Immigration Policy "Firm but Fair", and Failing?' *Political Studies*, 17/3: 196–214.

Connolly, T. (2000). 'Emigration from Ireland to Britain during the Second World War', in A. Bielenberg (ed.), *The Irish Diaspora*. Harlow: Longman, 51–64.

Constantine, S. (1990). 'Introduction: Empire Settlement and Imperial Harmony', in S. Constantine (ed.), *Emigrants and Empire: British Settlement in the Dominions between the Wars*. Manchester: Manchester University Press, 1–21.

Council of Europe (1995). *Recent Demographic Developments in Europe*. Strasbourg: Council of Europe Press.

Delaney, E. (2000*a*). *Demography and Society: Irish Migration to Britain, 1921–71*. Liverpool: Liverpool University Press.

—— (2000*b*). 'Placing Post-War Irish migration to Britain in a Comparative European Perspective', in A. Bielenberg (ed.), *The Irish Diaspora*. Harlow: Longman, 317–30.

Devis, T. (1985). 'International Migration: Return Migrant and Re-migrant Flows'. *Population Trends*, 41: 13–20.

Dex, S. (1986). 'Earnings Differentials of Second Generation West Indian and White School Leavers in Britain'. *Manchester School*: 162–79.

Dustmann, C., and Fabbri, F. (2003). 'Language Proficiency and Labour Market Performance of Immigrants in the UK'. *Economic Journal*, 113, July: 695–717.

—— —— Preston, I., and Wadsworth, J. (2003). *Labour Market Performance of Immigrants in the UK Labour Market*. Home Office Report, May.

Federowich, K. (1990) 'The Assisted Emigration of British Ex-servicemen to the Dominions, 1900–22', in S. Constantine (ed.), *Emigrants and Empire: British Settlement in the Dominions between the Wars*. Manchester: Manchester University Press, 45–71.

Fielding, A. J. (1995). 'Migration and Social Change: A Longitudinal Study of the Social Mobility of "Immigrants" in England and Wales'. *European Journal of Population*, 11: 107–21.

Garrard, J. A. (1971). *The English and Immigration, 1880–1910*. Oxford: Oxford University Press.

Gartner, L. P. (1960). *The Jewish Immigrant in England, 1880–1910*. Detroit: Wayne State University Press.

Hamnet, C. (1992). 'House Price Differentials, Housing Wealth and Migration', in T. Champion and T. Fielding (eds.), *Migration Patterns and Processes*, i: *Research Problems and Prospects*. London: Belhaven Press, 55–64.

Hansen, R. (2000). *Citizenship and Immigration in Post-War Britain*. Oxford: Oxford University Press.

Haskey, J. (1994). 'The Ethnic Minority Populations of Great Britain: Their Estimated Sizes and Age Profiles'. *Population Trends*, 84: 33–9.

—— and Scott, A. (2001). 'More Reliable Population Estimates and Proportions for Local Areas: Which Areas to Select and Other Choices to be Made—an Exploratory Analysis'. *Population Trends*, Autumn: 16–36.

Hatton, T. J., and Wheatley-Price, S. (1998). 'Migration, Migrants and Policy in the United Kingdom'. Unpublished paper, Centre for Economic Policy Research.

Holmes, C. (1988). *John Bull's Island: Immigration and British Society, 1871–1971*. London: Macmillan.

Howard, C. (1993). 'United Kingdom II: Immigration and the Law', in D. Kabat (ed.), *The Politics of Migration Policies*. New York: Centre for Migration Studies, 108–23.

Isaac, J. (1954). *British Post-War Migration*. Cambridge: Cambridge University Press, NIESR (National Institute of Economic and Social Research).

Jones, T. (1993). *Britain's Ethnic Minorities: An Analysis of the Labour Force Survey*. London: Policy Studies Institute.

Jones, C. (1997). *Immigration and Social Policy in Britain*. London: Tavistock.

Jones, K., and Smith, A. D. (1970). *The Economic Consequences of Commonwealth Immigration*. Cambridge: Cambridge University Press, NIESR (National Institute of Economic and Social Research).

Jupp, J. (1998). *Immigration*. Melbourne: Oxford University Press.

Kay, D., and Miles, R. (1992). *Refugees or Migrant Workers? European Volunteer Workers in Britain, 1946–51*. London: Routledge.

Kempton, J. (ed.) (2002). *Migrants in the UK: Their Characteristics and Labour Market Outcomes and Impacts*. Home Office, Research, Development & Statistics Directorate, Occasional Paper 82.

Kershaw, R., and Pearsall, M. (2000). *Immigrants and Aliens. A Guide to Sources on UK Immigration and Citizenship*. London: Public Record Office.

Layton-Henry, Z. (1992). *The Politics of Immigration: Immigration, 'Race' and 'Race' Relations in Post-War Britain*. Oxford: Blackwell.

Mason, D. (1995). *Race and Ethnicity in Modern Britain*. Oxford: Oxford University Press.

ONS (Office for National Statistics) (1998). 'Trends in Migration in the UK'. *Population Trends*. London: Her Majesty's Stationery Office.

—— (2001*a*). 'International Migration to and from the UK: Consistency and Implication for the Labour Market'. *Population Trends*. London: Her Majesty's Stationery Office.

—— (2001*b*). 'The Size and Characteristics of the Minority Ethnic Population of Great Britain: Latest Estimates'. *Population Trends*. London: Her Majesty's Stationery Office.

OPCS (Office of Population Censuses and Surveys) (1979). 'International Migration: Recent Trends'. *Population Trends*, 18: 24–7.

—— (1993). *International Migration, 1993*. London: Her Majesty's Stationery Office.

Patterson, S. (1969). *Immigration and Race Relations in Britain, 1960–67*. Oxford: Oxford University Press, Institute of Race Relations.

Payani, P. (1994). *Immigration, Ethnicity and Racism in Britain*. Manchester: Manchester University Press.

Peach, G. C. K. (1968). *West Indian Migration to Britain: A Social Geography*. Oxford: Oxford University Press, Institute of Race Relations.

—— Robinson, V., Maxted, J., and Chance, J. (1988). 'Immigration and Ethnicity', in F. H. Halsey, *British Social Trends since 1900*. Basingstoke: Macmillan, 561–615.

Rees, T. (1993). 'United Kingdom I: Inheriting the Empire's People', in D. Kabat (ed.), *The Politics of Migration Policies*. New York: Centre for Migration Studies, 87–107.

Ringe, M. J. (1993). *The Migration of Scientists and Engineers*. London: Royal Society.

Robinson, V. (1995). 'The Migration of East African Asians to the UK', in R. Cohen (ed.), *The Cambridge Survey of World Migration*. Cambridge: Cambridge University Press, 331–6.

Salt, J. (1995). 'Foreign Workers in the United Kingdom: Evidence from the Labour Force Survey'. *Employment Gazette*, January: 11–19.

—— and Kitching, R. (1992). 'The Relationship between International and Internal Labour Migration', in T. Champion and T. Fielding (eds.), *Migration Patterns and Processes*, i: *Research Problems and Prospects*. London: Belhaven Press, 148–68.

Shaw, C. (1988), 'Components of Growth in the Ethnic Minority Population'. *Population Trends*, 52: 26–30.

Shields, M. A., and Wheatley-Price, S. (2002). 'The English Language Fluency and Occupational Success of Ethnic Minority Immigrant Men Living in the English Metropolitan Areas'. *Journal of Population Economics*, 15: 137–60.

Sly, F. (1995). 'Ethnic Groups and the Labour Market: Analysis from the Spring 1994 Labour Force Survey'. *Employment Gazette*, 103/6: 251–82.

—— (1996). 'Ethnic Minority Participation in the Labour Market: Trends from the Labour Force Survey'. *Labour Market Trends*, 104/6: 259–69.

—— Price, A., and Risdon, A. (1997). 'Trends in Labour Market Participation by Ethnic Groups: 1984–1986: Analysis from the Spring 1994 Labour Market Survey'. *Labour Market Trends*, 105/8: 295–303.

Smith, T. E. (1981). *Commonwealth Migrations: Flows and Policies*. London: Macmillan.

Spencer, I. R. G. (1997). *British Migration Policy since 1939: Making of a Multi-Racial Britain*. London: Routledge.

Spencer, S. (ed.) (1994). *Strangers and Citizens: A Positive Approach to Migrants and Refugees*. London: Rivers Oram Press.

Teague, A. (1993). 'Ethnic Group: First Results from the 1991 Census'. *Population Trends*, 80: 12–17.

Walker, C., and Gee, M. (1979). 'Migration: The Impact on the Population'. *Population Trends*, 9: 24–6.

Walshaw, R. S. (1941). *Migration to and from the British Isles*. London: Jonathan Cape.

Wheatley-Price, S. (2001). 'The Employment Adjustment of Male Immigrants in England'. *Journal of Population Economics*, 14: 193–220.

Woolford, C. L. (1994). 'Irish Nationals in the British Labour Market'. *Employment Gazette*, 102/91: 29–32.

Index

Index

Index